# Gender Differences at Puberty

Puberty is one of the most important life transitions. There is no other period in the life cycle in which there is such significant, rapid, and simultaneous transformation in biology and social and psychological development. Change at puberty is both dramatic and universal, yet there are few researchers who study this important stage in the life course. Indeed, the study of biological and psychosocial changes at puberty is relatively recent. One of the most interesting aspects of puberty is that it marks a significant separation between the genders: physically, psychologically, and socially. This book focuses on the emergence of gender differences and provides an up-to-date summary of interdisciplinary research in the area, with contributions from an international team of leading experts in the field. Topics covered include biological aspects of puberty, body image, aggression, sexual abuse, opposite sex relationships, and psychopathology.

*Cambridge Studies on Child and Adolescent Health*

This series aims at publishing books on the health and disease status of children, adolescents, and young adults and on intervention strategies in medicine, psychology, sociology, public health, and political science. It is supported by the international research network Health Behavior in School Children (HBSC) and is sponsored by the World Health Organization (WHO) Regional Office for Europe.

# Gender Differences at Puberty

*Edited by*

Chris Hayward

*Department of Psychiatry and Behavioral Sciences*
*Stanford University School of Medicine*

PUBLISHED BY THE PRESS SYNDICATE OF THE UNIVERSITY OF CAMBRIDGE
The Pitt Building, Trumpington Street, Cambridge CB2 1RP, United Kingdom

CAMBRIDGE UNIVERSITY PRESS
The Edinburgh Building, Cambridge, CB2 2RU, UK
40 West 20th Street, New York, NY 10011–4211, USA
477 Williamstown Road, Port Melbourne, VIC 3207, Australia
Ruiz de Alarcón 13, 28014 Madrid, Spain
Dock House, The Waterfront, Cape Town 8001, South Africa

http://www.cambridge.org

First published 2003

Printed in the United Kingdom at the University Press, Cambridge

*Typeface* Plantin 10/12 pt.      *System* LATEX 2$_\varepsilon$   [TB]

*A catalogue record for this book is available from the British Library*

ISBN 0 521 80704 2 hardback
ISBN 0 521 00165 x paperback

This book would not have been written if it were not for the pioneering work of Jeanne Brooks-Gunn and her colleagues. Twenty years ago Jeanne Brooks-Gunn and Anne Petersen edited the first book to focus on gender issues at puberty, *Girls at puberty*. This ground-breaking volume spawned interest in an important and long-neglected area of research, namely what happens to girls at puberty. Jeanne Brooks-Gunn continues to lead and inspire faculty scholars, trainees, and students in their effort to understand the complex interplay between biology and psychosocial factors at puberty. We dedicate this book to her, for her unwavering commitment.

# Contents

# Figures

# Tables

# Contributors

ADRIAN ANGOLD, Associate Professor of Psychiatry and Behavioral Sciences, Duke University Medical Center

BONNIE L. BARBER, Associate Professor, School of Family and Consumer Sciences, University of Arizona

TANYA A. BERGEVIN, PH.D. Candidate, Centre for Research in Human Development, Concordia University

WILLIAM M. BUKOWSKI, Professor, Department of Psychology and Centre for Research in Human Development Principal, Loyola International College, Concordia University

ROBIN Z. COHEN, MSC, Banting Institute, University of Toronto

LAURA COMPIAN, PH.D. Candidate, Department of Psychiatry and Behavioral Sciences, Stanford University

E. JANE COSTELLO, Professor of Medical Psychology, Duke University Medical Center

JACQUELYNNE S. ECCLES, Professor of Developmental Education and Psychology, University of Michigan

PATRICIA FECHNER, Assistant Professor, Department of Pediatrics, Stanford University

XIAOJIA GE, Associate Professor and Associate Child Psychologist, University of California, Davis

ANDREW GOTOWIEC, Post-doctoral fellow, McMaster University

JULIA GRABER, Assistant Professor of Psychology, University of Florida

STEPHANIE R. HAWKINS, Research Clinical Psychologist

CHRIS HAYWARD, Associate Professor, Department of Psychiatry and Behavioral Sciences, Stanford University

JENICA HUDDLESTON, Human and Community Development, University of California, Davis

PAMELA JO JOHNSON, Division of Epidemiology University of Minnesota

LAURIE L. MESCHKE, Good Reason Consulting, Inc., Minneapolix

ALICE MICHAEL, Centers for Research on Women, Wellesly College

SAMANTHA PIA MILLER, Department of Psychiatry and Behavioral Sciences, Stanford University

EVA SCHMITT-RODERMUND, Institut für Psychologie, Lehrstuhl für Entwicklungspsychologie, Jena

KATHERINE SANBORN, Department of Psychiatry and Behavioral Sciences, Stanford University

MARY V. SEEMAN, Professor Emerita of Psychiatry, University of Toronto

RAINER SILBEREISEN, Professor of Developmental Psychology and, head of the department of Developmental Psychology, Friedrich Schiller University, Jena

HANS STEINER, Professor of Psychiatry, Stanford University

ERIC STICE, Associate of Psychology, University of Texas

KARINA WEICHOLD, Institut für Psychologie, Lehrstuhl für Entwicklungspsychologie, Jena

CAROL WORTHMAN, Samuel Candler Dobbs Professor of Anthropology, Emory University

# Preface

Following a relatively long period of juvenile growth and reproductive immaturity, adolescence commences with a series of rapid endocrinological changes and ends at the completion of body growth. During adolescence, males and females... show a spurt in growth, secondary sexual characteristics such as sexual dimorphism and body shape... and both sexes attain reproductive maturity. Concomitant with these physical and physiological changes it is clear that there are profound changes in social behavior.

E. Pusey, Behavioral changes at adolescence in chimpanzees,
*Behaviour*, 115(3–4), 204

This description reflects what we know about puberty in humans, although it was written by Anne Pusey to describe puberty in chimpanzees.

Puberty represents the most salient developmental milestone in early adolescence. Although it is commonly thought of as the emergence of secondary sexual characteristics, there are a multitude of other important biological, psychological, and social changes associated with puberty. In the biological sphere there are changes in sleep patterns, brain neurochemistry, and body habitus, in addition to hormonal changes, during puberty. In the psychological domain, there are dramatic shifts in identity, body image, and relationships with parents. Socially, the peer group becomes predominant, social awareness and social anxiety increase. There are important school transitions – elementary to middle school and middle school to high school – which youth have to navigate. It is at this time that experimentation with drugs escalates, sexual promiscuity begins, and risk-taking behavior becomes a way of life for a small subgroup of adolescents. Puberty is also of interest because males and females enter and complete pubertal development at different ages. There are interactions between gender-specific developmental changes and puberty. For example, the emergence of important gender differences in peer relationships, sexual activity, drug use, body image, depression, and anxiety occur at puberty. Why there is this divergence in life course between the genders at this critical developmental period is increasingly becoming the subject of scholarly inquiry.

The focus on the emergence of gender differences at puberty is based on the important observation that, during early adolescence, pubertal stage is generally a more important correlate of behavior than is chronological age. This finding requires focusing on pubertal development rather than on age, when considering the emergence of gender differences in risk-taking behavior, symptoms of depression, body image disturbances, and so forth. How developmental changes during puberty increase or lessen the risks for youth has been the focus of a number of research groups, nationally and internationally. Models in developmental psychology now emphasize the role of context in understanding the relationships between the biology of puberty and behavior. Research is beginning to describe the context-dependent ways in which puberty and its behavioral correlates interact. Importantly, the interactions between the social world of an adolescent and the biology of puberty may differ by gender. Understanding this research has important implications for those involved with adolescents, including parents, teachers, administrators, community youth group leaders, officials of the juvenile justice system, and health-care workers. This volume will describe and summarize these research efforts, as well as present the results of new investigations.

Finally, puberty should not be regarded as the cause of difficulties in young people; rather, it is a marker for a developmental phase that has important implications for the transition from childhood to adulthood. It is important to remember that most adolescents who traverse puberty do not suffer ill effects from this transition. For some, puberty may accentuate earlier childhood problems. For others, however, the transition does herald the beginning of a range of psychosocial problems, from substance abuse and emotional problems to disturbed body image and sexually acting out. We know a great deal about the patterns of these behaviors in relation to puberty; we know less about the explanations.

# Acknowledgments

Adela Martinez deserves special recognition for her assistance in editing this book. This book was partially supported from a grant from the W. T. Grant Foundation (Faculty Scholar award for Chris Hayward).

# 1    Methodological concerns in puberty-related research

*Chris Hayward*

### Defining puberty

Puberty is not a single event, but rather a complex metamorphosis. It is a cascade of changes that result in adult appearance, adult physiology, and altered identity. Although sexual dimorphism, differences in form and structure between males and females, are initiated at conception, some of the most salient biological differences between males and females emerge during pubertal transition. However, identifying exactly when puberty begins has been difficult. It is easier to know that puberty has already started than to pinpoint its exact onset, since the initiation of puberty is not completely understood.

As described by Patricia Fechner in chapter 2, puberty consists of both adrenarche and gonadarche. Adrenarche occurs when the adrenal gland begins to increase production of androgen in both males and females, and is responsible for the development of pubic and axillary hair. This begins much earlier than what is typically thought of as the age of onset of puberty, beginning normatively as early as 6 years of age and typically having started by 8 years of age. Gonadarche is characterized by the development of the gonads, with increased release of estrogen in females and testosterone in males, which results in breast development in girls and testicular enlargement in boys.

As puberty is a process and not an event, its definition partly depends on the purpose for which the definition is being used. It is not necessary to measure hormones to define puberty if the purpose of the definition is to determine rate of growth. On the other hand, if an understanding of the interplay between different aspects of puberty is desired then the definition and measurement need to be more complex. In determining the source of the decrement in body image that many girls experience at puberty, to take one specific example, it may be best to measure multiple characteristics of puberty (increase in body fat, breast development, hormones, etc.), as well as the contextual factors in which these biological changes occur (degree of weight-related teasing by peers, media-induced culture of the thin ideal, parent preoccupation with body weight and shape, etc.). Arguably, both the individual's pubertal changes and the context in which these changes occur constitute the best definition of puberty for understanding issues such as body image change. In fact, it can be argued that a full understanding of most psychological aspects of puberty requires measuring both the individual pubertal changes and the environmental factors that give these changes meaning. In this view, the definition of puberty is "purpose dependent" and in its more complex form includes interrelated biological, psychological, and social factors.

### Measuring puberty

Having argued that the definition of puberty can either be narrow (e.g., Tanner stage) or broad (e.g., Tanner stage, hormones, growth, social context, etc.), depending on the purpose for which the definition is to be used, then it follows that the appropriate measurement of puberty is also "purpose dependent." Different biological systems are developing at different rates and times and may have variable downstream effects (e.g., estrogen's effect on serotonin), intrapsychic meaning, and elicit different external responses. Although the measurement of puberty using different markers may yield highly correlated indicators, they are not equivalent. For example, puberty may be measured by assessing secondary sexual characteristics (e.g., Tanner staging either by physical exam or self-report), bone age, growth spurt, menarche, or hormonal indicators (estrogen, testosterone, or adrenal androgen, etc.). None of these represent a "gold standard," as each captures a different aspect of the pubertal process. Each indicator may be more or less an imperfect proxy for another. If the purpose of the measurement is to determine general categories (e.g., prepubertal or not), then any of these indicators may suffice. On the other hand, if the purpose is to determine any "direct effect" an indicator might have on an outcome (versus one indicator being a proxy for another), multiple indicators must be measured (see below).

Thus, the selection of the appropriate indicator of puberty is best based on the desired purpose, but in practice (clinical and research) it is also determined by convenience, feasibility, and cost. It is important to note, therefore, the limitations of various pubertal indicators. In early adolescent girls self-reported onset of first menses may be difficult to measure reliably (Petersen, 1983; Hayward, *et al.*, 1997). For example, a girl may have her first period followed by several months of being amenorrheic. On the other hand, in older adolescents and adults, menarche is a reliable measure of puberty (Petersen, 1983; Dubas, Graber, and Petersen, 1991; Brooks-Gunn and Warren, 1985). Menarche is also the most commonly used measure in psychological research, as it is easily collected. Unfortunately, there is no equivalently validated convenient measure of puberty for boys.

Self-reported Tanner stage can be measured in both sexes and has fairly good agreement with physician examination, but the validity of self-ratings may vary by ethnicity and degree of body image disturbance in girls (Litt, 1999; Hick and Katzman, 1999). Also, Tanner self-staging requires showing diagrams of genitalia. This can be problematic in non-clinical studies. For this reason, self-ratings that use a questionnaire index (e.g., the Petersen Development Scale) may be preferable (Petersen, et al., 1988) and can be given to both sexes. Physician visual inspection versus physical examination may confound puberty and obesity (Kaplowitz, et al., 2001). Measurements of hormonal indicators have methodological problems as well. Diurnal, menstrual cycle, and pubertal variations make cross-sectional measurements of sex hormone levels difficult to interpret. Measurements at the same time of day, at the same stage of the menstrual cycle in girls would be ideal. Longitudinal hormonal measurements are often more informative, allowing for estimates of rate of change and direction of change over time. Finally, because of the variability in the tempo of various aspects of puberty (e.g., female increase in body fat occurs later than height spurt), relationships between different indicators vary by pubertal stage (see chapter 8 below). There may be individual asynchronies in the sequencing of pubertal changes (e.g., delayed height spurt), which can have significant psychological effects (Eichorn, 1975). Ideally, multiple indicators of puberty measured over time provide the best characterization of the pubertal process. Short of this, qualifying inferences from measurements that are inevitably less than ideal continues to be the best protection against unwarranted conclusions.

## Differentiating different pubertal effects

As I have previously stated, different indicators of puberty may be more or less correlated. For example, teasing apart the effects of adiposity from timing of menarche (Striegel-Moore, et al., 2001) or the effect of Tanner stage from estrogen levels at puberty (Angold, et al., 1999) can be challenging. In studying how different aspects of puberty are related to outcomes, how can their effects be differentiated? Any apparent association between puberty and an outcome is going to be dependent on which pubertal process is measured. If body image worsens in most females at puberty this change will likely be associated with increases in estrogen, BMI, Tanner stage, height, and so forth. Which, if any, of these different components of puberty is most critical for understanding the development of body image disturbance in girls at puberty? The most common statistical method used to parcel effects is multiple regression, the results of which are partially dependent on the measurement characteristics of each variable and the degree of colinearity between variables. Highly correlated independent variables, such as different indicators of puberty, may yield unstable results. Dimensional variables and variables with a metric that has a broad distribution and low measurement error yield larger effect sizes. For example, BMI is frequently observed to be a more powerful predictor than self-reported pubertal stage in multiple regression analyses. Yet, BMI and Tanner stage are highly correlated. Which is more important? For the purposes of multiple regression, BMI has better measurement characteristics, as it offers a continuous measure usually with a broad distribution, whereas the measure of pubertal stage is ordinal and frequently the samples used are truncated at one of the extremes of the five Tanner stages. Self-reported Tanner stage is also less likely to be reliable than direct measurements of height and weight. By virtue of the different measurement characteristics and all other things being equal, BMI would be expected to have a better chance of showing more of an association than Tanner stage. Techniques such as centering and rescaling can address some of the differences in measurement characteristics of the different indicators of puberty, although not measurement unreliability. The problem of parceling effects from colinear variables is more insidious.

If the goal is to have an overall marker of puberty, then strategies to deal with colinearity can include creating an index (i.e., combining different indicators into one index) or factor analysis that produces a set of truly independent variables. However, if the intent is to determine the relative contribution of different (but correlated) aspects of puberty, then stratifying the sample on those factors of interest may be preferable. For example, examining the effects of BMI within Tanner stage groups on a particular outcome would allow for differentiating effects attributable to increasing BMI while holding pubertal stage constant. Similarly, examining effects of Tanner stage within different BMI levels allows an estimate of pubertal stage effects while holding BMI constant. Because stratifying a representative sample by two highly correlated variables will yield smaller numbers at the "corners" (e.g., low BMI at Tanner stage 5 and high BMI for Tanner 1), sampling stratification may be necessary to provide adequate power.

Finally, BMI and pubertal stage may interact in their effect on an outcome. Although including interaction terms is the preferred method for testing for interactive effects, negative findings may be subject to type II error, as more statistical power is required to observe significant interaction effects compared to main effects. This raises the practical problem of adequate sample sizes for teasing apart the main and interactive effects of correlated indicators of puberty; sample sizes of less than 100 subjects are rarely adequate and typically samples need to be quite large (e.g., 500–1000 subjects).

### Differentiating pubertal status and pubertal timing effects

Differentiating age from pubertal status effects is important in determining if outcomes occurring in early adolescence are part of "getting older" or are linked specifically to puberty (Angold and Worthman, 1998). Examining pubertal status effects within the age groups where variation in pubertal status is expected provides information about the relative contribution of pubertal status at different ages and vice versa. The age range in which this can be accomplished is limited and differs between the genders (later in boys). Figure 1.1 shows hypothetical data demonstrating age effects and not pubertal stage effects, while figure 1.2 shows the reverse. Figure 1.3 shows additive effects of age and pubertal status and figure 1.4 demonstrates an interaction between age and pubertal status. Interestingly, interactive effects between age and pubertal status suggest a pubertal timing effect. These two features of puberty, pubertal status and pubertal timing, are sometimes confused (Steinberg, 1987). Pubertal

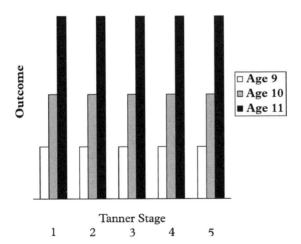

Figure 1.1 Hypothetical outcome data showing stratification by age and Tanner Stage. This figure shows an age effect but no pubertal stage effect.

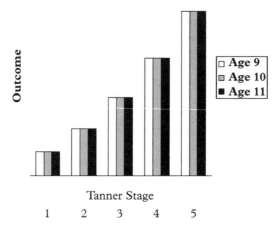

Figure 1.2  Hypothetical outcome data showing stratification by age and Tanner Stage. This figure shows a pubertal stage effect but no age effect.

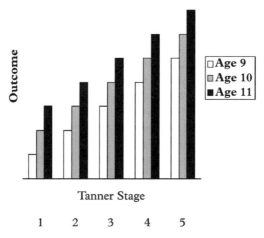

Figure 1.3  Hypothetical outcome data showing stratification by age and Tanner Stage. This figure shows an additive age and pubertal stage effect.

status refers to the level or stage of pubertal development, while pubertal timing refers to the age of a pubertal event and is often categorized early, on time, or late in comparison to a defined reference group. Measuring pubertal status effects requires a sufficient distribution of subjects in different pubertal stages. Obviously, pubertal status effects cannot be measured prior to puberty or after its completion.

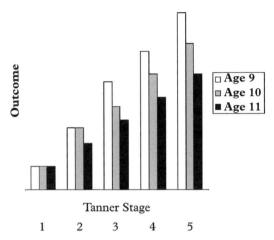

Figure 1.4 Hypothetical outcome data showing stratification by age and Tanner Stage. This figure shows an interaction effect between age and pubertal stage. The interaction in this figure represents an early pubertal timing effect.

Pubertal timing effects are, however, often confounded with pubertal status effects in cross-sectional studies limited to one age or grade. If more sexually mature fifth grade girls have higher depression scores, it is difficult to know if this is a status effect or a timing effect. The less sexually mature girls may or may not "catch up" when they proceed through puberty. Longitudinal studies or studies with sufficient age distributions across all levels of pubertal development can help differentiate status effects from timing effects (Angold and Worthman, 1998; Ge, Conger, and Elder, 2001). Also, both pubertal status and timing effects may be important. In other words, there may be a main effect for pubertal status and an interaction effect between age and status (i.e., a timing effect). This is graphically shown in figure 1.4.

Untangling short-term and long-term pubertal effects can also be difficult. For example, the sexually mature sixth grader may have more depression than the eighth grader at the same level of sexual maturation, but both may be similar by tenth grade. Cross-sectional studies in the peripubertal age range cannot differentiate short-term pubertal timing effects from long-term timing effects that persist after all subjects have completed puberty. Longitudinal studies that continue past the time when most subjects have completed puberty (Stattin and Magnussen, 1990) or studies of postpubertal subjects who retrospectively report their pubertal timing can both yield results that provide information about long-term pubertal

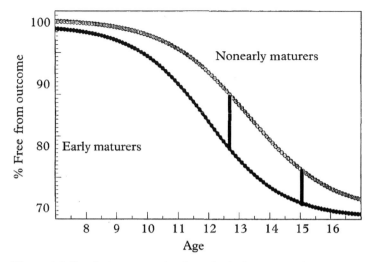

Figure 1.5 Survival curves using hypothetical outcome data comparing those with early pubertal timing and those with nonearly pubertal timing. This figure demonstrates a short-term early pubertal timing effect.

timing effects (Graber, *et al.*, 1997). However, the retrospective report of pubertal timing may be subject to recall bias. Figures 1.5, 1.6 and 1.7 show survival curves from hypothetical data to demonstrate short-term, long-term, and no pubertal timing effects.

It is also difficult to know the degree to which even purported long-term pubertal timing effects are related to the length of time between the onset of puberty and the measurement of the outcome. For example, if increasing levels of estrogen at puberty are found to be related to depression in girls with early onset of puberty, is this due to problems of being an "early bloomer" or to the effects of a longer exposure to estrogen? Measuring the outcome in all subjects at the same time interval from the onset of puberty while controlling for age may help. For example, if depression is measured at age 16 in subjects with pubertal onset at age 10, a comparable test would be rates of depression in 18-year-olds who had onset of puberty at age 12, adjusting for age effects. Statistically controlling for the number of years since pubertal onset might accomplish the same end.

In summary, evaluating status effects requires dividing samples into different levels of pubertal development during the peri-pubertal time period. Observing short-term pubertal timing effects requires knowing the age most subjects start puberty and for long-term pubertal timing

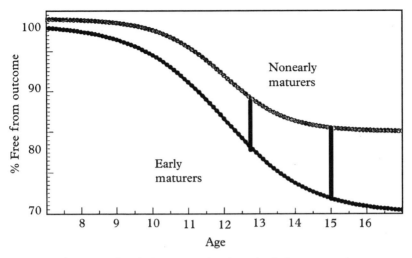

Figure 1.6 Survival curves using hypothetical outcome data comparing those with early pubertal timing and those with nonearly pubertal timing. This figure demonstrates a long-term early pubertal timing effect.

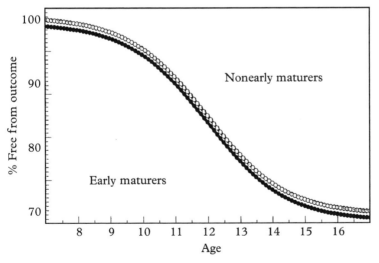

Figure 1.7 Survival curves using hypothetical outcome data comparing those with early pubertal timing and those with nonearly pubertal timing. This figure demonstrates no early pubertal timing effect.

effects most subjects must have completed puberty. Controlling for the length of time "exposed" to puberty may help separate effects that are related to the amount of time since pubertal onset versus effects of being an early maturer. Finally, most of the comments offered in reference to early maturation apply equally well to late maturation.

### Recent secular trend in the onset of secondary sexual characteristics but not menarche

One of the most puzzling recent findings in puberty research is the apparent decrease in the age of onset of secondary sex characteristics by approximately one year in Caucasians and African American girls in the United States over the last two decades, while the mean age of menarche has remained unchanged (Herman-Giddons, *et al.*, 1997). Is pubertal onset earlier but the tempo (duration of puberty) slower? This reported finding has received considerable attention in the media and has alarmed those who are concerned about the psychological well-being of girls who enter into puberty at a younger age. In this report the mean age of beginning breast development was 10 for Caucasian girls and just under 9 for African American girls. Previously, Tanner reported mean age for breast development onset to be 11.2 years of age (Marshall and Tanner, 1969). Similar secular trends were observed for pubic hair growth in girls. No decrease in age of onset at puberty was observed for boys.

The finding that the onset of secondary sex characteristics is occurring earlier in Caucasian and African American girls comes from one study, the Pediatric Research in Office Settings Network (Herman-Giddens, *et al.*, 1997). Consisting of trained pediatricians, this network reported staged breast and pubic hair development in over 17,000 children between the ages of 3 and 12. There are some notable limitations to this study. The sample, although large, is drawn from pediatric office visits and is not representative of the general population. Parents who were concerned about early breast development may have been more likely to bring their daughters to the pediatrician (although not necessarily state that as the reason for the visit) than those parents without this concern. This would bias the sample in favor of early maturers.

Another concern was that breast development staging was performed by visual inspection for 60 percent of the sample. In obese girls, increased fat can be mistaken for breast tissue. A follow-up study using the same sample addressed the role of BMI in explaining the reported findings (Kaplowitz, *et al.*, 2001). When the reanalysis included only the subsample (40%) that received breast examinations, the observation of earlier age of breast development persisted. Given the trend for increasing levels of obesity in youth, the follow-up study also examined the relationship between early onset of secondary sexual characteristics and obesity. They observed, as has been noted previously, that overweight girls tend to mature earlier than those girls that are not. However, the remaining unanswered question is whether earlier puberty in the US is a result of the increase in obesity in youth or, alternatively, the increase in body fat in young girls is a result of earlier puberty. Finally, it remains unclear how the development of secondary sexual characteristics could be decreasing while the mean age of menarche is not. Obviously, this is an area in need of further study as it is a significant change for girls to be developing breasts and pubic hair one year earlier than they were two to three decades ago.

### Ethnicity

Pubertal development varies considerably by ethnicity. For example African American girls have pubertal onset up to one year before Caucasian girls (Herman-Giddens, et al., 1997); and Asians appear to mature later than Caucasians (Hammer, et al., 1991). Few studies of the psychosocial aspects of puberty have included samples of multiple ethnic groups (see chapter 13 below for an exception). Studies that have compared puberty-related effects in African Americans versus Caucasians have generally observed ethnic differences. In general, the associations between pubertal status or pubertal timing and psychosocial factors are smaller in the African American samples (Striegel-Moore, et al., 2001; Hayward, Gotlib, Schraedley, and Litt, 1999; see chapter 13 below). It is useful to examine effects both within different ethnic groups and across groups. In examining effects of ethnicity it is also important to consider differences in socioeconomic status (SES). A recent study reported that apparent differences in age of onset of puberty between Caucasian and Latino girls was no longer apparent after controlling for SES (Obeidallah, et al., 2000).

If psychological changes at puberty are ethnic-group specific, does this suggest a greater role for sociocultural factors and a lesser role for biological factors in understanding psychosocial changes at puberty? Or are there ethnic differences in the biology of puberty? There are no clear answers to these questions. Although it is unlikely that the biological basis of puberty differs greatly between ethnic groups, biological effects of puberty may be dependent on cultural context. The effects of hormones or their downstream effects may be critical in one social environment but minimal in another.

Finally, we need to understand what it is about ethnic differences that lead to findings that vary across ethnic groups. What is it about African

American girls that appear to make them less vulnerable than Caucasian girls to the negative effects of early pubertal timing? Ethnicity is a construct that needs to be "unwrapped" before we will understand the meaning of the differences in the pyschosocial correlates of puberty by ethnic group.

## Summary

Methodological concerns will continue to limit our understanding of the pubertal transition and the emergence of gender differences at puberty (Alsaker, 1995; Angold and Worthman, 1993; Graber, Petersen, and Brooks-Gunn, 1996). Discerning mechanisms underlying associations between different indicators of puberty and psychosocial outcomes will require increasing methodological sophistication, as well as large sample sizes and measurements of multiple aspects of puberty. We have only scratched the surface in our understanding of how this developmental period affects developmental trajectories for youth. Glaring gaps in our knowledge base exist. We know little about changes in neuromodulation at puberty, cross-cultural comparisons of the pubertal transition, and the interactions between biological and psychosocial changes at puberty. Studies that combine methods from different disciplines, such as neurobiology, developmental psychology, anthropology, education, and sociology are needed. The importance of this developmental milestone deserves the attention of researchers and funding agencies alike, so that continued scientific inquiry can utilize the best and most up-to-date scientific methods from a variety of fields.

## References

Alsaker, F. D. (1995). Timing of puberty and reactions to pubertal changes. In M. Rutter (ed.), *Psychosocial disturbances in young people: challenges for prevention* (pp. 37–82). Cambridge: Cambridge University Press.

Angold, A., and Worthman, C. M. (1993). Puberty onset of gender differences in rates of depression: a developmental, epidemiologic and neuroendocrine perspective. *Journal of Affective Disorders*, **29**, 145–158.

Angold, A., Worthman, C. M., and Costello, E. J. (1998). Puberty and depression: the roles of age, pubertal status and pubertal timing. *Psychological Medicine*, **28**, 51–61.

Angold, A., Costello, E. J., Erkanli, A., and Worthman, C. M. (1999). Pubertal changes in hormone levels and depression in girls. *Psychological Medicine*, **29**, 1043–1053.

Brooks-Gunn, J., and Warren, M. P. (1985). Measuring physical status and timing in early adolescence: a developmental perspective. *Journal of Youth and Adolescence*, **14(3)**, 163–189.

Dubas, J. S., Graber, J. A., and Petersen, A. C. (1991). A longitudinal investigation of adolescents' changing perceptions of pubertal timing. *Developmental Psychology*, **27**, 580–586.

Eichorn, D. E. (1975). Asynchronizations in adolescent development. In S. E. Dragastin and G. H. Elder, Jr. (ed.), *Adolescence in the life cycle: psychological change and the social context* (pp. 81–96). New York: John Wiley.

Ge, X., Conger, R. D., and Elder, G. H. (2001). The relation between puberty and psychological distress in adolescent boys. *Journal of Research on Adolescence*, **11(1)**, 49–70.

Graber, J. A., Lewinsohn, P. M., Seeley, J. R., and Brooks-Gunn, J. (1997). Is Psychopathology associated with the timing of pubertal development? *Journal of the American Academy of Child and Adolescent Psychiatry*, **36(12)**, 1768–1776.

Graber, J. A., Petersen, A. C., and Brooks-Gunn, J. (1996). Pubertal process, methods, measures and models. In J. A. Graber, A. C. Petersen, and J. Brooks-Gunn (ed.), *Transitions through adolescence: interpersonal domains and context* (pp. 3–53). Mahwah, NJ: Lawrence Erlbaum.

Hammer, L., Wilson, D., Litt, I. F., Killen, J., Hayward, C., Miner, B., Vosti, C., and Taylor, C. B. (1991). Impact of pubertal development on body fat distribution among White, Hispanic and Asian female adolescents. *Journal of Pediatrics*, **118(6)**, 975–980.

Hayward, C., Gotlib, I. H., Schraedley, P. K., and Litt, I. F. (1999). Ethnic difference in the association between pubertal status and symptoms of depression in adolescent girls. *Journal of Adolescent Health*, **25**, 143–149.

Hayward, C., Killen, J. D., Wilson, D. M., Hammer, L. D., Litt, I. F., Kraemer, H. C., Haydel, F., Varady, A., and Taylor, C. B. (1997). Psychiatric risk associated with early puberty in adolescent girls. *Journal of the American Academy of Child and Adolescent Psychiatry*, **36(2)**, 255–262.

Herman-Giddens, M. E., Slora, E. J., Wasserman, R. C., Bourdony, C. J., Bhapkar, M. V., Koch, G. G., and Hasemeir, C. C. (1997). Secondary sexual characteristics and menses in young girls seen in office practice: a study from the Pediatric Research Office Settings Network. *Pediatrics*, **99**, 505–512.

Hick, K. M., and Katzman, D. K. (1999). Self-assessment of sexual maturation in adolescent females with anorexia nervosa. *Journal of Adolescent Health*, **24(3)**, 206–211.

Kaplowitz, P. B., Slora, E. J., Wasserman, R. C., Pedlow, S. E., and Herman-Giddens, M. E. (2001). Earlier onset of puberty in girls: relation to increased body mass index and race. *Pediatrics*, **108(2)**, 347–353.

Litt, I. F. (1999). Self-assessment of puberty: problems and potential (editorial). *Journal of Adolescent Health*, **24(3)**, 157.

Marshall, W. A., and Tanner, J. M. (1969). Variations in the pattern of pubertal change in girls. *Archives of Disease in Childhood*, **44**, 291–303.

Obeidallah, D. A., Brennan, R. T., Brooks-Gunn, J., Kindlon, D., and Earls, F. (2000). Socioeconomic status, race and girls' pubertal maturation: results from the Project on Human Development in Chicago Neighborhoods. *Journal of Research on Adolescence*, **10(4)**, 443–464.

Petersen, A. C. (1983). Menarche: meaning of measures and measuring meaning. In S. Golub (ed.), *Menarche: the transition from girl to woman* (pp. 63–76). Lexington, MA: Lexington Books.

Petersen, A. C., Crockett, L. J., Richards, M., and Boxer, A. (1988). A self-report measure of pubertal status: reliability, validity and initial norms. *Journal of Youth and Adolescence*, **17**, 117–133.

Stattin, H., and Magnusson, D. (1990). *Paths through life*, vol. II: *Pubertal maturation in female development*. Hillsdale, NJ: Lawrence Erlbaum.

Steinberg, L. (1987). Impact of puberty on family relations: effects of pubertal status and pubertal timing. *Developmental Psychology*, **23(3)**, 451–460.

Striegel-Moore, R. H., McMahon, R. P., Biro, F. M., Schreiber, G., Crawford, P. B., and Voorhees, C. (2001). Exploring the relationship between timing of menarche and eating disorder symptoms in black and white adolescent girls. *International Journal of Eating Disorders*, **30**, 421–433.

*Part 1*

# Sex differences in hormones and their effect at puberty

# 2 The biology of puberty: new developments in sex differences

*Patricia Y. Fechner*

At first glance puberty appears to be a discreet, isolated event that marks the transition from childhood to adulthood. In reality, though, it is part of a continuum of events that were initiated at conception. The hypothalamic gonadotropin releasing hormone (GnRH) pulse generator is initially active in fetal life and early infancy, but then suppressed during childhood; although at the onset of puberty it is reactivated. The etiology of this inhibition of the GnRH pulse generator is not known. It has been hypothesized that the onset of puberty is controlled by the brain "gonadostat," which is a model used to describe the regulation of the hypothalamic GnRH pulse generator. Initially, in fetal life the gonadostat is insensitive to the negative feedback of gonadal sex steroids, testosterone in males and estrogen in females. But by the third trimester, the gonadostat has undergone some maturation and becomes sensitive to the high levels of estrogen and progesterone, and LH (luteinizing hormone) and FSH (follicle stimulating hormone) become suppressed. Through infancy and early childhood this sensitivity increases and the GnRH pulse generator is suppressed by the low levels of sex steroids. This feedback system is approximately ten times more sensitive to sex steroids than is the adult feedback mechanism (Styne and Grumbach, 1991). Then just prior to the onset of puberty, the sensitivity of the gonadostat to the negative feedback of gonadal sex steroids decreases, which releases the hypothalamic–pituitary axis from inhibition. The consequent generation of GnRH pulses, and the increased sensitivity of the pituitary gonadotropic (LH and FSH producing) cells to GnRH, lead to increased LH and FSH secretion. The LH and FSH pulses secreted in response to the GnRH pulses occur first at night and then during the day. The gonads, in response to LH and FSH, enlarge, mature, and secrete increased amounts of gonadal sex steroids.

**Fetal life**

Even in fetal life, differences in the male and female pattern of gonadotropin secretion have been observed. LH and FSH are produced
by the gonadotropic cells of the pituitary gland and stimulate the ovaries
and testes to secrete estrogen and testosterone, respectively. The male fetus has a rise in both LH and FSH at 16 weeks, with a peak at 20 weeks,
followed by a gradual decline. Testosterone levels are initially elevated
in response to the placental HCG (human chorionic gonadotropin) and
then remain elevated with the LH rise and peak. In contrast, the female fetus has a slightly earlier rise in LH with a more gradual decline;
between 17 to 24 weeks of gestation LH and FSH levels are higher in
female fetuses. They are not exposed to the high testosterone levels that
the male fetus is exposed to during midgestation and this may account for
the higher gonadotropins in the female fetus seen at 17–26 weeks (Beck-
Peccoz, Padmanabhan, *et al.*, 1991). Both male and female fetuses are
exposed to extremely high levels of estrogen secondary to maternal fetoplacental production. The FSH values are higher in females than males
between 26 and 36 weeks gestation, but the mean LH levels are higher
in males (Massa, de Zegher, *et al.*, 1992). The decrease in LH and FSH
seen in both sexes during the third trimester is a consequence of the maturation of the negative feedback system of the gonadostat (Beck-Peccoz,
Padmanabhan, *et al.*, 1991).

**Infancy**

At birth there is a "mini-puberty," with elevated gonadotropin levels and
steroid hormone levels reaching the adult range. This occurs as a result
of inhibitory estrogen levels, produced by the fetoplacental unit falling
abruptly at birth. Males are born with an elevated testosterone level that
rapidly decreases in the first day of life and then rises again after one week.
In the male infant, both the LH and FSH fall back to prepubertal levels
at about three months of age; this decline leads to a fall in testosterone
levels from 200–300 ng/dl to prepubertal values of less than 10 ng/dl.
Females do not have this elevation of testosterone levels; the LH level is
increased only for several months, but the FSH level remains elevated
for the first few years of life. Estradiol measurements using current com-
mercial assays appear low in both sexes, but if an ultrasensitive biologic
assay is employed, differences become apparent. Females appear to have
almost ten times the amount of estradiol as compared to males in early
childhood. Other androgens and adrenal hormones are also transiently
elevated in the first year of life in both sexes. The rise in LH and FSH

seen in the first few months of life may be secondary to a lack of complete maturity of the gonadostat, so that it is insensitive to the presence of gonadal sex steroids.

## Childhood

During childhood there is quiescence; the gonadostat is very sensitive to low levels of sex steroids and there is inhibition of the GnRH pulse generator. Gonadotropin levels are low in both sexes, as are sex steroids. Abnormalities in puberty can occur during this period with the development of early or precocious puberty. The frequency and etiology of central precocious puberty between females and males are quite different; it occurs five times more frequently in girls than in boys and is idiopathic in more than 80–90 percent of the cases (Root, 2000). The converse is true in boys, where there is an equal or greater incidence of CNS etiologies compared to idiopathic etiologies of central precocious puberty (Bridges, Christopher, *et al.*, 1994). The reason for these differences is not known but may be related to the subtle differences in FSH levels.

## Puberty

Puberty occurs in the sexes as a result of increased pulses of gonadotropins, which initially occur at night creating a diurnal pattern and then occur throughout the day. During early puberty, females have an increase in FSH over LH production secondary to FSH's longer half-life and because of its decreased regulation by GnRH. The increased LH and FSH initiate gonadotropin-dependent follicular development in the ovaries, which stimulates them to produce the sex steroid estrogen. Estrogen-sensitive tissues, such as the breasts and uterus, then respond; breasts have an increase in the glandular, fatty, and connective tissues. Males have gonadal and adrenal development approximately six months to one year later than females. The reason for this difference is not known. As the testes begin to secrete testosterone under the stimulation of LH, they increase in size. A second source for testicular enlargement is due to the growth of the seminiferous tubules, which are involved in spermatogenesis.

The onset of puberty is characterized by the incipience of breast development in girls and testicular enlargement in boys. Usually these changes are so subtle that dating the development of the onset of puberty is difficult if not impossible. Clinically, the onset of puberty is discerned by physical examination consisting of visual inspection and palpation. Visual inspection alone may be misleading as girls with a lot of subcutaneous tissue might mistakenly be thought to have true breast buds when indeed all that is present is adipose tissue. Also, in boys the presence of a hydrocele may be mistaken for testicular enlargement if it is not carefully palpated. There is still some controversy as to what exactly represents the first sign of breast development or testicular enlargement (i.e., should it be 3 cc or 4 cc of testicular volume). By the time breast buds are palpable or testes are enlarged, the hormonal changes responsible for these transformations have already been in the early pubertal range for some time. Thus, while physical findings of puberty are not the most sensitive or accurate indicators of the onset of puberty, they are the most commonly used. Laboratory studies are not usually necessary to make a diagnosis of central puberty unless it occurs early.

Marshall and Tanner have classified breast development into five stages (Marshall and Tanner, 1969). Stage 1 is prepubertal, stage 2 is elevation of the breast and areola as one mound, stage 3 is further breast enlargement, stage 4 is the formation of a secondary mound by the areola and papilla, and stage 5 is the projection of the papilla only. In the United States breast development occurs between the ages of 8 and 13 years in girls. In a study by Roche *et al.* (Roche, Wellens, *et al.*, 1995) Tanner stage 2 breast development occurred at a mean age of 11.2 years in girls. Menarche, the onset of menses, occurs at Tanner stage 4 to 5. The mean age of menarche in the United States is 12.8 years.

Marshall and Tanner also developed Tanner stages for male genitalia (Marshall and Tanner, 1970). Tanner stage 1 in the male is the presence of prepubertal testes and penis. The earliest evidence of gonadarche in the male is the thinning of the scrotum and enlargement in testicular volume to greater than 4 cc. This is Tanner stage 2 and occurs at 11.6 years with a normal range of 9 to 13.5 years. Tanner stage 3 occurs when the testes increase further in size and the phallus begins to increase in length and breadth. Tanner stage 4 describes testes and phallus growth, which have further enlarged but are not yet the size found in adults. Tanner stage 5 describes genitalia that are adult in size.

Puberty consists of both gonadarche (originating from the gonads) and adrenarche (originating from the adrenal glands). The onset of pubic hair may be easier to determine by inspection than the presence of breast buds or testicular enlargement. Usually gonadarche and adrenarche occur in close approximation. However, they may occur independent of one another since gonadarche is in response to hormones secreted from the gonad and adrenarche is in response to hormones secreted from the adrenal gland. For example, premature adrenarche, the early onset of pubic or axillary hair, may occur years before the onset of breast development. In gonadal dysgenesis (failure of the testis to develop in a

46, XY individual), adrenarche will occur but gonadarche will not. In primary adrenal insufficiency, gonadarche can occur without significant adrenarche. Adrenarche is a result of an increase in adrenal androgen production in both males and females, which begins between the ages of 6 and 8 years. There is some androgen production from the ovaries, which may contribute to adrenarche, whereas in males, there is androgen production from both the testes and the adrenal glands. Pubic hair usually appears in girls between the ages of 8 and 13 years, versus 9 and 14 years in boys. There is no significant advancement in age of gonadarche in either sex; breast development and menarche do not occur earlier than normal (Grumbach and Styne, 1998). Premature adrenarche, the early onset of pubic or axillary hair in the absence of a known etiology, has been regarded as a normal variant of development. African American females may have the onset of adrenarche a year earlier than Caucasian females in the United States.

Tanner also developed a staging system for classification of pubic hair development in females and males. In females, stage 1 is again prepubertal with no pubic hair present, stage 2 is the presence of sparse growth of downy hair over the labia, and stage 3 is the presence of darker, coarser, and curlier hair extending to the pubes. Stage 4 is the presence of pubic hair that is adult in type, but which covers a smaller area. Stage 5 is the presence of pubic hair which is adult in both type and distribution, but is not present along the linea alba or medial thigh. Tanner stage 6 is the presence of pubic hair along the medial surface of the thigh, although this does not occur in all females. The mean age of Tanner stage 2 pubic hair was 11.0 years in the Roche study, versus 8.8 years in African American girls and 10.5 years in Caucasian girls as found in the Herman-Giddens et al. study (Herman-Giddens, Slora, et al., 1997). Similarly, stage 3 was attained on average by 11.8 years in the Roche study, versus 10.4 years in African American girls and 11.5 years in Caucasian girls. Thus, while the onset of pubarche appears much earlier in African American girls, the age of Tanner stage 3 is only 1.4 years earlier in the African American girls and 0.3 in Caucasian girls than what was reported by Roche et al. (Roche, Wellens, et al., 1995).

The Tanner staging for pubic hair in males is similar to that found in females. Stage 1 is prepubertal, stage 2 consists of hair at the base of the penis, and in stage 3 pubic hair is darker, coarser, curlier, and spreads over the pubes. In stage 4 pubic hair is adult in nature but distributed over a smaller area, and by stage 5 it is adult in nature and distribution. The onset of Tanner stage 2 in males had been reported to occur between 12.2 to 12.5 years. Herman-Giddens in the National Health and Nutrition Examination Study III found that there were ethnic differences in the onset of Tanner stage 2 pubic hair, with African Americans boys developing pubic hair at 11.2 years, nine months prior to Caucasians' 12.0 years and more than a year earlier than Mexican American boys' 12.3 years. However, all three ethnic groups attained Tanner stage 5 within five months of each other (Herman-Giddens, Wang, *et al.*, 2001).

Both females and males undergo a pubertal growth spurt, although there are a number of significant differences between the two sexes. First, the pubertal growth spurt occurs much earlier in females than in males, with girls being two years earlier on average. Thus, girls are shorter in stature than boys when they undergo their growth spurt. Second, this earlier growth spurt occurs at an earlier stage of puberty in girls than it does in boys, Tanner stage 2 for girls versus stage 4 for boys. In addition, the growth gained during this pubertal spurt is less in females than in males, as the peak growth velocity and duration of the growth spurt is less in females. All of these factors contribute to the 13 cm difference in final adult height between females and males.

Growth hormone and estrogen (extraglandular conversion of testosterone and androstenedione to estradiol in males) are responsible for the growth spurt. However, estrogen is a double-edged sword, as on the one hand it promotes growth but on the other has maturational effects on bones that lead to epiphyseal fusion of the long bones. Once the epiphyses are fused, longitudinal development can no longer occur and growth is complete. At puberty there is an increase in both the amplitude and frequency of growth hormone secretion, which results in higher basal levels of growth hormone and IGF-1 (insulin-like growth factor-1) production. Estrogen and, to a lesser extent, testosterone increase growth hormone production. In females increased growth hormone secretion occurs with the beginning of breast development and peaks at midpuberty. In contrast, males do not have the increase in growth hormone until Tanner stage 2, with a peak at stage 4 for genitalia. The pubertal growth spurt is in response to this increased growth hormone production. However, there is no correlation between the growth hormone or IGF-1 levels and the peak height velocity of the growth spurt. Estrogen may inhibit the normal suppression of growth hormone release by IGF-1, thus permitting the increase in growth hormone, which then causes the pubertal growth spurt. There is also increased local production of IGF-1 in cartilage and bone (Harris, Van Vliet, *et al.*, 1985). Estrogen does not only promote the pubertal growth spurt via growth hormone, it appears to be important in itself.

Body composition also differs in females and males at puberty. Prior to puberty there is an increase in lean body mass, which occurs at 6 years in girls and not until 9.5 years in boys. At adulthood, men have 1.5 times greater lean body mass and skeletal mass than women, and adult females have two times as much body fat as males. The distribution of fat is also different between males and females, with males accumulating fat around the abdomen and females at the hips. Increased testosterone production in men leads to higher hemoglobin and hematocrits.

Other changes that occur in both sexes at puberty include the development of axillary hair and acne. Males may have transient breast development, usually less than 4 cm, during midpuberty. As a result of the increased androgen production in the testes, the membranous and cartilaginous component of the vocal cords increase in length more in males than females, which results in a deepening of the voice. Males in response to the increased androgens also develop facial hair. Females who are exposed to excessive androgens via an adrenal secreting tumor can also undergo these changes.

The pattern of gonadotropin secretion differs between males and females. Gonadotropins, in both pubertal males and females, are secreted in a tonic or basal secretion, which is regulated by a negative feedback of the gonadal steroids and by inhibin, a hormone produced by the Sertoli cells in the testes and the granulosa cells in the ovaries. This is the sole control mechanism of gonadal steroid production in males, and is also one of the two control mechanisms of gonadal steroid production in females. Just prior to the onset of puberty there is a release in the inhibition of this negative feedback so that the LH and FSH begin to respond to GnRH. The gonadostat, which was at its most sensitive to negative feedback of gonadal steroids during midchildhood, becomes less sensitive and allows the hypothalamic GnRH pulse generator to respond to the low levels of gonadal steroids. Initially there is an increase in the GnRH pulse generator at night, with a corresponding increase in LH and FSH release (Apter, Butzow, et al., 1993). In females there is more FSH produced than LH. This may be secondary to the longer half-life of FSH and the differential regulation of LH and FSH by the GnRH (Kulin and Reiter, 1973; Winter and Faiman, 1973; Apter, Butzow, et al., 1993). This increase in FSH over LH is important in the growth and development of the follicular component of the ovary.

A second pattern of gonadotropin secretion is unique to the adult female. It is a positive feedback system, which refers to the midcycle LH surge that is secreted once the ovary has produced enough estrogen in preparation for ovulation. Autoamplification occurs at several levels. Estradiol increases the GnRH pulse amplitude in the hypothalamus, which sensitizes the pituitary to release more LH in response to the same amplitude of GnRH (Moll and Rosenfield, 1984). LH and FSH also become more sensitive to GnRH pulses secondary to estradiol and progesterone secretion patterns (March, Goebelsmann, *et al.*, 1979). The ovary becomes more sensitive to LH and FSH and produces more estradiol. Each menstrual cycle mimics the onset of puberty in that during the first half of the cycle (follicular phase) gonadotropins and ovarian sex steroids are low. FSH then begins to increase while LH begins to increase only at night in a pulsatile fashion. Estradiol levels increase as the follicle matures and FSH decreases. The dominant follicle becomes more sensitive to FSH so that lower levels do not inhibit its growth, whereas the other nondominant follicles undergo atresia in lower levels of FSH. Once estradiol reaches 200–300 pg/ml there is a midcycle LH surge that causes the dominant follicle to undergo ovulation. Estradiol also induces progesterone receptors in the hypothalamus and pituitary to rise slightly to contribute to the LH surge and to initiate a surge in FSH. Once the oocyte is released from the follicle, estradiol levels decline. The resultant corpus luteum begins to secrete progesterone, estradiol begins to rise again, and the elevated progesterone causes the gonadotropin pulses to decrease. If there is no pregnancy, the corpus luteum involutes with the decrease in progesterone and estradiol production. This then allows the FSH to increase more than LH, which then initiates a new cycle and, with the fall in progesterone and estradiol, menses occur.

A factor that has recently been postulated to have an effect on the onset of puberty is leptin. A great deal of research regarding leptin has been done in mice. Leptin-deficient mice have been found not to enter puberty, although when given leptin they do initiate puberty (Barash, Cheung, *et al.*, 1996). Leptin is produced by adipose cells; thus weight may play a role in the timing of the onset of puberty. Girls and boys who are obese tend to enter puberty at an earlier age than their peers. A comparison of leptin level in pubertal children shows that in females there is a continual rise in leptin as puberty progresses, with a peak at full pubertal maturation. In contrast, males have an increase in leptin level with a peak occurring in early midpuberty and then decreasing as they continue to progress through puberty (Garcia-Mayor, Andrade, *et al.*, 1997).

Recently there has been much controversy over whether or not there has been a secular trend to earlier onset of puberty in females and males. An observational study by Herman-Giddens *et al.* (Herman-Giddens, Bourdony, *et al.*, 2001) found that visual changes consistent with Tanner Stage II occurred at 8.9 ± 1.93 years in African Americans and 10.0 ± 1.82 years in Caucasians. This is in contrast to the previously held notion that breast development occurs at 11.2 years (Roche, Wellens, *et al.*, 1995). This study has led to many debates regarding the age at which initiation of breast and pubic hair development is normal (Kaplowitz and

Oberfield, 1999; Rosenfield, Bachrach, *et al.*, 2000). Criticisms regarding the Herman-Giddens (1977, 2001) studies include that the girls in the first study were not taken from a random sample of the population and thus that there may have been some ascertainment bias. Also, while the study reported an earlier onset of breast tissue, primarily by inspection only, there was no significant earlier onset of menarche, which is a more easily identified endpoint. The mean age of menarche has not changed from 12.8 years, with African American girls achieving menarche at age 12.2 years, approximately six months earlier than Caucasians girls, who start menarche at 12.9 years (MacMahon, 1973; Zacharias, Rand, *et al.*, 1976).

It is well known that moderate obesity is associated with earlier menarche (Hartz, Barboriak, *et al.*, 1979), and in the United States obesity has greatly increased in the last ten years. It appears that obese children tend to have skeletal bone ages that are one to two years in advance of their chronological age, although this is still within the normal range. It has been noted that African American females have higher caloric intakes and a higher incidence of obesity than Caucasian females (NHLBI Growth and Health Study, 1992). This may account for the earlier breast and pubic hair development and slightly earlier menarche that have been found in African American females. A follow-up study using the same data as in the Herman-Giddens study, but analyzing for the effect of body fat mass index, found that obesity played an important contributing factor in the earlier onset of breast development. This was more so for Caucasian females than African American females (Kaplowitz, Slora, *et al.*, 2001). Other factors, such as genetic and environmental factors, may play a role in why African Americans develop earlier than Caucasians.

Analysis of cross-sectional pubertal data obtained from the NHANES III study suggests that the mean age of Tanner Stage II for both male genitalia and pubic hair are occurring earlier than reported by Marshall and Tanner in 1970 (Herman-Giddens, Wang, *et al.*, 2001). These authors reported that the mean age of this stage for male genitalia is 10.1 years for Caucasians, 9.5 years for African Americans, and 10.4 years for Mexican Americans. Tanner staging was done by inspection only, with a total of 2114 boys examined, who represented 16,575,753 boys as per the NHANES III sampling strategies. This study did look at a random population of males, but the Tanner staging was done by inspection and did not include testicular volumes. A one-stage variance was permitted, which can be significant when determining the difference between Tanner Stage I and Stage II. Also, even though a younger age at initiation of puberty was reported, there was no difference in the number of boys who still had Tanner Stage I at 14 years. If puberty were occurring earlier, one would expect that everything would be shifted earlier as well (Reiter and Lee, 2001). Lee *et al.* (Lee, Guo, *et al.*, 2001) found that the lack of standardized criteria for male genital staging prohibited the determination of whether or not there is a secular trend for an earlier onset of puberty in males. Also, prior studies did not look at the same ethnic mix as current studies, and it is known that there are ethnic variations in the timing of the onset of puberty.

In general, obesity is becoming more prevalent in the preadolescent population and this may contribute to the perceived notion that puberty is starting earlier. It is felt by many pediatric endocrinologists that before any conclusions can be made regarding the earlier onset of puberty, a well-designed longitudinal study with careful physical exams is necessary (Rosenfield, Bachrach, *et al.*, 2000). While the use of laboratory studies is more accurate and can indicate the onset of puberty prior to any physical changes, it is not practical for screening in the general pediatric population. Pediatric endocrinologists investigate the etiology of precocious puberty in females and males in order to exclude a pathologic etiology of the early puberty. If there are secular trends for a younger age of onset, many normal children will undergo an evaluation that is not needed. On the other hand, if puberty is not occurring earlier, pediatric endocrinologists still need to evaluate the child with early puberty in order to avoid missing the diagnosis of a potentially life-threatening process.

Puberty is a time of physical change and increased emotions. This can be a very stressful period for an adolescent who is either developing earlier or later than his or her peers. For example, height, which is easily discernible to all, can vary over a foot in boys who are the same age. Thus, adolescents involved in sports may suddenly find themselves too short or thin to continue participating in their favorite sport. Adolescents may be treated as younger or older than they are, based on their physical development as opposed to their chronological age. For example, teachers and parents may have unattainable expectations for the child who looks older than his or her age. Individuals working with adolescents need to be aware of the wide range of normal pubertal development and that girls, in general, go through puberty earlier than boys.

### References

Apter, D., Butzow, T. L., *et al.* (1993). Gonadotropin-releasing hormone pulse generator activity during pubertal transition in girls: pulsatile and diurnal patterns of circulating gonadotropins. *Journal of Clinical Endocrinology and Metabolism*, **76**, 940.

Barash, I. A., Cheung, C. C., *et al.* (1996). Leptin is a metabolic signal to the reproductive system. *Endocrinology*, **137**, 3144–3147.

Beck-Peccoz, P., Padmanabhan, V., *et al.* (1991). Maturation of hypothalamic-pituitary gonadal function in normal human fetuses: circulating levels of gonadotropins, their common alpha subunit and free testosterone, and discrepancy between immunological and biological activities of circulating follicle-stimulating hormone. *Journal of Clinical Endocrinology and Metabolism*, **73**, 525–532.

Bridges, N. A., Christopher, J. A., *et al.* (1994). Sexual precocity: sex incidence and etiology. *Archives of Disease in Childhood*, **70**, 116–118.

Garcia-Mayor, R. V., Andrade, M. A., *et al.* (1997). Serum leptin levels in normal children: relationship to age, gender, body mass index, pituitary-gonadal hormones, and pubertal stage. *Journal of Clinical Endocrinology and Metabolism*, **82**, 2849–2855.

Grumbach, M. M., and Styne, D. M. (1998). Puberty: ontogeny, neuroendocrinology, physiology, and disorders. In J. D. Wilson, D. W. Foster, H. M. Kronenberg and P. R. Larsen (ed.), *Williams textbook of endocrinology*, 9th edn (pp. 1509–1625). Philadelphia, PN: W. B. Saunders.

Harris, D. A., Van Vliet, G., *et al.* (1985). Somatomedin-C in normal puberty and in true precocious puberty before and after treatment with a potent luteinizing hormone-releasing hormone agonist. *Journal of Clinical Endocrinology and Metabolism*, **61**, 152–159.

Hartz, A. J., Barboriak, P. N., *et al.* (1979). The association of obesity with infertility and related menstrual abnormalities in women. *International Journal of Obesity*, **3**, 57–73.

Herman-Giddens, M. E., Bourdony, C., *et al.* (2001). Early puberty: a cautionary tale. *Pediatrics*, **107(3)**, 609–610.

Herman-Giddens, M. E., Slora, E. J., *et al.* (1997). Secondary sexual characteristics and menses in young girls seen in office practice: a study from the Pediatric Research in Office Settings Network. *Pediatrics*, **99(4)**, 505–512.

Herman-Giddens, M. E., Wang, L., and Koch, G. (2001). Secondary sexual characteristics in boys: estimates from the National Health and Nutrition Examination Survey III, 1988–1994. *Archives of Pediatrics and Adolescent Medicine*, **155(9)**, 1022–1028.

Kaplowitz, P. B., and Oberfield, S. E. (1999). Reexamination of the age limit for defining when puberty is precocious in girls in the United States: implications for evaluation and treatment. Drug and Therapeutics and Executive Committees of the Lawson Wilkins Pediatric Endocrine Society. *Pediatrics*, **104**, 936–941.

Kaplowitz, P. B., Slora, E. J., *et al.* (2001). Earlier onset of puberty in girls: relation to increased body mass index and race. *Pediatrics*, **108(2)**, 347–353.

Kulin, H. E., and Reiter, E. O. (1973). Gonadotropins during childhood and adolescence: a review. *Pediatrics*, **51**, 260.

Lee, P. A., Guo, S. S., and Kulin, H. E. (2001). Age of puberty: data from the United States of America. *APMIS*, **109(2)**, 81–88.

MacMahon, B. (1973). Age at menarche. *National Health Survey*. US Department of Health, Education and Welfare, Health Resources Centre. Washington, DC, Government Printing Office, **133**, 74–1615.

March, C. M., Goebelsmann, U., *et al.* (1979). Roles of estradiol and progesterone in eliciting the midcycle luteinizing hormone and follicle-stimulating hormone surges. *Journal of Clinical Endocrinology and Metabolism*, **49**, 507.

Marshall, W. A., and Tanner, J. M. (1969). Variations in pattern of pubertal changes in girls. *Archives of Disease in Childhood*, **44**, 291–303.

Marshall, W. A., and Tanner, J. M. (1970). Variations in the pattern of pubertal changes in boys. *Archives of Disease in Childhood*, **45**, 13–23.

Massa, G., de Zegher, F., *et al.* (1992). Serum levels of immunoreactive inhibin, FSH, and LH in human infants at preterm and term birth. *Biology of Neonate*, **61**, 150–155.

Moll, G. W., Jr., and Rosenfield, R. L. (1984). Direct inhibitory effect of estradiol on pituitary luteinizing hormone responsiveness to luteinizing hormone releasing hormone is specific and of rapid onset. *Biology of Reproduction*, **30**, 59.

National Heart, Lung and Blood Growth and Health Study (1992). Obesity and cardiovascular disease risk factors in black and white girls. *American Journal of Public Health*, **82**, 1613–1620.

Reiter, E. O., and Lee, P. A. (2001). Have the onset and tempo of puberty changed? *Archives of Pediatrics and Adolescent Medicine*, **155(9)**, 988–989.

Roche, A. F., Wellens, R., *et al.* (1995). The timing of sexual maturation in a group of US white youths. *Journal of Pediatric Endocrinology and Metabolism*, **8**, 11–18.

Root, A. W. (2000). Precocious Puberty. *Pediatric Reviews*, **21**, 10–19.

Rosenfield, R. L., Bachrach, L. K., *et al.* (2000). Current age of onset of puberty. *Pediatrics*, **106**, 622.

Styne, D. M., and Grumbach, M. M. (1991). Disorders of puberty in the male and female. In S. S. C. Yen and R. B. Jaffe (ed.), *Reproductive Endocrinology: Physiology, Pathophysiology and Clinical Management* (pp. 511–554). Philadelphia, PN: W. B. Saunders.

Winter, J. S. D., and Faiman, C. (1973). Pituitary-gonadal relations in female children and adolescents. *Pediatric Research*, **7**, 948.

Zacharias, L., Rand, M., *et al.* (1976). A prospective study of sexual development in American girls: the statistics of menarche. *Obstetrics and Gynecology Survey*, **31**, 325–337.

# 3 Hormonal changes at puberty and the emergence of gender differences in internalizing disorders

*Katherine Sanborn and Chris Hayward*

As puberty is the most salient developmental milestone occurring during adolescence, there is speculation about the differential effects of puberty on the emergence of gender differences in internalizing disorders (depressive anxiety and eating disorders) during adolescence. Prior to adolescence the rates of internalizing disorders are slightly higher in boys or equal to that for girls. In early adolescence the rates of girls' internalizing disorders rise to at least two times those for boys (Angold and Worthman, 1993; Silberg, et al., 1999). Several authors have attempted to establish whether the key factor in the increase of internalizing symptoms and disorders during early adolescence is more linked to puberty specifically, or to increasing age (Angold, Costello, and Worthman, 1998; Angold and Rutter, 1992; Brooks-Gunn and Warren, 1989; Hayward, et al., 1999; Hayward, et al., 1992; Killen, et al., 1992; Paikoff, Brooks-Gunn, and Warren, 1991; Patton, Hibbert, and Carlin, 1996; Rutter, et al., 1989; Rutter, Tizard, and Whitmore, 1970; Susman, et al., 1987a; Warren and Brooks-Gunn, 1989; see chapter 8). Most studies comparing age effects and puberty effects in peri-pubertal adolescent girls have found an association with puberty but not with age in the emergence of internalizing symptoms and disorders. In a study of sixth and seventh grade girls, the relative importance of pubertal stage and age in frequencies of anxiety and eating disorder symptoms were compared (Hayward, et al., 1992; Killen, et al., 1992). The stronger predictor of panic attack occurrence and eating disorder symptoms was found to be pubertal stage, not age. The frequency of panic attack occurrence and eating disorder symptoms increased only slightly between the ages of 11 and 13 years, while they both increased dramatically with increasing pubertal stage. Similarly, Angold, Costello, and Worthman (1998; see chapter 8) reported that pubertal status was a stronger predictor of depression among adolescent girls than increasing age and Patton, Hibbert, and Carlin (1996) reported that menarcheal status was a better predictor of depression than was age in a representative sample of early adolescent girls in Australia. Taken together, these results support pubertal status, but not age, as a predictor of girl's internalizing symptoms during the peri-pubertal time period.

Not all studies find an association between puberty specifically and the emergence of internalizing symptoms in girls. In studies that have used smaller sample sizes (fewer than 110) and tested multiple predictors using multivariate methods with pubertal status as one of many predictors, pubertal status has not been found to be a predictor of depressive symptomatology (Brooks-Gunn and Warren, 1989; Paikoff, *et al.*, 1991; Susman, *et al.*, 1987b). Similarly, in a large clinical sample Angold and Rutter (1992) reported that age, but not pubertal status, predicted depression in adolescent girls. However, this study was constrained by the limited assessment of pubertal status. Finally, Hayward and colleagues (1999) used a representative cohort of 3,216 ethnically diverse adolescents to examine the association between pubertal status and adolescent girls' depressive symptoms. They found that in early adolescence pubertal status is a better predictor of depressive symptoms than chronological age in Caucasian, but not African American or Hispanic girls. While this study supports an association between puberty and depressive symptoms in Caucasians, it also suggests that pubertal status may not be a strong predictor of depression in non-Caucasian samples.

In summary, while not all studies find an association specifically between puberty and the increase in the rates of internalizing disorders in adolescent girls, studies of larger size and fewer methodological limitations do find a significant association, at least for Caucasian samples (Angold, *et al.*, 1998; Hayward, *et al.*, 1999; Patton, *et al.*, 1996; see chapter 8). These larger studies provide evidence that, for girls, puberty is associated with an increased rate of internalizing symptoms.

### Why puberty?

It is unclear why the increase in rates of internalizing symptoms in girls is associated with puberty. Multiple factors are associated with puberty and potentially contribute to the increase in internalizing disorders. Cognitive changes (Allgood-Merten, Lewinsohn, and Hops, 1990; Nolen-Hoeksema and Girgus, 1994), body image changes (Allgood-Merten, *et al.*, 1990; see chapter 4), the relative timing of puberty in relation to peers (Hayward, *et al.*, 1997; Nottleman, *et al.*, 1987; Peterson, Sarigiani, and Kennedy, 1991; Simmons, *et al.*, 1987; see chapter 12), the onset of puberty in relation to other life events (Brooks-Gunn and Warren, 1989; Koenig and Gladstone, 1998; Silberg, *et al.*, 1999), and hormonal effects have all been investigated (Angold, *et al.*, 1999; Brooks-Gunn and Warren, 1989; Dorn, *et al.*, 1996a; Dorn, *et al.*, 1996b; Nottleman, *et al.*, 1990; Slap, *et al.*, 1994; Susman, Dorn, and Chrousos, 1991; Susman, *et al.*, 1997; Susman, *et al.*, 1987a; Susman, *et al.*, 1987b; Susman, *et al.*, 1985; Warren and Brooks-Gunn, 1989; see chapter 8). Evidence supporting all of these potential factors has been found, however, no one factor alone is likely to account for the increased incidence of internalizing disorders in pubertal girls. It is more likely that multiple factors interact to produce the emergence of gender differences. While acknowledging this complexity, this chapter will focus on the hormonal aspects of puberty, which may be associated with the emergence of gender differences in the rates of internalizing symptoms. First, we review the evidence for and against an association between hormonal changes and the emergence of internalizing symptoms at puberty. We then discuss the limitations of hormonal studies to date, with a special focus on the unstudied potential "downstream effects" of hormones and the probable differential sensitivity of individuals to the effects of hormones.

### Hormonal studies

Studies in pubertal girls have found various, inconsistent associations between hormonal levels and internalizing symptoms (Angold, *et al.*, 1999; Brooks-Gunn and Warren, 1989; Dorn, *et al.*, 1996b; Goodyer, Herbert, Tamplin, and Altham, 2000a, 2000b; Nottleman, *et al.*, 1990; Nottleman, *et al.*, 1987; Paikoff, *et al.*, 1991; Slap, *et al.*, 1994; Susman, *et al.*, 1991; Susman, *et al.*, 1997; Susman, *et al.*, 1987a; Susman, *et al.*, 1987b; Susman, *et al.*, 1985). The practical limitations of these studies at least partly explain the inconsistent findings and make negative findings inconclusive. Many studies have theoretical limitations, in that they look at simple relationships between hormonal levels and symptoms. Several authors have suggested models for more complex hormonal–symptom relationships (Angold and Worthman, 1993; Brooks-Gunn, Graber, and Paikoff, 1994; Susman, 1997). The most recent studies examining associations between hormonal levels at puberty and internalizing symptoms are reviewed here, as earlier studies do not modify or contribute differently to the reports included here. Studies are included if they measured hormone levels (or other biological measures), pubertal status, and assessed for internalizing symptoms. The presentation of their results is organized around the hormones studied. The populations include community samples, as well as clinical populations, and most capture ages that include Tanner stages 1–5. Most use questionnaire measures of symptom clusters, while a few make use of structured diagnostic interviews. The majority also make use of cross-sectional design.

### Estrogen

Two of the four reviewed studies measuring estrogen levels found significant associations between estrogen and internalizing symptoms. Angold and colleagues (1999; see also chapter 8) found the increase in odds of depression for an increase of one-quarter of the observed range of the predictor to be 2.5 for estradiol. The relationship between estradiol and depression appeared to be linear in this study. Brooks-Gunn and colleagues (1989) found estradiol to be associated with girls' reports of depressive affect in a curvilinear fashion. Specifically, depressive affect was found to increase at the time of initial rise in estrogen and to plateau by mid to late puberty, around the time girls might begin to have menstrual periods. While this curvilinear relationship was found, social factors accounted for a larger proportion of the variance (8–18%), than did hormonal factors (1–4%). One year later, a significant linear effect of the estradiol levels obtained one year earlier was found on one of the two self-reports of current depressive affect (Paikoff, *et al.*, 1991). Overall, prior reports of depressive affect accounted for more variance than prior hormonal levels in this study.

### Testosterone

Associations between testosterone levels and internalizing symptoms in girls were found in two of the four studies measuring testosterone. Specifically, Susman and colleagues (1991) found that higher levels of negative affect were associated with higher testosterone levels (along with higher cortisol levels and lower dehydroepiandosterodione sulphate levels) in girls. Angold and colleagues (1999; see also chapter 8) found a fourfold increase in the odds of major depression associated with higher testosterone levels and that the relationship between testosterone and the rate of depression was nonlinear, with a sharp increase between the third and fourth quintiles of the testosterone range.

### Gonadotropin

Associations between internalizing symptoms and gonadotropin levels were found by two of the four reviewed studies. Nottlelman *et al.* (1987) found that in girls, higher FSH levels are associated with problems in body and self-image. Similarly, Slap and colleagues (1994) found a negative correlation between FSH and body image scores.

### Adrenal

Higher morning DHEA – but not cortisol – levels were associated with the development of major depression in boys and girls a year later in one recent study (Goodyer, *et al.*, 2000a; Goodyer, *et al.*, 2000b). Also, a more stress-reactive HPA axis has been found in those adolescents reporting behavior problems and symptoms of depression a year later (Susman, *et al.*, 1997). The gender differences in stress responses over the course of puberty have yet to be clarified, however.

### Oxytocin

While to the best of our knowledge there have not been any studies examining the associations between oxytocin and the emergence of gender differences in internalizing disorders during puberty, a theoretical model has been posed by Cyranowski and colleagues (2000). In animal studies, puberty is accompanied by a rise in oxytocin and associated increases in affiliative behavior (Cyranowski, *et al.*, 2000). Cyranowski and colleagues posit that it is this intensification of affiliative needs (secondary to increases in oxytocin), coupled with difficulties in the adolescent transition of high-risk girls, that increases their vulnerability to the depressogenic effects of negative life events.

### Limitations

As several authors reviewing the literature have concluded, the data supporting associations between hormonal changes at puberty and the emergence of gender differences in internalizing symptoms have been weak and inconsistent. However, it is unclear whether the lack of findings has been due to a lack of association or to study limitations. Buchanan and colleagues (1992) extensively reviewed the literature on the activational effects of hormones at puberty and found little evidence supporting associations between hormonal changes and internalizing symptoms. Similarly, the review by Nolen-Hoeksema and colleagues (1994) found little evidence for hormonal effects in the emergence of gender differences in internalizing disorders. The studies to date have had limitations that may significantly affect these conclusions, however. The numbers and types of subjects are major limitations in the studies reviewed. The study finding the strongest associations, that by Angold and colleagues (1999; see also chapter 8), was the one study with a larger sample size (465 subjects);

none of the others had much more than 100 subjects. The vast majority of the reviewed study subjects were Caucasian and middle class. This presents problems of generalizability, especially in light of a recent study finding the emergence of gender differences in internalizing disorders at puberty for Caucasians, but not Hispanics or African Americans (Hayward, *et al.*, 1999).

Also, authors frequently cite lack of control for menstrual cycle variations in hormonal measurements as a major limitation. In the NIMH-NICHD study, for example, 35 percent of the sample was menarcheal (Susman, *et al.*, 1987a; Susman, *et al.*, 1987b). Mean levels of estrogen can vary by threefold to fourfold over the course of the menstrual cycle (Casper, 1998). Therefore, when the menstrual cycle phase is uncontrolled, any absence of association between estradiol levels and symptoms are difficult to interpret. Indeed, it makes the associations between estradiol levels and internalizing symptoms found by Angold and colleagues (1999) and Brooks-Gunn, Paikoff and colleagues (1994) more striking. A similar explanation may account for the lack of concomitant associations found between internalizing symptoms, estradiol, and the gonadotropin. For example, one of the common findings was that of elevated FSH and body image disturbances; this association has been found in the absence of concomitant associations between estradiol and body image. This lack of relationship between estrogen and FSH levels has been hypothesized to be due to less cyclical variation in FSH levels compared to estrogen and LH; the larger variations in estradiol may make it a less recognizable marker for overall serum hormone concentrations (Slap, *et al.*, 1994). In addition to monthly variations in hormonal levels, during puberty there are also fluctuations in estrogen and testosterone levels throughout the day (Ankarberg and Norjavaara, 1999; Norjavaara, Ankarberg, and Albertsson-Wikland, 1996). Therefore, studies that used only one plasma sample for hormonal measurements have decreased the ability to find associations due to variance in hormonal levels.

Most of the studies reviewed are also limited by cross-sectional design or cross-sectional analysis of longitudinal data. While cross-sectional data has inherent limitations in elucidating the nature of associations, cross-sectional measurements of absolute hormone levels are particularly problematic.

Consistent with and expanding upon these limitations is the proposition that in order for associations to be found, a more complex understanding of the effects of hormones in the context of individual vulnerabilities may be required. A more complex understanding of hormonal effects requires examining internalizing symptoms in the context of downstream effects of hormones and understanding the biological changes at puberty in a broader way. Hormonal downstream effects may include acute hormonal neurotransmitter interactions, organizational effects, interactions between hormones, and the hypothalamic-pituitary-adrenal (HPA) axis or background CNS changes at puberty. Because data on adolescents is sparse, information from other areas, such as animal research and research in adult women, may be useful in understanding and providing direction for adolescent research. Even so, a deeper understanding of hormonal effects may not explain why the normal hormonal changes of puberty, which occur in every female, are associated with difficulties in particular individuals. Individual vulnerabilities or a differential sensitivity to the effects of normal hormonal changes has been implicated in the adult premenstrual syndrome literature (Schmidt, *et al.*, 1998). It may be that associations between the biological changes of puberty and the development of internalizing symptoms only emerge in the context of understanding differential sensitivities of vulnerable individuals. The rest of this chapter will discuss examples of potentially relevant downstream effects of hormones and potential factors conferring differential sensitivity to hormones in the production of internalizing symptoms at puberty.

*"Downstream effects" of hormones*

The downstream effects of gonadal hormones involve several potentially relevant interactions with systems associated with depression and anxiety symptoms. Gonadal hormones have direct modulatory or "activational" effects on neurotransmitter systems thought to be directly involved with the production of symptoms (Rubinow and Schmidt, 1996). Gonadal hormones also cause permanent structural changes, through effects known as organizational effects, which then influence vulnerability to the development of internalizing symptoms (Phoenix, *et al.*, 1959). They may affect the background "tone" or reactivity of the CNS to environmental stimuli through their interactions with major neurotransmitters such as GABA, increasing vulnerability to the development of internalizing symptoms (reviewed in Altemus and Arleo, 1999). And finally, they affect stress reactions via effects on the function of the hypothalamic pituitary axis (reviewed in Young and Korszun, 1999). These downstream effects are not meant to be inclusive, but to provide examples of approaches to understanding the roles that hormones may play in the emergence of gender differences in internalizing disorders at puberty. These downstream effects are shown schematically in figure 3.1.

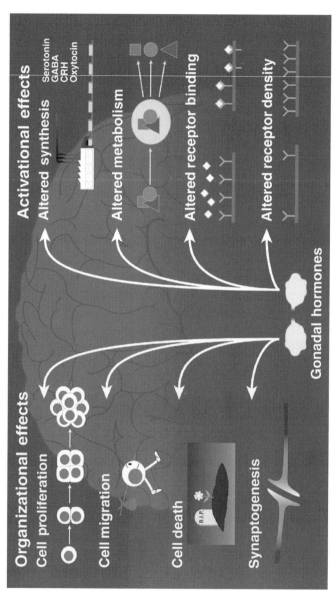

Figure 3.1 Potential CNS effects of estrogen at puberty. Reprinted with permission, Hayward and Sanborn (2002).

*Modulation of neurotransmitter systems' – "activational" effects*

The most direct downstream effect of hormones that may be associated with internalizing symptoms is the modulation of neurotransmitter systems involved in mood and affect regulation. Gonadal steroids (estrogen, androgens) account for the majority of the sexual dimorphism in neuroregulation (Rubinow and Schmidt, 1996). Estrogen, androgen (testosterone), and progesterone receptors are found throughout the brain, including areas of the brain thought to be involved in the regulation of mood and autonomic reactivity (Rubinow and Schmidt, 1996; Simerly, *et al.*, 1990). Also, estrogen, testosterone, and progesterone modulate multiple neurotransmitter systems thought to be involved in the production and regulation of affect (McEwen, 1991). They have been shown to modulate the serotonin (reviewed in Rubinow and Schmidt, 1996; Rubinow, Schmidt, and Roca, 1998), glutamate (Wong and Moss, 1992), GABA (Halbreich, *et al.*, 1996; Jung-Testas, *et al.*, 1989; Lambert, *et al.*, 1996), noradrenergic (reviewed in DeBattista, Smith, and Schatzberg, 1999), oxytocin, neurokinin, and cholcystokinin (reviewed in Rubinow and Schmidt, 1996; Rubinow, *et al.*, 1998), and dopamine systems (Attali, *et al.*, 1997; Halbreich and Lumley, 1993). The distribution of gonadal hormone receptors in the brain and the effects of individual hormones are sex specific. For example, estrogen increases 5-HT1 binding in the preoptic area in female rats and decreases binding in male rats (Fischette, Biegon, and McEwen, 1983). The effects of gonadal hormones on neurotransmitter systems and their relationship with the production of internalizing symptoms are probably complex, however. There is evidence that relative levels of combinations of hormones and the fluctuating nature of hormonal levels may be important in the production of internalizing symptoms (Altemus and Arleo, 1999).

A complete presentation of the specific effects of gonadal hormones and their combinations on neurotransmitter systems is outside the scope of this chapter, however an example may be illustrative. The interaction between estrogen and the serotonin neurotransmitter system has been of interest (Rubinow, *et al.*, 1998). Estrogen modulates serotonin function by affecting serotonin synthesis (Cone, Davis, and Goy, 1981), metabolism (Klaiber, *et al.*, 1979), receptor affinity (Rojansky, Halbreich, and Zander, 1991), and receptor density (reviewed by Biegon, 1990; McEwen, 1991) through both genomic and nongenomic mechanisms (McEwen, 1991); for reviews, see Halbreich, 1993 and DeBattista, 1999. The implications of estrogen's modulation of the serotonin systems are most likely complex and dependent on the balance between estrogen and other hormones. There is evidence that by itself estrogen primarily modulates the serotonin system in the direction of antidepressant effects. For example, studies of estrogen suggest that it increases the efficiency of serotonergic neurotransmission (Altemus and Arleo, 1999) through such mechanisms as decreases in 5-HT1 receptor density (Biegon, Reches, Snyder, and McEwen, 1983), increases in 5HT2 receptor density (Biegon, *et al.*, 1983; Fischette, *et al.*, 1983; Summer and Fink, 1995), and inhibition of monoamine oxidase activity (DeBattista, *et al.*, 1999; Luine, Khylchevskaya, and McEwen, 1975). However, the effects of estrogen on the serotonin system may be partially reversed by the effects of other hormones, such as testosterone. For example, testosterone administration has been found to cause reductions in serotonergic activity (Altemus and Arleo, 1999; Mendelson and McEwen, 1990). Therefore, the combined effects of gonadal hormones on other neurotransmitter systems, and the balance between various hormones, may be more useful measurements than individual, absolute hormonal levels.

In addition to looking at the relative levels of combinations of hormones, the dynamics of hormonal-level cyclicity may be informative in understanding potential associations between hormones and internalizing symptoms. The antidepressant effect of estrogen is clinically supported by studies finding that increases in estradiol improve depressive symptoms in hypoestrogenic women (Montgomery, *et al.*, 1987). Estradiol has been found to have a therapeutic effect in women with depression after surgical oophorectomy (Nathorst-Boos, von Schoultz, and Carlstrom, 1993) and to enhance antidepressant effectiveness (Schneider, Small, and Hamilton, 1997). At the same time, physiological levels of estrogen have been found to produce symptoms in women with a history of PMS (Schmidt, *et al.*, 1998). The absolute levels of estrogen may not be as important in determining whether estrogen acts as an antidepressant or a depressant as the rate and directions of change in those levels (Seeman, 1997). It is also possible that cyclical withdrawal of progestins and estrogens kindles neuronal systems and promotes anxiety states by mechanisms similar to those that have been implicated in the provocation of peri-menstrual epilepsy (Narbone, *et al.*, 1990; Seeman, 1997). Or similarly, these periods of withdrawal may generally increase women's stress responses in the similar way as anxiolytic withdrawal (Seeman, 1997).

Some authors have posited that the repeated cyclicity of hormonal changes may actually cause increases in neurotransmitter dysfunction over time. In their review of gender differences in neurotransmitters, Halbreich and Lumley (1993) found evidence for gender differences in the norepinephrine, serotonin, dopamine, and acetylcholine systems. For example, while there are some gender differences in the absolute levels of plasma 3-methoxy-4-hydroxyphenol-glycol (MHPG, main metabolite of NE), the major difference between men and women was in the rate of change in this metabolite with aging (Halbreich, *et al.*, 1987). Multiple differences in the serotonin system were also reviewed. It has been found that the aging process of some 5-HT systems might be less apparent in men than in women, and it might be different in different 5-HT systems. For example, the imipramine uptake (a proxy for serotonin function) in the cortex of normal controls and suicide subjects has been found to be significantly influenced by age and sex (Aurora and Meltzer, 1989). It is hypothesized that because not all serotonergic systems are impaired at the same rate, an age-related change in vulnerability to dysregulation of the system is implied (Halbreich, Rojansky, Zander, and Barkai, 1991). The gender differences in age-related neurotransmitter dysfunction might arise at puberty. There is evidence from animal data that gender differences in the serotonin system reaction to stress emerges in adolescence, presumably secondary to the effects of gonadal steroids. Prior to puberty, male and female rhesus monkeys have been found to have equivalent levels of 5-HIAA following separation, while during adolescence females have significantly higher separation levels of 5-HIAA than males (Higley, Suomi, and Linnoila, 1990). Similar associations between life events and neurotransmitter function over the course of puberty in humans have yet to be elucidated.

In summary, gonadal hormones have acute, modulatory effects on all the neurotransmitter systems thought to be involved in the production of internalizing symptoms. These effects are not only dependent on individual hormonal levels, but also on the relative balance between different hormones and their potentially oppositional or additive effects. In addition, the rates of change, direction of change, and cyclicity of hormonal levels over time may have implications for symptom production. These factors are a consideration for further research in the emergence of gender differences in internalizing disorders at puberty.

### "Organizational" effects

Newer data suggest that there may be important organizational effects of gonadal hormones on the CNS during puberty, as well as the acute modulatory or activational effects (Giedd, *et al.*, 1997; Romeo, Diedrich, and Sisk, 2000). Organizational effects of gonadal steroids are those effects which produce a permanent change in the structure or functional potential of the brain during specific developmental periods of time (Phoenix, *et al.*, 1959), and may confer a vulnerability effect to the development of internalizing disorders in females. The major organizational effects of gonadal hormones occur prenatally and produce most of the sexual di-morphism in brain morphology (Rubinow and Schmidt, 1996). However, puberty is also a developmental window during which steroid hormones are thought to effect sexual differentiation by gaining control over certain key maturational processes in the brain. These processes include influenc-ing cell proliferation, cell migration, ontogenetic cell death, and synap-togenesis (Casper, 1998; MacLusky and Naftolin, 1981; Phoenix, *et al.*, 1959). The resulting structural dimorphism may confer a functional dif-ference between males and females. For example, gender differences are very prominent in structural areas that have been suggested to be involved in regulation of normal and abnormal mood and behaviors, such as the hypothalamus, amygdala, and cortex (Goy and McEwen, 1980). Most of the research in organizational effects has been on prenatal development, however, with increasing technology there is preliminary evidence that the organizational effects of hormones at puberty may also prove rele-vant. In a MRI brain-imaging study intended to provide normative data, sex and age differences in brain morphology were found by Giedd and colleagues (1997) for a sample of 121 subjects ages 4–18. The amyg-dala increased significantly more in males than females and hippocampal volume increased more in females. This finding is consistent with the preponderance of androgen receptors in the amygdala and estrogen re-ceptors of rats in the hippocampus (Giedd, *et al.*, 1997). These data also suggest that the development of the brain continues through puberty with unknown implications for the emergence of gender differences in psychopathology. There has also been interest in the neuronal pruning that takes place under the influence of gonadal hormones and for which there may be a timing effect. There is evidence that the developmental timing of pruning may be sexually dimorphic and associated with other disorders, such as bipolar affective disorder and schizophrenia (Saugstad, 1994). This area, to the best of our knowledge, has yet to be explored in relation to the rise in gender differences in internalizing disorders at puberty.

**HPA axis effects**

Besides effects on neurotransmitter systems, gonadal hormones interact with other hormonal systems, which may be involved in the production of internalizing symptoms. One example is the hypothalamic-pituitary-adrenal (HPA) axis. There have been repeated links between HPA axis dysregulation and depressive disorders and gender differences in HPA axis function have been found in animals, healthy adults, and depressed adults. For an extensive review of this literature see Young and Korszun's review of 1999. Gonadal hormones may influence HPA axis function through effects on glucocorticoid receptors, on brain CRH systems or on pituitary responsiveness to CRH (Young and Korszun, 1999). These effects can be seen in healthy adults and there is evidence that estrogen may be partially responsible for the increased HPA stress response. For example, chronic estrogen treatment of ovariectomized female rats enhances their corticosterone response to stress and slows their recovery from stress (Burgess and Handa, 1992). Estrogen increases the stress response in men (Kirschbaum, Schommer, and Federenko, 1996), a lesser sensitivity to dexamethasone feedback (Altemus, Redwine, and Yung-Mei, 1997) and cortisol infusion (Young, 1995; Young, Haskett, and Watson, 1991) have been found during the luteal phase of the menstrual cycle. In addition to the HPA axis differences found between men and women without depression, depressed women have been found to have higher mean 24-hour plasma cortisol levels (Halbreich, et al., 1984; Young, et al., 1991) and increased central HPA axis drive in the evening (Young, Haskett, and Grunhaus, 1994), compared to depressed men.

These gender differences in the HPA axis function may emerge at puberty. Both male and female monkeys have been found to show slight decreases in separation-induced cortisol elevations at prepuberty, while males showed significantly reduced levels of cortisol increase in subsequent years and females showed stable increases (Higley, 1985; Suomi, 1991). Additionally, males' cortisol response to separation appeared blunted relative to that of females as they approached and entered puberty. This finding of suppressed or blunted cortisol response to challenge in adolescent males but not females has also been reported in at least two other monkey studies (Rasmussen and Suomi, 1989; Suomi, et al., 1989). Explanations for this blunted stress response in male monkeys include the effects of testosterone on the HPA axis and evolutionary considerations (Suomi, 1991).

There have been at least two studies in depressed adolescents examining stress responses, although neither did so in the context of pubertal changes. Dorn and colleagues (1996b) examined the hypothalamic-pituitary-adrenal response to stress across gender in both depressed and nondepressed adolescents. Unlike studies in adults, the depressed adolescents did not have elevated 24-hour UFC excretion, elevated morning serum cortisol, or elevated stimulated measures of cortisol following CRH when compared with controls. Also no blunting of ACTH response to CRH was observed, while this finding is commonly seen in adults with melancholic depression (Dorn, et al., 1996b; Gold, Goodwin, and

Chrousos, 1988). The depressed group of adolescents was found to have significantly lower concentrations of morning cortisol, similar to the pattern seen in adults with atypical, seasonal depression (Dorn, *et al.*, 1996b; Vanderpool, Rosenthal, and Chrousos, 1991). There was a "very robust" gender difference in plasma ACTH concentrations in the two CRH stimulation tests. Boys had significantly higher ACTH levels at baseline and higher areas under the ACTH curve. This is opposite to what has been observed in adults, where females had higher ACTH responses compared to males (Dorn, *et al.*, 1996b; Gallucci, Baum, and Laue, 1993; Vanderpool, *et al.*, 1991). Dorn and colleagues (1996b) suggest that the gender difference in adolescents could be due to differences in the peripheral metabolism of ACTH, resulting in changes of immunoreactivity, but not bioactivity or a different set point of the hypothalamic-pituitary-adrenal axis. They also suggest that the normal pattern of ACTH, cortisol responses to CRH, and the normal 24-hour free cortisol excretion, reflected normal negative feedback mechanisms at that age or that the subjects had atypical depression instead of melancholic depression. Limitations of this study include a small sample size and the stressor used did not produce a measured increase in cortisol, as expected.

In an arm of the NIMH-NICHD study, cortisol levels, observed distress behavior, behavior problems, and symptoms of anxiety and depression (Susman, *et al.*, 1997) were assessed in adolescent girls and boys. Cortisol levels were measured under a distress situation and behavior was recorded. Cortisol levels increased, decreased, or stayed the same in response to the stressor. Those whose cortisol levels increased in response to the stressor reported more behavior problems and symptoms of depression a year later than those whose cortisol decreased or remained the same. Girls tended to have higher cortisol levels and to exhibit more distress behaviors than boys. Interactions of sex and time of measurement and sex and situation also were found; the authors caution interpretation of these differences, however, because of the small sample size (Susman, *et al.*, 1997).

In summary, there are gender differences in the function of the HPA axis in both healthy and depressed adults, with most findings supporting an increased HPA reactivity to stress in females. These differences are thought to be due, in part, to gonadal hormones and their repeated fluctuating levels in women. Little is known about stress response changes over the course of puberty, however. Because of this link between internalizing symptoms, specifically depression and HPA dysfunction, an increased understanding of the changes between prepubertal stress responses and postpubertal stress responses may be particularly informative.

## Primary pubertal triggers – GABA/glutamate balance

Another way of looking at the potential associations between hormonal changes and the emergence of gender differences in internalizing disorders is related to the potential changes in CNS reactivity, via a shift in the balance between excitatory and inhibitory neurotransmitters at puberty. Indeed, there is evidence that there is a shift in the balance between the major excitatory neurotransmitter, glutamate, and the major inhibitory neurotransmitter, GABA, which is the trigger for puberty itself (Grumbach and Styne, 1998; Mitsushima, Hei, and Terasawa, 1994). The increases in gonadal hormones, in turn, further modulate these systems (Altemus and Arleo, 1999). Since both GABA and glutamate have been associated with anxiety and depressive disorders, this shift in the balance between excitatory and inhibitory neurotransmitters may have implications for internalizing disorders. We will focus on GABA because of recent evidence that the onset of puberty is triggered by decreases in hypothalamic GABA (Grumbach and Styne, 1998; Mitsushima, et al., 1994).

There is now considerable evidence that a decrease in the GABA-ergic influence in the hypothalamus triggers the onset of puberty in primates (Grumbach and Styne, 1998). With the approach of puberty in the rhesus monkey, GABA inhibition of the LHRH pulse generator decreases. In vivo studies of the median eminence of prepubertal, early pubertal, and midpubertal rhesus monkeys demonstrate striking decreases in GABA between the prepubertal and peri-pubertal period (Mitsushima, et al., 1994). This results in an augmentation of excitatory neurotransmitters and amino acids, such as glutamate, and ultimately the pulsatile release of gonadotropin in the pituitary. To date there are no similar studies measuring changes in central nervous system GABA in humans at pre- and postpuberty. In the only study of age trends, there was a downward trend in GABA levels between childhood and adulthood; however, this study did not include enough adolescent subjects to detect any change in early adolescence (Prosser, et al., 1997).

GABA has been implicated in both depression and anxiety. However, little is reported about gender differences in the psychiatric literature. Depressed subjects have been found to have lower mean plasma GABA levels compared to controls (Petty, 1995). In a recent study using MRS, abnormally low cortical GABA concentrations were observed in the brains of depressed versus nondepressed control subjects (Sanacora, et al., 1999). Evidence for the role of GABA in anxiety comes in part from the role of GABA in the mechanism of action of anxiolytic medications. Anxiolytics of the benzodiazepine class exert their primary effects by altering

GABA-ergic transmission. GABA also modifies and interacts with serotonergic and noradrenergic neurotransmitter systems (Petty, 1995). Therefore, the hypothesized effects of brain GABA on the risk for anxiety and depression may not be via direct effects, but mediated through other neurotransmitter systems known to be involved with anxiety and depression.

There are probably gender differences in the function of GABA neurotransmission due to gonadal hormones, with implications for anxiety and depression. While the trigger for puberty may be related to changes in GABA, the resulting increase in gonadal hormones then in turn may further modulate the GABA system. For example, estrogen has been found to increase GABA receptor binding and glutamic acid decarboxylase mRNA in the hippocampus, while progesterone reverses this increase in glutamic acid decarboxylase (Altemus and Arleo, 1999; Schumacher, Coirini, and McEwen, 1989; Weiland, 1992). The potential anxiolytic effect of estrogen is supported by the finding that estrogen-treated ovariectomized rats show increased activity in an open field test (McCarthy, Felzenberg, and Robbins, 1995). Little is known about the gender differences in human GABA neurotransmission and the implications of these differences in humans, however.

## Summary of downstream effects

While measuring direct gonadal hormonal levels individually has provided some insight into potential biological factors contributing to the emergence of gender differences in internalizing disorders at puberty, understanding the downstream effects of gonadal hormones on other systems may also prove informative.

## Differential sensitivity to the effects of hormones

Any explanation of the emergence of gender differences in internalizing symptoms at puberty must address the fact that every individual undergoes similar pubertal changes, yet only a minority develop symptoms. This issue raises the possibility that certain individuals enter puberty with underlying vulnerabilities to the effects of puberty in producing internalizing symptoms. One possibility is that individuals have neurotransmitter subtypes, which interact differently with gonadal hormones to produce an increased risk of developing symptoms. An illustrative example of this differential sensitivity to gonadal hormones comes from the adult literature on premenstrual syndrome (PMS) (Schmidt, *et al.*, 1998). Schmidt *et al.* (1998) showed that neither gonadal suppression nor replacement with estrogen or progesterone had any effect in women who do not normally have PMS, while women with a history of PMS showed return of symptoms at physiological levels of estrogen or progesterone. This finding is particularly relevant to hormonal investigations of mood disorders associated with puberty, because it suggests that there is a differential sensitivity to normal levels of hormones in some individuals and that investigating hormonal levels in isolation of the underlying vulnerabilities may not produce meaningful information. A greater understanding of the factors that could contribute to a differential sensitivity to hormones in relation to the production of internalizing symptoms is needed. The factors that are most likely involved in producing a differential sensitivity may be those that affect systems that are known to be associated with both internalizing symptoms and those known to be modulated by gonadal hormones or which change with puberty. Probably most relevant are those factors that are involved in stress responses and include genetic, social, traumatic, and temperamental factors that have been largely unexplored specifically in the context of hormonal changes at puberty.

### Genetic variation

Genetic differences could influence vulnerability to internalizing disorders at puberty in a number of ways that have yet to be explored. One hypothesized way is via variations in response to stressful life events. As far as we know, only one study has examined the associations between puberty, gender, stress response, genetic risk, and depressive symptoms (Silberg, *et al.*, 1999). Silberg *et al.* (1999) recently found that the emergence of gender differences in major depression in adolescence might be due to both an increased responsivity to stress and genetic risk. The study sample consisted of twin pairs from the Virginia Twin Study of Adolescent Behavioral Development: 182 prepubertal female, 237 prepubertal male, 314 pubertal female, and 171 pubertal male twin pairs. Past-year life events were analyzed and characterized as potentially within or beyond an individual's control; the authors used this categorization as they were interested in understanding the extent to which the genes for depression also increased the risk for experiencing negative life events. For the most part, the types of life events associated with depression did not differ significantly between boys and girls. Prior to age 12, boys and girls were quite similar in their level of depression, but the rates for girls show an increase over those for boys thereafter. Both boys and girls who experienced one or more negative life events showed an increase in depression after age 11, with girls having higher mean depression scores than boys. For girls without any notable life events in the past year, the age distribution of depression scores increased, although it was not as steep as those with a history of life events; this increase implicates factors other than life events in the age-related rise in depressive symptoms. Of those boys who did not experience any notable life event in the past year, the age distribution for the depression scores was nearly flat. The regression analysis indicated a significant main effect of total number of life events for both boys and girls, but a significant interaction between events and pubertal status and age only for girls. Twin correlations for depression indicated genetic influence, 0.37 monozygotic versus 0.09 dizygotic, in pubertal girls. The results from model fitting indicate a significant effect of genetic factors only in the adolescent girls, which accounts for approximately 28–30 percent of the overall variance in depression. The authors also concluded that the long-term stability of depression in pubertal girls is best explained by latent genetic factors, while the influence of genetic factors on the occurrence of life events is not stable and there is a developmentally related increase in genetic variance for life events. Part of the genetic risk for depression was posited to be attributable to a genetic predisposition to experiencing particular stressful life events. From the data on boys, the authors concluded that for boys, depression appears to be largely attributable to the occurrence of negative life events (Silberg, *et al.*, 1999). There could, of course, be many other types of genetic differences and experiential differences may be due to biological differences such as serotonin receptor sensitivity or density changes in response to estrogen.

### Social status

From animal research, there is evidence that neurotransmitter and hypothalamic-pituitary-adrenal (HPA) axis responses to stress vary by social status and changes in social status. Social experience, particularly dominance, may affect stress responses and have an additive effect along with gonadal hormones in increasing the risk for internalizing symptoms in reaction to stress. For example, Yeh, Fricke, and Edwards (1996) found that serotonergic stimulation caused increased firing in neurons from dominant crayfish, whereas the same stimulation caused decreased firing in neurons from subordinate animals (Leibenluft, 1999; Yeh, *et al.*, 1996). These differences were reversed if a subordinate crayfish triumphed in a subsequent dominance struggle. In another study, in monkeys, social status was manipulated so that half of the previously subordinate females became dominant and half of the previously dominant females became subordinate (Shively, Laber-Laird, and Anton, 1997). Current subordinates showed hyperactive HPA responses and more anxious and depressive behaviors. However, current subordinates with a history of social subordination were preferentially susceptible to a behavioral depression response compared to those that had previously been dominant. The social status of adolescent girls prior to and during puberty may, therefore, set the background for different responses to stressors and hormonal changes with unknown implications for the emergence of internalizing symptoms.

### History of trauma

Several studies have shown chronic changes in the HPA axis in response to early stress (for a thorough review see Weiss, 1999; Meaney, et al., 1996). The subsequent CRH hypersecretion is thought to increase vulnerability to depression either directly or in response to subsequent stressors (Weiss, Longhurst, and Mazure, 1999). It is possible that the hormonal changes at puberty further impair HPA axis function to a critical point in girls with a history of trauma. As previously mentioned in the section on downstream effects and the HPA axis, estrogen receptors have been linked to CRH regulatory mechanisms and therefore may affect HPA more acutely (Handa, et al., 1994; Weiss, et al., 1999), in addition to the hypothesized deteriorative effects on the HPA axis of chronically fluctuating hormone levels (Halbreich, et al., 1984; Halbreich and Lumley, 1993). In the opposite direction, parenting may protect against HPA overreactivity. Animals exposed to short periods of infantile stimulation or handling show decreased HPA axis responsivity to stress throughout their lives (Meaney, et al., 1996). In a similar way, family environment and parenting may influence the functional "resiliency" of the HPA axis to the effects of hormonal changes at puberty. While there have not been any studies to our knowledge linking parenting, biological changes, and the emergence of gender differences in internalizing disorders during puberty, there is evidence that the children of supportive parents have lower levels of internalizing symptoms during puberty (Scaramella, Conger, and Simons, 1999). A schematic of the possible interaction between a history of trauma and pubertal change is shown in figure 3.2.

### Temperament

The interaction between temperament and the emergence of gender differences in internalizing symptoms at puberty has been largely unexplored, yet variations in temperament have been found to increase risk for the development of certain disorders. In humans, two of the most studied early childhood temperamental traits with implications for later

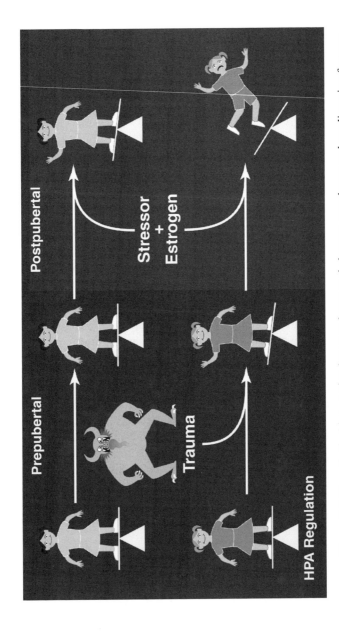

Figure 3.2 Hypothetical interaction between hormonal changes at puberty and predisposing factors: HPA axis disregulation in girls with a history of trauma. Reprinted with permission, Hayward and Sanborn (2002).

internalizing disorders are behavioral inhibition and negative affectivity. Behavioral inhibition is characterized by a cluster of behaviors which include withdrawal, shyness, avoidance, and fear of unfamiliar objects (Kagan, Resnick, and Snidman, 1988); these characteristics can have concomitant biological manifestations (increased salivary cortisol and high stable heart rates) (Kagan, et al., 1988). Several studies support behavioral inhibition as a risk factor for social anxiety disorder (Biederman, et al., 2001; Hayward, et al., 1998; Schwartz, Snidmen, and Kagan, 1999).

Negative affectivity is the temperamental trait characterized by sensitivity to negative stimuli (Watson and Clark, 1984). There is evidence that negative affectivity is a nonspecific risk factor for anxiety and depression (Brown, Chorpita, and Barlow, 1998; Spence, 1997; Zinbarg and Barlow, 1996). It is therefore possible that temperament sets the stage for hormonal changes to interact with stressors in the production of internalizing reactions to life events at puberty.

There is evidence from animal literature that temperamental reactivity is stable, even though the specific behaviors change over time. In monkeys, individual responses to separation have been found and followed longitudinally from birth to maturity (Suomi, 1991). Those monkeys exhibiting extreme reactions to separation during their first year of life were also likely to display extreme reactions in subsequent years, even if the form of the reactions changed over time. Likewise, those who displayed only mild reactions during their first year were unlikely to display extreme reactions in subsequent years. This relative consistency of individual reactivity over the course of development has implications for individuals having a differential sensitivity to developing internalizing disorders during puberty.

### Summary and conclusions

In conclusion, gender differences in the adult rates of internalizing disorders are one of the most consistent epidemiological findings in psychiatry. While it is fairly clear that these differences do not arise until early adolescence, it has been less clear, although probable, that puberty itself is the key event associated with the timing of the increase in internalizing symptoms and disorders in females. While this chapter has focused on potential biological factors, it is an artificial division to view this problem as being primarily either biological or psychosocial, as there are biological concomitants to psychosocial factors and vice versa. There is some evidence that the emergence of internalizing symptoms is associated with the rise of gonadal hormones in girls and that this association may be independent of the psychosocial effects arising from the concomitant morphological changes (See chapter 8). Specifically, associations have been found between rising levels of estrogen and testosterone and increased depressive symptoms; the associations have not been consistently observed, however. While this lack of consistency may eventually prove to be due to an actual lack of association, it may also be due to substantial study limitations, such as lack of control for menstrual cycle phase, cross-sectional design, and single, individual hormonal measurements. Data from animal and adult studies provide suggestions for other approaches. In general, it may be useful to view the hormonal changes of puberty by measuring hormonal levels in association with their "downstream" effects as well as internalizing symptoms. The balance between pubertal hormones and the dynamics of their changes over time, alterations in the function of other systems such as major neurotransmitters and the HPA axis, the triggers of puberty itself, and structural changes in the brain are all factors that have yet to be understood in the context of pubertal development. These biological factors do not occur in isolation, however, and their relationship to the development of internalizing symptoms is most likely dependent upon differential sensitivity to the effects of pubertal changes; understanding the emergence of symptoms means understanding the individual in the context of other factors. Individual context and the resulting vulnerabilities (or assets, for that matter) may provide the differentiating factors between the development and the non-development of symptoms. This context probably cannot be understood from cross-sectional studies or from the vantage of one theoretical framework. An individual's genetics, temperament, history of life events, and social status, for example, may all prove to differentiate, in the setting of puberty, between those girls who develop symptoms and those who do not. It will also inform the more general case, that is, the gender difference in rates of internalizing disorders.

## References

Allgood-Merten, B., Lewinsohn, P. M., and Hops, H. (1990). Sex differences and adolescent depression. *Journal of Abnormal Psychology*, **99**, 55–63.

Altemus, M., and Arleo, K. (1999). Modulation of anxiety by reproductive hormones. In E. Leibenluft (ed.), *Gender differences in mood and anxiety disorders: from bench to bedside* (vol. XVIII, pp. 53–89). Washington, DC: American Psychiatric Press.

Altemus, M., Redwine, L., and Yung-Mei, L. (1997). Reduced sensitivity to glucocorticoid feedback and reduced glucocorticoid receptor mRNA expression in the luteal phase of the menstrual cycle. *Neuropsychopharmacology*, **17**, 100–109.

Angold, A., and Rutter, M. (1992). The effects of age and pubertal status on depression in a large clinical sample. *Developmental Psychopathology*, **4**, 5–28.

Angold, A., and Worthman, C. M. (1993). Puberty onset of gender differences in rates of depression: a developmental, epidemiological and neuroendocrine perspective. *Journal of Affective Disorders*, **29**, 145–158.

Angold, A., Costello, E. J., Erkanli, A., and Worthman, C. M. (1999). Pubertal changes in hormone levels and depression in girls. *Psychological Medicine*, **29**, 1043–1053.

Angold, A., Costello, E. J., and Worthman, C. M. (1998). Puberty and depression: the roles of age, pubertal status and pubertal timing. *Psychological Medicine*, **28**, 51–61.

Ankarberg, C., and Norjavaara, E. (1999). Diurnal rhythm of testosterone secretion before and throughout puberty in healthy girls: correlation with 17beta-estradiol and dehydroepiandrosterone sulfate. *Journal of Clinical Endocrinology and Metabolism*, **84**, 975–984.

Attali, G., Weizman, A., Gil-Ad, I., and Rehavi, M. (1997). Opposite modulatory effects of ovarian hormones on rat brain dopamine and serotonin transporters. *Brain Research*, **756**, 153–159.

Aurora, R. C., and Meltzer, H. Y. (1989). [3H] Imipramine binding in the frontal cortex of suicides. *Psychiatry Research*, **30**, 125–135.

Biederman, J., Hirshfeld-Becker, D., Rosenbaum, J. F., Herot, C., Friedman, D., Snidman, N., Kagan, J., and Faraone, S. (2001). Further evidence of association between behavioral inhibition and social anxiety in children. *American Journal of Psychiatry*, **158**, 1673–1679.

Biegon, A. (1990). Effects of steroid hormones on the serotonergic system. In P. M. Whitaker-Zzmitia and S. J. Peroutka (ed.), *The neuropharmacology of serotonin*. New York: New York Academy of Sciences.

Biegon, A., Reches, A., Snyder, L., and McEwen, B. S. (1983). Serotonergic and noradrenergic receptors in the rat brain: modulation by chronic exposure to ovarian hormones. *Life Sciences*, **32**, 2015–2021.

Brooks-Gunn, J., and Warren, M. P. (1989). Biological and social contributions to negative affect in young adolescent girls. *Child Development*, **60**, 40–55.

Brooks-Gunn, J., Graber, J. A., and Paikoff, R. L. (1994). Studying links between hormones and negative affect: models and measures. *Journal of Research on Adolescence*, **4**, 469–486.

Brown, T., Chorpita, B., and Barlow, D. (1998). Structural relationships among dimensions of the DSM-IV anxiety and mood disorders and dimensions of negative affect, positive affect and autonomic arousal. *Journal of Abnormal Psychology*, **107**, 179–192.

Buchanan, C. M. (1989). Hormone concentrations and variability. Associations with self-reported moods and energy in early adolescent girls. Poster presentation at the biernnial meeting of the Society for Research on Child Development, Kansas City, MO.

Burgess, L., and Handa, R. (1992). Chronic estrogen-induced alterations in adrenocorticotropin and corticosterone secretion and glucocorticoid receptor-medicated functions in female rats. *Endocrinology*, **131**, 1261–1269.

Casper, R. (1998). Growing up female. In R. Casper (ed.), *Women's health: hormones, emotions, and behavior* (vol. XVIII, pp. 1–14). Cambridge: Cambridge University Press.

Casper, R. (ed.) (1998). *Women's health: hormones, emotions, and behavior*. Cambridge: Cambridge University Press.

Cone, R., Davis, G., and Goy, R. (1981). The effects of ovarian steroids on serotonin metabolism within grossly dissected and micro-dissected brain regions in ovariectomized rat. *Brain Research Bulletin*, 7, 639–644.

Cyranowski, J. M., Frank, E., Young, E., and Shear, M. K. (2000). Adolescent onset of the gender difference in lifetime rates of major depression: a theoretical model. *Archives of General Psychiatry*, 57, 21–27.

DeBattista, C., Smith, D., and Schatzberg, A. (1999). Modulation of monoamine neurotransmitters by estrogen: clinical implications. In E. Leibenluft (ed.), *Gender differences in mood and anxiety disorders – from bench to bedside* (vol. XVIII, pp. 137–166). Washington, DC: American Psychiatric Press.

Dorn, L. D., Burgess, E., Dichek, H. L., Putnam, F., Chrousos, G. P., and Gold, P. (1996a). Thyroid hormone concentrations in depressed and non-depressed adolescents: group difference and behavioral relations. *Journal of the American Academy of Child and Adolescent Psychiatry*, 35, 299–306.

Dorn, L. D., Burgess, E., Susman, E. J., von Eye, A., DeBellis, M., Gold, P., and Chrousos, G. P. (1996b). Response to oCRH in depressed and non-depressed adolescents: does gender make a difference? *Journal of the American Academy of Child and Adolescent Psychiatry*, 35, 764–773.

Fischette, C. T., Biegon, A., and McEwen, B. S. (1983). Sex differences in serotonin 1 receptor binding in rat brain. *Science*, 222, 333–335.

Gallucci, W., Baum, A., and Laue, L. (1993). Sex differences in sensitivity of the hypothalamic-pituitary-adrenal axis. *Health Psychology*, 12, 420–425.

Giedd, J. N., Castellanos, F. X., Rajapakse, J. C., Vaituzis, A. C., and Rapoport, J. L. (1997). Sexual dimorphism of the developing human brain. *Progress in Neuro-Psychopharmacology and Biological Psychiatry*, 21, 1185–1201.

Gold, P., Goodwin, F., and Chrousos, G. (1988). Clinical and biochemical manifestations of depression: relationship to the neurobiology of stress, part 1. *New England Journal of Medicine*, 319, 413–420.

Goodyer, I. M., Herbert, J., Tamplin, A., and Altham, P. M. (2000a). First-episode major depression in adolescents. Affective, cognitive and endocrine characteristics of risk status and predictors of onset. *British Journal of Psychiatry*, 176, 142–149.

Goodyer, I. M., Herbert, J., Tamplin, A., and Altham, P. M. (2000b). Recent life events, cortisol, dehydroepiandrosterone and the onset of major depression in high-risk adolescents. *British Journal of Psychiatry*, 177, 499–504.

Goy, R. W., and McEwen, B. S. (1980). *Sexual differentiation of the brain: based on a work session of the neuroscience research program*. Cambridge, MA: MIT Press.

Grumbach, M., and Styne, D. (1998). Puberty: ontogeny, neuroendocrinology, physiology, and disorders. In J. D. Wilson, D. W. Foster, H. M. Kronbenberg, and P. R. Larsen (ed.), *Williams textbook of endocrinology*, 9th edn (pp. 1509–1625). Philadelphia, PN: W. B. Saunders.

Halbreich, U., Asnis, G. M., Zumoff, B., Nathan, R. S., and Shindledecker, R. (1984). Effect on age and sex on cortisol secretion in depressives. *Psychiatry Research*, **13**, 221–229.

Halbreich, U., and Lumley, L. A. (1993). The multiple interactional biological processes that might lead to depression and gender differences in its appearance. *Journal of Affective Disorders*, **29**, 159–173.

Halbreich, U., Petty, F., Yonkers, K., Kramer, G., Rush, A., and Bibi, K. (1996). Low plasma gamma-aminobutyric acid levels during the late luteal phase of women with premenstrual dysphoric disorder. *American Journal of Psychiatry*, **153**, 718–720.

Halbreich, U., Rojansky, N., Zander, K. J., and Barkai, A. (1991). Influence of age, sex and diurnal variability on imipramine receptor binding and serotonin uptake in platelets of normal subjects. *Journal of Psychiatric Research*, **25**, 7–18.

Halbreich, U., Sharpless, N., Asnis, G. M., Endicott, J., Goldstein, S., Vital-Herne, J., Eisenberg, J., Zander, K., Kang, B., Shindledecker, R., and Yeh, C. (1987). Afternoon continuous plasma levels of 3-methoxy-4-hydroxyphenyl-glycol and age. *Archives of General Psychiatry*, **44**, 804–812.

Handa, R., Burgess, L., Kerr, J., and O'Keefe, J. (1994). Gonadal steroid hormone receptors and sex differences in the hypothalamo-pituitary-adrenal axis. *Hormones and Behavior*, **28**, 464–476.

Hayward, C., Gotlib, I. H., Schraedley, P. K., and Litt, I. (1999). Ethnic differences in the association between pubertal status and symptoms of depression in adolescent girls. *Journal of Adolescent Health*, **25**, 143–149.

Hayward, C., Killen, J., Hammer, L., Litt, I., Wilson, D., Simmonds, B., and Taylor, C. (1992). Pubertal stage and panic attack history in sixth- and seventh-grade girls. *American Journal of Psychiatry*, **149**, 1239–1243.

Hayward, C., Killen, J., Kraemer, H., and Taylor, C. (1998). Linking self-reported childhood behavioral inhibition to adolescent social phobia. *Journal of the American Academy of Child and Adolescent Psychiatry*, **37**, 1308–1316.

Hayward, C., Killen, J., Wilson, D., Hammer, L., Litt, I., Kraemer, H., Haydel, F., Varady, A., and Taylor, C. (1997). The psychiatric risk associated with early puberty in adolescent girls. *Journal of the American Academy of Child and Adolescent Psychiatry*, **36**, 255–262.

Hayward, C., and Sanborn, K. (2002). Puberty and the emergence of gender differences in psychopathology. *Journal of Adolescent Health*, **305**, 49–58.

Higley, J. D. (1985). Continuity of social separation behaviors from infancy to adolescence in rhesus monkeys (*Macaca mullata*). Unpublished dissertation, Madison.

Higley, J. D., Suomi, S. J., and Linnoila, M. (1990). Developmental influences on the serotonergic system and timidity in the non-human primate. In E. F. Coccaro and D. L. Murphy (ed.), *Serotonin in major psychiatric disorders*. Washington, DC: American Psychiatric Press.

Jung-Testas, I., Hu, Z. Y., Baulieu, E. E., and Robel, P. (1989). Steroid synthesis in rat brain cell cultures. *Journal of Steroid Biochemistry*, **34**, 511–519.

Kagan, J., Resnick, J. S., and Snidman, N. (1988). Biological bases of childhood shyness. *Science*, **240**, 167–171.

54     *Katherine Sanborn and Chris Hayward*

Killen, J. D., Hayward, C., Litt, I., Hammer, L. D., Wilson, D. M., Miner, B., Taylor, C. B., Varady, A., and Shisslak, C. (1992). Is puberty a risk factor for eating disorders? *American Journal of Diseases of Children*, **146**, 323–325.

Kirschbaum, C., Schommer, N., and Federenko, I. (1996). Short-term estradiol treatment enhances pituitary–adrenal axis and sympathetic responses to psychosocial stress in healthy young men. *Journal of Clinical Endocrinology and Metabolism*, **81**, 3639–3643.

Klaiber, E., Broverman, D., Vogel, W., and Kobayashi, Y. (1979). Estrogen therapy for severe persistent depressions in women. *Archives of General Psychiatry*, **36**, 550–554.

Koenig, L. J., and Gladstone, T. R. (1998). Pubertal development and school transition. Joint influences on depressive symptoms in middle and late adolescents. *Behavior Modification*, **22**, 335–357.

Lambert, J., Belelli, D., Hill-Venning, C., Callachan, H., and Peters, J. A. (1996). Neurosteroid modulation of native and recombinant GABA receptors. *Cellular and Molecular Biology*, **16**, 155–174.

Leibenluft, E. (ed.) (1999). *Gender differences in mood and anxiety disorders*, vol. III. Washington, DC: American Psychiatric Press.

Luine, V., Khylchevskaya, R., and Mc Ewen, B. (1975). Effect of gonadal steroids on activities of monoamine oxidase and choline acetylase in rat brain. *Brain Research*, **86**, 293–306.

MacLusky, N., and Naftolin, F. (1981). Sexual differentiation of the central nervous system. *Science*, **211**, 1294–1302.

McCarthy, M., Felzenberg, E., and Robbins, A. (1995). Infusions of diazepam and allopregnenolone into the midbrain central gray facilitate open field and reproductive behavior in female rats. *Hormones and Behavior*, **29**, 279–295.

McEwen, B. S. (1991). Non-genomic and genomic effects of steroids on neural activity. *Trends in Pharmacological Science*, **12**, 141–147.

Meaney, M. J., Diorio, J., Francis, D., Widdowson, J., LaPlante, P., Caldji, C., Sharma, S., Seckl, J. R., and Plotsky, P. M. (1996). Early environmental regulation of forebrain glucocorticoid receptor gene expression: implications for adrenocortical responses to stress. *Developmental Neuroscience*, **18**, 49–72.

Mendelson, S., and McEwen, B. (1990). Testosterone increases the concentration of ($^3$H)8-hydroxy-2-(di-n-propylamino)tetralin binding at $5\text{-}HT_{1A}$ receptors in the medial preoptic nucleus of the castrated male rat. *European Journal of Pharmacology*, **181**, 329–331.

Mitsushima, D., Hei, D., and Terasawa, E. (1994). Gamma-Aminobutyric acid is an inhibitory neurotransmitter restricting the release of luteinizing hormone-releasing hormone before the onset of puberty. *Proceedings of the National Academy of Sciences of the United States of America*, **91**, 395–399.

Montgomery, J. C., Brincat, M., Tapp, A., Appleby, L., Versi, E., Fenwick, P. B. C., and Studd, J. W. W. (1987). Effect of estrogen and testosterone implants on psychological disorders in the climacteric. *Lancet*, **7**, 297–299.

Narbone, M., Ruello, C., Oliva, A., Baviera, G., D'Amico, D., Bramanti, P., and DiPerri, R. (1990). Hormonal dysregulation and catmenial epilepsy. *Functional Neurology*, **5**, 49–53.

Nathorst-Boos, J., von Schoultz, B., and Carlstrom, K. (1993). Elective ovarian removal and estrogen replacement therapy – effects on sexual life, psychological well-being and androgen status. *Journal of Psychosomatic Obstetrics and Gynaecology*, **14**, 283–293.

Nolen-Hoeksema, S., and Girgus, J. (1994). The emergence of gender differences in depression during adolescence. *Psychological Bulletin*, **115**, 424–443.

Norjavaara, E., Ankarberg, C., and Albertsson-Wikland, K. (1996). Diurnal rhythm of 17 beta-estradiol secretion throughout pubertal development in healthy girls: evaluation by a sensitive radioimmunoassay. *Journal of Clinical Endocrinology and Metabolism*, **81**, 4095–4102.

Nottleman, E. D., Inoff-Germain, G., Susman, E. J., and Chrousos, G. P. (1990). Hormones behavior and puberty. In J. Bancroft and J. M. Reinisch (ed.), *Adolescence and puberty* (pp. 88–123). Oxford: Oxford University Press.

Nottleman, E. D., Susman, E. J., Dorn, L. D., Inoff-Germain, G., Cutler, G. B., Loriaux, D. L., and Chrousos, G. P. (1987). Developmental processes in early adolescence: relationships between adolescent adjustment problems and chronological age, pubertal stage, and puberty-related serum hormone levels. *Journal of Pediatrics*, **110**, 473–480.

Paikoff, R. L., Brooks-Gunn, J., and Warren, M. P. (1991). Effects of girls' hormonal status on depressive and aggressive symptoms over the course of one year. Special issue: the emergence of depressive symptoms during adolescence. *Journal of Youth and Adolescence*, **20**, 191–215.

Patton, G. C., Hibbert, M. E., and Carlin, J. (1996). Menarche and the onset of depression and anxiety in Victoria, Australia. *Journal of Epidemiology and Community Health*, **50**, 661–666.

Peterson, A. C., Sarigiani, P. A., and Kennedy, R. E. (1991). Adolescent depression: why more girls? *Journal of Youth Adolescence*, **20**, 247–271.

Petty, F. (1995). GABA and mood disorders: a brief review and hypothesis. *Journal of Affective Disorders*, **34**, 275–281.

Phoenix, C. H., Goy, R. W., Gerall, A. A., and Young, W. C. (1959). Organizing action of prenatally administered testosterone propionate on the tissues mediating mating behavior in the female guinea pig. *Endocrinology*, **65**, 369–382.

Prosser, J., Hughes, C., Sheikha, S., Kowatch, R., Kramer, G., Rosenbarger, N., Trent, J., and Petty, F. (1997). Plasma GABA in children and adolescents with mood behavior, and comorbid mood and behavior disorders: a preliminary study. *Journal of Child and Adolescent Psychopharmacology*, **7**, 181–199.

Rasmussen, K. L. R., and Suomi, S. J. (1989). Heart rate and endocrine responses to stress in adolescent male rhesus monkeys on Cayo Santiago. *Puerto Rican Health*, **8**, 65–71.

Rojansky, N., Halbreich, U., and Zander, K. (1991). Imipramine receptor binding and serotonin uptake in platelets of women with premenstrual changes. *Gynecologic and Obstetric Investigation*, **31**, 146–152.

Romeo, R., Diedrich, S., and Sisk, C. (2000). Effects of gonadal steroids during pubertal development on androgen and estrogen receptor-a immunoreactivity in the hypothalamus and amygdala. *Journal of Neurobiology*, **44**, 361–368.

Rubinow, D. R., and Schmidt, P. J. (1996). Androgens, brain, and behavior. *American Journal of Psychiatry*, **153**, 974–984.

Rubinow, D. R., Schmidt, P. J., and Roca, C. A. (1998). Estrogen-serotonin interactions: implications for affective regulation. *Biological Psychiatry*, **44**, 839–850.

Rutter, M., Angold, A., Taylor, E. J., Harrington, E. J., and Nicholls, J. (1989). Age and sex effects on depressive and other symptomatology. Paper presented at the annual meeting of the Society for Research in Child Development, Kansas City.

Rutter, M., Tizard, J., and Whitmore, K. (1970). *The selection of children with psychiatric disorder*. Harlow: Longman.

Sanacora, G., Mason, G., Rothman, D., Behar, K., Hyder, F., Petroff, O., Berman, R., Charney, D., and Krystal, J. (1999). Reduced cortical gamma aminobutyric acid levels in depressed patients determined by proton magnetic resonance spectroscopy. *Archives of General Psychiatry*, **56**, 1043–1047.

Saugstad, L. (1994). The maturational theory of brain development and cerebral excitability in the multifactorially inherited manic-depressive psychosis and schizophrenia. *International Journal of Psychophysiology*, **18**, 189–203.

Scaramella, L., Conger, R., and Simons, R. (1999). Parental protective influences and gender-specific increases in adolescent internalizing and externalizing problems. *Journal of Research on Adolescence*, **9**, 111–141.

Schmidt, P. J., Nieman, L. K., Danaceau, M. A., Adams, L. F., and Rubinow, D. R. (1998). Differential behavioral effects of gonadal steroids in women with and in those without premenstrual syndrome. *New England Journal of Medicine*, **338**, 209–216.

Schneider, L., Small, G., and Hamilton, S. (1997). Estrogen replacement and response to fluoxetine in a multi-center geriatric depression trial (Fluoxetine Collaborative Study Group). *American Journal of Geriatric Psychiatry*, **5**, 97–106.

Schumacher, M., Coirini, H., and McEwen, B. (1989). Regulation of high-affinity GABA-a receptors in the dorsal hippocampus by estradiol and progesterone. *Brain Research*, **487**, 178–183.

Schwartz, C. E., Snidmen, N., and Kagan, J. (1999). Adolescent social anxiety as an outcome of inhibited temperament in childhood. *Journal of the American Academy of Child and Adolescent Psychiatry*, **38**, 1308–1316.

Seeman, M. (1997). Psychopathology in women and men: focus on female hormones. *American Journal of Psychiatry*, **154**, 1641–1647.

Shively, C. A., Laber-Laird, K., and Anton, R. (1997). Behavior and physiology of social stress and depression in female cynomolgus monkeys. *Biological Psychiatry*, **41**, 871–872.

Silberg, J., Pickles, A., Rutter, M., Hewitt, J., Simonoff, E., Maes, H., Carbonneau, R., Murrelle, L., Foley, D., and Eaves, L. (1999). The influence of genetic factors and life stress on depression among adolescent girls. *Archives of General Psychiatry*, **56**, 225–232.

Simerly, R. B., Chang, C., Muramatsu, M., and Swanson, L. W. (1990). Distribution of androgen and estrogen receptor mRNA-containing cells in the rat brain: an in situ hybridization study. *Journal of Comparative Neurology*, **294**, 76–95.

Simmons, R. G., Burgeson, R., Carlton-Ford, S., and Blyth, D. A. (1987). The impact of cumulative change in early adolescence. *Child Development*, **58**, 1220–1234.

Slap, G. B., Khalid, N., Paikoff, R. L., Brooks-Gunn, J., and Warren, M. P. (1994). Evolving self-image, pubertal manifestations, and pubertal hormones: preliminary findings in young adolescent girls. *Journal of Adolescent Health*, **15**, 327–335.

Spence, S. (1997). Structure of anxiety symptoms among children: a confirmatory factor-analytic study. *Journal of Abnormal Psychology*, **106**, 280–297.

Summer, B. E., and Fink, G. (1995). Estrogen increases the density of 5-hydroxytryptamine(2A) receptors in cerebral cortex and nucleus accumbens in the female rat. *Journal of Steroid Biochemistry and Molecular Biology*, **54**, 15–20.

Suomi, S. J. (1991). Adolescent depression and depressive symptoms: insights from longitudinal studies with rhesus monkeys. *Journal of Youth and Adolescence*, **20**, 273–287.

Suomi, S. J., Scanlan, J. M., Rasmussen, K. L. R., Davidson, M., Boinski, S., Higley, J. D., and Marriott, B. (1989). Pituitary-adrenal response to capture in Cayo-derived M-Troop rhesus monkeys. *Puerto Rican Health Science Journal*, **8**, 171–176.

Susman, E. J. (1997). Modeling developmental complexity in adolescence: hormones and behavior in context. *Journal of Research on Adolescence*, **7**, 283–306.

Susman, E. J., Dorn, L. D., and Chrousos, G. P. (1991). Negative affect and hormone levels in young adolescents: concurrent and predictive perspectives. Special issue: the emergence of depressive symptoms during adolescence. *Journal of Youth and Adolescence*, **20**, 167–190.

Susman, E. J., Dorn, L. D., Inoff-Germain, G., Nottleman, E. D., and Chrousos, G. P. (1997). Cortisol reactivity, distress behavior, and behavioral problems and psychological problems in young adolescents: a longitudinal perspective. *Journal of Research on Adolescence*, **7**, 81–105.

Susman, E. J., Inoff-Germain, G., Nottleman, E. D., Loriaux, D. L., Cutler, G. B., and Chrousos, G. P. (1987a). Hormones, emotional dispositions and aggressive attributes in young adolescents. *Child Development*, **58**, 1114–1134.

Susman, E. J., Nottleman, E. D., Inoff-Germain, G., Dorn, L. D., and Chrousos, G. P. (1987b). Hormonal influences on aspects of psychological development during adolescence. *Journal of Adolescent Health Care*, **8**, 492–504.

Susman, E. J., Nottleman, E. D., Inoff-Germain, G., Dorn, L. D., Cutler, G. B., Loriaus, D. L., and Chrousos, G. P. (1985). The relation of relative hormonal levels and physical development and social-emotional behavior in young adolescence. *Journal of Youth and Adolescence*, **14**, 245–254.

Vanderpool, J., Rosenthal, N., and Chrousos, G. (1991). Evidence for hypothalamic CRH deficiency in patients with seasonal affective disorder. *Journal of Clinical Endocrinology and Metabolism*, **72**, 1382.

Warren, M. P., and Brooks-Gunn, J. (1989). Mood and behavior at adolescence: evidence for hormonal factors. *Journal of Clinical Endocrinology and Metabolism*, **69**, 77–83.

Watson, D., and Clark, L. A. (1984). Negative affectivity: the disposition to experience aversive emotional states. *Psychological Bulletin*, **96**, 465–490.

Weiland, N. (1992). Glutamic acid decarboxylase messenger ribonucleic acid is regulated by estradiol and progesteronin the hippocampus. *Endocrinology*, **131**, 2697–2702.

Weiss, E., Longhurst, J., and Mazure, C. (1999). Childhood sexual abuse as a risk factor for depression in women: psychosocial and neurobiological correlates. *American Journal of Psychiatry*, **156**, 816–828.

Wong, M., and Moss, R. L. (1992). Long-term and short-term electrophysiological effects of estrogen on the synaptic properties of hippocampal CA1 neurons. *Journal of Neuroscience*, **12**, 3217–3225.

Yeh, S. R., Fricke, R. A., and Edwards, D. H. (1996). The effect of social experience on serotonergic modulation of the escape circuit of crayfish. *Science*, **271**, 366–369.

Young, E. (1995). Glucocorticoid cascade hypothesis revisited: role of gonadal steroids. *Depression*, **3**, 1995.

Young, E., Haskett, R., and Grunhaus, L. (1994). Increased evening activation of the hypothalamic pituitary adrenal axis in depressed patients. *Archives of General Psychiatry*, **51**, 701–707.

Young, E., Haskett, R., and Watson, S. (1991). Loss of glucocorticoid fast feedback in depression. *Archives of General Psychiatry*, **48**, 693–699.

Young, E., and Korszun, A. (1999). Women, stress, and depression: sex differences in hypothalamic-pituitary-adrenal axis regulation. In E. Leibenluft (ed.), *Gender differences in mood and anxiety disorders* (vol. XVIII, pp. 31–52). Washington, DC: American Psychiatric Press.

Zinbarg, R., and Barlow, D. (1996). Structure of anxiety and the anxiety disorders: a hierarchical model. *Journal of Abnormal Psychology*, **105**, 181–193.

*Part 2*

# Girls at puberty

# 4 Puberty and body image

*Eric Stice*

Puberty represents a period of dramatic physiological change that is unparalleled in development (Connolly, Paikoff, and Buchanan, 1996). Not surprisingly, this maturational process has a profound impact on the psychological functioning of youth. One of the most intense changes to occur at puberty involves body image, which refers to cognitive and emotional perceptions of one's body. The changes in body image are particularly striking because they involve marked gender differences. Body dissatisfaction is the most widely studied aspect of body image disturbances, which afflict a large segment of the population and appear to have adverse sequela including eating pathology, anxiety, depression, low self-esteem, and unnecessary cosmetic surgery (Thompson, *et al.*, 1999). The aim of this chapter is to discuss (1) gender differences in body image perception in response to puberty, (2) the impact of sociocultural influences on this process, (3) the effects of changes in body image on broader psychological development, and (4) the limitations of the literature on this topic.

## Pubertal status versus timing

It is important to differentiate the effects of pubertal status from the effects of pubertal timing (Graber, Petersen, and Brooks-Gunn, 1996; see also chapter 1). Pubertal status refers to the level of pubertal development at a certain point in time, whereas pubertal timing refers to whether an individual's pubertal development occurs earlier, later, or at about the same time as most adolescents. There are several important implications for this distinction. First, studies on the effects of pubertal status must by definition occur when research participants are experiencing pubertal change. Second, studies on the effects of pubertal timing require that sufficient proportions of research participants have begun puberty so that they can be confidently classified with regards to timing of development (e.g., as early versus nonearly developers). Third, the effects of status and timing will often be confounded, with the precise degree of confounding a function of the age range of the sample. Although the conceptual distinction between these two aspects of pubertal development is quite important, they are often not clearly differentiated in the literature (Graber, *et al.*, 1996; see also chapter 7). It should be noted that the effects of perceived pubertal timing should be interpreted with caution, as studies suggest this variable lacks validity (See chapter 13 for alternative view). Specifically, research has found poor concordance between actual pubertal timing and perceived timing, and further that these two variables show differential relations to key criteria (e.g., body dissatisfaction; Gargiulo, *et al.*, 1987).

### Physiological changes associated with puberty

The physiological changes that characterize puberty are mediated by the endocrine system and include an accelerated growth rate, increased muscle development (both skeletal and smooth muscle), growth of pubic and axillary (underarm) hair, and growth in genitalia (Connolly, *et al.*, 1996; Tanner, 1978; see also chapter 2). Other changes that occur include increased acne and the development of sebaceous (oily) and apocrine (sweat) glands (Tobin-Richards, *et al.*, 1984). There are also several sex-specific changes: wherein boys experience facial hair growth, voice deepening, and the development of broader shoulders; girls experience breast development, menarche, and the development of broader hips (See chapter 2). Perhaps most germane with regard to body image, these changes collectively result in a marked increase in adipose tissue for girls and in muscle mass for boys by the completion of puberty.

### Cultural attractiveness ideals, pubertal development, and body image

The physiological changes wrought by puberty are thought to differentially interact with the socially defined attractiveness ideals for the two sexes. The current attractiveness ideal is ultraslender for females but muscular for males (Thompson, *et al.*, 1999). Thus, the dramatic increase in adipose tissue that occurs in puberty moves girls away from the sociocultural ideal of attractiveness. Theoretically, this divergence from the attractiveness ideal results in elevated body dissatisfaction for girls during adolescence (Graber, *et al.*, 1994; Petersen, Sarigiani, and Kennedy, 1991). The increase in height that accompanies puberty may also contribute to body dissatisfaction for girls. Specifically, because the growth spurt occurs approximately two years earlier than for boys, girls are often as tall or slightly taller than boys, which can be a source of concern as dating is initiated. In contrast, for boys, muscle mass and height increase during puberty, moving them toward the male attractiveness ideal, which theoretically leads to greater body satisfaction. Increased strength and height may also foster athletic ability, which enhances boys' standing among both peers and adults (Tobin-Richards, et al., 1984).

The timing of puberty is thought to amplify the differential effects pubertal development has on body image disturbances for the two genders. For instance, girls who experience the increase in adipose tissue before most of their female peers are thought to have the greatest body dissatisfaction because they are developmentally deviant. Similarly, boys who have an increase in muscle mass and height after most of their male peers are believed to experience the greatest body dissatisfaction. These theoretical predictions are an outgrowth of a developmental deviance perspective (Petersen and Crockett, 1985). Specifically, as girls enter puberty an average of two years before boys, the early maturing girls and late maturing boys deviate most widely from their larger peer groups. Thus, it might be expected that early maturing girls and late maturing boys would feel most out of sync with their peers and therefore experience the greatest body dissatisfaction (See chapters 7, 12, and 13).

An important implication of this theoretical account is that the relation between pubertal development and body dissatisfaction would be expected to be greatest for youth who have most strongly internalized the culturally promoted attractiveness ideals for the two sexes. That is, the effects of stage and timing of pubertal development should be most pronounced for girls and boys who report the strongest endorsement of the thin and muscular ideals (respectively). Furthermore, any other variables that may influence the degree of internalization of the attractiveness ideals, such as ethnicity and acculturation to mainstream values, would likewise qualify the relation between pubertal development and body image disturbances.

Studies have found that stage of pubertal development correlated positively with body dissatisfaction for girls but not for boys (Koff and Rierdan, 1993; Richards, et al., 1990; Simmons, Blyth, and McKinney, 1983). However, other studies have not observed significant effects for either sex (Cattarin and Thompson, 1994; Gargiulo, et al., 1987; Swarr and Richards, 1996). Because degree of pubertal development changes over time, it does not make sense to test for prospective effects of this variable. Accordingly, many researchers have focused on the effects of pubertal timing. Three studies found that early pubertal development was correlated with increased body dissatisfaction for girls (Cok, 1990; Simmons, Blyth, and McKinney, 1983; Stice, Presnell, and Bearman, 2001). There is also some evidence that late pubertal development is associated with increased body dissatisfaction in boys (Cok, 1990; Siegel, et al., 1999). However, other studies have not observed a significant correlation between early puberty and body dissatisfaction for girls (Gargiulo, et al., 1987; Smolak, Levine, and Gralen, 1993). A particularly illuminating study measured the correlation between pubertal timing and body dissatisfaction repeatedly over time and found that the correlations for girls ranged from $-0.09$ to $0.49$, with only two of the four being statistically significant (Wright, 1989). Similarly, this study found that the correlation between pubertal timing and body dissatisfaction for boys ranged from $-0.06$ to $0.43$, and only one of the four effects were significant. Whereas a number of prospective studies on this topic have been conducted (e.g., Simmons, Blyth, and McKinney, 1983; Smolak, Levine, and Gralen, 1993; Wright, 1989), none appeared to test for a prospective effect of early menarche on change in body dissatisfaction. The only study that tested whether early puberty predicted subsequent increases in body dissatisfaction among girls produced a nonsignificant effect (Stice and Whitenton, 2002).

Another important consideration is the magnitude, or potency, of these effects. Although most studies did not report effect sizes, metaanalytic procedures were used to estimate effect sizes and to calculate average effect sizes (Cooper and Hedges, 1994). If effect sizes were not reported, they were directly calculated by reconstituting the data (e.g., using weighted probability values to conduct a chi square test) or were estimated from the p-values using the formula provided in Rosenthal (1991). Average effect sizes were calculated using the fixed effects models detailed in Shadish and Haddock (1994). Averaging across the studies cited above, pubertal stage only accounted for 1.9 percent of the variance in body dissatisfaction and pubertal timing only accounted for 2.2 percent of the variance in body dissatisfaction. Given the magnitude of these effects, the inconsistent pattern of findings reported could have resulted because these effects are small and therefore not significant when using small sample sizes.

Although no studies could be found that directly tested whether internalization, acculturation, or ethnicity moderated the relation of pubertal stage and timing to body dissatisfaction, findings point to ethnic differences in several key variables. Emerging research suggests that puberty occurs earlier for girls in certain ethnic minority groups (e.g., African American) relative to Caucasians (Doswell, et al., 1998), and that girls from certain ethnic groups (e.g., African Americans, Native Americans, and Hispanics) show elevated rates of obesity relative to Caucasian girls (Rosner, et al., 1998; Siegel, et al., 1999; Troiano, et al., 1995). Although one might expect these girls to have more body image disturbances, it should be recalled that this relation is putatively qualified by the degree of thin ideal internalization. Consistent with the above theory, there is evidence that African American and Hispanic girls show a lesser degree of thin ideal internalization than do their Caucasian counterparts (Lopez, Blix, and Blix, 1995; Thompson, Corwin, and Sargent, 1997) and report correspondingly lower levels of body dissatisfaction (Robinson, *et al.*, 1996; Siegel, *et al.*, 1999; Story, *et al.*, 1995).

Interestingly, there is evidence that the relation between pubertal development and body dissatisfaction is qualified by another factor – concurrent life stressors. Specifically, research has found that the adverse effects of early puberty on body dissatisfaction for girls are amplified when they co-occur with other life stressors, such as school transitions (Blyth, Simmons, and Zakin, 1985). These results suggest that the coping resources of the adolescent may mitigate the negative effects of early puberty, and when they are overtaxed by other stressful life events the adverse effects are intensified.

In sum, there was mixed support for the assertion that pubertal stage was correlated with body dissatisfaction, and this effect was only observed for girls. There was also mixed support for the expectation that early puberty would be associated with body dissatisfaction for girls and late puberty would be associated with body dissatisfaction for boys. However, these effects appeared to be small in size. There was also some suggestion that they only occur for Caucasian girls. Finally, there was some evidence that the adverse effects of pubertal timing on body dissatisfaction are amplified when early development co-occurs with other life stressors.

### Consequences of body image disturbances

*Mood disturbances*

The body image disturbances resulting from pubertal development are in turn thought to increase the risk for mood disturbances (McCarthy, 1990; Petersen, Sarigiani, and Kennedy, 1991). Two theories have been advanced concerning the putative link between pubertal development and mood disturbances. The first, referred to as the gender intensification theory (Hill and Lynch, 1983), posits that the physical differentiation between girls and boys that results from puberty triggers an increased differentiation and development of gender roles, wherein boys are socialized to value independence and exploration and girls to value interpersonal relations. The greater reliance on interpersonal relationships for self-worth is thought to render girls more vulnerable to depression, because individuals are typically not able to control the emotional tone of these relationships. Greater subscription to the female gender role may also be associated with less active coping strategies, such as ruminative coping (Nolen-Hoeksema, 1994), which leaves girls more susceptible to depression. The second theory suggests that body dissatisfaction mediates the relation between pubertal development and depression for females (McCarthy, 1990; Nolen-Hoeksema, 1994). Presumably, dissatisfaction with one's body, either perceived excess weight for girls or perceived deficits in muscle mass for boys, promotes feelings of depression because appearance is a central evaluative dimension in western culture.

There has been mixed support for the suggestion that pubertal stage is related to mood disturbances, with some studies generating positive effects (Angold, Costello, and Worthman, 1998; Hayward, *et al.*, 1999; Patton, Hibbert, and Carlin, 1996; see also chapter 8) and other studies generating negative effects (Angold and Rutter, 1992; Paikoff, Brooks-Gunn, and Warren, 1991). Research has also suggested that there may be greater variability in negative mood states for pubertal girls relative to their prepubertal counterparts, though this effect does not seem to occur for males (Buchanan, 1991; Connolly, Paikoff, and Buchanan, 1996). Several studies have found that early puberty is associated with elevated depression for girls (Caspi and Moffitt, 1991; Graber, *et al.*, 1997; Rierdan and Koff, 1991; Siegel, *et al.*, 1999; Wichstrom, 1999; see also chapter 12). However, the relation of pubertal timing and depressive symptoms for girls has not been observed in other studies (Brooks-Gunn and Warren, 1989; Paikoff, Brooks-Gunn, and Warren, 1991). It is noteworthy that these effects were relatively small in magnitude. For example, averaging across these studies, early puberty only accounted for 2.0 percent of the variance in depressive symptoms for girls. Interestingly, there is some indication that late pubertal development among boys is associated with depressed affect (Nottelmann, *et al.*, 1987; Siegel, *et al.*, 1999; see also chapter 7). Research also suggests that girls experience a worsening of self-esteem with early puberty, whereas boys experience an increase in self-esteem (Tobin-Richards, *et al.*, 1984). Apparently, only one study has tested whether early menarche prospectively predicted depressive pathology – Hayward and associates (1997) found that early puberty only showed a marginally significant relation to subsequent onset of depressive pathology for girls (this effect accounted for less than 1 percent of the variance). Further support for the notion that early-puberty-induced body dissatisfaction might promote consequent depression is provided by the fact that body dissatisfaction predicted subsequent onset of depressive pathology (Rierdan, Koff, and Stubbs, 1989; Stice, *et al.*, 2000) and increases in depressive symptoms (Stice and Bearman, 2001). Additionally, the sex difference in depression is substantially reduced when body dissatisfaction is statistically controlled (Allgood-Merten, Lewinsohn, and Hops, 1990; Rierdan, Koff, and Stubbs, 1989; Siegel, *et al.*, 1999; Wichstrom, 1999). Somewhat surprisingly, body mass has not emerged as a prospective predictor of depression (Lewinsohn, *et al.*, 1994; Stice, *et al.*, 2000). This suggests that the attitudinal disturbances regarding body image that result from pubertal development may play a more important role in fostering depression than actual weight, or that it may be the changes in body shape rather than weight that promote depression.

There is emerging evidence that the relation between pubertal development and affective disturbances may be qualified by ethnicity. Hayward and associates (1999) found that pubertal status was correlated to depressive symptoms for Caucasian girls, but not African Americans and Hispanics (See chapter 13). This finding concurs with the notion that subscription to the thin ideal propagated by the mainstream culture is necessary for depression to result from puberty-induced body image disturbances.

It should also be noted that there is evidence that the adverse effects of early puberty on mood disturbances are amplified when accompanied by other developmental stressors, such as dating initiation and school transition (Simmons, *et al.*, 1979; Simmons, *et al.*, 1987). Again, this finding echoes the amplifying effects of life stressors on the relation of early pubertal timing to body dissatisfaction noted above.

In sum, there is support for the suggestion that pubertal stage and early puberty contribute to depression for girls, and that this effect may be mediated by body dissatisfaction. However, the effects are modest in magnitude and are potentially restricted to Caucasian girls. The evidence that pubertal timing is associated with depression has significant mental health implications. Depression is the most prevalent psychiatric problem for adolescents, with nearly 20 percent experiencing depression during their second decade of life (Lewinsohn, *et al.*, 1993). Furthermore, depression is associated with suicide attempts and predicts future adjustment problems, including academic failure, marital difficulties, unemployment, substance abuse, delinquency, and legal problems (Birmaher, *et al.*, 1996; Gotlib, Lewinsohn, and Seeley, 1998; Newcomb and Bentler, 1988).

*Eating disturbances*

Theoretically, the increase in adipose tissue that occurs in girls as they pass through puberty results in body dissatisfaction, dieting, and negative affect, which increase the risk for eating disturbances (McCarthy, 1990;

Polivy and Herman, 1985). More specifically, it has been proposed that elevated body mass results in body dissatisfaction because being overweight is not currently socially desirable. Perceived pressure to be thin from family, peers, and the media may exacerbate this process, as repeated messages that one is not attractive would promote discontent with one's body. Body dissatisfaction in turn may foster negative affect, because appearance is a central evaluative dimension for females in our culture. Elevated negative affect might leave girls vulnerable to binge eating, as some individuals are socialized to believe that eating provides comfort and distraction from adverse emotions. Body dissatisfaction is also thought to lead to dieting due to the common belief that this is an effective means of weight control; which in turn is theorized to result in a greater risk for bulimic pathology, as individuals may binge eat to counteract the effects of caloric deprivation. Furthermore, dieting might promote binge eating because breaking strict dietary rules can result in disinhibited eating (the abstinence–violation effect). Body dissatisfaction resulting from the increased adipose tissue may also directly motivate some girls to initiate more radical weight control behaviors, such as vomiting or laxative abuse.

Pubertal stage was associated with elevated eating pathology in some studies (Field, *et al.*, 1999b; Killen, *et al.*, 1992; Swarr and Richards, 1996), but others have generated null findings (Cattarin and Thompson, 1994; Leon, *et al.*, 1995). One study found that pubertal stage predicted an increased risk for subsequent development of eating pathology (Field, *et al.*, 1999a), and because they controlled for age this might be better conceptualized as reflecting pubertal timing. Early menarche has also been found to be associated with concurrent (Field, *et al.*, 1999b; Graber, *et al.*, 1994, 1997; Stice, Presnell, and Bearman, 2001) and subsequent eating pathology (Hayward, *et al.*, 1997). However, the relation between early menarche and eating pathology has not been found in other studies (Attie and Brooks-Gunn, 1989; Killen, *et al.*, 1994; Swarr and Richards, 1996). Again, these relations were rather small in magnitude. For example, averaging across studies, early menarche accounted for only 1.5 percent of the variance in eating pathology.

There is also support for the assertion that the relation between pubertal development and eating pathology is mediated by increases in body mass, body dissatisfaction, dieting, and negative affect. First, as noted above, there is evidence that pubertal stage and timing are associated with increases in body mass and body dissatisfaction (e.g., Richards, *et al.*, 1990; Simmons, Blyth, and McKinney, 1983). Second, early puberty has been found to be associated with elevated dieting (Field, *et al.*, 1999b; Stice, Presnell, and Bearman, 2001). Third, the research findings reviewed above provide evidence that pubertal stage and early puberty increased the risk for affective disturbances (e.g., Angold, Costello, and

Worthman, 1998; Caspi and Moffitt, 1991; see also chapter 8). Finally, body mass, body dissatisfaction, dieting, and negative affect have been found to increase the risk for subsequent development of eating pathology (Field, *et al.*, 1999a; Killen, *et al.*, 1994, 1996; Stice, Presnell, and Spangler, 2002; Wichstrom, 2000).

Although there appear to be no studies that have tested whether the relation between pubertal development and eating pathology is moderated by ethnicity, there are some suggestive findings. Specifically, research indicates that Caucasian girls generally report elevated eating pathology relative to ethnic minority girls (French, *et al.*, 1997; Gross and Rosen, 1988). However, other studies seem to suggest that girls from ethnic minority groups demonstrate similar rates of eating pathology to those observed in Caucasian girls (Childress, *et al.*, 1993; Story, *et al.*, 1995).

It should be noted that there is some indication that the adverse effects of early puberty on eating disturbances are amplified when accompanied by other developmental stressors, such as the onset of dating (Smolak, Levine, and Gralen, 1993). This finding echoes the interactive effects of menarche timing and life stressors in predicting body dissatisfaction and depressed affect, as previously discussed.

In sum, there is mixed support for the assertion that pubertal development contributes to eating pathology for girls and that this effect is mediated by body image disturbances, accompanying negative affect, and dieting. The inconsistent findings may have resulted because the magnitude of these effects is relatively small and therefore inconsistently observed in studies. Nonetheless, the association of pubertal development with eating pathology has serious public health implications, as eating disturbances are often chronic, result in psychosocial impairment, and can result in serious medical complications and a high mortality rate (Fairburn, *et al.*, 2000; Garfinkel, *et al.*, 1995). Moreover, relative to common psychiatric syndromes, eating disorders have the highest rates of treatment seeking, inpatient hospitalization, and suicide attempts (Newman, *et al.*, 1996).

**Methodological limitations of literature**

There were several methodological limitations of this literature that should be kept in mind when interpreting the above findings. First, many studies relied on self-report measures of menarche timing and psychopathology, rather than on structured interviews. Greater confidence could be placed in the findings if structured interviews had been used, because their assessment format allows questions to be clarified and provides in-depth definitions of specific concepts (e.g., binge eating episode), which are not possible with self-report measures. Second, the sole reliance on survey questionnaire data in many studies is likely to have artificially inflated the magnitude of the relations because of shared method bias; future studies should consider using multiple methods of data collection. Third, the majority of studies relied on adolescent-report data. Although adolescents are considered the most valid reporters for some factors (i.e., depression; Edelbrook, *et al.*, 1985), the fact that most of the data were self-report is likely to have inflated the magnitude of the relations because of shared reporter bias. This is particularly worrisome given the relatively small magnitude of the effects in this literature. Future research might make greater use of multiple reporter data (e.g., parental and teacher reports). Fourth, many studies focused on symptoms of body image disturbances, eating pathology, and depression, rather than on the diagnostic levels of these syndromes. Although the studies contribute to our understanding of these relations, it would be useful to ascertain whether early menarche is associated with clinically significant levels of these psychological disturbances. Fifth, many studies do not include both males and females, which hinders the ability to directly examine gender differences. Because males were under-represented in the studies, the results for boys should be interpreted with care. Sixth, few studies reported the effect sizes, which renders it difficult to determine the magnitude of the effect of pubertal development. Finally, several researchers who conducted longitudinal studies did not analyze their data in a way that establishes temporal precedence (e.g., Simmons, Blyth, and McKinney, 1983; Smolak, Levine, and Gralen, 1993; Wright, 1989). Even more surprising, a few of the investigators did not even apply inferential tests to determine whether the observed effects were likely to have occurred based on chance alone (e.g., Duncan, *et al.*, 1985; Petersen, *et al.*, 1994).

## Research and prevention implications

This literature review suggests several useful directions for future research. First, large-scale longitudinal studies that pinpoint more exactly the timing of change in body image, depression, and eating disturbances in relation to stage and timing of pubertal development are needed. As previously noted, it would be ideal if structured psychiatric interviews were used for this purpose, to insure that the psychological disturbances are clinically meaningful. Future research should also examine specific mood and eating disorder diagnoses, including major depression, bipolar disorder, dysthymia, anorexia nervosa, bulimia nervosa, and binge eating disorder. These disorders have qualitatively different symptom presentations and it is thus reasonable to suspect that they may have different risk factors. Research should also direct greater attention to factors that moderate the adverse effects of pubertal development. For example, it seems logical that early puberty would have more adverse effects among girls who have internalized the current thin ideal or who perceive greater pressure from family and peers to conform to this attractiveness ideal. In addition, future longitudinal studies should directly test the mediational processes that are theorized to account for the effects of early maturation on eating and mood disturbances.

Regarding prevention implications, the above findings suggest that early maturing girls constitute a high-risk group for body image, affective, and eating disturbances (see chapter 12). Thus, it might prove advantageous for prevention programs to directly target this group. The fact that other developmental stressors, such as school transitions and dating onset, amplify the adverse effects of early development, suggest that it might be beneficial to develop interventions that help adolescents negotiate these stressors more effectively (e.g., with coping skills training).

## Conclusions

Overall, research suggests that pubertal stage and timing of puberty show modest relations to body dissatisfaction. These effects differed by gender, with pubertal development apparently contributing to body dissatisfaction among girls, but promoting body satisfaction among boys. This differential change in body satisfaction for the two sexes appears to be rooted in the fact that puberty moves girls away from the thin ideal but moves boys toward the muscular ideal. Developmental deviance also seems to potentiate the effects of pubertal timing on body dissatisfaction, with early developing girls and late developing boys showing the greatest body image disturbances. The elevated body dissatisfaction in girls seems to increase the risk for both mood and eating disturbances, although these effects were relatively small in magnitude. Additionally, there was evidence that ethnicity and co-occurring developmental stressors moderated these relations. These findings suggest that the effects of pubertal development are imbedded in a complex matrix of psychosocial risk factors and that future research should focus greater attention on how these factors work together to promote body image disturbances during this important period of development.

## References

Allgood-Merten, B., Lewinsohn, P. M., and Hops, H. (1990). Sex differences and adolescent depression. *Journal of Abnormal Psychology*, **99**, 55–63.
Angold, A., and Rutter, M. (1992). The effects of age and pubertal status on depression in a large clinical sample. *Developmental Psychopathology*, **4**, 5–28.

Angold, A., Costello, E. J., and Worthman, C. W. (1998). Puberty and depression: the roles of age, pubertal status and pubertal timing. *Psychological Medicine*, **28**, 51–61.

Attie, I., and Brooks-Gunn, J. (1989). Development of eating problems in adolescent girls: a longitudinal study. *Developmental Psychology*, **25**, 70–79.

Birmaher, B., Ryan, N., Williamson, D., Brent, D., Kaufman, J., Dahl, R., Perel, J., and Nelson, B. (1996). Childhood and adolescent depression: A review of the past 10 years. Part 1. *Journal of the American Academy of Child and Adolescent Psychiatry*, **35**, 1427–1439.

Blyth, D. A., Simmons, R. G., and Zakin, D. F. (1985). Satisfaction with body image for early adolescent females: the impact of pubertal timing within different school environments. *Journal of Youth and Adolescence*, **14**, 207–225.

Brooks-Gunn, J., and Warren, M. P. (1989). Biological and social contributions to negative affect in young adolescent girls. *Child Development*, **60**, 40–55.

Buchanan, C. M. (1991). Pubertal status in early adolescent girls: relations to moods, energy, and restlessness. *Journal of Early Adolescence*, **11**, 185–200.

Caspi, A., and Moffitt, T. E. (1991). Individual differences are accentuated during periods of social change: the sample case of girls at puberty. *Journal of Personality and Social Psychology*, **61**, 157–168.

Cattarin, J. A., and Thompson, J. K. (1994). A three-year longitudinal study of body image, eating disturbance, and general psychological functioning in adolescent females. *Eating Disorders: Journal of Treatment and Prevention*, **2**, 114–125.

Childress, A. C., Brewerton, T. D., Hodges, E. L., and Jarrell, M. P. (1993). The Kids' Eating Disorder Survey (KEDS): a study of middle school students. *Journal of the American Academy of Child and Adolescent Psychiatry*, **32**, 843–850.

Cok, F. (1990). Body image satisfaction in Turkish adolescents. *Adolescence*, **25**, 409–413.

Connolly, S. D., Paikoff, R. L., and Buchanan, C. M. (1996). Puberty: the interplay of biological and psychosocial processes in adolescence. In G. R. Adams, R. Montemayor, and T. P. Gullotta (ed.), *Psychosocial development during adolescence* (pp. 259–299). Thousand Oaks, CA: Sage.

Cooper, H., and Hedges, L. V. (1994). *The handbook of research synthesis*. New York: Russell Sage Foundation.

Doswell, W., Millor, G., Thompson, H., and Braxter, B. (1998). Self-image and self-esteem in African American preteen girls: implications for mental health. *Issues in Mental Health Nursing*, **19**, 71–94.

Duncan, P. D., Ritter, P. L., Dornbusch, S. M., Gross, R. T., and Carlsmith, J. M. (1985). The effects of pubertal timing on body image, school behavior, and deviance. *Journal of Youth and Adolescence*, **14**, 227–235.

Edelbrook, C., Costello, A. J., Dulcan, M. K., Kalas, R., and Conover, N. C. (1985). Age difference in the reliability of the psychiatric interview of the child. *Child Development*, **56**, 265–275.

Fairburn, C. G., Cooper, Z., Doll, H. A., Norman, P. A., and O'Connor, M. E. (2000). The natural course of bulimia nervosa and binge eating disorder in young women. *Archives of General Psychiatry*, **57**, 659–665.

Field, A. E., Camargo, C. A., Taylor, C. B., Berkey, C. S., and Colditz, G. A. (1999a). Relation of peer and media influences to the development of purging behaviors among preadolescent and adolescent girls. *Archives of Pediatric Adolescent Medicine*, **153**, 1184–1189.

Field, A. E., Camargo, C. A., Taylor, C. B., Berkey, C. S., Frazier, L., Gillman, M. W., and Colditz, G. A. (1999b). Overweight, weight concerns, and bulimic behaviors among girls and boys. *Journal of the American Academy of Child and Adolescent Psychiatry*, **38**, 754–757.

French, S. A., Story, M., Neumark-Sztainer, D., Downes, B., Resnick, M., and Blum, R. (1997). Ethnic differences in psychosocial and health behavior correlates of dieting, purging, and binge eating in a population-based sample of adolescent females. *International Journal of Eating Disorders*, **22**, 315–322.

Garfinkel, P. E., Lin, E., Goering, P., Spegg, C., Goldbloom, D. S., Kennedy, S., Kaplan, A. S., and Woodside, D. B. (1995). Bulimia nervosa in a Canadian community sample: prevalence and comparison of subgroups. *American Journal of Psychiatry*, **152**, 1052–1058.

Gotlib, I. H., Lewinsohn, P. M., and Seeley, J. R. (1998). Consequences of depression during adolescence: marital status and martial functioning in early adulthood. *Journal of Abnormal Psychology*, **107**, 686–690.

Graber, J. A., Brooks-Gunn, J., Paikoff, R. L., and Warren, M. P. (1994). Prediction of eating problems: an eight-year study of adolescent girls. *Developmental Psychology*, **30**, 823–834.

Graber, J. A., Lewinsohn, P. M., Seeley, J. R., and Brooks-Gunn, J. (1997). Is psychopathology associated with the timing of pubertal development? *Journal of the American Academy of Child and Adolescent Psychiatry*, **36**, 1768–1776.

Graber, J. A., Petersen, A. C., and Brooks-Gunn, J. (1996). Pubertal processes: Methods, measures, and methods. In J. A. Graber, J. Brooks-Gunn, and A. C. Petersen (ed.), *Transitions through adolescence: interpersonal domains and context* (pp. 23–53). Hillsdale, NJ: Lawrence Erlbaum.

Gross, J., and Rosen, J. C. (1988). Bulimia in adolescents: prevalence and psychosocial correlates. *International Journal of Eating Disorders*, **7**, 51–61.

Hayward, C., Gotlib, I. H., Schraedley, P. K., and Litt, I. F. (1999). Ethnic differences in the association between pubertal status and symptoms of depression in adolescent girls. *Journal of Adolescent Health*, **25**, 143–149.

Hayward, C., Killen, J. D., Wilson, D. M., Hammer, L. D., Litt, I. F., Kraemer, H. C., Haydel, F., Varady, A., and Taylor, C. B. (1997). Psychiatric risk associated with early puberty in adolescent girls. *Journal of the American Academy of Child and Adolescent Psychiatry*, **36**, 255–262.

Hill, J. P., and Lynch, M. E. (1983). The intensification of gender-related role expectations during early adolescence. In J. Brooks-Gunn and A. C. Petersen (ed.), *Girls at puberty: biological and psychosocial perspectives* (pp. 201–228). New York: Plenum.

Killen, J., Hayward, C., Litt, I., Hammer, L., Wilson, D., Miner, B., Barr-Taylor, C., Varady, A., and Shisslak, C. (1992). Is puberty a risk factor for eating disorders? *American Journal of Diseases of Children*, **146**, 323–325.

Killen, J. D., Taylor, C. B., Hayward, C., Wilson, D., Haydel, K., Hammer, L., Simmonds, B., Robinson, T., Litt, I., Varady, A., and Kraemer, H. (1994). Pursuit of thinness and onset of eating disorder symptoms in a community sample of adolescent girls: a three-year prospective analysis. *International Journal of Eating Disorders*, **16**, 227–238.

Killen, J. D., Taylor, C. B., Hayward, C., Haydel, K. F., Wilson, D. M., Hammer, L., Kraemer, H., Blair-Greiner, A., and Strachowski, D. (1996). Weight concerns influence the development of eating disorders: a four-year prospective study. *Journal of Consulting and Clinical Psychology*, **64**, 936–940.

Koff, E., and Rierdan, J. (1993). Advanced pubertal development and eating disturbances in early adolescent girls. *Journal of Adolescent Health*, **14**, 433–439.

Leon, G. R., Fulkerson, J. A., Perry, C. L., and Early-Zald, M. B. (1995). Prospective analysis of personality and behavioral vulnerabilities and gender influences in the later development of disordered eating. *Journal of Abnormal Psychology*, **104**, 140–149.

Lewinsohn, P. M., Hops, H., Roberts, R. E., Seeley, J. R., and Andrews, J. A. (1993). Adolescent psychopathology: I. Prevalence and incidence of depression and other DSM III-R disorders in high school students. *Journal of Abnormal Psychology*, **102**, 133–144.

Lewinsohn, P. M., Roberts, R. E., Seeley, J. R., Rohde, P., Gotlib, I. H., and Hops, H. (1994). Adolescent psychopathology: II. Psychosocial risk factors for depression. *Journal of Abnormal Psychology*, **103**, 302–315.

Lopez, E., Blix, G., and Blix, A. (1995). Body image of Latinas compared to body image of non-Latina White women. *Health Values: Journal of Health Behavior, Education, and Promotion*, **19**, 3–10.

McCarthy, M. (1990). The thin ideal, depression, and eating disorders in women. *Behavioral Research and Therapy*, **28**, 205–218.

Newcomb, M. D., and Bentler, P. M. (1988). Impact of adolescent drug use and social support on problems of young adults: a longitudinal study. *Journal of Abnormal Psychology*, **97**, 64–75.

Newman, D. L., Moffitt, T. E., Caspi, A., Magdol, L., Silva, P. A., and Stanton, W. R. (1996). Psychiatric disorder in a birth cohort of young adults: Prevalence, comorbidity, clinical significance, and new case incidence from ages 11 to 21. *Journal of Consulting and Clinical Psychology*, **64**, 552–562.

Nolen-Hoeksema, S. (1994). An integrative model for the emergence of gender differences in depression in adolescence. *Journal of Research on Adolescence*, **4**, 519–534.

Nottelmann, E. D., Susman, E. J., Inoff-German, G., Cutler, G., Loriaux, D. L., and Chrousos, G. P. (1987). Gonadal and adrenal hormone correlates of adjustment in early adolescence. In R. M. Lerner and T. T. Foch (ed.), *Biological-psychosocial interaction in early adolescence* (pp. 303–323). Hillsdale, NJ: Lawrence Erlbaum.

Paikoff, R. L., Brooks-Gunn, J., and Warren, M. P. (1991). Effects of girls' hormonal status on depression and aggression over the course of one year. *Journal of Youth and Adolescence*, **20**, 191–215.

Patton, G. C., Hibbert, M. E., and Carlin, J. (1996). Menarche and the onset of depression and anxiety in Victoria, Australia. *Journal of Epidemiology and Community Health*, **50**, 661–666.

Petersen, A. C., and Crockett, L. (1985). Pubertal timing and grade effects on adjustment. *Journal of Youth and Adolescence*, **14**, 191–206.

Petersen, A. C., Leffert, N., Graham, B., Ding, S., and Overby, T. (1994). Depression and body image disorders in adolescence. *Women's Health Issues*, **4**, 98–108.

Petersen, A. C., Sarigiani, P. A., and Kennedy, R. E. (1991). Adolescent depression: why more girls? *Journal of Youth and Adolescence*, **20**, 247–271.

Polivy, J., and Herman, C. P. (1985). Dieting and binge eating: a causal analysis. *American Psychologist*, **40**, 193–204.

Richards, M. H., Boxer, A. M., Petersen, A. C., and Albrecht, R. (1990). Relation of weight to body image in pubertal girls and boys from two communities. *Developmental Psychology*, **26**, 313–321.

Rierdan, J., and Koff, E. (1991). Depressive symptomatology among very early maturing girls. *Journal of Youth and Adolescence*, **20**, 415–425.

Rierdan, J., Koff, E., and Stubbs, M. L. (1989). A longitudinal analysis of body image as a predictor of the onset and persistence of adolescent girls' depression. *Journal of Early Adolescence*, **9**, 454–466.

Robinson, T. N., Killen, J. D., Litt, I. F., Hammer, L. D., Wilson, D. M., Haydel, K. F., Hayward, C., and Taylor, C. B. (1996). Ethnicity and body dissatisfaction: are Hispanic and Asian girls at increased risk for eating disorders? *Journal of Adolescent Health*, **19**, 384–393.

Rosenthal, R. (1991). *Meta-Analytic Procedures for Social Research*. Thousand Oaks, CA; Sage.

Rosner, B., Prineas, R., Loggie, J., and Daniels, S. R. (1998). Percentiles for body mass index in US children 5 to 17 years of age. *Journal of Pediatrics*, **132**, 211–222.

Shadish, W. R., and Haddock, C. K. (1994). Combining estimates of effect size. In H. Cooper and L. V. Hedges (ed.), *The handbook of research synthesis* (pp. 261–281). Thousand Oaks, CA: Sage.

Siegel, J. M., Yancey, A. K., Aneshensel, C. S., and Schuler, R. (1999). Body image, perceived pubertal timing, and adolescent mental health. *Journal of Adolescent Health*, **25**, 155–165.

Simmons, R. G., Blyth, D. A., and McKinney, K. L. (1983). The social and psychological effects of puberty on white females. In J. Brooks-Gunn and A. Petersen (ed.), *Girls at puberty: biological and psychosocial perspectives* (pp. 229–272). New York: Plenum.

Simmons, R. G., Blyth, D. A., Van Cleave, E. F., and Bush, D. M. (1979). Entry into early adolescence: the impact of school structure, puberty, and early dating on self-esteem. *American Sociological Review*, **44**, 948–967.

Simmons, R. G., Burgeson, R., Carlton-Ford, S., and Blyth, D. A. (1987). The impact of cumulative change in early adolescence. *Child Development*, **58**, 1220–1234.

Smolak, L., Levine, M. P., and Gralen, S. (1993). The impact of puberty and dating on eating problems among middle school girls. *Journal of Youth and Adolescence*, **22**, 355–368.

Stice, E., and Bearman, S. K. (2001). Body image and eating disturbances prospectively predict growth in depressive symptoms in adolescent girls: a growth curve analysis. *Developmental Psychology*, **37**, 597–607.

Stice, E., Hayward, C., Cameron, R., Killen, J. D., and Taylor, C. B. (2000). Body image and eating related factors predict onset of depression in female adolescents: a longitudinal study. *Journal of Abnormal Psychology*, **109**, 438–444.

Stice, E., Presnell, K., and Bearman, S. K. (2001). Relation of early menarche to depression, eating disorders, substance abuse, and comorbid psychopathology among adolescent girls. *Developmental Psychology*, **37**, 608–619.

Stice, E., Presnell, K., and Spangler, D. (2002). Risk factors for binge eating onset: a prospective investigation. *Health Psychology*.

Stice, E., and Whitenton, K. (2002). Risk factors for body dissatisfaction in adolescent girls: a longitudinal investigation. Under review.

Story, M., French, S. A., Resnick, M. D., and Blum, R. W. (1995). Ethnic/racial and socioeconomic differences in dieting behaviors and body image perceptions in adolescents. *International Journal of Eating Disorders*, **18**, 173–179.

Swarr, A. E., and Richards, M. H. (1996). Longitudinal effects of adolescent girls' pubertal development, perceptions of pubertal timing, and parental relations on eating problems. *Developmental Psychology*, **32**, 636–646.

Tanner, J. M. (1978). *Fetus into man*. Cambridge, MA: Harvard University Press.

Thompson, S. H., Corwin, S. J., and Sargent, R. G. (1997). Ideal body size beliefs and weight concerns of fourth-grade children. *International Journal of Eating Disorders*, **21**, 279–284.

Thompson, J. K., Heinberg, L. J., Altabe, M., and Tantleff-Dunn, S. (1999). *Exacting beauty*. Washington, DC: American Psychological Association.

Tobin-Richards, M. H., Boxer, A. M., Kavrell, S. A., and Petersen, A. C. (1984). Puberty and its psychological and social significance. In R. M. Lerner and N. L. Galambos (ed.), *Experiencing adolescents: a sourcebook for parents, teachers, and teens* (pp. 17–50). New York: Garland.

Troiano, R. P., Flegal, K. M., Kuczmarski, R. J., Campbell, S. M., and Johnson, C. L. (1995). Overweight prevalence and trends for children and adolescents. *Archives of Pediatric Adolescent Medicine*, **149**, 1085–1091.

Wichstrom, L. (1999). The emergence of gender difference in depressed mood during adolescence: the role of intensified gender socialization. *Developmental Psychology*, **35**, 232–245.

Wright, M. R. (1989). Body image satisfaction in adolescent girls and boys: a longitudinal study. *Journal of Youth and Adolescence*, **18**, 71–83.

# 5 Gender differences in opposite sex relationships: interactions with puberty

*Laura Compian and Chris Hayward*

Pubertal maturation is the single most salient developmental change occurring during adolescence (Alsaker, 1996; Hayward, Killen, and Wilson, 1997). Puberty is unique in that it includes biological changes associated with the physical transition from a child's body to that of an adult, however, these changes also occur within a societal context that confers value upon this process (Graber, Petersen, and Brooks-Gunn, 1996). These physical changes take place against a backdrop of simultaneous changes occurring in a number of major domains of an adolescent's life (Brooks-Gunn and Graber, 1994). How these transitions interact may have implications for adjustment over time (Lerner, 1996; Lerner, *et al.*, 1996).

Although researchers are paying increased attention to the study of romantic involvement with the opposite sex during adolescence (Brown, Feiring, and Furman, 1999), relatively little work has been completed to link this body of literature with the preexisting research assessing the association between puberty and patterns of adjustment. Given that pubertal processes are directly related to physical and psychological sexual maturity (Brooks-Gunn and Reiter, 1990), it is important that researchers strive to understand the nature of these changes in relation to involvement with the opposite sex and how these interactions inform well-being. This chapter seeks to fill the gap by examining these associations as they vary by gender. Where possible, we will consider the influences of different forms of opposite sex involvement, because much of the research in this area has emphasized romantic relationships. This chapter will also reflect this trend. We will also examine possible explanations associated with reported gender differences, including differential capacities for intimacy and prior vulnerabilities.

## Association between pubertal processes and opposite sex involvement

Given that pubertal maturation and the onset of romantic involvement with the opposite sex coincide, researchers speculate that puberty may be directly related to the "kicking in" of the biologically based romantic attachment systems (Larson, Clore, and Wood, 1999). Evidence of this relationship is found in research indicating that the physical manifestations of pubertal maturation have been empirically linked with sexual motivation. The release of androgens, particularly testosterone, have been shown to increase interest in the opposite sex (Beach, 1974; Kinsey, *et al.*, 1953; Susman, *et al.*, 1985; Udry and Talbert, 1988). Similarly, Smith, Udry, and Morris (1985) surveyed 433 seventh, eighth, and ninth grade students to assess their reported sexual behavior, pubertal development, and their friends' involvement in sexual behavior. Results indicated that both boys and girls with increasing pubertal development were more likely to be involved sexually with the opposite sex than mere less developed adolescents.

Increased romantic involvement (i.e., dating, going steady, etc.) has been shown to occur more frequently in early maturing adolescents (McCabe, 1984). Smolak, Levine, and Gralen (1993) measured pubertal timing in relation to dating and eating disordered attitudes and found that early pubertal timing was, indeed, associated with higher levels of dating, as well as more disordered eating. Additional research suggests that puberty affects more than just the sexual desire of romantic involvement. Richards and Larson (1993) utilized the Experience Sampling Method (Larson and Csikszentmihalyi, 1983) to assess the daily subjective states of 459 fifth to ninth grade students. For both boys and girls, the strongest association between puberty and emotional experience was found with the specific feeling of being in love. Romantic and/or platonic involvement was not actually assessed in this study, only the adolescents' feelings. Although interpretation of these results is difficult given that pubertal status and timing is confounded, these results suggest that pubertal processes influence both the physical experience of sexual desire as well as the subjective mood state and feelings associated with involvement with the opposite sex.

These relationships have been shown to vary by gender. For girls, early maturation and more advanced pubertal status have consistently been linked to increased romantic and physical involvement with boys (Aro and Taipale, 1987; Crockett and Petersen, 1987; Simmons and Blyth, 1987; Stattin and Magusson, 1990). Flannery, Rowe, and Gulley (1993) measured both pubertal timing and pubertal status among boys and girls and found differing effects by gender. Pubertal status refers to the level of development on a set of physical indicators at a single point in time, whereas timing refers to whether an individual's overall development occurs earlier, later, or at about the same time as most adolescents (Graber, Petersen, and Brooks-Gunn, 1996; see also chapter 1). For girls, pubertal status predicted sexual experience and delinquency independent of age. For boys, the independent effects of pubertal status were weaker. Separate analyses of pubertal timing indicated that early maturing girls and boys engaged in more sexual activity and delinquent behavior than late maturers. Crockett and Petersen (1987) did find a positive association between pubertal status and romantic involvement for boys; however, other studies have found no relationship (Susman, et al., 1985; Udry and Billy, 1987).

Some researchers have suggested that romantic involvement during adolescence may be governed by age-graded social expectations rather than by physical changes (Dornbusch, et al., 1981; Garguilo, et al., 1987). There is evidence that the social context in which an adolescent resides has greater influence on the onset of dating than pubertal status or timing (Dornbusch, et al., 1981). Other studies have shown that both social context and pubertal maturation are important (Smith, Udry, and Morris, 1985); therefore, as with most developmental processes, the possibility exists that pubertal maturation and social context have a joint influence.

### Pubertal development and opposite sex involvement: relations with adjustment

Early pubertal maturation and co-occurring involvement with the opposite sex appears to be especially problematic for girls. Several studies have linked these simultaneous transitions to both internalizing and externalizing symptomatology. For instance, Levine and his colleagues (Levine, et al., 1994) found that recent and concurrent onset of menstruation along with dating was related to more weight management behavior in a sample of 382 sixth, seventh, and eighth grade girls. Similarly, Simmons and Blyth (1987) reported that girls' early pubertal maturation was associated with lower ratings of body image satisfaction, but was an advantage in terms of increased popularity with the opposite sex (see chapter 13). The advancement of secondary sexual characteristics among adolescent girls, including breast development, has been linked to both embarrassment in relation to the opposite sex (Rodriguez-Tomé, et al., 1993) and positive affect (Brooks-Gunn and Warren, 1988).

Recently, researchers have begun to tease apart the nature of the involvement with boys in an effort to further explicate the influence of these processes on eating-disordered behavior. An elegant demonstration of this is found in the work of Cauffman and Steinberg (1996). The authors asked seventh and eighth grade girls to self-report on their menarcheal status, dieting behaviors, and involvement with boys, using dating and different forms of heterosocial contact, including dating, physical involvement, and platonic involvement. Results indicated that social involvement with boys, on the whole, predicted higher disordered-eating scores. In addition, girls who were dating were more likely to be dieting and girls who were both dating and in the midst of puberty were the most likely to be dieting. Physical involvement with boys, including kissing and "making out," was associated with greater disordered eating and dieting.

Romantic involvement alone has also been linked with negative outcomes. Involvement in romantic relationships at an early age has been empirically associated with permissive sexual attitudes, premarital sexual experience, higher rates of drug use, minor delinquency, and behavioral difficulties, as well as lower levels of academic achievement (Brown and Theobald, 1996; Cauffman and Steinberg, 1996; Grinder, 1966; Konings, *et al.*, 1995; Miller, McCoy, and Olson, 1986; Neeman, Hubbard, and Masten, 1995). McDonald and McKinney (1994) found that high school girls who reported "going steady" were reporting the lowest self-esteem in comparison to girls who were not dating, girls who dated frequently, and boys in any category. In contrast, in the same study the authors found that boys who had "gone steady" in the past reported higher self-esteem than boys who had not, however, the more that boys reported that they valued dating, the lower their reported self-esteem. Similarly, sixth, seventh, and eighth grade boys who were "less enthusiastic" about dating were more likely to report lower ratings of self-esteem than their nondating peers or boys who were "very interested" in dating (Darling, *et al.*, 1999). Still other studies report no gender differences in overinvolvement in dating, level of dating experience, or self-reported quality of relationships in middle adolescence (Zimmer-Gembeck, Siebenbruner, and Collins, 2001).

Previous research suggests that entry into the world of romantic involvement is typically preceded by more platonic forms of involvement with the opposite sex (Brown, 1990; Maccoby, 1998). By middle school, interest in friendships and romantic relationships with the opposite sex increases, especially among girls (Savin-Williams and Berndt, 1990). Barriers to opposite sex involvement break down as "heterosexual attraction becomes an extraordinarily powerful force, opposing the forces of cross-sex avoidance" (Maccoby, 1998, p. 191). Boys and girls move from same-sex "gangs," typical of children ages 6 to 12, to larger heterosocial "crowds" beginning in early adolescence (Dunphy, 1969). Traditionally, same-sex peer groups begin to share association with opposite sex peer groups, becoming a loose association of several groups affording a more diverse social structure (Brown, 1990; Maccoby, 1998).

A study by Connolly and Johnson (1996) found that most fifth to eighth grade females spend time in opposite sex groups, 28 percent have a current or recent boyfriend, and 68 percent are interested in romantic relationships either currently or in the future. Dunphy (1963) indicated that same-sex peer groups serve primarily to socialize adolescents into appropriate heterosocial interest and behavior patterns. As group activities become more orientated to mixed-sex socializing, adolescents internalize new norms and standards for appropriate patterns of social activity (Gray and Steinberg, 1999) and tentatively explore the behavior and rituals of opposite sex involvement (Smith, et al., 1985).

Unfortunately, there are relatively few studies assessing the relationship between platonic involvement with boys, pubertal maturation, and socioemotional well-being. Our own research suggests that the way in which platonic involvement relates to pubertal status is uniquely different from the interaction between romantic involvement and sexual maturity (Compian, Hayward, and Gowen, accepted for publication). Utilizing a quantitative cross-sectional design, we assessed 157 sixth grade girls of varying ethnicities on measures of pubertal status, platonic and romantic involvement with boys, body image satisfaction, and depression symptoms. Our findings indicate that increased sexual maturity is related to higher levels of romantic involvement with boys, but the same is not true for platonic involvement. We also found an interaction between pubertal status, platonic involvement with boys, and body image satisfaction. Girls who were less sexually mature and who had high levels of platonic involvement reported the highest body image satisfaction. Results from this study raise some important points. First, our findings highlight the importance of considering different forms of involvement with boys separately when assessing the relationship between heterosocial involvement and socioemotional development.

In contrast, Ge, Conger, and Elder Jr., (1996) found that girls who were early maturing relative to their peers and who reported having both girls and boys in their friendship group during seventh grade reported the highest levels of psychological distress, including depression, anxiety, somatization, and hostility during the tenth grade. These results are in comparison to girls who reported having only females in their seventh grade friendship group. The authors know of no other studies that assess platonic involvement with boys in association with pubertal maturation; therefore, it is difficult to reconcile these findings.

However, there is a growing body of literature exploring the association between platonic involvement and socioemotional adjustment without an assessment of sexual maturation (Furman and Shaffer, 1999). For instance, Darling and her colleagues (Darling, et al., 1999) found that the quality of opposite sex platonic relationships was more important for adolescent girls' feelings of well-being in mixed-sex settings. That is, girls who reported greater comfort with the opposite sex reported higher assessments of global self-esteem. Boys who reported more girls in their peer group and who spent more time with their girlfriends outside of school reported higher social and romantic competence and comfort. Other research has shown that fifth and sixth grade girls who reported at least one reciprocal opposite sex friendship were better liked by boys, felt more integrated within their peer group, participated in more agentic activities, and were viewed by their same-sex peers as less withdrawn and powerless (McDougall, Hymel, and Zarbatany, 2000). In another sample, opposite sex friendships were found to be more supportive for boys than for girls in terms of esteem support (Kuttler, La Greca, and Prinstein, 1999). Opposite sex relationships may confer positive benefits, as there is reduced pressure to conform to "romantic social scripts" (Larson, Clore, and Wood, 1999) with the additional support, promotion of interpersonal competence, and increased recreational opportunities that accompany a social relationship (Brown, Feiring, and Furman, 1999; Hansen, Christopher, and Nangle, 1992; Savin-Williams and Berndt, 1990).

The contradictory nature of these findings is further confounded by the fact that each study has employed a slightly different interpretation of opposite sex involvement and friendship. Some studies have assessed the absolute number of opposite sex adolescents reported in the peer group (Ge, Conger, and Elder, 1996), while others have assessed reciprocal friendship pairings (Kuttler, La Greca, and Prinstein, 1999; McDougall, Hymel, and Zarbatany, 2000). These distinctions appear significant as the centrality and perceived nature of an opposite sex friendship is important to the adolescents involved in the relationship (Kovacs, Parker, and Hoffman, 1996). In addition, it is important for adolescents to establish for their peer audience whether opposite sex friends are "hanging around together," "just friends," "dating each other," or "boyfriend and girlfriend" (Rawlins, 1992). Some researchers suggest that opposite sex friendships are a less valued social achievement, much more difficult for others to understand, and are frequently doubted (Schofield, 1981).

It seems that depending upon the context, opposite sex friendships are either of high or low value. Bukowski, Sippola, and Hoza (1999) reported that children of both sexes who are either very popular or very unpopular are more likely than other children to have opposite sex friends. Among children without a same-sex friend, having an opposite sex friend is linked to higher levels of perceived well-being for boys and lower levels of well-being for girls. These results suggest that the contradictory nature of research exploring platonic opposite sex involvement across studies may be accounted for by the nature of interactions between involvement with the opposite sex and other indicators of social adjustment, such as same-sex friendship status.

## Socialized differences by gender in opposite sex relationships

Why do boys and girls experience the onset of opposite sex relationships differently? One theory suggests that the "separate worlds" in which boys and girls reside during childhood may differentially socialize them to interact with significant others in different ways when the two worlds collide in adolescence (Maccoby, 1995; Maccoby and Jacklin, 1987). One characteristic of interpersonal involvement, which has consistently varied by gender, is an individual's capacity for intimacy. Intimacy, typically defined as degree of self-disclosure (Monsour, 1992), is a useful marker for measuring the degree of closeness and connection of different kinds of relationships. To achieve intimacy, one must first be oriented to value and seek closeness. Second, one must be able to tolerate, and even embrace the intense emotions that are part of a close relationship. Finally, one must be capable of self-disclosure, mutual reciprocity, sensitivity to the feelings of others, and concern for others' well-being (Collins, *et al.*, 1997; Collins and Sroufe, 1999).

Previous research suggests that adolescent girls are much more comfortable and adept with intimacy than adolescent boys (Fischer, 1981). In a study by Fischer, Munsch, and Greene (1996) boys demonstrated a greater increase in intimacy from eighth to twelfth grade, however, girls were higher than boys on indices of intimacy at every time measured. For instance, Werebe (1987) reported that during adolescence, girls reported feeling almost as close with their boyfriends as they did with their same-sex friends, whereas boys report much more closeness with their same-sex friends. Boys' and girls' intentions for engaging in opposite sex involvement also reflect differing levels of comfort with intimacy. Girls reported that they are seeking a romantic love affair, while boys are more often attracted by sexuality alone, with continued loyalty to their same-sex peer group and its norms (Anderson, 1989; Zani, 1993). As couples embark on the first stages of intimacy, girls seek to prolong the early stages and delay intercourse; boys attempt to accelerate the pace at which physical intimacy increases (Maccoby, 1998).

These intentions are reflected in the desired qualities sought by boys and girls for potential romantic partners. In general, the characteristics considered most attractive during early adolescence are often more superficial (e.g., status, appearance) and general (e.g., nice personality) than those used to judge same-sex friends (Zani, 1993). Boys are more interested in the appearance and sexual activity of dating partners, while girls are more focused upon personality and behavioral factors (Zani, 1993). As a result, the possibility exists that adolescents may change the criteria by which they judge themselves due to the perceived value placed on certain characteristics in a potential dating partner (Darling, *et al.*, 1999). Maccoby (1998) writes: "Adolescent girls are perfectly aware of the importance of physical attractiveness in the eyes of the other sex, and many become intensely preoccupied with their hair-dos, their complexions, their clothes, and especially with controlling their weight" (p. 212). Boys, on the other hand, recognize that appearance is a less important factor in their attractiveness to girls and are less vulnerable to these superficial concerns. These reports suggest that adolescent girls' self-concept may be particularly susceptible during this process, as they are being evaluated by their external characteristics, whereas boys are assessed on constructs, which are more central to their true self.

There is also a degree of incongruence in the extent to which boys and girls expect to spend time with their romantic partner. Boys continue to participate in group activities while dating girls (Feiring, 1999). However, girls place greater import and value upon a relationship with the opposite sex, giving this type of relationship priority above all others (Feiring, 1999). Richards and colleagues (1998) found that girls reported spending twice as much time thinking about the opposite sex than did boys. In adolescence, girls begin to shift their time from youth and club activities to smaller friendship networks, attending heterosocial meeting places and eventually settling into a steady relationship with one boy (Coleman and Hendry, 1990). Previous research has shown that some girls continue to spend their leisure time with same-sex friends, adding romantic partners to their network of social relationships, while others replace their time with same-sex friends with the exclusive romantic relationship (Zimmer-Gembeck, 1999). The authors suggested that there may be individual or social influences that result in some girls maintaining involvement with their same-sex friends while others greatly limit the extent to which they socialize with same-sex friends once a romantic relationship has been established.

The onset of romantic relationships leaves many girls struggling to make sense of their new social role among same-sex and opposite sex peers. Same-sex friendships are often threatened because romantic relationships often create conflict over feelings of competition, jealousy, and disloyalty (Douvan and Adelson, 1966). Boys, on the other hand, tend to preserve their male friendships even when they engage in a steady dating relationship (Button, 1979). In turn, boys often complain about the responsibility of having to make choices, since their young partners feel the need to spend much of their free time as a pair (Zani, 1993). For boys, the romantic relationship is perceived as being important though demanding and, at times, all-consuming. Other research, however, shows that early adolescent boys in the sixth to eighth grades reported spending more time outside of school with their girlfriends than girls did with their boyfriends (Darling, *et al.*, 1999).

This inconsistency of reports may be explained by real or perceived differences between the sexes in terms of time spent with significant others. Because previous research has shown that boys often feel they are making a considerable sacrifice in terms of missed time spent with same-sex peers (Zani, 1993), they may perceive their time with their girlfriends as more time-consuming than it is in actuality. Or, likewise, girls may believe that they are not spending enough time with their boyfriends, and they may underestimate the time spent with their significant others. Either way, the research hints at an incongruence between the goals and desires for time spent with the opposite sex between boys and girls.

### Vulnerability in early romantic involvement with the opposite sex

Some researchers speculate that the negative outcomes associated with early romantic involvement may not be due directly to opposite sex involvement *per se*. Rather, prior vulnerabilities may predispose some adolescents to engage in relationships in such a way that their self-concept is compromised. Fischer, Munsch, and Greene (1996) wrote: "It may be that more vulnerable adolescents are more affected by the dark side [of romantic involvement with the opposite sex], indeed may even be more frequent victims of the dark side" (p. 115). In support of this theory, others have suggested that those with already low self-esteem may use early romantic involvement with the opposite sex as a confirmation of their self-worth (McDonald and McKinney, 1994). As such, going steady may be a form of compensatory behavior (Larson, Spreitzer, and Snyder, 1976). Thus, findings indicating that romantic involvement is related to negative socioemotional outcomes may be confounded by preexisting conditions.

Pawlby, Mills, and Quinton (1997) found that girls characterized as "high risk" began dating earlier and reported having a "solo" boyfriend more often than the "school comparison" group of girls. Further, high-risk girls were involved with boys who were on average two years older, often living on their own, and were more likely to be involved in problem behaviors. High-risk girls reported that their relationships were often fraught with volatility and subordination. These same girls also indicated that their boyfriends were the most important people in their social network. Viewing one's romantic relationship as the central contact for emotional support has been identified as a key problem, given that adolescent girls often feel abandoned by their same-sex friends, which creates more conflicts between female friends over feelings of competition, jealousy, and disloyalty (Douvan and Adelson, 1966). These findings suggest that girls who are already at risk for poor developmental outcomes may seek out romantic involvement with boys in an effort to enhance a poor self-concept. On many occasions, girls then become involved in relationships with boys that further contribute to an impaired sense of self.

Although compelling, we must emphasize that these are the results from one study. However, this line of research points to a new area of potential study. It would be useful to conduct longitudinal studies delineating the developmental sequelae of self-concept and other measures of adjustment among both boys and girls prior to puberty. This research would help answer the questions of who are the boys and the girls that begin early dating and are there meaningful individual differences between them and their nondating peers? Additionally, who are the boys and the girls that early-daters seek for partners? How does the status of these individuals contribute to positive and negative outcomes associated with opposite sex involvement?

## Conclusion

Preliminary evidence suggests that pubertal processes and involvement with the opposite sex are intimately related, however, this relationship appears to differ by gender. Increasing levels of sexual maturation are consistently related to higher levels of romantic involvement in girls (Aro and Taipale, 1987; Crockett and Petersen, 1987; Simmons and Blyth, 1987; Stattin and Magnusson, 1990), but there are inconsistent results for boys (Flannery, Rome, and Gulley, 1993; Susman, *et al.*, 1985; Udry and Billy, 1987). Other research suggests that increasing pubertal status is not linked with advanced levels of platonic opposite sex involvement with boys (Compian, *et al.*, accepted for publication). There is no information to date as to how pubertal development and platonic opposite sex involvement is related among adolescent boys. Understanding how these relationships interact is of the utmost importance, given that pubertal development, romantic involvement, and sometimes platonic involvement appear related to socioemotional well-being (Cauffman and Steinberg, 1996; Ge, Conger, and Elder, 1996; Levine, *et al.*, 1994; McDougall, Hymel, and Zarbatany, 2000; Simmons, *et al.*, 1987). Given that there are so few studies directly relating pubertal development, romantic and platonic involvement with the opposite sex, and socioemotional outcomes, the field is wide open. There is a large body of literature exploring the changing dynamics and nature of social relationships in adolescence (Brown, 1990), and there is an equal amount dedicated toward the study of pubertal maturation and its effects upon socioemotional well-being (Graber, Petersen, and Brooks-Gunn, 1996; see also chapters 12 and 13), however, there is little research combining the two.

Promising areas of research include further exploration of the distinction between romantic and platonic involvement in relation to pubertal status. How these relationships vary by gender is of high interest because the experience of involvement with the opposite-sex appears, particularly in the area of intimacy connection, to be different for boys and girls. Reported gender differences in comfort with intimacy among boys and girls prior to and during adolescence suggest that opposite sex relationships may occupy different levels of priority and import between the two sexes (Fischer, 1981; Fischer, Munsch, and Greene, 1996; Werebe, 1987). The centrality and importance of opposite sex relationships to the adolescent may be key in understanding how opposite sex involvement affects well-being and adjustment. This is another area for future consideration.

### References

Alsaker, F. D. (1996). Annotation: the impact of puberty. *Journal of Child Psychology and Psychiatry*, **37**(3), 249–258.

Anderson, E. (1989). Sex codes and family life among inner-city youth. In W. J. Wilson (ed.), *The ghetto underclass: Social science perspectives*, vol. DI. Thousand Oaks, CA: Sage.

Aro, H., and Taipale, V. (1987). The impact of timing of puberty on psychosomatic symptoms among fourteen- to sixteen-year-old Finnish girls. *Child Development*, **58**, 261–268.

Beach, F. A. (1974). Human sexuality and evolution. In A. Sadler (ed.), *Reproductive behavior*. New York: Plenum.

Brooks-Gunn, J., and Graber, J. A. (1994). Puberty as a biological and social event: implications for research on pharmacology. *Journal of Adolescent Health*, **15**(8), 663–671.

Brooks-Gunn, J., and Reiter, E. O. (1990). The role of pubertal processes. In S. S. Feldman and G. R. Elliot (ed.), *At the threshold: the developing adolescent* (pp. 16–53). Cambridge, MA: Harvard University Press.

Brooks-Gunn, J., and Warren, M. P. (1988). The psychological significance of secondary sexual characteristics in 9- to 11-year-old girls. *Child Development*, **59**(4), 1061–1069.

Brown, B. B. (1990). Peer groups and peer cultures. In S. S. Feldman and G. R. Elliot (ed.), *At the threshold: the developing adolescent* (pp. 171–196). Cambridge, MA: Harvard University Press.

Brown, B. B., Feiring, C., and Furman, W. (1999). Missing the love boat: why researchers have shied away from the adolescent romantic relationship. In W. Furman, B. B. Brown, and C. Feiring (eds.), *The development of romantic relationships during adolescence* (pp. 1–16). Cambridge: Cambridge University Press.

Brown, B. B., and Theobald, W. (1996). Is teenage romance hazardous to adolescent health? Paper presented at the biennial meeting of the Society for Research on Adolescence, Boston, MA, March.

Bukowski, W. M., Sippola, L. K., and Hoza, B. (1999). Same and other: interdependency between participation in same- and other-sex friendships. *Journal of Youth and Adolescence*, **28(4)**, 439–459.

Button, L. (1979). Friendship patterns. *Journal of Adolescence*, 2, 187–199.

Cauffman, E., and Steinberg, L. (1996). Interactive effects of menarcheal status and dating on dieting and disordered eating among adolescent girls. *Developmental Psychology*, **32(4)**, 631–635.

Coleman, J. C., and Hendry, L. (1990). *The nature of adolescence*, 2nd edn. London: Routledge.

Collins, W. A., Hennighausen, K. C., Schmit, D. T., and Sroufe, L. A. (1997). Developmental precursors of romantic relationships: a longitudinal analysis. In S. Shulman and W. A. Collins (ed.), *Romantic relationships in adolescence: developmental perspectives* (pp. 69–84). San Francisco, CA: Jossey-Bass.

Collins, W. A., and Sroufe, L. A. A. (1999). Capacity for intimate relationships: a developmental construction. In W. Furman and B. B. Brown (ed.), *The development of romantic relationships in adolescence* (pp. 125–147). Cambridge: Cambridge University Press.

Compian, L. J., Hayward, C., and Gowen, L. K. (accepted for publication). Peripubertal girls' romantic and platonic involvement with boys: associations with body image and depression symptoms. *Journal of Research on Adolescence*.

Connolly, J. A., and Johnson, A. M. (1996). Adolescents' romantic relationships and the structure and quality of their close interpersonal ties. *Personal Relationships*, **3(2)**, 185–195.

Crockett, L. J., and Petersen, A. C. (1987). Pubertal status and psychosocial development. Findings from the early adolescence study. In R. M. Lerner and T. T. Foch (ed.), *Biological-psychosocial interactions in early adolescence* (pp. 405–419). Hillsdale, NJ: Lawrence Erlbaum.

Darling, N., Dowdy, B. B., Van Horn, M. L., and Caldwell, L. L. (1999). Mixed-sex settings and the perception of competence. *Journal of Youth and Adolescence*, **28(4)**, 461–480.

Dornbusch, S. M., Carlsmith, J. M., Gross, R. T., Martin, J. A., Jennings, D., Rosenberg, A., and Duke, P. (1981). Sexual development, age and dating: a comparison of biological and social influences upon one set of behaviors. *Child Development*, **52**, 179–185.

Douvan, E., and Adelson, J. (1966). *The adolescent experience*. New York: Fawcett.

Dunphy, D. C. (1963). The social structure of urban adolescent peer groups. *Sociometry*, **26(2)**, 230–246.

Dunphy, D. C. (1969). *Cliques, crowds, and gangs*. Melbourne: Cheshire.

Feiring, C. (1999). Other-sex friendship networks and the development of romantic relationships in adolescence. *Journal of Youth and Adolescence*, **28(4)**, 495–512.

Fischer, J. L. (1981). Transitions in relationship style from adolescence to young adulthood. *Journal of Youth and Adolescence*, **10(1)**, 11–23.

Fischer, J. L., Munsch, J., and Greene, S. M. (1996). Adolescence and intimacy. In G. R. Adams, R. Montemayor, and T. P. Gulottoa (ed.), *Psychosocial development during adolescence*. Thousand Oaks, CA: Sage.

Flannery, D. J., Rowe, D. C., and Gulley, B. L. (1993). Impact of pubertal status, timing, and age on adolescent sexual experience and delinquency. *Journal of Adolescent Research*, **8(1)**, 21–40.

Furman, W., and Shaffer, L. A. (1999). A story of adolescence: the emergence of other sex relationships. *Journal of Youth and Adolescence*, **28(4)**, 513–522.

Garguilo, J., Attie, I., Brooks-Gunn, J., and Warren, M. (1987). Girls' dating behavior as a function of social context and maturation. *Developmental Psychology*, **23**, 730–737.

Ge, X., Conger, R. D., and Elder, G. H., Jr. (1996). Coming of age too early: pubertal influences on girls' vulnerability to psychological distress. *Child Development*, **67**, 3386–3400.

Graber, J. A., Petersen, A. C., and Brooks-Gunn, J. (1996). Pubertal processes: methods, measures, and models. In J. A. Graber, J. Brooks-Gunn, and A. C. Petersen (ed.), *Transitions through adolescence: interpersonal domains and contexts* (pp. 23–53). Mahwah, NJ: Lawrence Erlbaum.

Gray, M. R., and Steinberg, L. (1999). Romance and the parent–child relationship: a contextual perspective. In W. Furman, B. B. Brown, and C. Feiring (ed.), *The development of romantic relationships in adolescence* (pp. 235–265). Cambridge: Cambridge University Press.

Grinder, R. E. (1966). Relations of social dating attractions to academic orientation and peer relations. *Journal of Educational Psychology*, **57**, 27–34.

Hansen, D. J., Christopher, J. S., and Nangle, D. W. (1992). Adolescent heterosocial interactions and dating. In V. B. Van Hasselt and M. Hersen (ed.), *Handbook of social development: a lifespan perspective*. New York: Plenum.

Hayward, C., Killen, J. D., and Wilson, D. M. (1997). Psychiatric risk associated with early puberty in adolescent girls. *Journal of the American Academy of Child and Adolescent Psychiatry*, **36(2)**, 255–262.

Kinsey, A. C., Pomeroy, W. B., Martin, C. E., and Gebhard, P. H. (1953). *Sexual behavior in the human female*. Philadelphia, PN: W. B. Saunders.

Konings, E., Dubois-Arber, F., Narring, F., and Michaud, P. A. (1995). Identifying adolescent drug users: results of a national survey on adolescent health in Switzerland. *Journal of Adolescent Health*, **16**, 240–247.

Kovacs, D. M., Parker, J. G., and Hoffman, L. W. (1996). Behavioral, affective, and social correlates of involvement in cross-sex friendship in elementary school. *Child Development*, **67**, 2269–2286.

Kuttler, A. F., La Greca, A. M., and Prinstein, M. J. (1999). Friendship qualities and social-emotional functioning of adolescents with close, cross-sex friendships. *Journal of Research on Adolescence*, **9(3)**, 339–366.

Larson, D. L., Spreitzer, E. A., and Snyder, E. E. (1976). Social factors in the frequency of romantic involvement among adolescents. *Adolescence*, **11(41)**, 7–12.

Larson, R. W., Clore, G. L., and Wood, G. A. (1999). The emotions of romantic relationships: do they wreak havoc on adolescents? In W. Furman, B. B. Brown, and C. Feiring (ed.), *The development of romantic relationships during adolescence* (pp. 19–49). Cambridge: Cambridge University Press.

Larson, R. W., and Csikszentmihalyi, M. (1983). The experience sampling method. In H. Reis (ed.), *New directions for naturalistic methods in the behavioral sciences*. San Francisco, CA: Jossey-Bass.

Lerner, R. M. (1996). Relative plasticity, integration, and temporality. *Developmental Psychology*, **32(4)**, 781–786.

Lerner, R. M., Lerner, J. V., von Eye, A., Ostrom, C. W., Nitz, K., Talwar-Soni, R., and Tubman, J. G. (1996). Continuity and discontinuity across the transition of early adolescence: a developmental contextual perspective. In J. A. Graber, J. Brooks-Gunn, and A. C. Petersen (ed.), *Transitions through adolescence: interpersonal domains and context* (pp. 3–22). Hillsdale, NJ: Lawrence Erlbaum.

Levine, M. P., Smolak, L., Moodey, A. F., Shuman, M. D., and Hessen, L. D. (1994). Normative developmental challenges and dieting and eating disturbances in middle school girls. *International Journal of Eating Disorders*, **15(1)**, 11–21.

Maccoby, E. E. (1995). The two sexes and their social systems. In P. Moen and G. H. Elder, Jr. (ed.), *Examining lives in context: perspectives on the ecology of human development* (pp. 347–364). Washington, DC: American Psychological Association.

Maccoby, E. E. (1998). Cross-sex encounters. In E. E. Maccoby (ed.), *The two sexes: growing apart, coming together* (pp. 59–74). Cambridge, MA: Belknap Press, Harvard University Press.

Maccoby, E. E., and Jacklin, C. N. (1987). Gender segregation in childhood. In H. W. Reese (ed.), *Advances in child development and behavior* (pp. 239–287). San Diego, CA: Academic Press.

McCabe, M. P. (1984). Toward a theory of adolescent dating. *Journal of Adolescence*, **19**, 159–170.

McDonald, D. L., and McKinney, J. P. (1994). Steady dating and self-esteem in high school students. *Journal of Adolescence*, **17**, 557–564.

McDougall, P., Hymel, S., and Zarbatany, L. (2000). Cross-gender friendship in preadolescence: are there associated benefits? Paper presented at the Biennial Meeting of the Society for Research on Adolescence, Chicago, IL.

Miller, B. C., McCoy, J. K., and Olson, T. D. (1986). Dating age and stage as correlates of adolescent sexual attitudes and behavior. *Journal of Adolescent Research*, **1(3)**, 361–371.

Monsour, M. (1992). Meanings of intimacy in cross- and same-sex friendships. *Journal of Social and Personal Relationships*, **9**, 277–295.

Neeman, J., Hubbard, J., and Masten, A. S. (1995). The changing importance of romantic relationship involvement to competence from late childhood to late adolescence. *Development and Psychopathology*, **7**, 727–750.

Pawlby, S. J., Mills, A., and Quinton, D. (1997). Vulnerable adolescent girls: opposite sex relationships. *Journal of Child Psychology and Psychiatry*, **38(8)**, 909–920.

Rawlins, W. K. (1992). *Friendship matters: communication, dialects, and the life course*. New York: De Gruyter.

Richards, M. H., Crowe, P. A., Larson, R., and Swann, A. (1998). Developmental patterns and gender differences in the experience of peer companionship during adolescence. *Child Development*, **69(1)**, 154–163.

Richards, M. H., and Larson, R. (1993). Pubertal development and the daily subjective states of young adolescents. *Journal of Research on Adolescence*, **32(2)**, 145–169.

Rodriguez-Tomé, K., Bariaud, F., Cohen Zardi, M. F., Delmas, C., Jeanvoine, B., and Szlagyi, P. (1993). The effects of pubertal changes on body image and relations with peers of the cross-sex in adolescence. *Journal of Adolescence*, **16**, 421–438.

Savin-Williams, R. C., and Berndt, T. J. (1990). Friendship and peer relations. In S. S. Feldman and G. R. Elliot (ed.), *At the threshold: the developing adolescent* (pp. 277–307). Cambridge, MA: Harvard University Press.

Schofield, J. W. (1981). Complementary and conflicting identities: images and interaction in an interracial school. In S. R. Asher and J. M. Gottman (ed.), *The development of children's friendships* (pp. 53–90). Cambridge: Cambridge University Press.

Simmons, R. G., and Blyth, D. A. (1987). *Moving into adolescence: the impact of pubertal change and school context*. Hawthorne, NY: Aldine.

Simmons, R. G., Burgeson, R., Carlton-Ford, S., and Blyth, D. A. (1987). The impact of cumulative change in adolescence. *Child Development*, **58**, 1220–1234.

Smith, E., Udry, J. R., and Morris, N. M. (1985). Pubertal development and friends: a biosocial explanation of adolescent sexual behavior. *Journal of Health and Social Behavior*, **26**, 183–192.

Smolak, L., Levine, M. P., and Gralen, S. (1993). The impact of puberty and dating on eating problems among middle school girls. *Journal of Youth and Adolescence*, **22(4)**, 355–368.

Stattin, H., and Magnusson, D. (1990). Pubertal maturation in female development. In D. Magnusson (ed.), *Paths through life*. Hillsdale, NJ: Lawrence Erlbaum.

Susman, E. J., Nottlemann, E. D., Inoff-Germain, G. E., Dorn, L. D., Cutler, G. B., Loriaux, D. L., and Chrousos, G. P. (1985). The relation of relative hormonal levels and physical development and social-emotional behavior in young adolescents. *Journal of Youth and Adolescence*, **14**, 245–264.

Udry, J. R., and Billy, J. O. (1987). Initiation of coitus in early adolescence. *American Sociological Review*, **52**, 841–855.

Udry, J. R., and Talbert, L. M. (1988). Sex hormone effects on personality at puberty. *Journal of Personality and Social Psychology*, **54**, 291–295.

Werebe, M. J. G. (1987). Friendship and dating relationships among French adolescents. *Journal of Adolescence*, **10**, 269–289.

Zani, B. (1993). Dating and interpersonal relationships in adolescence. In S. Jackson and H. Rodriguez-Tome (ed.), *Adolescence and its social worlds* (pp. 95–119). Hillsdale, NJ: Lawrence Erlbaum.

Zimmer-Gembeck, M. J. (1999). Stability, change and individual differences in involvement with friends and romantic partners among adolescent females. *Journal of Youth and Adolescence*, **28**(4), 419–438.

Zimmer-Gembeck, M. J., Siebenbruner, J., and Collins, W. A. (2001). Diverse aspects of dating: associations with psychosocial functioning from early to middle adolescence. *Journal of Adolescence*, **24**, 313–336.

# 6 Aggression, psychopathology, and delinquency: influences of gender and maturation – where did all the good girls go?

*Stephanie R. Hawkins, Samantha Pia Miller, and Hans Steiner*

> I don't know why I did it, I don't know why I enjoyed it, and I don't know why I'll do it again.
> Bart Simpson, young character from *The Simpsons*, US animated
> television show

In this chapter we will summarize the problems of aggression and their relationship to gender and maturation. We will first discuss aggression as a normative behavior and examine gender differences and their relationship to puberty. We will then focus on psychopathological forms of aggression, such as disruptive behavior disorders, again relating them to gender and pubertal development; we will conclude with a discussion of gender differences in delinquency. In each of these subsections, we will cite research that approaches the topic from an experimental, naturalistic, and clinical perspective.

## Aggression as a normative behavior: gender differences

To understand gender differences in aggression and violence, one can take a developmental approach and examine the presence of aggression through the various life stages (Loeber and Hay, 1997). During infancy signs of frustration and rage can be observed, though significant gender differences cannot be detected. Research conducted by Weinberg and colleagues (1999) found gender differences in the emotional expressiveness among infants, although it is unclear if these differences are precursors to aggression. Infant girls were able to regulate their emotional states better than infant boys, who were more likely to show anger. During the toddler stage minimal gender differences were found to exist, but research findings are conflicted. For example, Fagot and Kavanagh (1990) found parents reported that boys exhibited more negative behaviors than girls, whereas Hay and colleagues (1995) found the opposite, with girls identified as more aggressive than boys.

93

Gender differences in aggression become more pronounced when peer interactions increase. As age increases from infancy forward, mobility increases, and with it the potential to be physically aggressive. Additionally, emotions differentiate, going from states of indiscriminate upset to frustration, anger, and intent to hurt in the span of five years. With the influence of socialization, however, there is a gradual decrease in physical aggression and an increase in verbal aggression, as language is acquired and more refined means of emotional expression predominate. This change from overt aggressive acts to covert aggressive acts is most pronounced in females, with males showing a greater frequency of overt aggression (Alan Sroufe, *Emotional Development*, 1999 book). During this time boys continue to exhibit higher rates of physical aggression than girls. Although this is true, girls have been found to use more verbal, indirect, and covert aggression than physical aggression. Examples here include character defamation, gossip, ostracism, and peer alienation (Bjorkquist, Osterman, and Kaukiainen, 1992; Cairns, *et al.*, 1989; Crick, 1995; Crick and Grotpeter, 1995). Differential pathways for the development of aggression in boys and girls appear during the elementary school years.

In middle childhood the development and use of interpersonal skills may be responsible for the observed decrease in aggression for boys and girls. Due to an increase in physical strength and the availability and lethality of weapons, aggressive acts increase in severity and can cause injury or death (Reiss and Roth, 1993; Johnson, *et al.*, 1995). While there is an overall increase in aggression and violent offenses in both genders during adolescence, it is clear that the gender differential in favor of boys is maintained throughout this crucial period of development (see figure 6.1).

### Hormones and aggression

Biological differences may account for some of the gender disparities in aggression and delinquency rates. Several researchers assert that biological processes can explain physically aggressive behaviors. In animals and humans impulsivity, sensation seeking, dominance, and aggression are behaviors typically associated with the presence of androgens. Conversely, castration of male mice decreases their aggressive behaviors (Gartner and Witaker-Azmitia, 1996). On the other hand, in certain strains, female mice injected with testosterone become as aggressive as the males. In humans, the fact that increased testosterone levels have been found in some adult violent crime offenders (Archer, 1991) seems to confirm the relationship between aggression and masculinizing hormones.

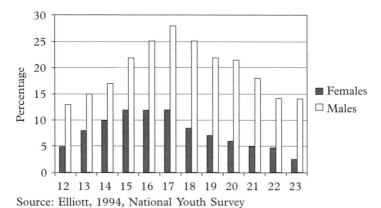

Source: Elliott, 1994, National Youth Survey

Figure 6.1 Age-specific prevalence of self-reported violent offending

The presence of androgenic hormones also results in permanent changes in both brain structure and function (Rubinow and Schmidt, 1996). The effects of hormones, however, are not simply confined to aggressive acts. For example, behaviors besides aggression that are attributed to gender differences in brain organization due to masculinizing hormones, include different rates of language acquisition, visual-spatial abilities, and motor activation.

Regarding humans, Rubinow and Schmidt (1996) suggest that in addition to regulating aggression, androgens in humans also effect cognition, personality, sexuality, and emotion; these effects may be related to gender differences in pharmacokinetics and to different responses to psychiatric treatment. The Susman and colleagues' 1996 study on adolescent boys and girls found that impulsivity predicted elevated testosterone in girls, suggesting that this may be the female correlate to male aggressive or dominant behavior. As with other hormones, the biological and behavioral effects of androgens in humans and animals seem highly complex, nonlinear, and, very often, context dependent. It seems clear that to fully understand androgen activity and its relationship to aggression, steroid hormone action, metabolism, receptor functioning, and gene regulation, and how all these variables vary in a context-dependent way, must be further studied. For example, primate research has shown that there is a drop in testosterone levels when a monkey falls in the dominance hierarchy. Similarly, with humans, testosterone levels drop with a decrease in self-esteem, such as in officer selection when one fares badly (Rutter and Cesaer, 1991).

It has been postulated that due to gender-related hormonal differences, for the most part, females have a biological defense against these stereotypical male behaviors (Rutter and Cesaer, 1991), although this "defense" is compromised when females are overexposed to male hormones in utero. High levels of testosterone in utero are thought to increase sensitivity to this hormone during puberty. Thus, females with increased androgen levels can exhibit characteristically male traits during puberty, including aggression. The behavioral consequences associated with increased testosterone levels are thought to be determined by the relative density of androgen receptors (Simon, *et al.*, 1996).

While it is tempting to ascribe a special role to sex hormones in the development of differential patterns of aggressivity from puberty onward, the literature strongly supports the role of several neurotransmitter systems, especially the serotenergic and noradrenergic norepinephrine system. Tryptophan hydroxylase (TPH), a catalyst in producing hydroxylation, the rate-limiting step in 5-HT synthesis, monoamine oxidase (MAO-A), and catechol-O-methyltransferase (COMT) are all important enzymes in the catabolism of catecholamines, including norepinephrine. The TPH, MAO-A, and COMT genotypes show associations with violent behavior that are largely limited to males. In addition, males are more likely than females to develop alcoholism, particularly the type-2 alcoholism that is associated with aggression (Volavka, 1999).

Following from this genetic evidence, it is likely that there are strong developmental gender differences in these and other hormonal and neurotransmitter systems. For example, underlying gender differences in behavior such as aggression, postmortem female human brains appear to have a greater density of cortical serotonin innervation than male brains (Gartner and Witaker-Azmitia, 1996). It is interesting to note that whole blood serotonin levels predicted violent behavior in men but not in women (Moffit, *et al.*, 1997; Moffit, *et al.*, 1998). In their naturalistic animal study, Mehlman and colleagues (1994) examined male rhesus monkeys and found a clear inverse relationship between the cerebral spinal fluid 5-hydroxyindoleacetic acid (CSF 5-HIAA) and increased aggression. As well, CSF 5-HIAA was much lower in monkeys that were wounded when compared to those that were not wounded, and also in monkeys that exhibited increased risk-taking behavior (i.e., leaping behaviors in the forest canopy) and aggression.

Similarly, in humans, suicidal behavior among incarcerated murderers is associated with significantly lower CSF 5-HIAA, when compared with murderers who have never attempted suicide. Youths convicted of homicide with elevated anxiety levels present a pattern of elevated CSF 5-HIAA levels (Lidberg, *et al.*, 2000). Risk-taking behavior in humans may also be explained by Raine's (1996) study, which showed those with antisocial behavior displayed underarousal in skin conductance and heart rate levels. Thus, it is plausible that those who have chronically under-aroused autonomic nervous systems are, perhaps, seeking stimulation in their risk-taking and often violent behavior.

While the predominant and scientifically strongest biological evidence comes from studies on animals, this research nonetheless offers convincing evidence for a biological system that, in interaction with the environment, plays a strong role in determining violent behavior for humans. For example, De Kloet and colleagues (1996) used genetically selected mice and rats to show that individual reaction patterns to stress (active versus passive) depends on genotype as well as early experiences of mother–pup interaction. Maternal deprivation proved to have long-term effects on corticosteroid receptor levels, showing that critical life experiences can trigger gene expressions that ultimately lead to increased vulnerability for aggressive behavior. This research proposed that during development, corticosteroids program a stress-reaction pattern for life. Specifically, genetically selected aggressive mice show low amounts of corticosteroid hormone with high amounts of serotonin receptor expression in the limbic areas. From this evidence it seems that the limbic serotenergic receptors also play an important role in aggression regulation.

*Aggression evolves in specific pathways*

Beyond the examination of developmental aggression, several researchers have postulated the pathways by which antisocial behaviors develop. The social-interactional model developed by Patterson and colleagues (1989) focused on the primary contexts of social learning. They theorized that factors such as a parent's involvement in crime, socioeconomic disadvantage, child temperament, and marital conflict may contribute to the development of antisocial behaviors in children, given ineffective parenting practices. The first phase of this model postulates that maladaptive parent–child interactions and unsuccessful parenting techniques are factors that contribute to a child's coercive and antisocial behaviors, including aggression. The second phase of this model focuses on the aggressive behaviors that may interfere with academic achievement and the development of positive relationships with peers. As the child develops and expands his/her social interactions, these aggressive behavior patterns continue in the school setting. Academic failure and peer rejection may be the result of this trajectory; according to Coie and colleagues (1998), aggression is highly correlated with rejection by most peer groups. Thus, aggressive children tend to associate with peers similar to them in terms of behaviors and values. Compounding the problem, deviant peer groups may have limited opportunities to engage in positive peer interactions, which subsequently increases their risk for aggressive and delinquent behaviors (Petersen and Crockett, 1985; Petersen, Leffert, and Graham, 1995).

Loeber and Dishion (1983) examined the pattern of male aggression in order to detect if the pathway to violence occurs in a deliberate fashion; they found support for three developmental pathways during childhood and adolescence. The "authority conflict pathway" develops first and tends to involve boys prior to age 12; it begins with stubborn behavior, followed by defiance, and finally avoidance such as truancy and running away. Secondly there is the "covert pathway," which consists of concealing problem behaviors; it begins with behaviors such as lying and shoplifting, followed by property damage (including vandalism and fire-setting), and lastly more serious forms of property crimes, such as burglary. The third pathway, encompassing increasingly aggressive acts, is the "overt pathway." Youths during this stage begin with bullying behaviors and annoying others, which can progress to physical fighting followed by more violent behaviors such as attacking someone, strong-arming, and rape. Loeber and Dishion postulated that individuals are not limited to one pathway and may, in fact, progress simultaneously along more than one pathway toward serious antisocial behavior.

Regardless of the pathway taken, research indicates early aggression is predictive of different manifestations of violence later (Stattin and Magnusson 1989). Puberty allows for biological maturity sooner than social maturity is permitted in western society, and for those who mature early, sooner than chronological age warrants (Moffitt, 1993; Caspi, *et al.*, 1993). Delinquency can be viewed as an attempt to consolidate these maturity gaps. Adolescents may obtain a "pseudo" social maturity by engaging in delinquent behaviors and demonstrating their autonomy from parental and social control (Moffitt, 1993). Deviant activities need the support of a peer group for their initiation and maintenance. In an attempt to understand the deviant activities of girls and, more specifically, some of the dynamics involved in girls' delinquency, Caspi and colleagues (1993) examined the role of biological maturation and behavioral changes in different contexts during adolescence. They found that preexisting behavior problems tend to be accentuated when an adolescent goes through a period of change that is novel and ambiguous, such as maturation, particularly when maturation occurs before the norm for same-age peers. Due to feeling isolated from same-age and same-sex peers, Newcomb and colleagues (1993) suggest, early maturing girls tend to associate more with boys and older peers who adhere to more deviant behavioral standards. This supports Caspi and colleagues' (1993) view that there are two factors necessary for the initiation and maintenance of female delinquency: puberty and boys. This research highlights the fact that chronological age may not be the best scale for understanding aggressive behaviors and the pathway to delinquency; rather, biological age may matter more and provide improved explanations for girls' delinquency.

## The psychopathology of aggression: conduct disorder

*Mental health and aggression*

An aspect that is essential to understanding juvenile delinquency is the mental health of the juvenile. A juvenile's mental state prior to, during, and after committing an offense provides useful information for interventions. Acting-out, disruptive, and aggressive behaviors are the primary reasons for a child's referral to the mental health services (Achenbach and Howell, 1993). It is important to discern whether these antisocial behavior patterns involve psychological impairments, or if they are realistic responses to environmental stimuli.

While it is clear that not all antisocial behaviors are pathological, research indicates that a significant number of youth in the juvenile justice system meet criteria for diagnosable mental illnesses (Davis, *et al.*, 1991). Juvenile delinquency is often associated with the diagnoses of Conduct Disorder, and, to a lesser degree, Oppositional Defiant Disorder. Conduct Disorder is characterized by a consistent pattern of aggressive and antisocial behaviors that disregard the rights of others and may involve the infliction of pain.

Research suggests most youth diagnosed with Conduct Disorder will be apprehended as delinquent; however there will only be a small amount of delinquent youth that meet diagnostic criteria for Conduct Disorder (Moffitt, 1993). The caution here is that the label Conduct Disorder (a diagnosable mental illness) can be misapplied to youth whose behaviors may be delinquent and possibly a reaction to their immediate social context.

Gender differences exist in the onset of Conduct Disorder, with girls typically having a later onset of the disorder than boys. However, research suggests that during adolescence the rate of Conduct Disorder among both sexes tends to become even. It may be that the rates of Conduct Disorder among males and females are similar throughout the developmental process, but because of males' use of overt aggression and females' use of covert behavior it is more difficult to detect Conduct Disorder in girls.

Preliminary results from a study assessing mental health issues among incarcerated juveniles reveal interesting findings with regard to gender.

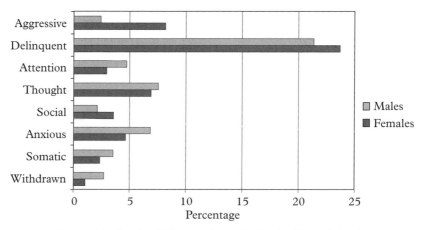

Figure 6.2  Gender differences in clinically significant behaviors

Consistent with established research, 92 percent of the 3,600 youth assessed were male. This study utilized the Achenbach Child Behavior Checklist as a screen for mental health problems, followed by a more comprehensive clinical interview. The Achenbach dichotomizes behavior problems into externalizing and internalizing behaviors. Externalizing behaviors consist of impulsive, aggressive, and antisocial actions, whereas internalizing behaviors encompass anxious, withdrawn, dysphoric, and somaticizing behaviors.

A striking finding exists when gender differences were examined in self-reported problem behaviors; girls identified their behaviors as being significantly more aggressive and delinquent than boys (see figure 6.2). The aggressive and delinquent behavior subscales of the Achenbach Child Behavior Checklist are associated with a diagnosis of Conduct Disorder. This idea of gender differences and delinquency will now be explored.

**Gender differences and delinquency**

Historically, delinquency and violence have been male-focused; reports consistently show the incarceration rates of males as outnumbering those of females. However, this has not always been the case; since the inception of juvenile institutions, girls have had a significant presence. In January 1825 the first "House of Refuge" was opened in New York City; it and others that followed were essentially the first residential institutions for juveniles who committed crimes or who were considered "at risk" for criminality. The New York City House of Refuge opened its doors to six girls and three boys; this gender disparity continued after the establishment of the first juvenile court in 1899. Female delinquency was considered primarily sexual, practically all girls appearing before the juvenile court were charged with immorality or unruliness (Grosser, 1952; Scholssman and Wallach, 1978; Sheldon, 1981). Thus, the gender disparity appeared to have been directly related to the juvenile justice system's obsession with precocious female sexuality and indirectly related to society's view of girls and puberty. This is evidenced by the following statement by a judge explaining the gender disparity among incarcerated youth during the early 1970s: "I figure if a girl is about to get pregnant, we'll keep her until she's sixteen and then Aid to Dependent Children will pick her up" (Chesney-Lind, 1989).

Gender differences and delinquency continue to center around issues relating to puberty. This is also a time when the prevalence of delinquent behaviors tends to increase (Magnusson, 1988; Silbereisen and Kracke, 1993; Simmons and Blythe, 1987; McGee and Williams, 1999; Moffitt, 1990; see also chapter 12). Puberty appears to affect social-emotional functioning differently, depending, in part, on its timing during the life course (Ge, et al., 1996; see also chapters 10 and 13). Early-maturing adolescents have less time to adapt to the new tasks of adolescence, and therefore may be at a greater risk for delinquent behavior (Petersen and Crockett, 1985; see also chapter 12). Body image disturbances, lower academic success, and conduct problems in school are some of the difficulties experienced by early-maturing girls (Simmons and Blythe, 1987; see also chapters 12 and 13). These difficulties may be due to the fact that early-maturing girls are more physically developed, yet psychologically immature and socially vulnerable. They have to learn how to negotiate the new demands placed on them due to their maturational status without the support of same-age peers and in settings that often offer a number of opportunities and reinforcements for delinquent behavior (Caspi, et al., 1993; Udry and Talbert, 1988; see also chapter 12).

*Girls and delinquency: current times*

While the majority of American girls can be described using the nursery rhyme "Sugar, spice, and everything nice," the increasing contact of girls with the juvenile justice system suggests "gangs, guns, and girls on the run" is an appropriate description for many girls. For more than a decade the United States has been plagued by a youth violence epidemic. According to the Office of Juvenile Justice and Delinquency Prevention, juvenile courts in the United States processed approximately 1,755,100 delinquency cases in 1997 (Scahill, 2000). Significant gender differences exist in delinquency rates, with males being more likely than females to commit crimes; it is believed that this difference may have been responsible for the lack of attention focused on female juvenile offenders. However, statistics indicating that adolescent girls make up the fastest-growing segment of the juvenile justice system has forced a shift in the focus of America's attention (Scahill, 2000).

"What About Girls," an appropriately titled fact sheet from the Office of Juvenile Justice and Delinquency Prevention (OJJDP), reports that between 1992 and 1996 the number of juvenile females arrested for Violent Crime Index Offenses increased by 25 percent, while there were no increases in arrests for male juveniles for the same offenses (Budnick and Shields-Fletcher, 1998). Overall, the number of delinquency cases involving females increased by 83 percent between 1988 and 1997; in contrast, there was only a 39 percent increase for males during the same time period (Scahill, 2000). It is important to note, however, that overall the female delinquency rate is still lower than the male rate.

Striking differences exist between genders when physical aggression is examined (Eagly and Steffen, 1986; Hyde, 1984). This is made clear by the fact that most homicides and other serious violent crimes are likely to be committed by men (Harries, 1990). Indirect aggression, characterized by alienation, ostracism, and character defamation, are more typical of girls (Cairns, *et al.*, 1989; Lagerspetz, Bjorkqvist, and Peltonen, 1988). These gender differences are due, in part, to differences in social context. The peer interactions of boys, characterized by large groups and high levels of physical activity, often lead to physical aggression. In contrast, girls tend to participate in smaller peer groups, an environment that is conducive to their use of indirect aggression (Lagerspetz, *et al.*, 1998). While the expression of aggression displays gender differences, the context in which actions occur may differ for males and females. Males tend to act out in the community, whereas females move their aggression to intimate relationships. This is supported by research suggesting that the majority of women convicted for violent crimes attacked people familiar to them, such as family members or neighbors (McClintock, 1963). Similarly, delinquent girls are more likely than delinquent boys to offend against people with whom they have a relationship (Supplemental Homicide Reports, 1993; Sondheimer, 2001).

### The role of status offenses

According to the Juvenile Detention and Correction Facility Census (JDCFC) of 1987, delinquent offenses are acts that would be considered crimes if committed by adults, whereas status offenses are delinquent acts that would not be considered crimes if committed by adults (Calhoun, Jurgens, and Chen, 1993). There seems to be a long-standing disparity in the types of act that identify males and females as juvenile delinquents (Schwartz, *et al.*, 1990; Figueira-McDonough, 1985). Female delinquency and status offenses are closely linked. Although boys are as likely as girls to run away from home, skip classes, and engage in disorderly conduct (i.e., commit status offenses), girls are more likely to be arrested and referred to court on these charges.

Many girls have found themselves victims of circumstance when it comes to the juvenile justice system. Calhoun and colleagues (1993) contend that over 75 percent of female juvenile delinquents have been sexually abused at an early age. The effects of sexual abuse may include behaviors such as running away from home, difficulties in school, and truancy (Brown and Finklehor, 1986). The courts recognize many of these behaviors as delinquent and impose additional trauma into the lives of the young women by treating them as criminals, often returning them home to the situations from which they were trying to escape.

*Violence and female delinquency*

Although juvenile crimes, like adult crimes, are dominated by males, female delinquents are becoming increasingly more comfortable in the territory once considered the exclusive domain of "bad boys" (Calhoun, *et al.*, 1993). Is this a new phenomenon? There is research that suggests it is not. [Researchers here critiqued the notion that girls are becoming more violent over time; examples from the media have been cited showing that girls becoming more violent is not a new concern.] For instance, a 1971 *New York Times* article of 1971 entitled Crime rate of women up sharply over men's, echoes current reports suggesting that the growth in delinquency cases involving females between 1988 and 1997 surpassed the growth for males in all offense categories (Scahill, 2000). [However, the reported increase in violent crimes committed by girls should be taken with caution. It should be acknowledged that the increases observed may appear significant, however,] closer analysis of the data reveals that the rise in arrests of girls more or less parallels increases in the arrests of males, and reflects overall changes in juvenile delinquency acts.

[Although it is important to elucidate the value of not taking data as given, the question of girls becoming more involved in violent] delinquent acts is an important issue and does not appear to be an artifact of the media. A study conducted by the California Youth Authority found that the percentage of girls who were incarcerated for murder was greater than the percentage of boys incarcerated for the same offense. Similar

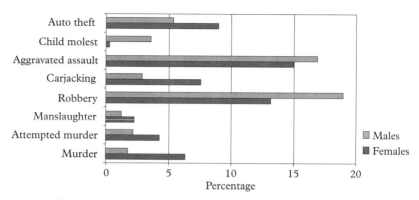

Figure 6.3 Gender differences in committing offenses

results were found in other offense categories (see figure 6.3). Although this study did not address the change in adolescent girls' involvement with violent crime over time, it does elucidate the type of crimes with which adolescent girls are currently involved and the gender differences that exist in those crime categories. It is clear that adolescent girls are engaging in violent delinquent acts and it is important to explore and develop an understanding for this phenomenon. The issue of violence and female delinquency can be depicted in the case of Melissa.

Melissa was interviewed during her detainment in a county juvenile hall in California. She was arrested on charges of carrying a concealed weapon, possession of an illegal substance with the intent to sell, and resisting arrest. Melissa was an intelligent young woman with a great sense of humor hidden behind a hard exterior. Melissa's presence in the juvenile hall made the staff vigilant and the other girls detained in the hall scared. She described her childhood as "okay," yet revealing that she witnessed domestic violence and often took on the role of primary caretaker for her younger siblings. Melissa indicated her mother suffers from a mental illness and has been hospitalized on several occasions. As Melissa entered adolescence, her older brother, who is involved in the sale of drugs, elucidated the choices she would have in life. He told her "either make money for yourself or you can be like most girls and become someone's 'hoe, who ends up with a bunch of kids." Melissa indicated she chose the former and was very successful with her drug business, and that she was not afraid to kill someone if the situation demanded that action.

The case of Melissa is interesting in that it shows an adolescent girl who is negotiating the demands of her environment, with what appears to be no prosocial support. Her brother serves as a delinquent role model and as research suggests, she is reinforced for participating in delinquent activities (Giordano, 1978; Caspi, *et al.*, 1993). It is clear that males engage in more delinquent acts and commit more crimes than females, but the types of behaviors and crimes with which females engage suggest that the gender difference many believe is so great is not, in fact, as remarkable.

## Conclusion

The scope of the problem of aggression, psychopathology, and violent acts among juveniles is alarming. Similar to many other domains of functioning, puberty is a defining period for gender differences to emerge in aggressive behaviors, psychopathology, and delinquent acts. The influences shaping these gender differences are varied. Maturation, self-regulation, and environment all play a role and interact in complicated ways that allow researchers to provide statements about the role of gender differences that are speculative, at best. However, the nascent research focusing on aggression, psychopathology, and delinquency gives promise to the field.

Gender differences in aggression do not appear until toddlerhood and the existence and stability of the gender differences during this developmental period is questionable. Clear signs of gender differences emerge during the preschool years. This coincides with an increase in peer interactions and these gender differences are relatively stable throughout the life course. It is also believed that biological processes may explain some of the gender differences that exist in aggressive behaviors. The interactions of biological processes and social interactions lay the foundation for explaining the various pathways with which aggression can evolve into delinquent and violent behaviors.

This chapter highlights the fact that delinquent acts tend to be the end result of aggressive behaviors, despite the specific development pathway for aggression. The role of puberty becomes particularly salient when examining the pathway of aggression. The case has been stated that puberty allows for biological maturity before adolescents are socially and psychologically mature and before western society encourages and support this maturity. Delinquent behaviors can be viewed as an attempt to reduce the resultant gap between an adolescent's biological and social maturity. Studies examining the behaviors among early-maturing adolescents compared to adolescents who mature within the normal range lend support to this notion (see chapter 12). In fact, research suggests that the role of puberty in understanding aggressive behaviors and delinquent acts is paramount. Following from this, it may be that one's biological age provides a greater understanding of aggressive behaviors and delinquent acts than does one's chronological age. The role of psychopathology in the expression of aggression and delinquent acts adds another dimension to the exploration of gender differences and maturation. The most compelling argument for gender difference and psychopathology as it relates to aggressive and delinquent behaviors is based on the expression of aggression research. More specifically, males and females tend to aggress differently, with males more likely to engage in overt aggression and females more likely to engage in covert, indirect, or relational aggression. Although the popular belief is that conduct disorder is more prevalent in boys than girls, some research suggests the prevalence of this disorder is similar between genders during adolescence and also that it is likely the use of covert aggression allows the behaviors of girls who are consistent with a diagnosis of conduct disorder to go unnoticed.

The study of puberty among girls has been extant because the onset of menarche is a biological marker that can be easily measured. Where there is a dearth of information is in the literature on girls and delinquency and the pathways for the development of delinquent acts. The research cited in this chapter provides a foundation that can be used to further the study of the influences of gender and maturation on aggression, psychopathology, and delinquency. It points to the specific need for research on girls and delinquency, taking into account the role of puberty, aggression, and psychopathology.

## References

Achenbach, T. M., and Howell, C. T. (1993). Are American children's problems getting worse? A thirteen-year comparison. *Journal of the American Academy of Child and Adolescent Psychiatry*, **32(6)**, 1145–1154.
Archer, J. (1991). The influence of testosterone on human aggression. *British Journal of Psychology*, **82**, 1–28.
Balthazar, M. L., and Cook, R. J. (1984). An analysis of the factors related to the rate of violent crimes committed by incarcerated female delinquents. *Journal of Offender Counseling, Services and Rehabilitation Special Issue: Gender Issues, Sex Offenses, and Criminal Justice: Current Trends*, **9(1–2)**, 103–118.
Bjorkqvist, K., Osterman, K., and Kaukiainen, A. (1992). The development of direct and indirect aggressive strategies in males and females. In K. Bjorkqvist and P. Niemela (ed.), *Of mice and women: Aspects of female aggression* (pp. 51–64). San Diego, CA: Academic Press.
Brody, L. R., Lovas, G. S., and Hay, D. H. (1995). Gender differences in anger and fear as a function of situational context. *Sex Roles*, **32(1–2)**, 47–78.
Browne, A., and Finklehor, D. (1986). Initial and long-term effects: a review of the research. In D. Finklehor (ed.), *A sourcebook on child sexual abuse* (pp. 143–179). London: Sage.
Budnick, K., and Shields-Fletcher, E. (1998). What About Girls? (OJJDP Fact Sheet, Sept 1998, 84) Washington DC: US. Dept of Justice.

Cairns, R. B., Cairns, B. D., Neckerman, H. J., and Ferguson, L. L. (1989). Growth and aggression: I. Childhood to early adolescence. *Developmental Psychology*, **25(2)**, 320–330.

Calhoun, G., Jurgens, J., and Chen, F. (1993). The neophyte female delinquent: a review of the literature. *Adolescence*, **28(110)**, 461–471.

Caspi, A., Lynam, D., Moffitt, T. E., *et al.* (1993). Unraveling girls' delinquency: biological, dispositional, and contextual contributions to adolescent misbehavior. *Developmental Psychology*, **29(1)**, 19–30.

Chesney-Lind, M., and Sheldon, R. (1998). Girls, delinquency, and Juvenile Justice (2nd ed). Belmont, CA: Wadsworth.

Coie, J., Terry, R., Lenox, K., Lochman, J., and Hyman, C. (1998). Childhood peer rejection and aggression as predictors of stable patterns of adolescent disorder: erratum. *Development and Psychopathology*, **10(3)**, 587–588.

Crick, N. R. (1995). Relational aggression: the role of intent attributions, feelings of distress, and provocation type. *Development and Psychopathology*, **7(2)**, 313–322.

Crick, N. R., and Grotpeter, J. K. (1995). Relational aggression, gender, and social psychological adjustment. *Child Development*, **66(3)**, 710–722.

Davis, D. L., Bean, G. J., Schumacher, J. E., *et al.* (1991). Prevalence of emotional disorders in a juvenile justice institutional population. *American Journal of Forensic Psychology*, **9(1)**.

De Kloet, E., Korte, S., Rots, N., and Kruk, M. (1996). Stress hormones, genotype, and brain organization: implications for aggression. *Annals of the New York Academy of Sciences*, **794**, 179–189.

Eagly, A. H., and Steffen, V. J. (1986). Gender and aggressive behavior: a meta-analytic review of the social psychological literature. *Psychological Bulletin*, **100(3)**, 309–330.

Fagot, B. I., and Kavanagh, K. (1990). Sex differences in responses to the stranger in the Strange Situation. *Sex Roles*, **23(3–4)**, 123–132.

Figueira-McDonough, J. (1985). Are girls different? Gender discrepancies between delinquent behavior and control. *Child Welfare Special Issue: Toward a Feminist Approach to Child Welfare*, **64(3)**, 273–289.

Gartner, J., and Witaker-Azmitia, P. (1996). Developmental factors influencing aggression: animal models and clinical correlates. *Annals of the New York Academy of Sciences*, **794**, 113–119.

Ge, X., Best, K. M., Conger, R. and D., *et al.* (1996). Parenting behaviors and the occurrence and co-occurrence of adolescent depressive symptoms and conduct problems. *Developmental Psychology*, **32(4)**, 717–731.

Giordano, P. C. (1978). Girls, guys, and gangs: the changing social context of female delinquency. *Journal of Criminal Law and Criminology*, **69**, 126–132.

Grosser, G. (1952). Juvenile delinquency and contemporary American sex roles. Ph.D. dissertation. Harvard University.

Hall, G. S. (1907). *Aspects of child life and education*. London: Routledge/ Thoemmes Press.

Harries, K. D. (1990). *Serious violence: patterns of homicide and assault in America*. Springfield, CA: Charles C. Thomas.

Hay, D. F., Castle, J., Stimson, C. A., and Davies, L. (1995). The social construction of character in toddlerhood. In M. Killen and D. Hart (ed.), *Mortality in everyday life: developmental perspectives* (pp. 23–51). Cambridge: Cambridge University Press.

Hyde, J. S. (1984). How large are gender differences in aggression? A developmental meta analysis. *Developmental Psychology*, **20(4)**, 722–736.

Johnson, E. O., Arria, A. M., Borges, G., *et al.* (1995). The growth of conduct problem behaviors from middle childhood to early adolescence: sex differences and the suspected influence of early alcohol use. *Journal of Studies on Alcohol*, **56(6)**, 661–671.

Kupfer, D. J., Foster, F. G., Detre, T. P. (1975). Sleep EEG and motor activity as indicators of affective states. *Neuropsychobiology*, **1(5)**, 296–303.

Lagerspetz, K. M., Bjoerkqvist, K., and Peltonen, T. (1998). Is indirect aggression typical of females? Gender differences in aggressiveness in 11- to 12-year-old children. *Aggressive Behavior*, **14(6)**, 403–414.

Lewis, T., Bjorkquist, D. C. (1992). Needs assessment: a critical reappraisal. *Performance Improvement Quarterly*, **5(4)**, 33–54.

Lidberg, L., Belfrage, H., Bertilsson, L., Evenden, M., and Asberg, M. (2000). Suicide attempts and impulse control disorder are related to low cerebrospinal fluid 5-HIAA in mentally disordered violent offenders. *Acta psychiatrica Scandinavica*, **101(5)**, 395–402.

Loeber, R., and Dishion, T. J. (1983). Early predictors of male delinquency: a review. *Psychological Bulletin*, **94**, 68–99.

Loeber, R., and Hay, D. (1997). Key issues in the development of aggression and violence from childhood to early adulthood. *Annual Review of Psychology*, **48**, 371–410.

Loeber, R., and Stouthamer-Loeber, M. (1998). Development of juvenile aggression and violence: some common misconceptions and controversies. *American Psychologist*, **53(2)**, 242–259.

Maccoby, E. E., and Jacklin, C. N. (1980). Sex differences in aggression: a rejoinder and reprise. *Child Development*, **51(4)**, 964–980.

Magnusson, D. (1988). *Individual development from an interactional perspective: a longitudinal study*. Hillsdale, NJ: Lawrence Erlbaum.

McClintock, C. G. (1963). Group support and the behavior of leaders and nonleaders. *Journal of Abnormal and Social Psychology*, **67(2)**, 105–113.

McGee, R., and Williams, S. (1999). Environmental risk factors in oppositional-defiant disorder and conduct disorder. In Herbert C. Quay and Anne E. Hogan (ed.), *Handbook of disruptive behavior disorders* (pp. 419–440). New York: Plenum.

Mehlman, P., Higley, J., Faucher, I., Lilly, A., Taub, D., Vickers, J., Suomi, S., and Linnoila, M. (1994). Low CSF 5-HIAA concentrations and severe aggression and impaired impulse control in non-human primates. *American Journal of Psychiatry*, **151(10)**, 1485–1492.

Moffitt, T. E. (1990). Juvenile delinquency and attention deficit disorder: boys' developmental trajectories from age 3 to age 15. *Child Development*, **61(3)**, 893–910.

Moffitt, T. E. (1993). Adolescence-limited and life-course-persistent antisocial behavior. A developmental taxonomy. *Psychological Review*, **100**, 674–701.

Moffitt, T. E., Brammer, G., Caspi, A., Fawcett, J., Raleigh, M., Yuwiler, A., and Silva, P. (1998). Whole blood serotonin relates to violence in an epidemiological study. *Biological Psychiatry*, 43(6), 446–457.

Moffitt, T. E., Caspi, A., Fawcett, P., Brammer, G., Raleigh, M., Yuwiler, A., and Silva, P. (1997). Whole blood serotonin and family background relate to male violence. *Biosocial Bases of Violence*, 231–249.

Newcomb, A. F., Bukowski, W. M., and Pattee, L. (1993). Children's peer relations: a meta-analytic review of popular, rejected, neglected, controversial, and average sociometric status. *Psychological Bulletin*, 113(1), 99–128.

Patterson, G. R., DeBaryshe, B. D., and Ramsey, E. (1989). A development perspective on antisocial behavior. *American Psychologist*, 44, 329–335.

Pepler, D. J. and Slaby, R. G. (1994). Theoretical and developmental perspectives on youth and violence. In Leonard D. Eron and J. H. Gentry (ed.), *Reason to hope: a psychosocial perspective on violence and youth* (pp. 27–58). Washington, DC: American Psychological Association.

Petersen, A. C., and Crockett, L. (1985). Pubertal timing and grade effects on adjustment. Special issue: time of maturation and psychosocial functioning in adolescence. *Journal of Youth and Adolescence*, 14(3), 191–206.

Petersen, A. C., Leffert, N., and Graham, B. L. (1995). Adolescent development and the emergence of sexuality. *Suicide and Life-Threatening Behavior*, 25, 4–17.

Raine, A. (1996). Autonomic nervous system factors underlying disinhibited, antisocial, and violent behavior. *Annals of the New York Academy of Sciences*, 794, 46–60.

Reichel, H., and Magnusson, D. (1988). The relationship of intelligence to registered criminality: an exploratory study. Report from the Department of Psychology, University of Stockholm (27 pages).

Reiss, A. J., and Roth, J. A. (1993). *Understanding and preventing violence*, vol. I. Washington, DC: National Academy Press.

Rubinow, D., and Schmidt, P. (1996). Androgens, brain, and behavior. *American Journal of Psychiatry*, 153(8), 974–984.

Rutter, M., and Cesaer, P. (1991). *Biological risk factors for psychosocial disorders*. Cambridge: Cambridge University Press.

Scahill, M. (2000). Female Delinquency Cases (OJJDP Fact Sheet 16, Nov. 2000) Washington DC: Department of Justice.

Schlossman, S., and Wallach, S. (1978). The crime of precocious sexuality: female delinquency in the progressive era. *Harvard Educational Review*, 48, 65–94.

Schwartz, C. E., Dorer, D. J., Beardslee, W. R., et al. (1990). Maternal expressed emotion and parental affective disorder: risk for childhood depressive disorder, substance abuse, or conduct disorder. *Journal of Psychiatric Research*, 24(3), 231–250.

Shelden, R. G. (1981). Sex discrimination in the juvenile justice system: Memphis, Tennessee, 1900–1917. In M. Q. Warren (ed.), *Comparing male and female offenders*. Thousand Oaks, CA: Sage.

Silbereisen, R. K., and Kracke, B. (1993). Variation in maturational timing and adjustment in adolescence. In S. Jackson and H. Rodriguez-Tome (ed.), *Adolescence and its social worlds* (pp. 67–94). Hillsdale, NJ: Lawrence Erlbaum.

110    *Stephanie Hawkins, Samantha Pia Miller, and Hans Steiner*

Simon, N., McKenna, S., Lu, S., and Cologer-Clifford, A. (1996). Development and expression of hormonal systems regulating aggression. *Annals of the New York Academy of Sciences*, **794**, 8–17.

Simmons, R. G., and Blythe, D. A. (1987). Moving into adolescence: the impact of pubertal change and school context. New York: De Gruyter.

Sondheimer, D. L. (2001). Young female offenders: increasingly visible yet poorly understood. *Gender Issues*, **19(1)**, 79–90.

Stattin, H., and Magnusson, D. (1989). The role of early aggressive behavior in the frequency, seriousness, and types of later crime. *Journal of Consulting and Clinical Psychology*, **57**, 710–718.

Steiner, H., and Cauffman, E. (1998). Juvenile justice, delinquency, and psychiatry. *Child and Adolescent Psychiatric Clinics of North America*, **7(3)**, 653–672.

Supplemental Homicide Reports (1993). Federal Bureau of Investigation, Washington, DC.

Susman, E., Granger, D., Murowchick, E., Ponirakis, A., and Worral, B. (1996). Gonadal and adrenal hormones: developmental transitions and aggressive behavior. *Annals of the New York Academy of Sciences*, **794**, 18–30.

Udry, J. R., and Talbert, L. M. (1988). Sex hormone effects on personality at puberty. *Journal of Personality and Social Psychology*, **54(2)**, 291–295.

Volavka, J. (1999). The neurobiology of violence: an update. *Journal of Neuropsychiatry and Clinical Neurosciences*, **11(3)**, 307–314.

Websdale, N., and Chesney-Lind, M. (1998). Doing violence to women: research synthesis on the victimization of women. In L. H. Bowker (ed.), *Masculinities and violence* (pp. 55–81). Thousand Oaks, CA: Sage.

Weinburg, M. K., Tronick, E. Z., Cohn, J. F., and Olson, K. L. (1999). Gender differences in emotional expressivity and self-regulation during early infancy. *Developmental Psychology*, **35(1)**, 175–188.

Williams, J. M., and Dunlop, L. C. (1999). Pubertal timing and self-reported delinquency among male adolescents. *Journal of Adolescence*, **22(1)**, 157–171.

Wilson, J. J., Rojas, N., Haapanen, R., Duxbury, E., and Steiner, H. (2001) Substance abuse and criminal recidivism: a prospective study of adolescents. *Child Psychiatry and Human Development*, **31(4)**, 297–312.

*Part 3*

# Boys at puberty

# 7  Boys at puberty: psychosocial implications

*Jenica Huddleston and Xiaojia Ge*

> I am pretty confused. I wonder whether I am weird or normal. My body
> is starting to change. I get nervous in the locker room during PE class.
>
> Mike, age 11

> I am fourteen already. But I still look like a kid. I got teased a lot,
> especially by other guys. I am always the last one picked for sides in
> basketball because I am so short. Girls don't seem to be interested in
> me either because most of them are taller than I am.
>
> Robert, age 14

Although pubertal development in boys has fascinated people for centuries, scientific inquiry into this area did not begin until the middle of
the twentieth century. Approximately a dozen well-researched articles
have appeared in the past decade that provide excellent overviews on
the study of psychosocial implications of pubertal changes (e.g., Alsaker,
1995, 1996; Brooks-Gunn, Graber, and Paikoff, 1994; Brooks-Gunn,
Petersen, and Compas, 1995; Brooks-Gunn and Reiter, 1990; Buchanan,
Eccles, and Becker, 1992; Connolly, Paikoff, and Buchanan, 1996;
Graber, Petersen, and Brooks-Gunn, 1996; Paikoff and Brooks-Gunn,
1991; Susman, 1997; Susman and Petersen, 1992). This chapter will
focus on studies of the psychosocial implications of pubertal changes in
boys; it will not be an exhaustive review, but, rather, will serve to highlight some of the important areas of research related to pubertal changes
among boys. This chapter is structured in five sections. First, the physical and physiological changes that boys experience during puberty will
be discussed. Then a brief review of some studies that relate hormonal
changes to boys' psychosocial adjustment will be followed by a discussion
of the two concepts frequently used in studying boys' pubertal transition:
pubertal status and pubertal timing. A large portion of this chapter will
be devoted to a review and discussion of the studies on the effect of
pubertal timing on boys' psychosocial adjustment, as the majority of
these studies have compared boys with different maturational timing and
researchers have generally noted the greater importance of pubertal

timing. The chapter will end with a discussion and suggestions for future research.

## Boys at puberty: physical and physiological changes

Along with the dramatic increase in body weight, body composition also changes during puberty. These changes, however, are quite different for boys and girls. While girls experience a greater and faster increase in body fat than boys, boys experience a greater and faster muscular growth than girls. Muscle mass increases for a longer time in boys than in girls; whereas girls reach the lean muscle mass of a young woman by about 15–16 years of age, boys reach the lean muscle mass of a young man at about 19–20 years of age (Rogol, Clark, and Roemmich, 2000). On average, girls' growth is smaller in magnitude in almost all dimensions when compared to boys, with the exception of hip width (Tanner, 1989). These sex differences in height and weight growth and in body composition at puberty result in the typical adult female and male body types (Rogol, Clark, and Roemmich, 2000). Before puberty, boys and girls have approximately similar levels of strength, lean body mass, skeletal mass, and body fat. By the end of pubertal development, however, boys are stronger and have more lean body mass, skeletal mass, and less body fat than girls (Grumbach and Styne, 1992; Tanner, 1989).

Growth of the testes, the male primary sexual characteristic, is most commonly the first sign of puberty in boys, which begins about six months after girls begin their pubertal development (Brooks-Gunn and Reiter, 1990; Grumbach and Styne, 1992). An acceleration of penis growth occurs about a year after this original testicular growth and lasts approximately two years (Tanner, 1989). Secondary sexual characteristics that develop during puberty include growth and changes in genital and pubic hair in boys. These changes and their variations have been carefully described by Marshall and Tanner (1970) and can be categorized into five stages. Other detectable signs, such as the growth of facial and underarm hair and the deepening of the voice, occur gradually at puberty and do not attain adult form until very late in adolescence. During puberty, boys' skin changes as well; the development of sweat glands and increased oiliness of the skin give rise to acne and skin eruption, a common sight in middle and high school that often creates agony among teenage boys.

## Hormonal correlates of psychosocial development in boys

Researchers have long been wondering about the role that hormones play in the psychosocial development of adolescents. Observed effects of outward morphological changes may simply be a manifestation of the underlying hormonal processes that directly contribute to psychosocial adjustment, indicated through internalizing and externalizing problems (Brooks-Gunn, Graber, and Paikoff, 1994; Petersen and Taylor, 1980; Susman, 1997). This section will briefly review some of the more recent studies. Interested readers are referred to Buchanan and colleagues (1992), who have provided a comprehensive and detailed review of the links between hormones and psychosocial adjustment for both girls and boys.

The most consistent results regarding hormone effects involve relationships between testosterone and various types of externalizing behaviors. Testosterone level is related to criminality in adult males (Dabbs and Hargrove, 1997), to dominance (Mazur and Booth, 1998) and aggression in 7- to 14-year-old boys (Scerbo and Kolko, 1994), and to lower frustration tolerance among older adolescents (Olweus, *et al.*, 1988). It is also related to certain types of aggression under provocative conditions (Olweus, 1986; Olweus, *et al.*, 1988).

At the pubertal transition, changes in adrenal and gonadal hormones may render adolescents vulnerable to dysregulation in emotions and behaviors. Indeed, these hormones were found to account for variance in antisocial behavior not accounted for by stage of puberty (physical maturation), and psychological, family, and peer processes. In Susman's study, 6–8 percent of the variance in antisocial behavior was explained by one hormone, whereas multiple hormones explained up to 43 and 45 percent of the variances in rebellious and delinquent behavior, respectively. Correlational studies also report relationships between adrenal and gonadal steroid levels and depressed affect and behavior problems (e.g., Angold, Costello, and Worthman, 1998; Brooks-Gunn and Warren, 1989; Nottelmann, *et al.*, 1990; Susman, *et al.*, 1987). Recently, Finkelstein and colleagues (1997, 1998) conducted a double-blind sex hormone treatment study that shows an administration of low-dose estrogen (early puberty levels) and mid-dose testosterone (midpuberty) significantly increased overt aggression in girls and boys, respectively, and sexual behavior in boys. These experimental model findings provide strong support for the causal role of hormone changes in antisocial behavior during the pubertal transition.

There is some evidence that indicates that adrenal androgens are related to dominance (Inoff-Germain, *et al.*, 1988), depression (Angold, Costello, and Worthman, 1998; Susman, *et al.*, 1987), aggressive affect (Brooks-Gunn and Warren, 1989), and sexual activities (Udry, *et al.*, 1985; Udry and Talbert, 1988). Boys with Conduct Disorder had significantly higher levels of dehydroepiandrosterone (DHEA) and dehydroepiandrosterone sulfate (DHEAS), with higher levels related to the intensity of aggression and delinquency (Van Goozen, *et al.*, 1998). In prepubertal boys, severe antisocial behavior and aggression were positively related to higher serum concentrations of adrenal androgens, and concentrations of adrenal androgens were higher in antisocial boys than in controls (Van Goozen, *et al.*, 1998).

The sign of the relationships (positive or negative) are not always consistent across studies and are different for boys and girls, however. In studies by Susman and colleagues (1987) and Schaal and colleagues (1996) it was a decreased level, as opposed to an increased level, of testosterone that was characteristic of antisocial boys. In some studies (e.g., Susman, *et al.*, 1987; Angold, Costello, and Worthman, 1998), lower estrogen and testosterone levels are significantly associated with higher levels of symptoms of anxiety and depression. But in other studies (e.g., Brooks-Gunn and Warren, 1989), higher estrogen and testosterone are associated with more internalizing symptoms. Given the consistent findings that testosterone is significantly related to aggression in older adolescents (Olweus, 1986; Olweus, *et al.*, 1988), these results appear to suggest that internalizing and externalizing problems may be related to rapid change or increases in testosterone. It is also interesting to note that Susman and her colleagues (Susman, *et al.*, 1985; Susman, Dorn, and Chrousos, 1991; Susman, *et al.*, 1987) found that boys with low-for-age gonadal activity and high-for-age andostenedione manifested more negative affect. This research suggests that it may be important to consider the effect of pubertal timing – pubertal changes relative to a person's age.

In addition to adrenal androgens and sex steroids, cortisol has also been identified as a potential source of vulnerability to externalizing behavior during the pubertal transition (Susman, *et al.*, 1997). With respect to cortisol reactivity, Susman and colleagues (1997) found that low baseline cortisol followed by an increase in cortisol levels (cortisol reactivity), in a novel situation, predicted depression and conduct disorder symptoms one year later in both boys and girls.

### Measuring pubertal status and pubertal timing

The two most frequently used measures in studying boys at puberty are pubertal status and pubertal timing. Pubertal status refers to the physical and physiological maturational levels of an individual at a given point in time, relative to the overall pubertal process, whereas pubertal timing refers to whether an individual's maturation is earlier, on time, or later in comparison to same-age peers. While pubertal status only makes reference to an individual himself (e.g., "his skin starts changing" or "he is at Tanner stage 2"), the assessment of pubertal timing makes reference to a comparison group (e.g., "he matured earlier than most of his classmates"). Pubertal status is intricately confounded with pubertal timing, because measuring pubertal timing requires knowledge of an individual's pubertal status (see chapter 1). Pubertal timing, however, differs from pubertal status in that it requires additional information of that individual's chronological age (e.g., "he started puberty early for his age") and the norm of maturational levels for that age group (e.g., "he started puberty early for his age when most of his classmates had not started"). It is interesting to note that while pubertal status does not need to refer to age, its variability is age-limited. That is, variability between individuals does not appear before puberty and it disappears as the development becomes complete. When assessing pubertal status, therefore, it is important to consider age range when its variability can be observed. Moreover, pubertal status, when assessed at a particular time point for a same-age same-sex group during an early year, could be an indicator of pubertal timing.

Although puberty is a continuous process, researchers often categorize the development of specific maturational characteristics into stages in order to make comparisons among individuals. Pubertal status has been measured by (1) development of primary and secondary sex characteristics, (2) other physical changes (e.g., x-ray of skeletal or bone age), and (3) levels of hormones. Marshall and Tanner (1970) detailed the changes in primary and secondary sex characteristics that develop during puberty. Variations in development have been carefully categorized into five stages (Tanner stages – see Marshall and Tanner, 1970), which have been widely used to indicate pubertal developmental status (see chapter 2). Typically, a physician or trained nurse conducts a physical examination to determine a child's stage of development. Another method, which some researchers have used, is to ask children and adolescents to rate themselves based on photographs of individuals at different Tanner stages (Tanner self-staging). The stages of puberty as described by Tanner are mainly based on adolescents of European decent. Relatively little information, however, exists regarding pubertal changes in populations of other ethnicities (see chapters 1 and 13).

Although Tanner self-staging has been considered accurate, having to show pictures or portraits of unclothed individuals to children is often a concern for parents and school officials. In response to this concern, Petersen and her colleagues (1988) developed a self-report measure, the Pubertal Developmental Scale (PDS), based on pencil-and-paper responses to a questionnaire about the degrees of voice change, height and weight growth, underarm hair, skin change, and pubic hair. The responses can either be used as a scale or translated into the correspond-ing Tanner stages. Perhaps due to its unobtrusive nature and convenience of use, the PDS quickly became a widely used instrument, both for urban and rural populations (Robertson, *et al.*, 1992). Although frequently used, the reliability of self-reported measures of pubertal development continues to be a topic of debate.

Even less intrusive, though more debatable in accuracy, is the obser-vation of visible signs of pubertal development, such as height, weight, muscle development, and facial and body hair, to determine pubertal development, as was done by Savin-Williams and Small (1986) and Steinberg (1987). Early archival studies measured pubertal development by skeletal age or bone age, with the use of x-rays (Jones and Bayley, 1950; Mussen and Jones, 1957). The costs and risks associated with x-ray expo-sure led to a virtual discontinuation of this method. Peak height velocity has also been used to determine pubertal status in studies such as those by Petersen and Crockett (1985) and Simmons and colleagues (1987). Less frequently used are measures of hormones, such as testosterone or estro-gen, to determine pubertal status. Levels of androgens have fairly high correlations with pubic hair development, but associations with other secondary sex characteristics are less conclusive. Interested readers are recommended to consult Graber, Petersen, and Brooks-Gunn (1996), who have provided the most detailed and up-to-date exposition of the measurement issues of puberty.

The determination of pubertal timing for boys, however, is more dif-ficult than for girls, because unlike girls, whose age at menarche is often conveniently used as an indicator of timing, boys do not have an equally salient event as a clear marker. Although spermarche is often speculated to be of equal importance to menarche, it is rarely used in research due to the difficulties in accurate assessment of the first nocturnal emission or reluctance for adolescents to offer information about masturbation. Therefore, measuring the pubertal timing of boys commonly involves an assessment of their pubertal developmental levels that are adjusted for their chronological age. For example, Susman and colleagues (1985) and Ge, Conger, and Elder (2001a) standardized pubertal developmental levels within their subjects' age.

Other methodological issues arise for measuring boys' pubertal timing as well. First, it is often difficult to determine which are the most appro-priate age cohorts to assess to cover the full range of early, on-time, and late maturing boys. Second, even given consensus on age range, there are no commonly accepted criteria for how to classify boys into differ-ent timing groups. Cut-offs for timing groups vary from study to study, making comparisons of findings more difficult. A third issue involves the differences between perceived and objective or calculated pubertal timing. Individuals may perceive themselves as off-time compared to their peers, when objective measures indicate otherwise. Dubas, Graber, and Petersen (1991) found perceived timing only moderately related to objective measures of timing, but perceived timing rather than objective timing was more strongly related to behavior.

## The effect of pubertal timing on boys

### Two theories and four variants

The majority of studies concerning boys at puberty have revolved around the effect of maturational timing on adolescent social and psychological adjustment. Two principal theoretical predictions, the deviance and stage termination hypotheses, have been advanced that focus on the disparities between chronological age, social timing, and biological maturation that frequently occur during the early years of adolescent growth (Petersen and Taylor, 1980).

The deviance hypothesis predicts that early-maturing girls and late maturing boys will manifest more psychosocial adjustment problems than their on-time peers. Because the early-maturing girls and late maturing boys experience their onset of puberty much farther in a continuum from "normal" maturational timing, this departure from the socially expected scheduling of life sequence places them in a deviant category compared to their on-time peers. On the other hand, transitions that occur at expected ages and conform to the social clock are socially predictable and desirable; on-time adolescents should thus be less affected than should their early- or late developing peers.

This theoretical prediction (called variant 1), as was originally conceived, pooled girls and boys together in a continuum of pubertal maturational timing. A variant of this deviance hypothesis (called variant 2) suggested that one should compare early, on-time, and late onsets of maturation within gender, rather than lumping boys and girls together. Thus, according to this variant, it is plausible that boys may only compare their levels of maturation with other boys and are less sensitive to how girls develop, and vice versa. From this perspective, those for whom puberty started earlier or later than their same-sex peers would be at higher risk for adjustment problems than their on-time maturing same-sex peers. Thus, both early- and late maturing boys would fall into this "deviant" category and should be compared to on-time maturing boys.

The alternative theoretical prediction, the stage termination hypothesis, posits that adolescents who mature early rather than late would experience higher levels of psychosocial adjustment difficulties (Ge, Conger, and Elder, 1996; Peskin, 1973; Petersen and Taylor, 1980). According to this line of reasoning, chronologically ordered developmental tasks in one stage need to be successfully completed in order to move to the next developmental stage. Maturing too early may shorten the preparatory time for children to acquire, assimilate, and strengthen adaptive and coping skills necessary to confront new challenges in adolescence, thus placing early maturers at risk for psychosocial maladjustment. Because early-maturing girls reach puberty earlier than other girls and much earlier than boys, they are the group that should be most negatively affected compared to the rest of their peers. According to this hypothesis (variant 1), early-maturing boys would not be affected because they were not the earliest maturing group when both girls and boys were considered together. However, if the preparatory tasks or rates of accomplishment of these tasks differ by gender, and if boys' comparative reference group consisted of only their same-sex peers, it would be the early-maturing boys that would be negatively affected. When considered within gender, the second variant of the stage termination hypothesis (variant 2) predicts that early-maturing boys would be the ones negatively affected. In the sections that follow we will briefly review some of the relevant literature that bears on the pubertal timing effect on boys.

*Pioneering studies, 1950–75*

The California and Fels longitudinal growth studies (Clausen, 1975; Jones, 1957, 1965; Jones and Bayley, 1950; Mussen and Jones, 1957, 1958; Peskin, 1967, 1973) have made significant contributions to our understanding of boys at puberty. The early research focus of these studies was largely on the psychological, social, and behavioral implication of the differential timing of puberty in developing teenagers. These studies, in general, painted a positive portrait for early-maturing boys, positing that they had significantly reduced feelings of inadequacy, rejection, and inferiority (Mussen and Jones, 1957), and that they were more relaxed and less tense and depressed (Clausen, 1975; Jones and Bayley, 1950). They were also less likely to show signs of guilt or to manifest negative self-concept, as compared to late maturing boys. Follow-up studies of these same boys suggested that the early-maturing boys appeared better adjusted and healthier psychologically as adults in their early and late 30s (Jones, 1957, 1965). When examined as adults, these early-maturing males made a better impression, were more responsible, and had more control of others and higher levels of socialization than those who had matured later (Jones, 1957, 1965).

Although these studies generally considered early-maturing boys to be more well adjusted socially and psychologically as compared to later maturing boys, there were some inconsistent findings. An analysis of the data from the Berkeley Guidance Study by Peskin (1967) found that, contrary to other research, early-maturing boys, as compared to later maturing boys, tended to have more mood problems (e.g., temper tantrums and anxiety) than the previous research had indicated. Similar inconsistent findings were also reported regarding aggression. While Mussen and Jones (1958) found a significantly higher level of aggression among late maturing boys, these same authors (Mussen and Jones, 1957) and Peskin (1973) reported an opposite finding that indicated a higher level of aggression among early-maturing boys. Furthermore, Peskin (1973) found that temper tantrums occurred significantly more often and with greater severity in early-maturing boys.

Whereas the original results from these early studies suggested positive effects of early maturation on boys' development, especially in social domains such as social prestige, popularity, and leadership (Clausen, 1975; Jones and Bayley, 1950; Jones, 1965; Weatherley, 1964), Jones and Bayley (1950) and others reported that later maturing boys showed higher levels of eagerness, social initiative, and sociability. Similarly, Peskin (1973) found that late maturing boys tended to have positive social skills that early-maturing boys lacked, such as higher levels of social initiation and lower social submission. Significant differences were found between timing groups on measures of leadership (Weatherley, 1964) and social acceptance (Mussen and Jones, 1958) in some early studies, while others did not find support for this.

*Summary* These early pioneering studies opened up an unexplored field of research by directing attention to the psychosocial significance of differential maturational timing. These studies suggested that early-maturing boys are, in general, at an advantage when compared to their later maturing peers. The advantage for early-maturing boys was manifested in social, psychological, and behavioral terms, especially in socially related attributes (e.g., social popularity) and interactions. These studies, when considered together with their results on girls, supported the deviance hypothesis (variant 1); most of the studies found that early-maturing boys were better off than their late maturing counterparts. It should also be mentioned that the earlier research came almost exclusively from the Berkeley Guidance and Oakland Growth studies conducted in the Bay area of northern California; inconsistent findings did emerge in these studies. Particularly noteworthy are Peskin's (1967, 1973) findings that support the stage termination hypothesis (variant 2). These findings left unsettled the question of whether early maturation confers an advantage to boys or not.

*Deepening the understanding, 1975–97*

The pioneering studies conducted at the University of California at Berkeley did not bring immediate and widespread academic responses and attention to the implication of differential pubertal timing until the 1980s. Publications related to the psychosocial implication of puberty only appeared sporadically between 1975 and 1983 (e.g., Steinberg and Hill, 1978). Three important publications in the 1980s marked a significant expansion of the knowledge on the psychosocial implications of human puberty: the publication of *Girls at puberty* (Brooks-Gunn and Petersen, 1983), a two-volume special issue in the *Journal of Youth and Adolescence* (1985), and *Biological-psychosocial interactions* (Lerner and Foch, 1987). Although the publication of *Girls at puberty* has contributed significantly to the knowledge of female pubertal maturation and stimulated more studies in that area, it was exclusively devoted to the study of girls, which is only tangentially relevant to this chapter. The two special issues in the *Journal of Youth and Adolescence*, targeting the area of maturational timing and psychosocial functioning, helped increase the knowledge related to both boys and girls. Approximately half of the studies in these issues included boys in their samples, though no articles were devoted exclusively to boys. At this time, girls were still the primary focus of investigation, but research related to pubertal timing and psychosocial functioning was gaining momentum and a further investigation related to the male experience was beginning.

These new studies on the psychosocial implications of pubertal timing for boys mostly focused on internalizing symptoms, externalizing problems, social adjustment, and family relations. Internalizing symptoms generally refer to the situation in which an individual's psychological difficulties are turned inward, resulting in more psychological or emotional symptoms, such as depressed moods, anxiety, or signs of withdrawal. Externalizing problems, on the other hand, refer typically to the situation in which an individual's psychological difficulties are turned outward and are manifested in behavior or actions that are readily visible to others, such as aggression, delinquent acts, conduct problems, and cruelty to people or animals. Because of their high co-occurrence, researchers often examine externalizing problems together with substance use and abuse, including tobacco, alcohol, and drugs.

*Internalizing symptoms*

Research conducted during this period continued to show pubertal timing effects on depressed mood, anxious feelings, and other areas of emotions among boys. It remained unclear, however, whether it was only the late maturing boys who were negatively affected, or both early- and late maturing boys. The former would support variant 1, while the latter would support variant 2 of the deviance hypothesis. For example, Susman and colleagues (Susman, Dorn, and Chrousos, 1991; Susman, *et al.*, 1985) showed that early-maturing boys were significantly higher on measures of negative and sad affect compared to their late maturing peers. Contrary to the earlier study by Jones and Bayley (1971), who reported that later maturing boys had higher levels of anxiety, Susman and colleagues (1991) found earlier maturing boys to be more anxious than on-time and late maturing boys. Similarly, Petersen and Crockett (1985) found that early-maturing boys had significantly higher levels of psychopathology, while late maturing boys were considered best off with the lowest levels of psychopathology, when all three timing groups were compared.

These findings of early-maturing boys being negatively affected lend support for variant 2 of the stage termination hypothesis, whereby only early-maturing boys were expected to show more symptoms. Other studies reported results that are consistent with variant 2 of the deviance hypothesis. For example, Alsaker (1992) reported that both early- and late maturing boys manifested higher levels of depressive tendencies compared to those who were considered on-time. In a study by Nottelmann and colleagues (1987) it was late maturing boys who reported a sadder affect. Similarly, Crockett and Petersen (1987) also showed that seventh and eighth grade boys who were still prepubertal had higher levels of sad affect than those who were pubertal, which supports the deviance hypothesis.

*Externalizing problems*

Interestingly, during this period the majority of studies conducted on deviant behavior and its relationship to pubertal timing consistently point to the negative side of early maturation for boys. Early-maturing boys were found to have higher rates of deviance (Duncan, *et al.*, 1985; Flannery, Rowe, and Gulley, 1993), were more likely to use tobacco and drugs, engage in sexual activity (Flannery, Rowe, and Gulley, 1993), and have higher levels of alcohol consumption (Andersson and Magnusson, 1990; Silbereisen and Kracke, 1993). Findings from these studies appear to support the stage termination hypothesis (variant 2) for boys. It is important to note, however, that the longitudinal study by Andersson and Magnusson (1990) found that the trend reversed in early adulthood; it was the late maturing boys who had significantly higher levels of registered alcohol abuse.

## Social adjustment

Several studies examined the self-concept, feelings, self-image, and social popularity of boys as related to pubertal timing. Consistent with earlier findings from archival studies (Mussen and Jones, 1957, 1958), Petersen and Crockett (1985) found that early-maturing boys have an advantage over their peers in self-image and popularity. This finding was further confirmed by a series of subsequent investigations (Alsaker, 1992; Blyth, *et al.*, 1981; Duncan, *et al.*, 1985; Nottelmann, *et al.*, 1987; Simmons and Blyth, 1987) that reported early-maturing boys enjoyed a higher level of self-esteem overall when compared to their later maturing peers, with an exception of those early-maturing boys with higher levels of life transitional stress (Blyth, *et al.*, 1981). It appears that body image and satisfaction with various physical characteristics are the most consistent findings in favor of early-maturing boys.

## Family relations

Studies on changes in family relations during this period present inconsistent findings. Steinberg and Hill and their colleagues (Hill, *et al.*, 1985; Steinberg, 1981; Steinberg and Hill, 1978) conducted a series of the most extensive research. These studies reported that the relationship with parents appeared to change for boys at puberty, with increased mother–son conflict and emotional distance for boys at or near puberty. While Steinberg (1987) found an increased level of conflict and decreased level of closeness with parents (mothers) among early-maturing boys, Savin-Williams and Small (1986), on the other hand, reported higher levels of family conflict for later maturing boys. Simmons and Blyth (1987) found that the relationships between family conflict and pubertal timing varied according to the timing of assessment. Early-maturing boys were found to have increased family conflict early on (sixth and eighth grades), whereas later maturing boys had this same increase in family conflict later (tenth grade), when they were experiencing heightened pubertal changes. Paikoff and Brooks-Gunn (1991) provided an excellent and detailed discussion on this topic.

*Summary*    Differences in findings characterize the studies of various domains of psychosocial adjustment during this period. Interesting patterns, however, began to emerge to provide further stimuli for future studies. One of the most significant findings involves the results that early-maturing boys were not necessarily better adjusted. Early maturation did not confer boys with much advantage psychologically, as suggested by earlier studies; rather, they seemed to be at a disadvantage in many areas. Although some studies of internalizing symptoms were consistent with variant 2 of the deviance hypothesis, in that boys who matured off-time manifested a higher level of symptoms, many other studies reported that only early-maturing boys displayed a higher level of internalizing symptoms when compared to their on-time and late maturing peers. The results for externalizing problems during this period particularly indicate support for variant 2 of the stage termination hypothesis, as most studies show a higher level of problems (aggression, delinquency, and conduct problems) for early-maturing boys. The supportive evidence for this variant is especially consistent in the domain of substance use and abuse (i.e., drugs, alcohol, and tobacco).

The findings that early-maturing boys may be at risk for psychosocial maladjustment provided researchers with a challenge to reevaluate the earlier statements that early pubertal timing is an advantage for boys. For example, Alsaker (1992), while finding more negative adjustment patterns for late maturing boys, also pointed out a lack of evidence for early maturation as an advantage. Indeed, most of the classic studies on boys were conducted several decades ago with relatively crude measures of psychosocial adjustment by contemporary standards and geographically limited samples. The early results may not be generalizable to contemporary teenage boys because the social meaning of puberty may have changed over the years. Based on an extensive review, Alsaker (1995) called for a reevaluation of the relationship between puberty and adjustment outcomes among boys.

*Recent developments, 1997–present*

Several large-scale studies that were carried out recently on the relationship between pubertal timing and adolescent outcomes mainly focused on two broad categories of maladjustment: internalizing symptoms and externalizing problems. With respect to internalizing symptoms such as depression, anxiety, signs of withdrawal, and somatic complaints, the symptom levels were found to differ significantly among early-, on-time, and late maturing boys. In a large epidemiological study conducted in Oregon,

Graber and colleagues (1997) found late maturing boys to display higher levels of internalizing behaviors (e.g., tendency to worry, hypomanic behavior, anxiety, and sleep problems) compared to their on-time peers. This study also found both early- and late maturing boys to show significantly higher rates of depression than on-time maturing boys. In either instance, it was the off-time maturing boys who manifested higher levels of internalizing symptoms in comparison to on-time boys, consistent with variant 2 of the deviance hypothesis. Clear support for variant 1 of the deviance hypothesis came from another large-scale investigation conducted by Siegel and colleagues (1999) in the Los Angeles area. This study found that, overall, early-maturing girls and late maturing boys manifested a significantly higher level of depressive symptoms.

More recently, Ge and colleagues (2001a) have reported results consistent with variant 2 of the stage termination hypothesis. In this longitudinal study with European American rural boys, internalized distress, including symptoms of depression, anxiety, and somatization, was found to be higher for early-maturing boys compared to both their on-time and late maturing counterparts. Also, in support of the stage termination hypothesis, Ge and colleagues (in press) reported higher levels of internalizing symptoms, including diagnosable symptoms of major depression, social anxiety, and generalized anxiety for early-maturing boys in a large-scale study of 867 African American 11-year-old boys and 11-year-old girls. The results, however, remain inconclusive with regard to the deviance hypothesis, since the subjects were only 11 years old and late maturers were not distinguishable from on-time maturers.

In terms of externalizing behaviors, research on problem behaviors and pubertal timing still indicate mixed results for early- and late maturing boys. Findings related to delinquent behavior indicate a distinct disadvantage for off-time maturing boys, consistent with variant 2 of the deviance hypothesis. In a recent study by Williams and Dunlop (1999), both early- and late maturing boys were found to have significantly higher rates of delinquency than did their on-time maturing peers. On the other hand, a study investigating hostile feelings found an advantage for late maturing boys, with early-maturing boys displaying significantly higher levels of hostile feelings, compared to both late and on-time maturing boys (Ge, *et al.*, 2001a). Ge and colleagues (2002) also reported significant differences between timing groups for clinically diagnosed externalizing behaviors, including symptoms of attentional deficit/hyperactive disorder, oppositional defiance disorder, and conduct disorder. In addition, early-maturing boys were found to be more likely to associate with deviant peers. As noted, this study is silent regarding whether late maturing boys would be negatively affected because of subjects' age.

Studies of pubertal timing and risky health behaviors continued to show support for the stage termination hypothesis (variant 2), with early-maturing boys being found to be at higher risk for health-compromising behaviors, such as early onset of sexual activity, tobacco and alcohol use and abuse. For example, Kaltiala-Heino and colleagues (2001) reported that early-maturing boys were more likely to engage in early sexual activity. In a study conducted by Graber and colleagues (1997), early-maturing boys had a significantly increased rate of tobacco use; they also found a significantly lower level of substance abuse among late maturing boys than among on-time maturing boys. A more recent Norwegian study also reported that early-maturing boys had increased alcohol use, including frequency of use and intoxications and units consumed (Wichstrom, 2001).

*Summary*    Literature on the relationship between internalizing behaviors and pubertal timing indicate mixed findings as to whether early- or late maturing boys are better or worse off. However, a trend is beginning to appear, showing that in many instances early-maturing boys, in addition to their late maturing peers, appear to be more maladjusted than are on-time maturing boys. Similarly, a consistent pattern has emerged in the studies related to externalizing behaviors, suggesting early maturation as a risk factor for externalizing problems among boys. Contrary to the image painted by early research and still presented in many child development textbooks, early-maturing boys are not at an advantage; rather, they may be at a distinct disadvantage compared to on-time and late maturing boys. This is particularly evident in the area of substance use, where early-maturing boys have been found to be more likely to experiment with tobacco, alcohol, and drugs than on-time and late maturing boys.

Studies on puberty conducted before this period were based on relatively small samples, almost exclusively white, middle-class adolescents, with little attention paid to ethnic minority children. More recent studies have tended to have large and sometimes epidemiological samples, with clinical diagnostic assessment of the outcome variables (e.g., Ge, *et al.*, in press; Graber, *et al.*, 1997). A particularly welcoming trend in more recent studies involves an inclusion of more diverse samples. For example, Ge and colleagues (in press) based their study on a large sample of African American children and their families. The study by Siegel and colleagues (1998) included a sample with diverse populations of Caucasian, African,

Latino, and Asian American adolescents. In the latter study, with such a diverse sample, these authors were able to show that the relationship between depressive symptoms and puberty varied by ethnicity, with a stronger link among Latino boys.

## Conclusion

As a transitional period between childhood and adulthood, puberty is a time during which pervasive physical change occurs, reproductive ability is achieved, and profound psychological changes take place. Although the majority of boys at puberty adapt well to these changes, pubertal changes do contribute to the turbulence and stress experienced by some adolescent boys. Research on psychosocial implications of pubertal changes for boys has been accumulating to provide us with an increasingly clearer picture of what actually happens for boys socially and psychologically during this transition. Several notable shifts in the conception of the problems faced by boys at puberty can be delineated on the basis of the present review. First, although early maturation was historically perceived to be socially and psychologically favorable for boys, this view is gradually being modified on the basis of research findings over the last few decades. Emerging from the cumulative research is a perspective that recognizes that both earlier and later timing of puberty may have a major impact on multiple dimensions of psychological functioning in boys. Early pubertal timing may be accompanied by some negative psychosocial consequences; this appears to be particularly consistent in the areas of externalizing problems, including substance use and abuse, delinquency, and aggression.

Second, the studies conducted during the past half-century suggest some major inconsistencies regarding the relationships between timing of puberty, behavior, adjustment, and psychopathology. As noted, studies were often conducted with different measures, methods, and analytical strategies, under different conceptual frameworks (i.e., deviance or stage termination hypotheses), at different ages of outcome assessment, and with relatively small and convenient samples from very limited ecological settings. These methodological and theoretical differences probably contributed to the inconsistencies in the findings. What emerges from the inconsistent findings, interestingly, is an increased recognition among researchers concerning the complexity of the relationship between puberty and behavior. Steinberg (1988) suggested that the relationship between biological change and social relations might very well be reciprocal and involve complex interplay between the two. Following this direction, there has been a welcome shift in research attention toward the interplay of puberty and contexts in several studies (e.g., Ge, *et al.*, in press; Siegel, *et al.*, 1998).

Third, longitudinal studies that follow pubertal experiences over time began to help clarify the life course significance of the pubertal transition. During the last half-century, the majority of studies were either cross-sectional or short-term, making difficult any long-term generalization. These cross-sectional studies have made significant contributions to our awareness of the importance of pubertal changes in social and emotional development. However, whether the pubertal effect represents only a temporary perturbation or a long-lasting impact can only be determined by longitudinal research. Of note, some recent longitudinal studies have begun to show that timing of puberty appears to have long-term implications, at least among rural European American adolescents. For example, Ge, Conger, and Elder (2001b), show that early-maturing boys continue to report higher internalized distress and externalized hostility, even as late as the end of the high school years.

Just as adolescence is a transitional period, the research on boys at puberty is in transition. We know much more now than was known fifty years ago about boys' pubertal experiences and their social and psychological implications. The fruits of the past fifty years of research are most clearly visible in our increased knowledge of implication of maturational timing. The study of boys at puberty, however, lags far behind the study on girls. Little is known about how the pubertal transition exerts its impact on different aspects of social and psychological adjustment. It remains uncertain if it is pubertal timing or pubertal status that matters more to boys' adjustment and whether the pubertal transition affects girls and boys in the same way. The mechanisms through which the pubertal changes influence male adolescents' psychosocial adjustments remain elusive. Do hormonal changes play a direct role in the behavioral changes observed in boys, or is the role of hormonal changes in behavior mainly indirect? How do the physiological changes interact with social contextual factors to influence boys' adjustment? These questions provide the next generation of researchers with challenges as well as opportunities.

### References

Alsaker, F. D. (1992). Pubertal timing, overweight, and psychological adjustment. *Journal of Early Adolescence*, **12**, 396–419.

Alsaker, F. D. (1995). Timing of puberty and reactions to pubertal changes. In M. Rutter (ed.), *Psychosocial disturbances in young people: challenges for prevention* (pp. 37–82). Cambridge: Cambridge University Press.

Alsaker, F. D. (1996). Annotation: the impact of puberty. *Journal of Child Psychology and Psychiatry*, **37**, 249–258.

Andersson, T., and Magnusson, D. (1990). Biological maturation in adolescence and the development of drinking habits and alcohol abuse among young males: a prospective longitudinal study. *Journal of Youth and Adolescence*, **19**, 33–41.

Angold, A., Costello, E. J., and Worthman, C. (1998). Puberty and depression: the role of age, pubertal status and pubertal timing. *Psychological Medicine*, **28**, 51–61.

Blyth, D. A., Simmons, R. G., Bulcroft, R., Felt, D., Van Cleave, E. F., and Bush, D. M. (1981). The effects of physical development on self-image and satisfaction with body-image for early adolescent males. In *Research in community and mental health* (vol. II, pp. 43–73). Greenwich, CT: JAI Press.

Brooks-Gunn, J., Graber, J. A., and Paikoff, R. (1994). Studying links between hormones and negative affect: models and measures. *Journal of Research on Adolescence*, **4**, 469–486.

Brooks-Gunn, J., and Petersen, A. C. (1983). *Girls at puberty: biological and psychosocial perspectives*. New York: Plenum.

Brooks-Gunn, J., Petersen, A., and Compas, B. (1995). Physiological processes and the development of childhood and adolescent depression. In I. M. Goodyer (ed.), *The depressed child and adolescent: developmental and clinical perspectives* (pp. 171–193). Cambridge: Cambridge University Press.

Brooks-Gunn, J., and Reiter, E. O. (1990). The role of pubertal processes. In S. S. Feldman and G. R. Elliott (ed.), *At the threshold: the developing adolescent* (pp. 16–53). Cambridge, MA: Harvard University Press.

Brooks-Gunn, J., and Warren, M. P. (1989). Biological and social contributions to negative affect in young adolescent girls. *Child Development*, **60**, 40–55.

Buchanan, C. M., Eccles, J., and Becker, J. B. (1992). Are adolescents the victims of raging hormones: evidence for activational effects of hormones on moods and behavior at adolescence. *Psychological Bulletin*, **111**, 62–107.

Clausen, J. A. (1975). The social meaning of differential physical and sexual maturation. In S. E. Dragastin and Elder, G. H., Jr. (ed.), *Adolescence in the life cycle: Psychological change and social context* (pp. 25–47). Washington, DC: Hemisphere.

Connolly, S. D., Paikoff, R. L., and Buchanan, C. M. (1996). Puberty: the interplay of biological and psychosocial processes in adolescence. In G. R. Adams, Montemayor, R., and Gullotta, T. P. (ed.), *Psychosocial development during adolescence* (pp. 259–299). Thousand Oaks, CA: Sage.

Crockett, L., and Petersen, A. C. (1987). Pubertal status and psychosocial development: findings from the early adolescence study. In R. M. Lerner and T. T. Foch (ed.), *Biological-psychosocial interactions in early adolescence* (pp. 173–188). Hillsdale, NJ: Lawrence Erlbaum.

Dabbs, J., and Hargrove, M. F. (1997). Age, testosterone, and behavior among female prison inmates. *Psychosomatic Medicine*, **59**, 477–480.

Dubas, J. S., Graber, J. A., and Petersen, A. C. (1991). A longitudinal investigation of adolescents' changing perceptions of pubertal timing. *Developmental Psychology*, **27**, 580–586.

Duncan, P., Ritter, P., Dornbusch, S., Gross, R., and Carlsmith, J. (1985). The effect of pubertal timing on body image, school behavior, and deviance. *Journal of Youth and Adolescence*, **14**, 227–236.

Finkelstein, J. W., Susman, E. J., Chinchilli, V., Dorcangelo, M. R., Kunselman, S. J., Schwab, J., Demers, L. M., Liben, L., and Kulin, H. E. (1998). Effects of estrogen or testosterone on self-reported sexual responses and behaviors in hypogonadal adolescents. *Journal of Clinical Endocrinology and Metabolism*, **83**, 2281–2285.

Finkelstein, J. W., Susman, E. J., Chinchilli, V., Kunselman, S. J., Dorcangelo, M. R., Schwab, J., Demers, L. M., Liben, L., Lookingbill, M. S., and Kulin, H. E. (1997). Estrogen or testosterone increases self-reported aggressive behavior in hypogonadal adolescents. *Journal of Clinical Endocrinology and Metabolism*, **82**, 2433–2438.

Flannery, D. J., Rowe, D. C., and Gulley, B. L. (1993). Impact of pubertal status, timing, and age on adolescent sexual experience and delinquency. *Journal of Adolescent Research*, **8**, 21–40.

Ge, X., Brody, G. H., Conger, R. D., Simons, R. L., and Murry, V. M. (2002). Contextual amplification of pubertal transition effects on deviant peer affiliation and externalizing behavior among African American children. *Developmental Psychology*, **38**, 42–54.

Ge, X., Brody, G. H., Conger, R. D., and Simons, R. L. (in press). Pubertal maturation and African American children's internalizing and externalizing symptoms. *Journal of Youth and Adolescence*.

Ge, X., Conger, R. D., and Elder, G. H., Jr. (1996). Coming of age too early: pubertal influences on girls' vulnerability to psychological distress. *Child Development*, **67**, 3386–3400.

Ge, X., Conger, R. D., and Elder, G. H., Jr. (2001a). The relationship between puberty and psychological distress in boys. *Journal of Research on Adolescence*, **11**, 49–70.

Ge, X., Conger, R. D., and Elder, G. H., Jr. (2001b). Pubertal transition, stressful life events, and the emergence of gender differences in depressive symptoms. *Developmental Psychology*, **37**, 404–417.

Graber, J. A., Lewinsohn, P. M., Seeley, J., and Brooks-Gunn, J. (1997). Is psychopathology associated with the timing of pubertal development? *Journal of American Academy of Child and Adolescent Psychiatry*, **36**, 1768–1776.

Graber, J. A., Petersen, A., and Brooks-Gunn, J. (1996). Pubertal processes: methods, measures, and models. In J. A. Graber, J. Brooks-Gunn, and A. Petersen (ed.), *Transitions through adolescence: interpersonal domains and context* (pp. 23–53). Hillsdale, NJ: Lawrence Erlbaum.

Grumbach, M. M., and Styne, D. M. (1992). Puberty: ontogeny, neuroendocrinology, physiology, and disorders. In J. D. Wilson and P. W. Foster (ed.), *Williams textbook of endocrinology* (pp. 1139–1231). Philadelphia, PN: W. B. Saunders.

Hill, J. P., Holmbeck, G. N., Marlow, L., Green, T. M., and Lynch, M. E. (1985). Pubertal status and parent-child relations in families of seventh-grade boys. *Journal of Early Adolescence*, **5**, 31–44.

Inoff-Germain, G., Arnold, G. S., Nottelmann, E. D., Susman, E. J., Cutler, G. B., Jr., and Chrousos, G. P. (1988). Relations between hormone levels and observational measures of aggressive behavior of early adolescents in family interactions. *Developmental Psychology*, **24**, 129–139.

Jones, M. C. (1957). The later careers of boys who were early- or late-maturing. *Child Development*, **28**, 113–128.

Jones, M. C. (1965). Psychological correlates of somatic development. *Child Development*, **36**, 899–911.

Jones, M. C., and Bayley, N. (1950). Physical maturing among boys as related to behavior. *Journal of Educational Psychology*, **41**, 129–148.

Jones, M. C., and Bayley, N. (1971). Physical maturing among boys as related to behavior. In M. C. Jones, N. Bayley, J. W. MacFarlane, and Honzik (ed.), *The course of human development* (pp. 252–257). Waltham, MA: Xeroz College Publishing.

Kaltiala-Heino, R. A., Rimpela, M., Rissanen, A., and Rantanen, P. (2001). Early puberty and early sexual activity are associated with bulimic-type eating pathology in middle adolescence. *Journal of Adolescent Health*, **28**, 346–352.

Lerner, R. M., and Foch, T. T. (ed.) (1987). *Biological-psychosocial interactions in early adolescence: a lifespan perspective*. Hillsdale, NJ: Lawrence Erlbaum.

Marshall, W. A., and Tanner, J. M. (1970). Variations in patterns of pubertal changes in boys. *Archives of Disease in Childhood*, **45**, 15–23.

Mazur, A., and Booth, A. (1998). Testosterone and dominance in men. *Behavioral and Brain Sciences*, **21**, 353–397.

Mussen, P. H., and Jones, M. C. (1957). Self-conceptions, motivations, and interpersonal attitudes of late- and early-maturing boys. *Child Development*, **28**, 243–256.

Mussen, P. H. and Jones, M. C. (1958). The behavior-inferred motivations of late- and early-maturing boys. *Child Development*, **29**, 61–67.

Nottelmann, E. D., Inoff-Germain, G., Susman, E. J., and Chrousos, G. P. (1990). Hormones and behavior at puberty. In J. Bancroft and J. M. Reinisch (ed.), *Adolescence and puberty* (pp. 88–123). Oxford: Oxford University Press.

Nottelmann, E. D., Susman, E. J., Inoff-Germain, G., Cutler, G., Loriaux, D. L., and Chrousos, G. P. (1987). Developmental processes in early adolescence: relations between adolescent adjustment problems and chronological age, pubertal stage, and pubertal-related serum hormone levels. *Journal of Pediatrics*, **110**, 473–480.

Olweus, D. (1986). Aggressions and hormones: behavioral relationships with testosterone and adrenaline. In D. Olweus, J. Block, and M. Radke-Yarrow (ed.), *Development of antisocial and prosocial behavior: research, theories, and issues* (pp. 51–72). San Diego, CA: Academic Press.

Olweus, D., Mattson, A., Schalling, D., and Low, H. (1988). Circulating testosterone levels and aggression in adolescent males: a causal analysis. *Psychosomatic Medicine*, **50**, 261–272.

Paikoff, R., and Brooks-Gunn, J. (1991). Do parent–child relationships change during puberty? *Psychological Bulletin*, **110**, 47–66.

Peskin, H. (1967). Pubertal onset and ego functioning. *Journal of Abnormal Psychology*, **72**, 1–15.

Peskin, H. (1973). Influence of the developmental schedule of puberty on learning and ego functioning. *Journal of Youth and Adolescence*, **2**, 273–290.

Petersen, A. C., and Crockett, L. (1985). Pubertal timing and grade effects on adjustment. *Journal of Youth and Adolescence*, **14**, 191–206.

Petersen, A. C., and Taylor, B. (1980). The biological approach to adolescence: biological change and psychological adaptation. In J. Anderson (ed.), *Handbook of adolescent psychology* (pp. 117–155). New York: Wiley.

Robertson, E. B., Skinner, M. L., Love, M. M., Elder, G. H., Jr., Conger, R. D., Dubas, J. S., and Petersen, A. C. (1992). The pubertal development scale: a rural and suburban comparison. *Journal of Early Adolescence*, 12, 174–186.

Rogol, A. D., Clark, P. A., and Roemmich, J. N. (2000). Growth and pubertal development in children and adolescents: effects of diet and physical activity. *American Journal of Clinical Nutrition*, 72, 521S–528S.

Savin-Williams, R. C., and Small, S. A. (1986). The timing of puberty and its relationship to adolescent and parent perceptions of family interactions. *Developmental Psychology*, 22, 342–347.

Scerbo, A. S., and Kolko, D. J. (1994). Salivary testosterone and cortisol in disruptive children: relationship to aggressive, hyperactive, and internalizing behaviors. *Journal of the American Academy of Child and Adolescent Psychiatry*, 33, 1174–1184.

Schaal, B., Tremblay, R., Soussignan, B., and Susman, E. J. (1996). Male pubertal testosterone linked to high social dominance but low physical aggression: a seven-year longitudinal study. *Journal of the American Academy of Child Psychiatry*, 35, 1322–1330.

Siegel, J. M., Aneshensel, C. S., Taub, B., Cantwell, D. P., and Driscoll, A. K. (1998). Adolescent depressed mood in a multiethnic sample. *Journal of Youth and Adolescence*, 27, 413–427.

Siegel, J. M., Yancey, A. K., Aneshensel, C. S., and Schuler, R. (1999). Body image, perceived pubertal timing, and adolescent mental health. *Journal of Adolescent Health*, 25, 155–165.

Silbereisen, R. K., and Kracke, B. (1993). Variation in maturational timing and adjustment in adolescence. In S. Jackson, and H. Rodriguez-Tome (ed.) *Adolescence and its social worlds* (pp. 67–94). Hillsdale, NJ: Lawrence Erlbaum.

Simmons, R. G., and Blyth, D. A. (1987). *Moving into adolescence: the impact of pubertal change and school context*. Hawthorne, NY: De Gruyter.

Simmons, R. G., Burgeson, R., Carlton-Ford, S., and Blyth, D. A. (1987). The impact of cumulative change in early adolescence. *Child Development*, 58, 1220–1234.

Steinberg, L. D. (1981). Transformation in family relations at puberty. *Developmental Psychology*, 17, 833–840.

Steinberg, L. (1987). Impact of puberty on family relations: effects of pubertal status and pubertal timing. *Developmental Psychology*, 23, 451–460.

Steinberg, L. (1988). Reciprocal relations between parent–child distance and pubertal maturation. *Developmental Psychology*, 24, 122–128.

Steinberg, L., and Hill, J. P. (1978). Patterns of family interaction as a function of age, the onset of puberty, and formal thinking. *Developmental Psychology*, 14, 683–684.

Susman, E. J. (1997). Modeling developmental complexity in adolescence: hormones and behavior in context. *Journal of Research on Adolescence*, 7, 283–306.

Susman, E. J., Dorn, L. D., and Chrousos, G. P. (1991). Negative affect and hormone levels in young adolescents: concurrent and predictive perspectives. *Journal of Youth and Adolescence*, 20, 167–190.

Susman, E. J., Dorn, L. D., Inoff-Germain, G., Nottelmann, E. D., and Chrousos, G. P. (1997). Cortisol reactivity, distress behavior, and behavioral and psychological problems in young adolescents: a longitudinal perspective. *Journal of Research on Adolescence*, 7, 81–105.

Susman, E. J., Inoff-Germain, G., Nottelmann, E. D., Loriaux, D. L., Cutler, G. B., Jr., and Chrousos, G. P. (1987). Hormones, emotional disposi- tions, and aggressive attributes in young adolescents. *Child Development*, 58, 1114–1134.

Susman, E. J., Nottelmann, E. D., Inoff-Germain, G. E., Dorn, L. D., Cutler, G. B., Jr., Loriaux, D. L., and Chrousos, G. P. (1985). The relation of relative hormonal levels and physical development and social-emotional behavior in young adolescents. *Journal of Youth and Adolescence*, 14, 245–264.

Susman, E. J., and Petersen, A. C. (1992). Hormones and behavior in adoles- cence. In E. R. McAnarney, R. E. Kreipe, D. P. Orr, and G. D. Comerci (ed.), *Textbook of adolescent medicine* (pp. 125–133). New York: W. B. Saunders.

Tanner, J. M. (1989). *Fetus into man: physical growth from conception to maturity*. Cambridge, MA: Harvard University Press.

Udry, R. J., and Talbert, L. M. (1988). Sex hormone effects on personality at puberty. *Journal of Personality and Social Psychology*, 54, 291–295.

Udry, R. J., Billy, J. O. G., Morris, N. M., Groff, T. R., and Raj, M. H. (1985). Serum androgenic hormones motivate sexual behavior in adolescent boys. *Fertility and Sterility*, 43, 90–94.

Van Goozen, S. H. M., Matthys, W., Cohen-Kettenis, P. T., Thisjssen, J. H. H., and van Engeland, H. (1998). Adrenal androgens and aggression in conduct disorder prepubertal boys and normal control. *Biological Psychiatry*, 43, 156–158.

Weatherley, D. (1964). Self-perceived rate of physical maturation and personality in late adolescence. *Child Development*, 35, 1197–1210.

Wichstrom, L. (2001). The impact of pubertal timing on adolescents' alcohol use. *Journal of Research on Adolescence*, 11, 131–150.

Williams, J. M., and Dunlop, L. C. (1999). Pubertal timing and self-reported delinquency among male adolescents. *Journal of Adolescence*, 22, 157–171.

# Part 4

# Puberty and psychopathology

# 8    Puberty and depression

*Adrian Angold, Carol Worthman, and E. Jane Costello*

In this chapter we will examine evidence concerning the emergence of an excess of unipolar depression in females during adolescence. We will also present new data from the Great Smoky Mountains Study (GSMS) in support of an approach that combines consideration of both the endocrinology of puberty and the effects of stress on depression.

**The phenomenon to be explained**

Numerous adult studies from around the world have documented that women have 1.5 to 3 times more current and lifetime unipolar depression than men (Bebbington, *et al.*, 1981; Bland, Newman, and Orn, 1988a; Bland, Newman, and Orn, 1988b; Blazer, *et al.*, 1994; Canino, *et al.*, 1987; Cheng, 1989; Hwu, Yeh, and Chang, 1989; Kessler, *et al.*, 1994; Kessler, *et al.*, 1993; Lee, Han, and Choi, 1987; Weissman, *et al.*, 1993; Weissman, *et al.*, 1996; Weissman and Klerman, 1977; Wells, *et al.*, 1989; Wittchen, *et al.*, 1992). In later life (after age 55), the female excess of depressions probably diminishes; mostly on account of falling rates in women (Bebbington, 1996; Bebbington, *et al.*, 1998; Jorm, 1987).

Retrospective data from adults suggested that the female excess did not appear until adolescence (Burke, *et al.*, 1990; Kessler, *et al.*, 1993), and the child and adolescent epidemiological literature agrees that rates of unipolar depression in prepubertal girls are not higher than those in prepubertal boys (Anderson, *et al.*, 1987; Angold, Costello, and Worthman, 1998; Angold, Costello, and Worthman, 1999; Angold and Rutter, 1992; Bird, *et al.*, 1988; Cohen and Brooks, 1987; Cohen, Cohen, and Brook, 1993a; Cohen, *et al.*, 1993b; Costello, Stouthamer-Loeber, and DeRosier, 1993; Fleming and Offord, 1990; Guyer, *et al.*, 1989; Hankin, *et al.*, 1998; Kashani, *et al.*, 1987; Kashani, *et al.*, 1989; Lewinsohn, Gotlib, and Seeley, 1995; McGee, *et al.*, 1992; McGee, *et al.*, 1990;

McGee and Williams, 1988; Nolen-Hoeksema, Girgus, and Seligman, 1991; Reinherz, *et al.*, 1993b; Rutter, *et al.*, 1976; Velez, Johnson, and Cohen, 1989). Indeed, there is growing evidence that depression is more common in boys before adolescence (Anderson, *et al.*, 1987; Angold, Costello, and Worthman, 1998; Costello, *et al.*, 1988; Hankin, *et al.*, 1998; McGee, *et al.*, 1990).

However, by far the largest and best-documented effect of adolescence on depression is the very large increase in prevalence of depression in girls (Anderson, *et al.*, 1987; Angold, Costello, and Worthman, 1998; Angold, Costello, and Worthman, 1999; Angold and Rutter, 1992; Bird, *et al.*, 1988; Cohen and Brooks, 1987; Costello, Stouthamer-Loeber, and DeRosier, 1993; Fleming and Offord, 1990; Guyer, *et al.*, 1989; Hankin, *et al.*, 1998; Kashani, *et al.*, 1987; Kashani, *et al.*, 1989; Lewinsohn, Gotlib, and Seeley, 1995; Lewinsohn, *et al.*, 1993; McGee, *et al.*, 1992; McGee, *et al.*, 1990; McGee and Williams, 1988; Nolen-Hoeksema, Girgus, and Seligman, 1991; Reinherz, *et al.*, 1993a; Reinherz, *et al.*, 1993b; Rutter, *et al.*, 1976; Velez, Johnson, and Cohen, 1989). The four child and adolescent general population studies of effects of age on depression diagnoses, with sufficient extension at the lower end of the age range and adequate sample size to allow sufficiently narrow age groupings, all agree that this change only becomes apparent at or after age 13 (Angold, Costello, and Worthman, 1998; Cairney, 1998; Hankin, *et al.*, 1998; McGee, *et al.*, 1992; Velez, Johnson, and Cohen, 1989).

Thus the question "Why does depression become more common in girls than boys during adolescence?" largely reduces to the question "Why does the prevalence of depression increase in girls during adolescence?" The remainder of this chapter will focus on the latter question.

It comes as no surprise that a substantial change in the prevalence of depression occurring during adolescence led to the suggestion that the changes of puberty might in some way be responsible. This idea has spawned many studies, but it is only recently that studies of sufficient size to disentangle a variety of putative pubertal and other effects have begun to clarify the situation. For instance, it was only with the appearance of larger general population-based studies that the timing (in terms of age) of the increased prevalence of depression ruled out the possibility that it might be related to adrenarche (occurring around age 6–8 years), rather than puberty. However, puberty is a complex developmental process, and before turning to the evidence relating depression and puberty a brief diversion into the physiology of puberty is required (see also chapter 2).

## Physiology of female puberty and its implications for the study of psychopathology

*Changes in the hypothalamo-pituitary-gonadal (HPG) axis*

Although the HPG and hypothalamo-pituitary-adrenal (HPA) axes show a brief burst of activity in the first months after birth (Skuse, 1984), circulating concentrations of gonadotropins and gonadal and adrenal steroids are very low in early- to mid-childhood. An increase in adrenal androgen output (adrenarche) occurs at around 6–8 years (DePeretti and Forest, 1976; Ducharme, *et al.*, 1976; Lashansky, *et al.*, 1991; Parker, *et al.*, 1978; Reiter, Fuldauer, and Root, 1977; Sizonenko and Paunier, 1975). Adrenarche precedes the earliest changes of puberty on the HPG axis by about two years, and was initially thought to act as a trigger for its onset (Collu and Ducharme, 1975). It is now known that this is untrue (Counts, *et al.*, 1987; Korth-Schutz, Levine, and New, 1976; Wierman, *et al.*, 1986), but adrenarche is still suspected to play a facilitative role in the initiation of puberty.

Luteinizing hormone-releasing hormone (LHRH) pulse amplitude and pulse frequency both increase across the late prepubertal to early and mid stages of puberty (Hale, *et al.*, 1988; Landy, *et al.*, 1992), and show progressive diminution of diurnal variation in early to mid puberty. These changes, in turn drive increased gonadotropin (luteinizing hormone [LH] and follicle stimulating hormone [FSH]) pulse frequency and amplitude. Early puberty is marked by the appearance of frequent, closely sleep-entrained nighttime pulses of LH, beginning in late childhood (Dunkel, *et al.*, 1990; Wu, *et al.*, 1990). LHRH pulse frequency decreases in late puberty in females (although amplitude continues to increase in males) as its release becomes more sensitive to negative feedback control from gonadal steroids (Dunger, *et al.*, 1991; Marshall, *et al.*, 1991; Wennink, *et al.*, 1989). An important sex difference established over the course of puberty is that females develop pulsatile gonadotropin releasing hormone (GnRH) secretion along with fluctuating estradiol and progesterone (Marshall, *et al.*, 1991). Maturation of this pattern extends from before menarche to several months or years beyond in the course of establishing regular ovulation and luteal function (Vihko and Apter, 1980; Wennink, *et al.*, 1990).

*Secondary sex characteristics and menarche*

Puberty is a gradual event mediated through physiological mechanisms that are operative at ages 8–12 years, or one to three years prior to the onset of morphological puberty (the growth spurt and appearance of secondary sex characteristics) and well before menarche (Wennink, *et al.*, 1989; Wennink, *et al.*, 1990; Wu, *et al.*, 1990; see also chapter 2). In other words, the physiological changes of early puberty long predate the appearance of the features upon which most research on the relationship between puberty and psychopathology has been based. For instance, in our data from the GSMS, there is a substantial linear relationship between FSH and age (Pearson $r = .35$, $p < .0001$) in girls aged 9 and above in Tanner stage 1 (i.e., girls showing no secondary sex characteristics at all) that is not reflected in morphological status. Similarly, once Tanner stage 5 is reached, there is still continuing hormonal change, but again it is not reflected in body morphology, at least as measured by the Tanner scheme. Indeed, as girls begin to cycle, age and Tanner stage can have relatively little effect on levels of FSH, LH, and estrogen, because their levels become primarily controlled by the menstrual cycle.

The key point here is that, at different stages of puberty, the correlations among the various manifestations of puberty change dramatically. This, in turn, means that the best marker for a given effect of puberty on psychopathology can be expected to change depending on the developmental range covered in a particular study (see chapter 1). For instance, if an effect of puberty on depression were in reality caused by changes in androgen and estrogen levels, but direct hormonal measures are not available to a particular study, whether age, pubertal status, pubertal timing or some other "superficial" marker of pubertal status appeared to have an effect on depression would depend in part on the distribution of developmental levels of participants in the study.

*The implications of variations in end-organ sensitivity to sex steroids*

Neuroendocrine changes are obviously grossly reflected in morphological signs of puberty, such as growth and the development of secondary sex characteristics; for example, those rated by Tanner's pubertal stages (Apter, 1980; Burr, *et al.*, 1970; Lee and Migeon, 1975; Lee, *et al.*, 1975; Sizonenko, *et al.*, 1970; Sizonenko and Paunier, 1975). The causal cascade in morphological development commences from maturation of CNS-generated pulsatility of gonadotropin release that stimulates activity of the peripheral glands (gonads and adrenals) (Hayes and Crowley, 1998; McCann, *et al.*, 1998; Ojeda and Ma, 1998; Phillips, *et al.*, 1997; Veldhuis, 1996). Rising levels of gonadal and adrenal steroid hormones, in turn, stimulate development of secondary sex characteristics (see chapter 2). In girls, breast development is driven by rising estrogen levels, while the emergence of pubic and axillary hair is associated with increasing androgens. The primary source of estrogens is the ovary, while androgens are primarily produced in adrenals (with increasing contributions from the ovary, which begin to fluctuate as ovarian cyclicity becomes established). Hence, it has been argued that morphological development represents a bioassay for cumulative steroid exposure.

However, hormone levels explain on average less than half the variance in morphological pubertal development and growth in girls (Nottelmann, *et al.*, 1987b). Sex characteristic development is modulated by end-organ sensitivity, which is controlled by the number and type of tissue receptors and other intracellular conditions (aromatase and other steroid metabolic enzymes; tyrosine kinases and other secondary messengers) (Layman, 1995). Furthermore, responses by these peripheral target tissues may be but a poor reflection of the central impact of steroid hormones at puberty. The discovery of two major classes of estrogen receptors, alpha and beta (Murphy, *et al.*, 1997), with numerous variants in each receptor type (Lu, *et al.*, 1998), has revealed new complexities in estrogen action. Mapping of ER distribution by density and subtype in the brain and periphery has demonstrated patterns of differential expression of both types across (and even within) brain regions (Laflamme, *et al.*, 1998; Mitchner, Garlick, and Ben-Jonathan, 1998; Osterlund, *et al.*, 1998), but also identified tissue-distinctive ER expression in peripheral target tissues such as the breast (Murphy, *et al.*, 1997). The upshot of such findings is that we cannot expect sex steroid effects on breast tissue to be a very precise mirror of their impact in the CNS. Although little is actually known about the mechanisms by which sex steroids might be related to developmental risk for psychopathology (reviewed in Seeman, 1997; Young and Korszun, 1998; see also chapter 3), present evidence suggests that, in the absence of highly locale-specific probes for estrogen action in the CNS, circulating levels of steroids probably represent the best general measure of CNS steroid exposure.

*There is no single "best measure" of puberty*

Lest it seem that we are arguing that hormonal measures will provide a "better" measure of puberty, let us be clear that this is not so. Puberty is a complex, multifaceted phenomenon. There can be no single "best" measure of puberty (see chapter 1). Rather, we want to indicate the need to recognize that hormones, Tanner stage, and menarche (to name but three aspects) are all measures of correlated, but meaningfully different aspects. We have argued that circulating hormone levels are likely to be the

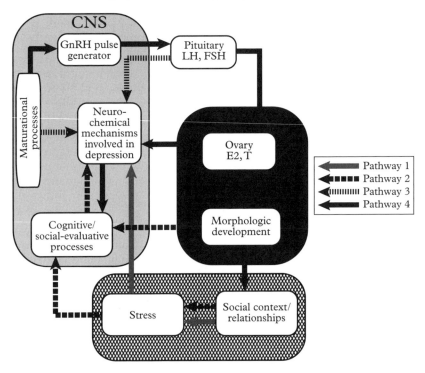

Figure 8.1  Four potential pathways linking puberty and depression

best available correlate of hormonal actions in the CNS. But we are also quite sure that self-report of breast development is a better measure of breast development than is circulating estrogen level. Different theories of the relationship between puberty and depression have concentrated attention on the potential effects of different aspects of puberty, and it seems likely that this has led to much confusion.

## Potential pathways from puberty to depression

We have found it helpful to think of four basic types of pathways by which puberty might affect depression. These are summarized in figure 8.1. The three large shaded areas divide the potential causes of depression into three broad groups: CNS effects (both physiological and psychological), peripheral physiological manifestations of puberty (both hormonal and morphologic), and extra-organismic (environmental, social, or otherwise). The pituitary sits at the interface between the two major intra-organismic compartments.

*Pathway 1*

The first and simplest pathway indicts changes in levels of extra-organismic risk factors in the causation of increased levels of depression. Simply put, more bad things happen to older girls, so they become depressed more often. Here puberty is simply a marker for the changing circumstances faced by adolescents as they age, and is not directly involved in the generation of depression at all. The other three pathways all depend upon effects of puberty directly.

*Pathway 2*

The second pathway implicates psychosocial and/or experiential changes contingent upon the morphological changes of puberty (such as breast development). The basic idea is that changed body morphology impacts upon girls' self-perceptions and/or the reactions of others to them, in such a way as to increase the risk for depression.

A number of studies of menarche or morphological development (secondary sex characteristics – usually measured by Tanner stages; Tanner, 1962) have suggested that the timing of pubertal status may be significantly related to mood or other disturbances, as measured by a wide variety of scales (Angold and Rutter, 1992; Brooks-Gunn and Warren, 1989; Ge, Conger, and Elder, 1996; Olweus, *et al.*, 1988; Paikoff, Brooks-Gunn, and Warren, 1991; Susman, *et al.*, 1987b; see also chapters 12 and 13). Early puberty has been associated with problem behaviors in girls, but with good adjustment in boys (see Stattin and Magnusson [1990] for a review; see also chapters 7, 12, and 13). Stattin and Magnusson (1990) argued from their influential longitudinal study that the negative effects of early development in girls were generated by the impact of early maturity on girls' social lives, and their early introduction to sexual life, for which they might be cognitively unready. However, these effects had largely disappeared by the time the girls were in mid-adolescence, whereas the female excess of depressive disorders continues throughout adulthood. Overall, the scale-based pubertal timing literature contains many failures to replicate findings from study to study (Cairns and Cairns, 1994; Greif and Ulman, 1982; Stattin and Magnusson, 1990), and it is uncertain how much of this is because different studies have used different designs and different measures of psychopathology and puberty. However, it cannot be said, by any means, to have provided very solid support for the idea that early puberty is a major factor in the emergence of the female excess of depression.

Studies of pubertal timing and depressive diagnoses are few and far between. Hayward and colleagues (1997) found that onsets of internalizing symptoms measured by various scales were associated with earlier puberty. However, the effect for depression scores alone was not significant. In a much smaller subset of girls followed into high school, they also reported a nonsignificant association (OR = 1.7) between earlier pubertal timing and the development of interview-based diagnoses of "internalizing disorders" (any depression, subclinical bulimia, social phobia, agoraphobia, or panic disorder).

Graber and colleagues' study from the Oregon Adolescent Depression Project (Graber, *et al.*, 1997) produced contradictory results. Self-reported early maturers (the adolescents were asked whether they thought they were early, on-time, or late) had higher lifetime rates of depression than on-time maturers (30.2% vs. 22.1%), but late maturers had the highest lifetime rates overall (33.8%). Both of these effects were statistically significant. On the other hand, rates of current major depression were lowest in the early maturers (2.3%), intermediate in the on-time group (3.5%), and highest in the late maturers (3.9%). None of these differences was statistically significant.

### Pathway 3

The third alternative implicates brain maturational changes occurring around the onset of puberty in both the initiation of puberty itself and in the alterations of mood regulation that exacerbate risk for depression at the CNS level (see chapter 3). These changes may then generate or exacerbate depressive mood changes and depressive cognitive styles. In other words, it suggests that changes indexed by gonadotropin secretion should be most closely linked to changes in rates of depression. As indicated in figure 8.1, such effects might be mediated by the tropic hormones themselves, or operate through quite separate mechanisms that correlate with tropic hormone status.

The previous evidence relating to these possible pathways has been minuscule. In the NIMH study of puberty and psychopathology, FSH levels correlated with negative emotional tone in girls but not boys (Nottelmann, *et al.*, 1990; Susman, *et al.*, 1985).

### Pathway 4

Pathway four in figure 8.1 represents models that focus on the CNS effects of steroid hormones. Such models posit that the effects of puberty on depression are not dependent upon the effects of body morphology on self-image, social and sexual behavior, or changing levels of stress dependent upon them (or any other such thing), but instead are dependent upon the effects of peripherally synthesized steroid hormones on brain functioning (or structure, or both; see chapter 3).

Previous evidence for the effects of sex steroids on depression has been suggestive, but far from definitive. The NIMH study of puberty and psychopathology (Nottelmann, *et al.*, 1987a; Nottelmann, *et al.*, 1987b; Susman, *et al.*, 1987a; Susman, *et al.*, 1987b) found negative associations between the testosterone–estradiol ratio, sex hormone binding globulin, and androstenedione concentration and negative emotional tone in boys. Researchers also reported an association of early maturation (measured by estradiol and testosterone–estradiol ratio) with reduced negative emotional tone in boys, but more negative emotional tone in girls. Brooks-Gunn and Warren (1989) found that negative affect increased in 10- to 14-year-old girls during rapid estrogen rise. A one-year follow-up of 72 girls (Paikoff, *et al.*, 1991) found a significant linear relationship between estradiol level at time 1 and depression one year later according to one depression scale, but no such effect in relation to two other depression scales.

None of these hormonal studies had sufficient power to tease apart the possible contributions of age itself, the indirect psychosocial impacts of morphologic pubertal status, and the more direct impact of the different groups of hormones that change at puberty. In addition, all of them used depression scale scores only, rather than interview-based diagnoses.

It will be immediately apparent that these four pathways are not mutually exclusive, and that effects could operate at all of these levels. Our interest in the rest of this chapter is in trying to determine which of these possible pathways contributes to increasing rates of depression in girls in the Great Smoky Mountains Study (GSMS). We begin with a brief overview of the design of the GSMS.

## An overview of the methods of the Great Smoky Mountains Study

A detailed account of the study design and instrumentation used can be found in earlier literature (Angold, Costello, and Worthman, 1999; Costello, *et al.*, 1996).

*Sampling frame*

A representative sample of 4,500 children aged 9, 11, and 13, recruited through the Student Information Management System of the public school systems of eleven counties in western North Carolina, was selected using a household equal probability design. As close as possible to the child's birthday, a screening questionnaire was administered to a parent (usually the mother), either by telephone or in person. This consisted of fifty-five questions from the Child Behavior Checklist about the child's behavior ("externalizing") problems, together with some basic demographic and service use questions. All children scoring above a pre-determined cutoff score of 20 (designed to include about 25% of the population) on the behavioral questions, plus a 1 in 10 random sample of those scoring below the cutoff, were recruited for the longitudinal study. Eighty percent of eligible families agreed to participate in the interviews for at least one wave (1,073 of 1,346). A 100 percent oversample of American Indian children was also collected, but data from this sample are not included here.

Shortly after being screened, eligible children and one of their parents were interviewed. They were reinterviewed using very similar assessment protocols at multiple follow-up waves, one, two, and three years later. Here we present data from the first three annual waves of data collection, because we only had funding to complete hormone assays on these waves. The sample considered here, therefore, consists of 465 girls aged 9–15 on whom we had a total of 1,283 interview observations from the first three waves of data collection.

Because sexual development is a sensitive topic, we showed the Tanner stage assessment to parents before giving it to the children, and specifically asked permission to use it. At each wave, between 2.6 percent and 7.5 percent of parents refused to have the scale administered to their female children. However, refusal to complete the Tanner stage assessment was not significantly related to depression scores or diagnoses, so it seems unlikely that this additional source of missing data was a source of bias in the results.

At each wave, between 22.8 percent and 24.8 percent of female participants refused to give blood for hormone measurements (separate consent for the finger prick procedure used here was sought). Again, there was no significant relationship between depression status and missing hormone data, so again it seems unlikely that the results will be substantially biased by missing data in this area. Numbers of girls with hormone data at each wave were: wave 1 N = 339; wave 2 N = 333; wave 3 N = 310.

## Measures

### Psychiatric symptoms and disorders

Children and parents were interviewed using the Child and Adolescent Psychiatric Assessment (CAPA; Angold, *et al.*, 1995), which generates a Diagnostic and Statistical Manual of Mental Disorders (DSM-IV) (American Psychiatric Association, 1994). Diagnoses were generated from symptom codings by computer algorithms. If either parent or child reported a symptom as present in the past three months, it was counted toward the relevant CAPA/DSM-IV scale score or diagnosis. This three-month "primary period" was selected rather than, say, a one year or lifetime period, because shorter recall periods are associated with more accurate recall (see, e.g., Angold, et al., 1996). We considered three depression diagnoses: DSM-IV major depressive episode, dysthymia, and depression not otherwise specified (NOS). The last of these diagnostic categories comprised individuals who met the DSM-IV experimental criteria for Minor Depressive Disorder (American Psychiatric Association, 1994, p. 719).

The CAPA also contains a section covering the occurrence during the last three months of thirty-eight life events (Costello, et al., 1998). Apart from a simple count of the number of such events that occurred, three subscales counted loss (N = 11), violence-related (N = 13), and social network related (N = 9) events.

*Pubertal morphologic status*

Self-ratings of pubertal morphologic status based on the standard Tanner staging system (Tanner, 1962) were performed with the aid of schematic drawings of secondary sexual characteristics (breasts and pubic hair). Such ratings correlate well with physical examination based on Tanner stages (Dorn, et al., 1990; Duke, Litt, and Gross, 1980; Frankowski, et al., 1987; Morris and Udry, 1980; Schlossberger, Turner, and Irwin, 1992). Each child was provided with sex-appropriate schematic drawings and requested to rate herself on each dimension. Both self-ratings were averaged to yield a single individual score (ranging from I = prepubertal, to V = adult level of development).

*Blood spot collection and hormonal assays*

Hormone samples were obtained at the beginning of the interview session, as follows: two finger-prick samples were collected at 20-minute intervals, applied to specially prepared paper, immediately refrigerated upon drying, and express-shipped (without refrigeration) to the laboratory within two weeks of collection. Samples were then stored at −23 degrees C until they were assayed.

Blood spot FSH and LH were measured using modifications of commercially available fluoroimmunometric kits for assay of these hormones in serum or plasma (DELFIA; Wallac, Inc., Gaithersburg, MD). The blood spot testosterone (T) and estradiol (E2) assays are modifications of commercially available serum/plasma radioimmunoassay kits (Binax, South Portland, ME; Pantex, Santa Monica, CA; DSL, Webster, TX; and Pantex, respectively). Complete details of protocol, validation, performance, sample stability, and comparability to plasma or serum values for each blood spot assay are provided elsewhere (Worthman and Stallings, 1997a; Worthman and Stallings, 1997b). To minimize effects of pulsatility, hormone values for each observation were taken as the average of the two blood spot samples. Formulae for conversion of blood spot assay values to serum/plasma equivalents are given in Worthman and Stallings (1997a). All values presented here represent plasma/serum total T and E2 (i.e., bound plus unbound) equivalents, and hence are comparable to the extant literature based on that medium.

Bioavailability of testosterone and estradiol are regulated by their carrier protein, SHBG, which exhibits greater affinity for T than E2 and, along with albumin, leaves less than a tenth of either hormone unbound in circulation (Knochenhauer, *et al.*, 1998; Pugeat, *et al.*, 1996; Zeginiadou, *et al.*, 1997). There is an age-related decline in SHBG levels during both childhood and adolescence in girls (Bedcarras, *et al.*, 1998; reviewed in Worthman, 1999), which has fueled speculation that altered steroid bioavailability plays a role in somatic and psychological development. Nevertheless, very few studies of psychobehavioral correlates of puberty in girls have measured SHBG to evaluate its possible moderating role. Those that have, have reported mixed results, from no or uncertain effect (Halpern and Suchindran, 1997; Susman, Dorn, and Chrousos, 1991) to enhanced relationships between androgens and emotional regulation and aggression in boys, but not in girls (Inoff-Germain, *et al.*, 1988; Susman, *et al.*, 1987a) when SHBG concentrations are factored in.

### Analytic strategy

The presence of repeated measures and screen-stratified sampling required the use of weighted analyses to generate unbiased population parameter estimates and of "sandwich" type variance corrections (Diggle, Liang, and Zeger, 1994; Pickles, Dunn, and Vazquez-Barquero, 1995) to produce appropriate confidence intervals and p values. These were obtained using generalized estimating equations (GEE) in SAS PROC GENMOD.

## A summary of previous findings

Our first foray into this area (Angold, Costello, and Worthman, 1998) involved analyses of age, pubertal timing, and Tanner stage on the probability of depression in both boys and girls over the first four annual waves of the GSMS (we could use four waves because the hormone data, available only for three waves, were not involved). To make a long story short, we found that Tanner stage provided a better fit to the prediction of depression than did age, and that once Tanner stage was controlled, there was no significant effect of age on depression diagnoses (while the effect of Tanner stage was significant). There was no effect on depression of the timing of puberty, whether measured by age of onset of menarche, or achievement of particular Tanner stages. These findings suggested that some aspect of puberty itself was related to increasing prevalence of depression, and that pubertal stage was not just a marker for nonpubertal age-related factors. However, it appeared that it was achieving a particular developmental level that was important, not the age at which that level was achieved. At this point, a version of pathway 2 involving pubertal status (but not timing) effects was still viable, but could not be differentiated from possible effects through pathways 3 and 4.

We then went on to examine a variety of HPG axis hormonal effects on depression in girls alone (Angold, Costello, and Worthman, 1999). We focused on girls because only they had Tanner-stage-dependent increases in depression. The results here were striking: Both T and E2 levels had strong independent effects on depression, but even more notable was the fact that T and E2 accounted for all of the effects of Tanner stage (the OR for Tanner stage fell from 3.4 to 1.0 when these hormones were included). There were also indications that the effects of T on depression were nonlinear – being manifested only above a certain threshold. We shall return to the threshold issue later. For now, we simply note that explanations in terms of pathway 2 are not compatible with these findings.

We also measured levels of FSH and LH and found that they had no effect on depression rates over and above those accounted for by T and E2. There was, therefore, no support for pathway 3. This leaves pathway 4 as the sole recipient of support among the explanations involving puberty directly. However, it was still possible that increased levels of stress in adolescence might be responsible for part of the increase. Indeed, if changes in stress were more strongly correlated with steroid hormone levels than either age or Tanner stage, then the whole apparent effect of T and E2 could be the result of confounding. This latter scenario seems rather implausible, but it is at least a theoretical possibility.

Our next aim is to test the predictions of pathway 1 using life events as a marker for stress. As a prelude to that, however, we first return to the question of the existence of a sex steroid threshold in the prediction of depression.

*Sex steroid threshold*

At the intracellular level, these apparent effects of both testosterone and estradiol could represent only an estrogenic effect, since when behavioral effects of testosterone in animals have been investigated at the level of the brain receptors involved, most have proved to occur via estrogen receptors following intracellular aromatization of testosterone to estrogen (Hutchison, *et al.*, 1990; Rasmussen, *et al.*, 1990). Since estrogen is the latest of the hormones studied here to begin to rise in puberty, an intracellular estrogen effect could first appear as an effect of peripheral testosterone and only later manifest directly as an effect of peripheral estrogen. In our analyses so far, we have treated T and E2 separately. This adds complexity to explanatory statistical models, and, if both were acting at the same receptors in their effects on depression, then the combined level of T and E2 would actually be a more physiologically appropriate index of pubertal status for our purposes.

We therefore developed a combined sex steroid level (SSL) by simply summing the measured molarities of T and E2 (an appropriate combinatorial approach because one molecule of T is aromatized to one molecule of E2). We then divided the distribution of SSLs into deciles, and plotted the prevalences of depression in those deciles (figure 8.2). This plot shows even more pronounced threshold effects than did that for T alone. The curve appears to have three regions. First there is a flat portion with very low levels of depression corresponding to SSLs up to 1.3 nanomolar. The second region with rates of depression about five times as high is generated by SSLs between 1.3 nanomolar and 2.3 nanomolar. The final region involving a further quadrupling of the rate of depression is associated with SSL levels above 2.3 nanomolar. We divided the observations into SSL groups based on these three cut points. The differences between them were all significant (1 vs. 2: OR=4.6, 95% CI 1.4–15.9, p=.01; 2 vs. 3: OR=4.41, 95% CI 1.3–15.4, p=.02; 1 vs. 3: OR=20.2, 95% CI 7.0–57.9, p<.0001).

Since the effect of E2 considered alone had appeared to be linear in our previous analyses, we then fitted a model to the depression data that included SSL reduced to the trichotomy just described, and added E2 as an additional predictor. E2 had no significant residual effect on the probability of depression (OR=1.01, p=.08). There was similarly no residual effect of T (OR=1.01, p=.6).

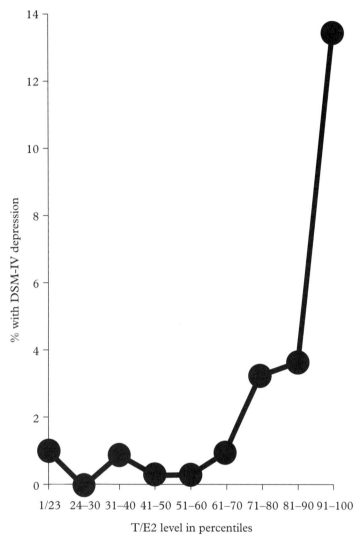

Figure 8.2  Relationship between sex steroid level and depression

## The prevalence of life events in mature and immature girls

There is no doubt that a variety of family and environmental acute and chronic stressors and problems are associated with depression (and a variety of other problems) in children and adolescents (see, e.g., Compas, Grant, and Ey, 1994; Goodyer and Altham, 1991; Goodyer, Wright, and

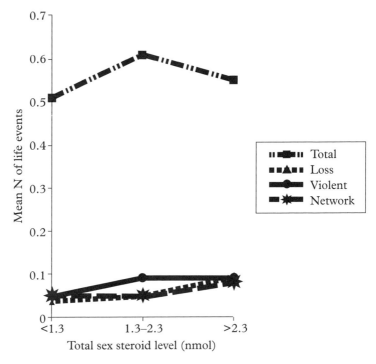

Figure 8.3 Relationship between sex steroid level and mean life event counts

Altham, 1990; Goodyer, 1990; Goodyer, 1995; Goodyer, *et al.*, 1993; Goodyer, Kolvin, and Gatzanis, 1986; Goodyer, Kolvin, and Gatzanis, 1987; Jensen, *et al.*, 1991; Laitinen-Krispijn, *et al.*, 1999; Lewinsohn, *et al.*, 1995; Lewinsohn, Rohde, and Seeley, 1998; Olsson, *et al.*, 1999; Sandberg, 2001; Williamson, *et al.*, 1998).

Pathway 1 depends upon mature girls suffering higher levels of stress than do immature girls. In beginning to test for such effects we decided to look at the relationships among age, life events in the three months preceding the interview, and depression. Since the distribution of life events was radically positively skewed, we used Poisson regression for the analysis. We fitted four models, one for the number of each subtype of life events, and one for the total number of life events during the last three months. The results were clear cut, as shown in figure 8.3. In no case were there significantly more life events in more mature girls (p values for all comparisons >.18). This can hardly have been the result of a "power problem," because we know we had sufficient power to find a difference in rates of depression between mature and immature girls with high statistical confidence. If a substantial cause of depression were to have been changing rates of life events, then we must have had good power to detect it. So at this point, pathway 1 has failed the test, along with pathways 2 and 3. Pathway 4, on the other hand, has received substantial support.

### The effects of life events in mature and immature girls

It is all very well to say that pathway 4 is supported by our data, but what does that mean? At this point it means that we have established a strong connection between SSL and a black box that we have conveniently labeled "neurochemical mechanisms involved in depression." It is completely unclear what those mechanisms are, or how they relate to other risk factors for depression. It is obviously not the case that having an SSL above 1.3 nanomolar is "the cause of depression." If it were, then all physiologically normal women of reproductive age would be depressed all the time. The enormous literature on psychosocial predictors of depression in adults shows, without a shadow of doubt, that other factors need to be taken into account. The question, then, is "What are the mechanisms by which higher levels of sex steroids lead to increased rates of depression?"

One possibility is that there is an increase in mature girls' "sensitivity" to the depressogenic effects of negative life experiences (see chapter 3). This implies the presence of an interaction between life events and SSL, such that life events have relatively little impact in the immature and a larger impact in the mature girls. To examine this possibility, we fitted a series of logistic regression models with depression as the outcome and numbers of life events (total, network, loss, violent), SSL status, and the interaction of life events and SSL status as the predictors. The results are shown in table 8.1. In every case, the OR for the effect of life events was smaller in the more mature girls. However, none of the interaction terms was significant, so we may conclude that there were no significant differences in the effects of life events on depression between the more and less mature girls. In other words, the more mature girls were not more sensitive to the depressogenic effects of life events than the less mature girls. Our results, therefore, agree with those of Goodyer and colleagues (1990), who reported that pubertal status made no difference to the effects of life events on depression and anxiety in a comparison of clinic cases and normal controls.

Table 8.1. *The effects of life events on the probability of being depressed in immature and mature girls (logistic regression results)*

| Type of life event | Immature OR (95% CI) | Mature OR (95% CI) |
|---|---|---|
| Any | 1.9 (1.4–2.7) | 1.8 (1.1–2.7) |
| Violent | 3.8 (1.4–10.5) | 2.8 (0.6–13.4) |
| Loss | 9.2 (2.5–34.1) | 2.5 (0.4–13.9) |
| Network | 2.7 (1.2–6.2) | 1.7 (0.5–5.8) |

## Conclusions

To date, our findings point towards sex steroids having an effect on adolescent girls' likelihood of becoming depressed, that is, independent of body morphology, the timing of pubertal changes, or stress levels. We want to emphasize again that this does not mean that we believe stress is not an important component in the etiology of depression. We have seen that in both immature and more mature girls recent life events have very substantial effects on the probability of depression. The point is that the effects of pubertal hormonal status cannot be explained either by changes in levels of life events or by changing sensitivity to the depressogenic effects of life events. Of course, it remains possible that changing rates of other specific types of stressor (perhaps family relationship difficulties or negative parenting styles) might explain these effects, but our work suggests, at the very least, that the effects of puberty on depression cannot be explained by any general change in susceptibility to stressors. Explanations in terms of changing levels of stress also fail to provide any parsimonious account of our findings. In order to "explain" the puberty effect, a stressor would have to be substantially more closely confounded with total sex steroid level than with secondary sex characteristics. We can think of no likely mechanism by which such a situation might arise. On the other hand, we know that estrogen has effects on CNS monoaminergic systems, so pathway 4 in figure 8.1 is physiologically plausible, as well as being supported by our data.

However, we do not know how changes in the central mechanisms related to depression are impacted by changes in peripheral sex steroids. We are currently pursuing further analyses that we hope will shed light on that key question.

## References

American Psychiatric Association (1994). *Diagnostic and statistical manual of mental disorders, fourth edition (DSM-IV)*. Washington, DC: American Psychiatric Press.

Anderson, J. C., Williams, S., McGee, R., and Silva, P. A. (1987). DSM-III disorders in preadolescent children: prevalence in a large sample from the general population. *Archives of General Psychiatry*, **44**, 69–77.

Angold, A., and Rutter, M. (1992). The effects of age and pubertal status on depression in a large clinical sample. *Development and Psychopathology*, **4**, 5–28.

Angold, A., Costello, E. J., and Worthman, C. M. (1998). Puberty and depression: the roles of age, pubertal status, and pubertal timing. *Psychological Medicine*, **28**, 51–61.

Angold, A., Costello, E. J., and Worthman, C. M. (1999). Pubertal changes in hormone levels and depression in girls. *Psychological Medicine*, **29**, 1043–1053.

Angold, A., Erkanli, A., Costello, E. J., and Rutter, M. (1996). Precision, reliability and accuracy in the dating of symptom onsets in child and adolescent psychopathology. *Journal of Child Psychology and Psychiatry*, **37**, 657–664.

Angold, A., Prendergast, M., Cox, A., Harrington, R., Simonoff, E., and Rutter, M. (1995). The Child and Adolescent Psychiatric Assessment (CAPA). *Psychological Medicine*, **25**, 739–753.

Apter, D. (1980). Serum steroids and pituitary hormones in female puberty: a partly longitudinal study. *Clinical Endocrinology*, **12**, 107–120.

Bebbington, P. (1996). The origins of sex differences in depressive disorder: bridging the gap. *International Review of Psychiatry*, **8**, 295–332.

Bebbington, P. E., Dunn, G., Jenkins, R., Lewis, G., Brugha, T., Farrell, M., and Meltzer, H. (1998). The influence of age and sex on the prevalence of depressive conditions: report from the National Survey of Psychiatric Morbidity. *Psychological Medicine*, **28**, 9–10.

Bebbington, P. E., Hurry, J., Tennant, C., Sturt, E., and Wing, J. K. (1981). Epidemiology of mental disorders in Camberwell. *Psychological Medicine*, **11**, 561–579.

Bedcarras, P. M. G., Ayuso, S., Escobar, M. E., Bergada, C., and Campo, S. (1998). Characterization of serum SHBG isoforms in prepubertal and pubertal girls. *Clinical Endocrinology*, **49**, 603–608.

Bird, H. R., Canino, G., Rubio-Stipec, M., Gould, M. S., Ribera, J., Sesman, M., Woodbury, M., Huertas-Goldman, S., Pagan, A., Sanchez-Lacay, A., and Moscoso, M. (1988). Estimates of the prevalence of childhood maladjustment in a community survey in Puerto Rico: the use of combined measures. *Archives of General Psychiatry*, **45**, 1120–1126.

Bland, R. C., Newman, S. C., and Orn, H. (1988a). Lifetime prevalence of psychiatric disorders in Edmonton. *Acta Psychiatrica Scandinavica*, **77**, 24–32.

Bland, R. C., Newman, S. C., and Orn, H. (1988b). Period prevalence of psychiatric disorders in Edmonton. *Acta Psychiatrica Scandinavica*, **77**, 33–42.

Blazer, D. G., Kessler, R. C., McGonagle, K. A., and Swartz, M. S. (1994). The prevalence and distribution of major depression in a national community sample: the National Comorbidity Survey. *American Journal of Psychiatry*, **151**, 979–986.

Brooks-Gunn, J., and Warren, M. P. (1989). Biological and social contributions to negative affect in young adolescent girls. *Child Development*, **60**, 40–55.

Burke, K. C., Burke, J. D., Regier, D. A., and Rae, D. S. (1990). Age at onset of selected mental disorders in five community populations. *Archives of General Psychiatry*, 47, 511–518.

Burr, I. M., Sizonenko, P. C., Kaplan, S. L., and Grumbach, M. M. (1970). Hormonal changes in puberty. 1. Correlations of serum luteinizing hormone and follicle-stimulating hormone with stages of puberty, testicular size and bone age in normal boys. *Pediatric Research*, 4, 25–35.

Cairney, J. (1998). Gender differences in the prevalence of depression among Canadian adolescents. *Canadian Journal of Public Health*, 89, 181–182.

Cairns, R. B., and Cairns, B. D. (1994). *Lifelines and risks: pathways of youth in our time*, 1st edn. Cambridge: Cambridge University Press.

Canino, G. J., Bird, H. R., Shrout, P. E., Rubio-Stipec, M., Bravo, M., Martinez, R., Sesman, M., and Guevara, L. M. (1987). The prevalence of specific psychiatric disorders in Puerto Rico. *Archives of General Psychiatry*, 44, 727–735.

Cheng, T. A. (1989). Sex difference in the prevalence of minor psychiatric morbidity: a social epidemiological study in Taiwan. *Acta Psychiatrica Scandinavica*, 80, 395–407.

Cohen, P., and Brook, J. (1987). Family factors related to the persistence of psychopathology in childhood and adolescence. *Psychiatry*, 50, 332–345.

Cohen, P., Cohen, J., and Brook, J. (1993a). An epidemiological study of disorders in late childhood and adolescence: 2. Persistence of disorders. *Journal of Child Psychology and Psychiatry*, 34, 869–877.

Cohen, P., Cohen, J., Kasen, S., Velez, C. N., Hartmark, C., Johnson, J., Rojas, M., Brook, J., and Streuning, E. L. (1993b). An epidemiological study of disorders in late childhood and adolescence: 1. Age- and gender-specific prevalence. *Journal of Child Psychology and Psychiatry and Allied Disciplines*, 34, 851–867.

Collu, R., and Ducharme, J. R. (1975). Role of adrenal steroids in the regulation of gonadotropin secretion at puberty. *Journal of Steroid Biochemistry*, 6, 869–872.

Compas, B. E., Grant, K. E., and Ey, S. (1994). Psychosocial stress and child and adolescent depression: can we be more specific? In W. M. Reynolds and H. F. Johnston (ed.), *Handbook of Depression in children and adolescents* (pp. 509–523). New York: Plenum.

Costello, E. J., Angold, A., Burns, B. J., Stangl, D. K., Tweed, D. L., Erkanli, A., and Worthman, C. M. (1996). The Great Smoky Mountains Study of Youth: goals, designs, methods, and the prevalence of DSM-III-R disorders. *Archives of General Psychiatry*, 53, 1129–1136.

Costello, E. J., Angold, A., March, J., and Fairbank, J. (1998). Life events and post-traumatic stress: the development of a new measure for children and adolescents. *Psychological Medicine*, 28, 1275–1288.

Costello, E. J., Costello, A. J., Edelbrock, C., Burns, B. J., Dulcan, M. K., Brent, D., and Janiszewski, S. (1988). Psychiatric disorders in pediatric primary care: prevalence and risk factors. *Archives of General Psychiatry*, 45, 1107–1116.

Costello, E. J., Stouthamer-Loeber, M., and DeRosier, M. (1993). Continuity and change in psychopathology from childhood to adolescence. Paper delivered at the Annual meeting of the Society for Research in Child and Adolescent Psychopathology, Santa Fe, NM.

Counts, D. R., Pescovitz, O. H., Barnes, K. M., Hench, K. D., Chrousos, G. P., Sherins, R. J., Comite, F., Loriaux, D. L., and Cutler, G. B. (1987). Dissociation of adrenarche and gonadarche in precocious puberty and in isolated hypogonadotropic gypogonadism. *Journal of Clinical Endocrinology and Metabolism*, **64**, 1174–1178.

DePeretti, E., and Forest, M. G. (1976). Unconjugated dehydroepiandrosterone plasma levels in normal subjects from birth to adolescence in human: the use of a sensitive radioimmunoassay. *Journal of Clinical Endocrinology and Metabolism*, **43**, 962–969.

Diggle, P. J., Liang, K. Y., and Zeger, S. L. (1994). *Analysis of Longitudinal Data*. Oxford: Clarendon.

Dorn, L. D., Susman, E. J., Nottelmann, E. D., Inoff-Germain, E. D., and Chrousos, G. P. (1990). Perceptions of puberty: adolescent, parent, and health care personnel. *Developmental Psychopathology*, **26**, 322–329.

Ducharme, J. R., Forest, M. G., DePeretti, E., Sempe, M., Collu, R., and Bertrand, J. (1976). Plasma adrenal and gonadal sex steroids in human pubertal development. *Journal of Clinical Endocrinology and Metabolism*, **42**, 458–467.

Duke, P. M., Litt, I. F., and Gross, R. T. (1980). Adolescents' self-assessment of sexual maturation. *Pediatrics*, **66**, 918–920.

Dunger, D. B., Villa, A. K., Matthews, D. R., Edge, J. A., Jones, J., Rothwell, C., Preece, M. A., and Robertson, W. R. (1991). Pattern of secretion of bioactive and immunoreactive gonadotropins in normal pubertal children. *Clinical Endocrinology*, **35**, 267–275.

Dunkel, L., Alfthan, H., Stenman, U. H., and Perheentupa, J. (1990). Gonadal control of pulsatile secretion of luteinizing hormone and follicle stimulating hormone in prepubertal boys evaluated by ultrasensitive time-resolved immunofluorometric assay. *Journal of Clinical Endocrinology and Metabolism*, **70**, 107–114.

Fleming, J. E., and Offord, D. R. (1990). Epidemiology of childhood depressive disorders: a critical review. *Journal of the American Academy of Child and Adolescent Psychiatry*, **29**, 571–580.

Frankowski, B., Duke-Duncan, P., Guillot, A., McDougal, D., Wasserman, R., and Young, P. (1987). Young adolescents' self-assessment of sexual maturation. *American Journal of Diseases of Children*, **141**, 385–386.

Ge, X., Conger, R. D., and Elder, G. H. (1996). Coming of age too early: pubertal influences on girls' vulnerability to psychological distress. *Child Development*, **67**, 3386–3400.

Goodyer, I. M. (1990). *Life experience, development, and child psychopathology*. Chichester, UK: John Wiley.

Goodyer, I. M. (1995). Life events and difficulties: their nature and effects. In I. M. Goodyer (ed.), *The depressed child and adolescent: developmental and clinical perspectives* (pp. 171–193). Cambridge: Cambridge University Press.

Goodyer, I., and Altham, P. M. E. (1991). Lifetime exit events and recent social and family adversities in anxious and depressed school-age children and adolescents – II. *Journal of Affective Disorders*, **21**, 229–238.

Goodyer, I. M., Cooper, P. J., Vize, C. M., and Ashby, L. (1993). Depression in 11–16-year-old girls: the role of past parental psychopathology and exposure to recent life events. *Journal of Child Psychology and Psychiatry*, **34**, 1103–1115.

Goodyer, I. M., Kolvin, I., and Gatzanis, S. (1986). Do age and sex influence the association between recent life events and psychiatric disorders in children and adolescents? A controlled enquiry. *Journal of Child Psychology and Psychiatry*, **27**(5), 681–687.

Goodyer, I. M., Kolvin, I., and Gatzanis, S. (1987). The impact of recent undesirable life events on psychiatric disorders in childhood and adolescence. *British Journal of Psychiatry*, **151**, 179–184.

Goodyer, I., Wright, C., and Altham, P. (1990). The friendships and recent life events of anxious and depressed school-age children. *British Journal of Psychiatry*, **156**, 689–698.

Graber, J. A., Lewinsohn, P. M., Seeley, J. R., and Brooks-Gunn, J. (1997). Is psychopathology associated with the timing of pubertal development? *Journal of the American Academy of Child and Adolescent Psychiatry*, **36**, 1768–1776.

Greif, E. B., and Ulman, K. J. (1982). The psychological impact of the menarche on early adolescent females: a review of the literature. *Child Development*, **53**, 1413–1430.

Guyer, B., Lescohier, I., Gallagher, S. S., Hausman, A., and Azzara, C. V. (1989). Intentional injuries among children and adolescents in Massachusetts. *New England Journal of Medicine*, **321**, 1584–1589.

Hale, P. M., Khoury, S., Foster, C. M., Beitins, I. Z., Hopwood, N. J., Marshall, J. C., and Keich, R. P. (1988). Increased luteinizing hormone pulse frequency during sleep in early to midpubertal boys. *Journal of Clinical Endocrinology and Metabolism*, **66**, 785–791.

Halpern, C. T. R. U. J., and Suchindran, C. (1997). Testosterone predicts initiation of coitus in adolescent females. *Psychosomatic Medicine*, **59**, 161–171.

Hankin, B. L., Abramson, L. Y., Moffitt, T. E., Silva, P. A., McGee, R., and Angell, K. E. (1998). Development of depression from preadolescence to young adulthood: emerging gender differences in a ten-year longitudinal study. *Journal of Abnormal Psychology*, **107**, 128–140.

Hayes, F. J., and Crowley, W. F. J. (1998). Gonadotropin pulsations across development. *Hormone Research*, **49**, 163–168.

Hayward, C., Killen, J. D., Wilson, D. M., Hammer, L. D., Litt, I. F., Kraemer, H. C., Haydel, F., Varady, A., and Taylor, C. B. (1997). Psychiatric risk associated with early puberty in adolescent girls. *Journal of the American Academy of Child and Adolescent Psychiatry*, **36**, 255–261.

Hutchison, J. B., Schumacher, M., Steimer, T., and Gahr, M. (1990). Are separable aromatase systems involved in hormonal regulation of the male brain? *Journal of Neurobiology*, **21**, 743–759.

Hwu, H. G., Yeh, E. K., and Chang, L. Y. (1989). Prevalence of psychiatric disorders in Taiwan defined by the Chinese Diagnostic Interview Schedule. *Acta Psychiatrica Scandinavica*, **79**, 136–147.

Inoff-Germain, G., Nottelmann, E. D., Arnold, G. S., and Susman, E. J. (1988). Adolescent aggression and parent–adolescent conflict: relations between observed family interactions and measures of the adolescents' general functioning. *Journal of Early Adolescence*, **8**, 17–36.

Jensen, P. S., Richters, J., Ussery, T., Bloedau, L., and Davis, H. (1991). Child psychopathology and environmental influences: discrete life events versus ongoing adversity. *Journal of the American Academy of Child and Adolescent Psychiatry*, **30**, 303–309.

Jorm, A. F. (1987). Sex and age differences in depression: a quantitative synthesis of published research. *Australian and New Zealand Journal of Psychiatry*, **21**, 46–53.

Kashani, J. H., Beck, N. C., Hoeper, E. W., Fallahi, C., Corcoran, C. M., Mcallister, J. A., Rosenberg, T. K., and Reid, J. C. (1987). Psychiatric disorders in a community sample of adolescents. *American Journal of Psychiatry*, **144**, 584–589.

Kashani, J. H., Orvaschel, H., Rosenberg, M. A., and Reid, J. C. (1989). Psychopathology in a community sample of children and adolescents: a developmental perspective. *Journal of the American Academy of Child and Adolescent Psychiatry*, **28**, 701–706.

Kessler, R. C., McGonagle, K. A., Nelson, C. B., Hughes, M., Swartz, M., and Blazer, D. G. (1994). Sex and depression in the National Comorbidity Survey: II. Cohort effects. *Journal of Affective Disorders*, **30**, 15–26.

Kessler, R. C., McGonagle, K. A., Swartz, M. S., Blazer, D. G., and Nelson, C. B. (1993). Sex and depression in the National Comorbidity Survey: I. Lifetime prevalence, chronicity and recurrence. *Journal of Affective Disorders*, **29**, 85–96.

Knochenhauer, E. S., Boots, L. R., Potter, H. D., and Azziz, R. (1998). Differential binding of estradiol and testosterone to SHBG. Relation to circulating estradiol levels. *Journal of Reproductive Medicine*, **43**, 665–670.

Korth-Schutz, S., Levine, L. S., and New, M. I. (1976). Serum androgens in normal prepubertal and pubertal children and in children with precocious adrenarche. *Journal of Clinical Endocrinology and Metabolism*, **42**, 117–124.

Laflamme, N., Nappi, R. E., Drolet, G., Labrie, C., and Rivest, S. (1998). Expression and neuropeptidergic characterization of estrogen receptors (ER alpha and ER beta) throughout the rat brain: anatomical evidence of distinct roles of each subtype. *Journal of Neurobiology*, **36**, 357–378.

Laitinen-Krispijn, S., Van der Ende, J., Hazebroek-Kampschreur, A. A. J. M., and Verhulst, F. C. (1999). Pubertal maturation and the development of behavioural and emotional problems in early adolescence. *Acta Psychiatrica Scandinavica*, **99**, 16–25.

Landy, H., Beopple, P. A., Mansfield, M. J., Charpie, P., Schoefeld, D. I., Link, K., Romero, G., Crawford, J. D., Crigler, J. F., Blizzard, R. M., and Crowley, W. F. (1992). Sleep modulation of neuroendocrine function: developmental changes in gonadotropin-releasing hormone secretion during sexual maturation. *Pediatric Research*, **213**, 217.

Lashansky, G., Saenger, P., Fishman, K., Gautier, T., Mayes, D., Berg, G., DeMartino-Nardi, J., and Reiter, E. (1991). Normative data for adrenal steroidogenesis in a healthy pediatric population: age- and sex-related changes after adrenocorticotropin stimulation. *Journal of Clinical Endocrinology and Metabolism*, **73**, 674–686.

Layman, L. C. (1995). Molecular biology in reproductive endocrinology. *Current Opinion in Obstetrics and Gynecology*, 75, 328–339.

Lee, C. K., Han, J. H., and Choi, J. O. (1987). The epidemiological study of mental disorders in Korea (IX): alcoholism, anxiety, and depression. *Seoul Journal of Psychiatry*, 12, 183–191.

Lee, P. A., and Migeon, C. J. (1975). Puberty in boys: correlation of plasma levels of gonadotropins (LH, FSH), androgens (testosterone, androstene-dione, dehydroepiandrosterone and its sulfate), estrogens (estrone and estradiol), and progestins (progesterone and 17-hydroxyprogesterone) with physical changes. *Journal of Clinical Endocrinology and Metabolism*, 41, 556–562.

Lee, P. A., Xenakis, T., Winer, J., and Matsenbaugh, S. (1975). Puberty in girls: correlation of serum levels of gonadotropins, prolactin, androgens, estrogens, and progestins with physical changes. *Journal of Clinical Endocrinology and Metabolism*, 43, 775–784.

Lewinsohn, P. M., Gotlib, I. H., and Seeley, J. R. (1995). Adolescent psychopathology: IV. Specificity of psychosocial risk factors for depression and substance abuse in older adolescents. *Journal of the American Academy of Child and Adolescent Psychiatry*, 34, 1221–1229.

Lewinsohn, P. M., Hops, H., Roberts, R. E., Seeley, J. R., and Andrews, J. A. (1993). Adolescent psychopathology: I. prevalence and incidence of depression and other DSM-III-R disorders in high school students. *Journal of Abnormal Psychology*, 102, 133–144.

Lewinsohn, P. M., Rohde, P., and Seeley, J. R. (1998). Major depressive disorder in older adolescents: prevalence, risk factors, and clinical implications. *Clinical Psychology Review*, 18, 765–794.

Lu, B., Leygue, E., Dotzlaw, H., Murphy, L. J., Murphy, L. C., and Watson, P. H. (1998). Estrogen receptor-beta mRNA variants in human and murine tissues. *Molecular and Cellular Endocrinology*, 138, 199–203.

Marshall, J. C., Dalkin, A. C., Haisenieder, D. J., Paul, S. J., Ortolano, G. A., and Kelch, R. P. (1991). Gonadotropin-releasing hormone pulses: regulators of gonadotropin synthesis and ovulatory cycles. *Recent Programs of Hormone Research*, 47, 155–187.

McCann, S. M., Kimura, M., Walczewska, A., Karanth, S., Rettori, V., and Yu, W. H. (1998). Hypothalamic control of FSH and LH by FSH-RF, cytokines, leptin and nitric oxide. *Neuroimmunomodulation*, 5, 193–202.

McGee, R., and Williams, S. (1988). A longitudinal study of depression in 9-year-old children. *Journal of the American Academy of Child and Adolescent Psychiatry*, 27, 342–348.

McGee, R., Feehan, M., Williams, S., and Anderson, J. (1992). DSM-III disorders from age 11 to age 15 years. *Journal of the American Academy of Child and Adolescent Psychiatry*, 31, 51–59.

McGee, R., Feehan, M., Williams, S., Partridge, F., Silva, P. A., and Kelly, J. (1990). DSM-III disorders in a large sample of adolescents. *Journal of the American Academy of Child and Adolescent Psychiatry*, 29, 611–619.

Mitchner, N. A., Garlick, C., and Ben-Jonathan, N. (1998). Cellular distribution and gene regulation of estrogen receptors alpha and beta in the rat pituitary gland. *Endocrinology*, 139, 3976–3983.

Morris, N. M., and Udry, J. R. (1980). Validation of a self-administered instrument to assess stage of adolescent development. *Journal of Youth and Adolescence*, **9**, 271–280.

Murphy, L. C., Dotzlaw, H., Leygue, E., Douglas, D., Coutts, A., and Watson, P. H. (1997). Estrogen receptor variants and mutations. *Journal of Steroid Biochemistry and Molecular Biology*, **62**, 363–372.

Nolen-Hoeksema, S., Girgus, J. S., and Seligman, M. E. P. (1991). Sex differences in depression and explanatory style in children. *Journal of Youth and Adolescence*, **20**, 233–245.

Nottelmann, E. D., Inoff-Germain, G., Susman, E. J., and Chrousos, G. P. (1990). Hormones and behavior at puberty. In J. Bancroft and J. M. Reinisch (ed.), *Adolescence and puberty* (pp. 88–123). Oxford: Oxford University Press.

Nottelmann, E. D., Susman, E. F., Dorn, L. D., Inoff-Germain, G., Loriaux, D. L., Cutler, G. B., and Chrousos, G. P. (1987a). Developmental processes in early adolescence: relations among chronological age, pubertal stage, height, weight, and serum levels of gonadotropins, sex steroids, and adrenal androgens. *Journal of Adolescent Health Care*, **8**, 246–260.

Nottelmann, E. D., Susman, E. J., Inoff-Germain, G., Cutler, G. B., Loriaux, D. L., and Chrousos, G. P. (1987b). Developmental processes in early adolescence: relationships between adolescent adjustment problems and chronological age, pubertal stage, and puberty-related serum hormone levels. *Journal of Pediatrics*, **110**, 473–480.

Ojeda, S. R., and Ma, Y. J. (1998). Epidermal growth factor tyrosine kinase receptors and the neuroendocrine control of mammalian puberty. *Molecular and Cellular Endocrinology*, **140**, 101–106.

Olsson, G. I., Nordström, M. L., von Knorring, H. A., and von Knorring, A. L. (1999). Adolescent depression: social network and family climate – a case-control study. *Journal of Child Psychology and Psychiatry*, **40**, 227–237.

Olweus, D., Mattsson, A., Schalling, D., and Low, H. (1988). Circulating testosterone levels and aggression in adolescent males: a causal analysis. *Psychosomatic Medicine*, **50**, 261–272.

Osterlund, M., Kuiper, G. G., Custafsson, J. A., and Hurd, Y. L. (1998). Differential distribution and regulation of estrogen receptor-alpha and -beta mRNA within the female rat brain. *Brain Research: Molecular Brain Research*, **54**, 175–180.

Paikoff, R. L., Brooks-Gunn, J., and Warren, M. P. (1991). Effects of girls' hormonal status on depressive and aggressive symptoms over the course of one year. *Journal of Youth and Adolescence*, **20**, 191–215.

Parker, L. N., Sack, J., Fisher, D. A., and Odell, W. D. (1978). The adrenarche: Prolactin, gonadotropins, adrenal androgens, and cortisol. *Journal of Clinical Endocrinology and Metabolism*, **46**, 396–404.

Phillips, D. J., Albertsson-Wikaland, K., Eriksson, K., and Wide, L. (1997). Changes in the isoforms of luteinizing hormone and follicle-stimulating hormone during puberty in normal children. *Journal of Clinical Endocrinology and Metabolism*, **82**, 3103–3106.

Pickles, A., Dunn, G., and Vazquez-Barquero, J. (1995). Screening for stratification in two-phase ('two-stage') epidemiological surveys. *Statistical Methods in Medical Research*, **4**, 73–89.

Pugeat, M., Crave, J. C., Tourniaire, J., and Forest, M. G. (1996). Clinical utility of sex hormone binding globulin measurement. *Hormone Research*, 45, 148–155.

Rasmussen, J. E., Torres-Aleman, I., MacLusky, N. J., Naftolin, F., and Robbins, R. J. (1990). The effects of estradiol on the growth patterns of estrogen receptor-positive hypothalamic cell lines. *Endocrinology*, 126, 235–240.

Reinherz, H. Z., Giaconia, R. M., Lefkowitz, E. S., Pakiz, B., and Frost, A. K. (1993a). Prevalence of psychiatric disorders in a community population of older adolescents. *Journal of the American Academy of Child and Adolescent Psychiatry*, 32, 369–377.

Reinherz, H. Z., Giaconia, R. M., Pakiz, B., Silverman, A. B., Frost, A. K., and Lefkowitz, E. S. (1993b). Psychosocial risks for major depression in late adolescence: a longitudinal community study. *Journal of the American Academy of Child and Adolescent Psychiatry*, 32, 1155–1163.

Reiter, E. O., Fuldauer, V. G., and Root, A. W. (1977). Secretion of the adrenal androgen, dehydroepliandrosterone sulfate, during normal infancy, childhood, and adolescence, in sick infants, and in children with endocrinologic abnormalities. *Journal of Pediatrics*, 90, 76–80.

Rutter, M., Graham, P., Chadwick, O. F. D., and Yule, W. (1976). Adolescent turmoil: fact or fiction? *Journal of Child Psychology and Psychiatry*, 17, 35–56.

Sandberg, S., Rutter, M., Pickles, A., McGuinness D., and Angold, A. (2001). Do high-threat life events really provoke the onset of psychiatric disorder in children? *Journal of Child Psychology and Psychiatry*, 42, 523–532.

Schlossberger, N. M., Turner, R. A., and Irwin, C. E. (1992). Validity of self-report of pubertal maturation in early adolescents. *Journal of Adolescent Health*, 13, 109–113.

Seeman, M. V. (1997). Psychopathology in women and men: focus on female hormones. *American Journal of Psychiatry*, 154, 1641–1647.

Sizonenko, P. C., Burr, I. M., Kaplan, S. L., and Grunbach, M. M. (1970). Hormonal changes in puberty II. Correlation of serum luteinizing hormone and follicle stimulating hormone with stages of puberty and bone age in normal girls. *Pediatric Research*, 4, 36–45.

Sizonenko, P. C., and Paunier, L. (1975). Hormonal changes in puberty III: Correlation of plasma dehydroepiandrosterone, testosterone, FSH, and LH with stages of puberty and bone age in normal boys and girls and in patients with Addison's disease or hypogonadism or with premature or late adrenarche. *Journal of Clinical Endocrinology and Metabolism*, 41, 894–904.

Skuse, D. (1984). Extreme deprivation in early childhood. *Journal of Child Psychology and Psychiatry*, 25, 543–572.

Stattin, H., and Magnusson, D. (1990). *Paths through life*, vol. II, *Pubertal maturation in female development*. Hillsdale, NJ: Lawrence Erlbaum.

Susman, E. J., Dorn, L. D., and Chrousos, G. P. (1991). Negative affect and hormone levels in young adolescents: concurrent and predictive perspectives. *Journal of Youth and Adolescence*, 20, 167–190.

Susman, E. J., Inoff-Germain, G., Nottelmann, E. D., Loriaux, D. L., Cutler, G. B., and Chrousos, G. P. (1987a). Hormones, emotional dispositions, and aggressive attributes in young adolescents. *Child Development*, 58, 1114–1134.

Susman, E. J., Nottelmann, E. D., Inoff-Germain, G., Dorn, L. D., and Chrousos, G. P. (1987b). Hormonal influences on aspects of psychological development during adolescence. *Journal of Adolescent Health Care*, **8**, 492–504.

Susman, E. J., Nottelmann, E. D., Inoff-Germain, G. E., Dorn, L. D., Cutler, G. B., Loriaus, D. L., and Chrousos, G. P. (1985). The relation of relative hormonal levels and physical development and social-emotional behavior in young adolescents. *Journal of Youth and Adolescence*, **14**, 245–264.

Tanner, J. M. (1962). *Growth at adolescence: with a general consideration of the effects of hereditary and environmental factors upon growth and maturation from birth to maturity.* Oxford: Blackwell Scientific.

Veldhuis, J. D. (1996). Neuroendocrine mechanisms mediating awakening of the human gonadotropic axis in puberty. *Pediatric Nephrology*, **10**, 304–317.

Velez, C. N., Johnson, J., and Cohen, P. (1989). A longitudinal analysis of selected risk factors of childhood psychopathology. *Journal of the American Academy of Child and Adolescent Psychiatry*, **28**, 861–864.

Vihko, H., and Apter, D. (1980). The role of androgens in adolescent cycles. *Journal of Steroid Biochemistry*, **12**, 369–373.

Weissman, M. M., Bland, R., Joyce, P. R., Newman, S., Wells, J. E., and Wittchen, H. U. (1993). Sex differences in rates of depression: cross-national perspectives. *Journal of Affective Disorders*, **29**, 77–84.

Weissman, M. M., Bland, R. C., Canino, G. J., Faravelli, C., Greenwald, S., Hwu, H. G., Joyce, P. R., Karam, E. G., Lee, C. K., Lellouch, J., Lepine, J. P., Newman, S. C., Rubio-Stipec, M., Wells, J. E., Wickramaratne, P. J., Wittchen, H., and Yeh, E. K. (1996). Cross-national epidemiology of major depression and bipolar disorder. *Journal of the American Medical Association*, **276**, 293–299.

Weissman, M. M., and Klerman, G. L. (1977). Sex differences and the epidemiology of depression. *Archives of General Psychiatry*, **34**, 98–111.

Wells, J. E., Bushnell, J. A., Hornblow, A. R., Joyce, P. R., and Oakley-Browne, M. A. (1989). Christchurch Psychiatric Epidemiology Study. Part I, Methodology and lifetime prevalence for specific psychiatric disorders. *Australian and New Zealand Journal of Psychiatry*, **23**, 315–326.

Wennink, J. M. B., Delemarre-van de Waal, H. A., Schoemaker, R., Schoemaker, H., and Schoemaker, J. (1989). Luteinizing hormone and follicle stimulating hormone secretion patterns in boys throughout puberty measured using highly sensitive immunoradiometric assays. *Clinical Endocrinology*, **31**, 551–564.

Wennink, J. M. B., Delemarre-van de Waal, H. A., Schoemaker, R., Schoemaker, H., and Schoemaker, J. (1990). Luteinizing hormone and follicle stimulating hormone secretion patterns in girls throughout puberty measured using highly sensitive immunoradiometric assays. *Clinical Endocrinology*, **33**, 333–344.

Wierman, M. E., Beardsworth, D. E., Crawford, J. D., Crigler, J., JF, Mansfield, M. J., Bode, H. H., Boepple, P. A., Kushner, D. C., and Crowley, J., WF (1986). Adrenarche and skeletal maturation during luteinizing hormone releasing hormone analogue suppression of gonadarche. *Journal of Clinical Investigation*, **77**, 121–126.

Williamson, D. E., Birmaher, B., Frank, E., Anderson, B., Matty, M. K., and Kupfer, D. J. (1998). Nature of life events and difficulties in depressed adolescents. *Journal of the American Academy of Child and Adolescent Psychiatry*, 37, 1049–1057.

Wittchen, H.-U., Essau, C. A., von Zerssen, D., Krieg, J. C., and Zaudig, M. (1992). Lifetime and six-month prevalence of mental disorders in the Munich Follow-up Study. *European Archives of Psychiatry and Clinical Neuroscience*, 241, 247–258.

Worthman, C. (1999). Epidemiology of human development. In C. Panter-Brick and C. Worthman (ed.), *Hormones, health, and behavior: a socio-ecological and lifespan perspective* (pp. 47–104). Cambridge: Cambridge University Press.

Worthman, C. M., and Stallings, J. F. (1997a). Hormone measures in fingerprick blood spot samples: new field methods for reproductive endocrinology. *American Journal of Physical Anthropology*, 103, 1–21.

Worthman, C. M., and Stallings, J. F. (1997b). Hormone measures in fingerprick blood spot samples: new field methods for reproductive endocrinology. *American Journal of Physical Anthropology*, 103, 1–21.

Wu, F. C., Butler, G. E., Kelnar, C. J. H., and Sellar, R. E. (1990). Patterns of pulsatile luteinizing hormone secretion before and during the onset of puberty in boys: a study using an immunoradiometric assay. *Journal of Clinical Endocrinology and Metabolism*, 70, 629–637.

Young, E., and Korszun, A. (1998). Psychoneuroendocrinology of depression. Hypothalamic pituitary-gonadal axis. *Psychiatric Clinics of North America*, 21, 309–323.

Zeginiadou, T., Kolias, S., Kouretas, D., and Antonoglou, O. (1997). Nonlinear binding of sex steroids to albumin and sex hormone binding globulin. *European Journal of Drug Metabolism and Pharmacokinetics*, 22, 229–235.

# 9   Puberty and schizophrenia

*Andrew Gotowiec, Mary V. Seeman, and
Robin Z. Cohen*

Clinical lore links puberty with the onset of schizophrenia, but few empirical studies exist to connect the two events. One hypothesis is that
a central nervous system protective role for female hormones, especially estrogens, may underlie such a relationship. In this chapter we
describe our own empirical observations, discuss possible interpretations, note the limitations of each, and suggest some directions for future
research.

## Schizophrenia

Schizophrenia is a major psychotic disorder that affects approximately
one percent of the adult population worldwide (Warner and de Girolamo,
1995); the impact of the disease is considerable, for society and for the
individual. In the United States, for example, patients with schizophrenia
occupy approximately 25 percent of hospital beds (Eaton, 1991). For the
individual, schizophrenia presents with symptoms that make all aspects
of life difficult. Active psychotic symptoms include hallucinations in various sensory domains, mainly auditory. Also characteristic are delusions
or false beliefs, usually of a persecutory nature. Schizophrenia often leaves
thought, speech, and behavior disorganized. Perhaps more problematic
are deficit or negative symptoms, such as apathy, lack of motivation, loss
of previous pleasures and interests, and a tendency toward social isolation.
Increasingly, investigators have recognized that even more fundamental
symptoms are cognitive, such as attentional problems, memory problems,
and difficulties with reasoning. Clinical presentations are heterogeneous;
the exact constellation of symptoms varies among individuals, within individuals, and changes over time (Liddle, 1999). In contrast to depressive
and anxiety syndromes, schizophrenia is at least as common in men as in
women and appears to affect men more severely than women, at least in
the first several decades after onset.

   Like its clinical presentation, schizophrenia's causes are probably
heterogeneous, but are as yet unknown. Familial associations strongly

implicate genetic factors; monozygotic twins have concordance rates for the disorder four times higher than dizygotic twins or other full siblings. First-degree relatives of an affected person are at approximately ten times greater risk of developing schizophrenia than are members of the general population. The inheritance pattern suggests a complex disorder to which many interlinked genes contribute.

Genes related to schizophrenia are probably turned on by specific epigenetic factors controlled by unknown chemical messengers. Current thinking is that something occurs during fetal life to activate the responsible genes, many years before the onset of symptoms. For example, second trimester maternal nutritional deficiency or infection is positively associated with risk for schizophrenia (Susser, *et al.*, 1996), as is maternal–fetal Rh incompatibility (Hollister, Laing, and Mednick 1996). Increased risk is also associated with low birth weight, prolonged labor and fetal distress, among other pre- and perinatal complications (Brixley, *et al.*, 1993; McGrath, *et al.*, 1994). Researchers have noted a slight preponderance of winter or early spring births among affected individuals (Kunugi, *et al.*, 1996; Mednick and Hollister, 1995; Welham, Pemberton, and McGrath, 1996). Some account for this relationship in terms of maternal exposure to infectious illnesses that are common in the northern hemisphere's colder weather. It is possible, however, that environmental factors operating not during fetal development but at a time more proximal to the time of symptom onset (i.e., adolescence) activate, or facilitate the expression of, relevant genes. For instance, alcohol and drug use in adolescence has been associated with an enhanced risk of developing schizophrenia (Mueser, *et al.*, 1990; Mueser, Yarnold, and Bellack, 1992).

Although the presentation of schizophrenia may vary by cultural setting (Jablensky, 1995), no population or culture yet studied is free of schizophrenia. In fact, prevalence rates are remarkably similar across countries. The course and outcome of schizophrenia appear more favorable in less industrialized, compared with more industrialized, countries (Warner and de Girolamo, 1995; Jablensky, 1995). The protection does not extend to migrants from these countries to Europe or North America, however. This suggests that environmental factors associated with specific ways of life, such as communal social support, may be able to modulate the severity of the expression of schizophrenia genes. This hypothesis is untested; the finding of superior outcomes in nonindustrialized countries is itself open to criticism. On the other hand, a late onset of illness and relatively less severe early course in women is a more robust finding, replicated across the world.

## Gender differences in schizophrenia

The peak of schizophrenia incidence occurs between the ages of 17 and 25. First emergence of symptoms in childhood or in late adult life is comparatively uncommon. Because of the association of first onset to early adulthood, clinicians and researchers have long debated the role of pubertal factors in creating a permissive internal environment favoring the emergence of symptoms. Gender differences in this respect deserve attention. Before age 14, gender ratios in schizophrenia incidence are essentially one to one (Frazier, *et al.*, 1997; Galdos, Van Os, and Murray, 1993), but after age 14 the pattern changes. For example, Castle and colleagues' (1995) examination of the distribution of onset age showed an early peak (age 19–23) in men, with a subsequent, uniform decline in the incidence. In contrast, women had a later onset peak (age 25–29) followed by a second, lower peak between the ages of 45 and 54 (i.e., immediately postmenopause; see Häfner, *et al.*, 1993; Häfner, *et al.*, 1998). Later in life the picture changes again; 80 percent of late onset schizophrenia occurs in women, but by the end of life the gender ratio in prevalence is roughly equal (Castle and Murray, 1991, 1993; Howard, Almeida, and Levy, 1994). The gender difference in the age distribution of incidence rates is well established across the globe (Jablensky, 1995; Warner and de Girolamo, 1995).

As stated previously, the early course of schizophrenia is less severe in women than in men (Harrison, *et al.*, 1996; Davidson, *et al.*, 1999; Häfner, *et al.*, 1993). Premorbid deficit, often a predictor of later outcomes, is less pronounced in women (Castle, *et al.*, 1995; Castle and Murray, 1993; Foerster, *et al.*, 1991; Goldstein, 1988; McGlashan and Bardensein, 1990; Shtasel, *et al.*, 1992). For example, Shtasel and colleagues (1992) found women scored higher than men on measures of premorbid adjustment during childhood, adolescence, and adulthood. They also found that females with schizophrenia had higher scores than their male counterparts on measures of social functioning and engagement. Moreover, direct measures of outcome, including symptom severity, relapse rates, and social and occupation function, all favor women with schizophrenia over men with the disorder (Andia and Zisook, 1991; Angermeyer, Kuhn, and Goldstein, 1990), at least in the first fifteen years after onset. After that period, when women are postmenopausal, outcomes in men and women are indistinguishable (Jonsson and Nyman, 1991; Leff, *et al.*, 1992; Opjordsmoen, 1991). Clinical reports note not only postmenopausal but also premenstrual and postpartum worsening of women's symptoms (for a review, see Seeman and Lang, 1990).

## Gender difference in puberty and schizophrenia

The onset at puberty and the gender differences in onset age and course have led to several conjectures about possible relationships between schizophrenia and pubertal events. Pubertal events can shift family relations in the direction of either upsetting or enhancing supportive relationships; loss of supportive relationships may dispose vulnerable individuals to the emergence of symptoms. Anthropological observations suggest that across cultures menarche brings daughters closer into the family fold while puberty in sons is accompanied by greater social activity outside the family, with a noticeable shift in the son's locus of activity from within to without the family (Schlegel and Barry, 1991). The family's potential as a supportive resource may, in part, explain gender differences in the onset age and early course of schizophrenia. The anthropological observations suggest that the same general maturational process (i.e., the advent of puberty) brings women into closer contact with a potentially protective family and casts the young male away from the safety of the family nest. However, no data exist with which to directly test these hypotheses as they apply to schizophrenia.

Existing data do not necessarily clarify the picture. High family-expressed emotion, for instance, has been associated with early relapse of schizophrenia symptoms (Leff, *et al.*, 1992). High-expressed emotion has been found to be present more often in the families of men with schizophrenia than in women (Leff and Vaughn, 1981, 1989; Vaughn, 1989). Some psychological studies suggest that menarche is associated with increased family conflict (Paikoff and Brooks-Gunn, 1991; see also chapter 10). However, these observations are cross-sectional, with little longitudinal data available; that is, we do not know that conflict at a single point in time is necessarily associated with diminished family cohesion for girls. We also do not know if such general observations pertain equally to families of preschizophrenic women, who may tend premorbidly to be quiet and withdrawn (i.e., not eliciting much conflict). Existing data do suggest that pubertal maturation is associated with increased conflict between mothers and sons, with relatively fewer attempts at assertiveness by boys directed at their fathers (Paikoff and Brooks-Gunn, 1991; see also chapter 12). The relationship between pubertal events and a variety of psychosocial variables, however, has been much more thoroughly studied among females than among males.

Biologically focused hypotheses have been easier to test in animals than in humans. For example, information is beginning to accumulate about the relationship between pubertal stages and neurodevelopmental processes that may ultimately lead, in the genetically predisposed, to the emergence of psychosis. The postulate is that maturational events in the brain, such as neuronal pruning (Huttenlocher, 1984), are hormonally facilitated. The actions of hormones on faulty neural wiring laid down in fetal life (O'Connell, et al., 1997; Weinberger, 1987) have been implicated in impaired adult circuitry that eventually manifests as psychosis (Saugstad, 1989, 1994). Synaptic pruning is only one of several events taking place in the central nervous system during the pubertal years. Rapidly occurring alterations in hormone levels may provide a "permissive" or alternatively a "hostile" environment to other concurrent events, such as myelination (Benes, 1989; Galdos, et al., 1993).

Pubertal development may influence the eventual outcome of an early neuronal insult. Animal models provide examples of how a congenital lesion can remain dormant until sexual maturation, and then produce profound behavioral effects (Goldman and Alexander, 1977). Researchers frequently focus on the ventral hippocampal (VH) region of the brain, as a potential site of brain impairment in schizophrenia. Lipska and colleagues (Lipska, Jaskiw, and Weinberger, 1993; Lipska and Weinberger 1993a, 1993b, 1995) presented a lesioning model by which male rats with neonatal VH lesions did not differ from sham-operated rats when tested before puberty on a variety of dopamine-related parameters. However, after puberty VH-lesioned animals showed behavioral changes consistent with dopamine hyperactivity. These changes seemed permanent in the rat, but antipsychotic treatment (i.e., anti-dopaminergic treatment) reversed the behaviors to a considerable degree. Analogous to the clinical observation that stressful experiences exacerbate schizophrenia symptoms (Norman and Malla, 1993; Walker, et al., 1996), exposure to stress in these animals magnified the effects of the VH lesion. Ellenbroek, van Den Kroonenberger, and Cools (1998) developed another rat model, this one based on early maternal separation. Maternal deprivation, lasting twenty-four hours, results in a disturbance of sensorimotor gating (i.e., disruption of prepulse inhibition) in adult rats. This brain wave response to a sensory stimulus is currently one of the best trait markers for human schizophrenia (Cadenhead, et al., 2000; Perry, Geyer, and Braff, 1999). Just as in the Lipska and Weinberger model, the prepulse inhibition disruption in the experimental rats emerges only after puberty; antipsychotic agents reverse it. Delayed emergence of behavioral abnormalities following early hippocampal damage has been reported in monkeys as well as rats. As in rats, severe behavioral impairments in the experimental monkeys are evident in adulthood, but not in early life (Beauregard, Malkova, and Bachevalier, 1991).

## The role of stress

Response to stress is relevant here. Although the notion that adolescence is inevitably a period of storm and stress has been largely rejected, theorists and researchers agree that adolescence – the years of pubertal development – remains a period of enhanced vulnerability (Arnett, 2000). For example, Dorn and Chrousos (1997) suggest that biological transitions such as puberty are times of both psychological and physical vulnerability. The changes in the biological response to stressors that accompany puberty could be one critical trigger to the onset of schizophrenia. Sachser, Durchlag, and Hirzel (1998) have explored the special challenges of puberty across mammalian social systems. They discuss two predominant forms of social relation: dominance relationships and social bonding. During periods of instability, as in puberty, when adolescents are learning social skills and negotiating for hierarchical status, distinct increases in the activity of pituitary-adrenocortical and sympathetic-adrenomedullary stress systems occurred in all mammalian species the researchers studied. However, once individuals establish dominance hierarchies, stress levels fall. Similarly, successful social bonding is a second route to the alleviation of arousal and the reduction of stress. The anthropological observations described earlier suggested that postpubertal males find their locus of activity outside the family. It may be, therefore, that the establishment of dominance hierarchies is more salient, and thus more stressful, for males than for females.

Stressful experiences, however triggered, provoke a release of glucocorticoids, the body's hormonal response to stress. A threshold level of glucocorticoids is essential for neuron development, neuron survival, and for brain plasticity. The exceedingly high levels attained during extremely stressful periods, however, may cause neuronal loss. This is even more likely to happen if the brain has previously suffered an insult from anoxia, trauma, exogenous toxins, or from the action of endogenous excitatory neurotransmitters such as glutamate (Reagan and McEwen, 1997), to name only a few possibilities. As discussed earlier, associations have been found between the occurrence of schizophrenia and very early brain insult.

The hypothalamic-pituitary-adrenal axis, which mediates the stress response, changes with pubertal development. Corticosterone receptors in the rat exhibit a peak at puberty and subsequently decline (Meaney, Sapolsky, and McEwen, 1985). In humans, there is a gradual increase in baseline levels of cortisol from childhood, with a marked increase during adolescence (Kiess, *et al.*, 1995). Some have reported a greater cortisol response in women, especially depressed women, than in men; other studies report higher levels of cortisol in postpubertal males (Young, 1995). High cortisol release has been associated with both social inhibition (Granger, Weisz, and Kauneckis, 1994) and social disinhibition in males (Bell, et al., 1993), as well as depression (Dabbs and Hopper, 1990). Preexisting response dispositions and pubertal stage may determine the specifics of the behavioral reaction to the stress (Stansbury and Gunnar 1994). In keeping with anthropological observations, males probably experience stress during the adolescent period differently than women, at different time points, and in response to different stressors. In males and females with schizophrenia, cortisol levels are elevated over normal (Walker and Diforio, 1997). In schizotypal personality disorder, which is considered part of the spectrum of schizophrenia and which may be a diagnosis marking the early stages of the illness, baseline cortisol levels are already elevated (Walker, et al., 1996).

Stressors may occur in the psychosocial or in the biological domain; infection, for instance, is a common potential stressor on a vulnerable brain. Several infectious agents, including herpes simplex and human immunodeficiency viruses, can infect neurons and produce schizophrenia-like symptoms. This observation, the winter birth excess described earlier, and the excess of schizophrenia births to mothers exposed to viral infections during their pregnancy have contributed to the hypothesis that complex viral-host interactions contribute to the etiology of schizophrenia. The speculation is that something reactivates a latent viral infection during periods of relative immunosuppression (Waltrip, Carrigan, and Carpenter, 1990). Study of the effects of sex hormones on a variety of immune functions suggests that, after puberty, women's immune response is more active than men's. Sex hormone receptors are found on T cells, B cells, and mononuclear macrophages, all critical constituents of the immune system (Athreya, Rettig, and Williams, 1998; Bijlsma, et al., 1999; Friedman and Waksman, 1997; Gaillard and Spinedi, 1998). The male hormone, testosterone, appears to have an immunosuppressive effect (Kanda, Truchida, and Tamaki, 1996; Paavonen, 1994; Cutolo, et al., 1995; Zuk, 1996). Although no direct evidence exists, the postpubertal emergence of schizophrenia symptoms during a time of relative immunosuppression in men may thus reflect a reactivation of latent viral infection acquired early in life, perhaps during gestation.

**Estrogens exert central nervous system protection**

All hormones are known to interact in the body, therefore, one cannot attribute neuronal protection to the action of one hormone alone. For simplicity, however, this chapter focuses on the potentially protective role of estrogen. Estrogens can exert protective actions on neurons in many ways. Whether these protective capabilities come into play or not depends on developmental (i.e., maturational stage) factors, interactive (host-environment) factors, and tissue-specific factors. Tissue-specific means that protection may exist for some brain cells and not for others. Estrogens act through intracellular receptors directly on the DNA of specific cells, thus altering their functions. Such genomic effects have delayed onset and prolonged duration.

Estrogens also act directly through membrane receptors; such nongenomic action is rapid and transient. Indirect action of estrogens, via cells that do not themselves exhibit steroid receptors, may occur by the estrogen-facilitated release or inhibition of neurotransmitters on neighbouring cells (for a recent review, see McEwen and Alves, 1999). Under specific conditions and in specific tissues, estrogens have been found to increase neuron survival and facilitate neurite outgrowth. They have been shown to protect against oxidative damage to neurons and against amyloid toxicity, glucose deprivation, and glutamate toxicity, and to also inhibit programmed cell death (apoptosis). Estrogens influence serotonin, acetylcholine, noradrenaline, and dopamine transmission, sometimes via membrane effects, sometimes via transsynaptic regulation of adjacent neurons, and sometimes via genomic effects. The effects on the dopamine system (a system strongly implicated in schizophrenia) are complex; low doses stimulate dopamine release and enhance dopamine binding to its receptor, higher doses exert a net antidopaminergic effect. It is important to note that most of the effects described have been observed in laboratory experiments with rodents. The assumption that the same mechanisms operate in humans remains, for the most part, to be tested.

Estrogens increase synaptic connections in the hippocampus and promote the formation of new neurons in the hippocampal dentate gyrus during adulthood. They protect against brain damage secondary to glucocorticoid release in response to stress, ischemia, and traumatic lesions. They act on glial cells to increase their plasticity and on endothelial cells of blood vessels to facilitate glucose uptake and transport. In this way, they exert an important influence on energy metabolism in the brain and on the functionality of the blood-brain barrier (McEwen and Alves, 1999).

Intracellular estrogen receptors, both estrogen-receptor alpha and estrogen-receptor beta, are present in many areas of the adult brain putatively involved in schizophrenia (i.e., hippocampus, cortex, and amygdala). They are present in males and females, but are distributed differently. The same brain tissue may respond differently in the two sexes to the same hormone, probably because of priming or organizational effects that have taken place during early, critical periods of brain development.

## Estrogen and schizophrenia

We decided to examine the estrogen-protection hypothesis as it might apply to schizophrenia, by exploring the relationship between pubertal events and schizophrenia onset in women and in men. We predicted that the onset of schizophrenia symptoms in women would be negatively correlated with time at onset of puberty (i.e., menarche). In other words, the earlier menarche occurs, the earlier high estrogen levels could exert their positive or protective effects on the developing brain and, thus, delay the onset of brain impairment.

We predicted that early puberty in men would not exert similarly protective effects; however, we were unsure what relationship to expect between pubertal events and schizophrenia onset in men. If the tempo of pubertal stages roughly correlates with the pace of brain development, earlier puberty should, without estrogen's protective effect, be associated with earlier brain maturity and, therefore, with earlier schizophrenia onset. This suggests a positive association between puberty and schizophrenia onset. On the other hand, early adrenarche and puberty may be protective in boys as well as in girls; adrenals produce estrogens and about 1 percent of androgens produced in adrenals and testes are aromatized to estrogens within neural cells. Thus, one would predict a negative association between markers of age at puberty and age at schizophrenia onset that is similar, albeit weaker, to the one predicted for women.

The foregoing notwithstanding, some research has associated testosterone levels with forms of aggression such as impulsivity, antisocial behavior, risk-taking, head trauma, and substance abuse. All of these may trigger psychosis directly or may lead to rebellion, social alienation, isolation, and loss of social support, factors that indirectly contribute to speeding the onset of psychotic symptoms. The testosterone–aggression connection is a complex and controversial one, first "proven" in 1849 by Berthold, who transplanted rooster testes into capons whereupon the capons "crowed lustily, often engaged in battle with each other and the other cockerels." This association, however, is much disputed (Campbell, Muncer, and Odber, 1997; Dabbs, *et al.*, 1995; Mazur and Booth, 1998; Tremblay, *et al.*, 1998). These observations, taken together, left us unsure as to what hypothesis to make about an association between puberty and schizophrenia onset in males.

## Methods

*Participants*

Males and females with DSM-IV diagnoses of schizophrenia or schizoaffective disorder took part in the study. Thirty-five females and 45 males within ten years of their first diagnosis provided written informed consent to take part. Of these eighty, 24 females (68.6%) and 33 males (73.3%) had a mother willing to participate and allowed us to contact her. The Centre for Addiction and Mental Health, Clarke Division, Toronto, was the recruitment site for most participants. Diagnoses made by experienced clinicians following case conferences were confirmed by DTREE, a computer-assisted diagnostic algorithm (First, Williams, and Spitzer, 1997).

*Measures and procedure*

Our aim was to establish each participant's age at onset of schizophrenia and age at onset of puberty. Since both schizophrenia and puberty evolve over several years, we needed to identify events that would serve as proxy time points for these constructs. We also wanted to measure possible confounding variables, which could bring forward or delay schizophrenia onset, regardless of hormonal influence. These included family history of schizophrenia, obstetric complication, head injury, and alcohol and/or other psychoactive drug use. Each onset date was established following an interview with the patient, an interview with the mother, and a review of the psychiatric record.

To determine puberty onset we used the Maturational Timing Questionnaire (MTQ; Gilger, Geary, and Eisele, 1991), a seven-item scale. We defined first menstrual period as puberty onset in women because of its ease of recall (Casey, *et al.*, 1991; Koo and Rohan, 1997), although we recognize that it is a relatively late pubertal event. We used voice change as the equivalent pubertal event in men, because in 80 percent of instances there was concordance between mother and son on the timing of this event. Concordance for other male puberty milestones was far lower.

To establish schizophrenia onset, we used the Interview for the Retrospective Assessment of the Onset of Schizophrenia (IRAOS, for onset). With the help of this semistructured interview, we delineated three separate onsets: age at first odd behavior, age at first psychotic symptoms, and age at first psychiatric hospitalization. The IRAOS is based on the Present State Examination and the International Classification of Disorders and has been adapted to DSM-IV. It is built around memorable events (summer vacations, specific school events, etc.), which help date the beginning of various signs and symptoms of schizophrenia or its prodrome. The IRAOS's developers have shown interrater reliability of 77–97 percent (Häfner, *et al.*, 1992; Maurer and Häfner, 1995).

We interviewed the patient and the patient's mother separately using the IRAOS. When they did not agree on time points, we had agreed beforehand that the mother's word would win out when it came to age at first odd behavior, since behavior is most objectively assessed by someone other than oneself. The patient's estimate won out over the mother's when it came to defining the onset of the first psychotic symptom, since only the person experiencing it can be sure (Hambrecht and Häfner, 1997). In fact, since we were asking about the age in years (a twelve-month range) at which these changes took place, there was very little disagreement between the two informants.

For family history, we used the Family History Questionnaire, based on the Research Diagnostic Criteria (RDC) Family History Schedule for Psychiatric Disorder in First-Degree Relatives (Endicott and Spitzer, 1978), administered to the mother, or, if she were unavailable, to the patient. We scored presence of family history as "zero" if there were none, "one" if it were suspected, and, "two" if it were definitely present. For obstetric complications, we used the Obstetric Complication Scale (Lewis, Owen, and Murray, 1989), which includes seventeen items addressing the prenatal, perinatal, and postnatal period. Administered to mothers, it produced scores of "zero" for no complications, "one" for one or more equivocal but not definite complications, and "two" for one or more definite complications. We asked about head injury severe enough to lead to a loss of consciousness and occurring before the first psychotic symptom; we scored head injury as present or absent.

For substance use, we used the IRAOS (for substance use), which is a semistructured interview developed to assess retrospectively the onset age, frequency, and persistence of psychoactive drug and alcohol use (Hambrecht and Häfner, 1996). We scored only patients who used drugs and/or alcohol before the onset of any psychotic symptom, and we scored the severity of use on a seven-point scale. In cases of discrepancy between patient and mother, we gave the participant's report greater weight.

As shown in table 9.1, for each definition of schizophrenia onset, as expected, men were younger than women. The differences were statistically significant for age at first psychotic symptoms ($t(78) = 3.22$, $p < .010$) and age at first psychiatric hospital admission ($t(78) = 3.56$, $p < .001$). Women were younger than men at puberty onset ($t(78) = 5.36$, $p < .001$), which we expected. Another expected finding was that men

Table 9.1. *Descriptive statistics and associations: females versus males*

| | Scores | | | | Correlation with puberty onset | |
|---|---|---|---|---|---|---|
| | Females | | Males | | Females | Males |
| Measure | Mean | SD | Mean | SD | [r] | [r] |
| Puberty onset (age yrs) | 12.7 | 1.3 | 14.5 | 1.6 | | |
| Odd behavior (age yrs) | 19.9 | 5.9 | 18.6 | 5.9 | −0.31 | 0.18 |
| Psychotic symptoms (age yrs) | 26.7 | 6.8 | 22.4 | 5.1 | −0.55* | 0.11 |
| Hospital admission (age yrs) | 29.0 | 6.9 | 24.2 | 5.0 | −0.57* | 0.26 |

*Notes:* females $n = 35$; males $n = 45$; *$p < .01$

used more alcohol and drugs than women ($t(76) = 2.01, p < .05$). None of the other variables distinguished men and women.

Table 9.1 also shows the zero-order correlations among the schizophrenia and puberty onset measures. Two of the onset age definitions for schizophrenia were negatively associated with age at puberty in women: age at first psychotic symptoms and age at first hospitalization. The corresponding correlations for males were in the opposite direction, but not statistically significant. For each pair, the correlations between age at schizophrenia onset and age at puberty for males and females are significantly different. Figure 9.1 displays the relationship between one onset definition, age at first psychotic symptoms, and age at puberty for females and for males. Regression lines display the negative relationship for females, while for males the relationship is much weaker and in the opposite direction. As assessed by means of partial correlations, none of the additional variables, alcohol or substance use, family history, head injury, or obstetric complications accounted for the relationships observed.

We concluded from the study, recognizing its many limitations, that something about early puberty in women delayed the onset of frank psychotic symptoms, whereas early puberty in men did not work in the same way. Since researchers generally think schizophrenia to be a developmental process, one prediction could have been that early puberty in both sexes, being an index of relatively rapid development, would be associated with an early onset of psychotic symptoms. Though not statistically significant, the association observed for men suggests this theoretically logical association; however, the results in women contradict it and are interesting for that reason. In line with the estrogen hypothesis, we suggest that the early arrival of menarche brings sufficient titres of estrogen on

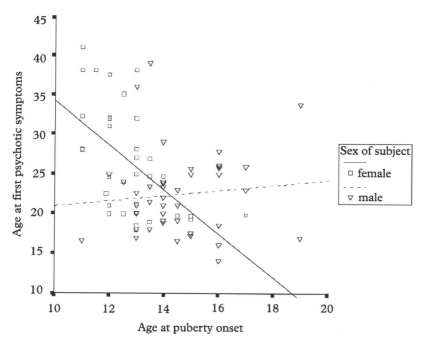

Figure 9.1 Comparison of the relationship between age first psychotic symptoms and puberty onset for females and males

board to buffer whatever neuronal toxicity is operative during this stage of evolution of the schizophrenia process.

Comparatively early puberty in women means more than higher levels of estrogens. Several studies have shown, for example, a positive association between age at menarche and young women's predisposition to anxiety and depression (Angold, Costello, and Worthman, 1998; Cyranowski, et al., 2000; see also chapter 12). Researchers have advanced many hypotheses to account for this association; some explanations focus on psychosocial factors (see chapter 13). Since girls reach puberty earlier than boys, early-maturing girls are off-time for both their same- and opposite-gender age mates (see chapters 7 and 12). Thus, without the resources of same-age peers, they are exposed to a social world of older people – including, for example, the sexual interest of older males – for which they may be unprepared (see chapter 10). Some have advanced hormonally based explanations for this association (Angold, et al., 1999; see also chapter 8). Early puberty in girls is associated with diminished body image (Moffitt, Belsky, and Silva, 1992); this may be associated with depression (see chapter 4). Some have even reversed the usually assumed causal direction to suggest that depression and/or anxiety may themselves cause early puberty (Moffitt, Belsky, and Silva, 1992; see also chapters 10 and 11). Whatever the cause and direction of causation, overall, early puberty appears to be a risk factor for various manifestations of psychopathology in young women (see chapter 12). Paradoxically, early menarche protects women, at least temporarily, from schizophrenia, and this temporary protection is important. Delayed onset is associated with superior outcome after an initial episode of illness: better symptom resolution, higher social and occupational functioning, and lesser likelihood of relapse. In other words, the association between early puberty and later schizophrenia onset informs not only theory about the etiology of schizophrenia, but also points to possible ways of delaying onset and improving outcome. For these reasons, examining the world of young men and young women during the pubertal years is important.

## References

Andia, A. M., and Zisook, S. (1991). Gender differences in schizophrenia: a literature review. *Annals of Clinical Psychiatry*, **3**, 333–340.

Angermeyer, M. C., Kuhn, L., and Goldstein, J. M. (1990). Gender and the course of schizophrenia: differences in treated outcomes. *Schizophrenia Bulletin*, **16**, 293–307.

Angold, A., Costello, E. J., Erkanli, A., and Worthman, C. M. (1999). Pubertal changes in hormone levels and depression in girls. *Psychological Medicine*, **29**, 1043–1053.

Angold, A., Costello, E. J., and Worthman, C. M. (1998). Puberty and depression: the roles of age, pubertal status and pubertal timing. *Psychological Medicine*, **28**, 51–61.

Arnett, J. J. (2000). Adolescent storm and stress, reconsidered. *American Psychologist*, **54**, 317–326.

Athreya, B. H., Rettig, P., and Williams, W. V. (1998). Hypophyseal-pituitary-adrenal axis in autoimmune and rheumatic diseases. *Immunology Research*, **18**, 93–102.

Beauregard, M., Malkova, L., and Bachevalier, J. (1991). Is schizophrenia a result of early damage to the hippocampal formation? A behavioral study on primates. *Society Neuroscience Abstracts*, **364**, 1.

Bell, I. R., Martino, G. M., Meredith, K. E., Schwartz, G. E., Siani, M. M., and Morrow, F. D. (1993). Vascular disease risk factors, urinary free cortisol, and health histories in older adults: shyness and gender interactions. *Biological Psychology*, **35**, 37–49.

Benes, F. M. (1989). Myelination of cortical-hippocampal relays during late adolescence. *Schizophrenia Bulletin*, **15**, 585–593.

Bijlsma, J. W., Cutolo, M., Masi, A. T., and Chikanza, I. C. (1999). The neuroendocrine immune basis of rheumatic diseases. *Immunology Today*, **20**, 298–301.

Brixley, S. N., Gallagher, B. J., McFalls, J. A., and Parmelee, L. F. (1993). Gestational and neonatal factors in the etiology of schizophrenia. *Journal of Clinical Psychology*, **49**, 447–456.

Cadenhead, K. S., Light, G. A., Geyer, M. A., and Braff, D. L. (2000). Sensory gating deficits assessed by the P50 event-related potential in subjects with schizotypal personality disorder. *American Journal of Psychiatry*, **157**, 55–59.

Campbell, A., Muncer, S., and Odber, J. (1997). Aggression and testosterone: testing a bio-social model. *Aggressive Behavior*, **23**, 229–238.

Casey, V. A., Dwyer, J. T., Coleman, K. A., Krall, E. A., Gardner, J., and Valadian, I. (1991). Accuracy of recall by middle-aged participants in a longitudinal study of their body size and indices of maturation earlier in life. *Annals of Human Biology*, **18**, 155–66.

Castle, D. J., and Murray, R. M. (1991). The neurodevelopmental basis of sex differences in schizophrenia. *Psychological Medicine*, **21**, 565–575.

Castle, D. J., and Murray, R. M. (1993). The epidemiology of late-onset schizophrenia. *Schizophrenia Bulletin*, **19**, 691–700.

Castle, D. J., Abel, K., Takei, N., and Murray, R. M. (1995). Gender differences in schizophrenia: hormonal effects or subtypes? *Schizophrenia Bulletin*, **21**, 1–12.

Cutolo, M., Sulli, A., Barone, A., Scriolo, B., and Accardo, S. (1995). The role of androgens in the pathophysiology of rheumatoid arthritis. *Fundamental and Clinical Immunology*, **3**, 9–18.

Cyranowski, J. M., Frank, E., Young, E., and Shear, M. K. (2000). Adolescent onset of the gender difference in lifetime rates of major depression. *Archives of General Psychiatry*, **57**, 21–27.

Dabbs, J. M., and Hopper, C. H. (1990). Cortisol, arousal, and personality in two groups of normal men. *Personality and Individual Differences*, **11**, 931–935.

Dabbs, J. M., Carr, S., Frady, R., and Riad, J. (1995). Testosterone, crime, and misbehavior among 692 male prison inmates. *Personality and Individual Differences*, **18**, 627–633.

Davidson, M., Reichenberg, A., Rabinowitz, J., Weiser, M., Kaplan, Z., and Mark, M. (1999). Behavioral and intellectual markers for schizophrenia in apparently healthy male adolescents. *American Journal of Psychiatry*, **156**, 1328–1335.

Dorn, L. D., and Chrousos, G. P. (1997). The neurobiology of stress: understanding regulation of affect during female biological transitions. *Seminars in Reproductive Endocrinology*, **15**, 19–35.

Eaton, W. W. (1991). Update on the epidemiology of schizophrenia. *Epidemiology Review*, **13**, 320–328.

Ellenbroek, B. A., van den Kroonenberg, P. T., and Cools, A. R. (1998). The effects of an early stressful life event on sensorimotor gating in adult rats. *Schizophrenia Research*, **30**, 251–260.

Endicott, J., and Spitzer, R. L. (1978). A diagnostic interview: the schedule for affective disorders and schizophrenia. *Archives of General Psychiatry*, **35**, 837–844.

First, M. B., Williams, J. B. W., and Spitzer, R. L. (1997). *DTREE for Windows: the DSM IV expert computer program*. Toronto: Multi Health Systems.

Foerster, A., Lewis, S. W., Owen, M. J., and Murray, R. M. (1991). Pre-morbid adjustment and personality in psychosis: effects of sex and diagnosis. *British Journal of Psychiatry*, **158**, 171–176.

Frazier, J. A., Alaghband-Rad, J., Jacobsen, L., Lenane, M. C., Hamburger, S., Albus, K., Smith, A., McKenna, K., and Rapoport, J. L. (1997). Pubertal development and onset of psychosis in childhood onset schizophrenia. *Psychiatry Research*, **70**, 1–7.

Friedman, A., and Waksman, Y. (1997). Sex hormones and autoimmunity. *Israeli Journal of Medical Science*, **33**, 254–257.

Gaillard, R. C., and Spinedi, E. (1998). Sex- and stress-steroid interactions and the immune system: evidence for a neuroendocrine-immunological sexual dimorphism. *Domestic Animal Endocrinology*, **15**, 345–352.

Galdos, P. M., Van Os, J. J., and Murray, R. M. (1993). Puberty and the onset of psychosis. *Schizophrenia Research*, **10**, 7–14.

Gilger, J. W., Geary, D. C., and Eisele, L. M. (1991) Reliability and validity of retrospective self-reports of the age of pubertal onset using twin, sibling, and college student data. *Adolescence*, **26**, 41–53.

Goldman, P. S., and Alexander, G. E. (1977). Maturation of prefrontal cortex in the monkey revealed by local reversible cryogenic depression. *Nature*, **267**, 613–615.

Goldstein, J. M. (1988). Gender differences in the course of schizophrenia. *American Journal of Psychiatry*, **145**, 684–689.

Granger, D. A., Weisz, J. R., and Kauneckis, D. (1994). Neuroendocrine reactivity, internalizing behavior problems, and control-related cognitions in clinic-referred children and adolescents. *Journal of Abnormal Psychology*, **103**, 259–266.

Häfner, H., an der Heiden, W., Behrens, S., Gattaz, W. F., Hambrecht, M., Löffler, W., Maurer, K., Munk-Jorgensen, P., Nowotny, B., Riecher-Rössler A., and Stein, A. (1998). Causes and consequences of the gender difference in age at onset of schizophrenia. *Schizophrenia Bulletin*, **24**, 99–113.

Häfner, H., Maurer, K., Löffler, W., and Riecher-Rössler, A. (1993). The influence of age and sex on the onset and early course of schizophrenia. *British Journal of Psychiatry*, **162**, 80–86.

Häfner, H., Riecher-Rössler, A., Fatkenheuer, B., Maurer, K., Meissner, S., Löffler, W., and Patton, G. (1992). Interview for the retrospective assessment of the onset of schizophrenia (IRAOS). *Schizophrenia Research*, **6**, 209–223.

Hambrecht, M., and Häfner, H. (1996). Substance abuse and the onset of schizophrenia. *Biological Psychiatry*, **40**, 1155–1163.

Hambrecht, M., and Häfner, H. (1997). Sensitivity and specificity of relatives' reports on the early course of schizophrenia. *Psychopathology*, **30**, 12–19.

Harrison, G., Croudace, T., Mason, P., Glazebrook, C., and Medley, I. (1996). Predicting the long-term outcome of schizophrenia. *Psychological Medicine*, **26**, 697–705.

Hayward, C., Killen, J. D., Wilson, D. M., Hammer, L. D., Litt, I., Kraemer, H. C., Haydel, F., Varady, A., and Taylor, C. B. (1997). Psychiatric risk associated with early puberty in adolescent girls. *Journal of the American Academy of Child and Adolescent Psychiatry*, **36**, 255–262.

Hollister, J. M., Laing, P., and Mednick, S. A. (1996). Rhesus incompatibility as a risk factor for schizophrenia in male adults. *Archives of General Psychiatry*, **53**, 19–24.

Howard, R., Almeida, O., and Levy, R. (1994). Phenomenology, demography and diagnosis in late paraphrenia. *Psychological Medicine*, **24**, 397–410.

Huttenlocher, P. R. (1984) Synapses: elimination and plasticity in developing human cerebral cortex. *American Journal of Mental Deficiency*, **88**, 488–496.

Jablensky, A. (1995). Schizophrenia: the epidemiological horizon. In S. R. Hirsch and D. R. Weinberger (ed.), *Schizophrenia* (pp. 206–252). Oxford: Blackwell Scientific.

Jonsson, H., and Nyman, A. K. (1991). Predicting long-term outcome in schizophrenia. *Acta Psychiatrica Scandinavica*, **83**, 342–346.

Kanda, N., Tsuchida, T., and Tamaki, K. (1996). Testosterone inhibits immunoglobulin production by human peripheral blood mononuclear cells. *Clinical and Experimental Immunology*, **106**, 410–415.

Kiess, W., Meidert, A., Dressendorfer, R. A., Schriever, K., Kessler, U., Konig, A., Schwarz, H. D., and Strasburger, C. J. (1995). Salivary cortisol levels throughout childhood and adolescence: relation with age, pubertal stage and weight. *Pediatric Research*, **37**, 502–506.

Koo, M. M., and Rohan, T. E. (1997). Accuracy of short-term recall of age at menarche. *Annals of Human Biology*, **24**, 61–64.

Kunugi, H., Nanko, S., Takei, N., Saito, K., Murray, R. M., and Hirose, T. (1996). Perinatal complications and schizophrenia: data from the maternal and child health handbook in Japan. *Journal of Nervous and Mental Disorder*, **184**, 542–546.

Leff, J. P., and Vaughn, C. E. (1981). The role of maintenance therapy and relatives' expressed emotion in relapse of schizophrenia: a two-year follow-up. *British Journal of Psychiatry*, **139**, 102–104.

Leff, J., and Vaughn, C. E. (1989). The interaction of life events and relatives' expressed emotion in schizophrenia and depressive neurosis. In T. W. Miller (ed.), *Stressful life events* (pp. 377–391). Madison, CT: International Universities Press.

Leff, J., Sartorius, N., Jablensky, A., Korten, A., and Emberg, G. (1992). The International Pilot Study of Schizophrenia: five-year follow-up findings. *Psychological Medicine*, **22**, 131–145.

Lewis, S. W., Owen, M. J., and Murray, R. M. (1989). Obstetric complications and schizophrenia. In S. C. Schulz and C. A. Tamminga (ed.), *Methodology and mechanism in schizophrenia: scientific progress*. Oxford: Oxford University Press.

Liddle, P. F. (1999). The multidimensional phenotype of schizophrenia. In C. A. Tamminga (ed.), *Schizophrenia in a molecular age*. Washington, DC: American Psychiatric Press.

Lipska, B. K., and Weinberger, D. R. (1993a). Cortical regulation of the mesolimbic dopamine system: implications for schizophrenia. In P. W. Kalivas (ed.), *The mesolimbic motor circuit and its role in neuropsychiatric disorders* (pp. 329–349). Boca Raton, FL: CRC Press.

Lipska, B. K., and Weinberger, D. R. (1993b). Delayed effects of neonatal hippocampal damage on the haloperidol-induced catalepsy and apomorphine-induced stereotypic behaviors in the rat. *Developmental Brain Research*, 75, 213–222.

Lipska, B. K., and Weinberger, D. R. (1995). Genetic variation in vulnerability to the behavioral effects of neonatal hippocampal damage in rats. *Proceedings of the National Academy of Science, USA*, 92, 8906–8910.

Lipska, B. K., Jaskiw, G. E., and Weinberger, D. R. (1993). Postpubertal emergence of hyper-responsiveness to stress and to amphetamine after neonatal excitotoxic hippocampal damage: a potential animal model of schizophrenia. *Neuropsychopharmacology*, 9, 67–75.

Maurer, K., and Häfner, H. (1995). Methodological aspects of onset assessment in schizophrenia. *Schizophrenia Research*, 15, 265–276.

Mazur A., and Booth, A. (1998). Testosterone and dominance in men. *Behavioral and Brain Sciences*, 21, 353–397.

McEwen, B. S., and Alves, S. E. (1999). Estrogen actions in the central nervous system. *Endocrine Reviews*, 20, 279–307.

McGlashan, T. H., and Bardenstein, K. K. (1990). Gender differences in affective, schizoaffective, and schizophrenic disorders. *Schizophrenia Bulletin*, 16, 319–329.

McGrath, J. J., Pemberton, M. R., Welham, J. L., and Murray, R. M. (1994). Schizophrenia and the influenza epidemics of 1954, 1957 and 1959: a southern hemisphere study. *Schizophrenia Research*, 14, 1–8.

Meaney, M. J., Sapolsky, R. M., and McEwen, B. S. (1985). The development of the glucocorticoid receptor system in the rat limbic brain. I: ontogeny and autoregulation. *Developmental Brain Research*, 18, 159–164.

Mednick, S. A., and Hollister, J. M. (1995). *Neural development and schizophrenia: theory and research*. New York: Plenum.

Moffit, T. E., Belsky, J., and Silva, P. A. (1992). Childhood experience and the onset of menarche: a test of a sociobiological model. *Child Development*, 63, 47–58.

Mueser, K. T., Yarnold, P. R., and Bellack, A. S. (1992). Diagnostic and demographic correlates of substance abuse in schizophrenia and major affective disorder. *Acta Psychiatrica Scandinavica*, 85, 48–55.

Mueser, K. T., Yarnold, P. R., Levinson, D. F., Singh, H., Bellack, A. S., Kee, K., Morrison, R. L., and Yadalam, K. G. (1990). Prevalence of substance abuse in schizophrenia: demographic and clinical correlates. *Schizophrenia Bulletin*, 16, 31–56.

Norman, R. M., and Malla, A. K. (1993). Stressful life events and schizophrenia. I: a review of the research. *British Journal of Psychiatry*, 162, 161–166.

O'Connell, P., Woodruff, P. W. R., Wright, I., Jones, P., and Murray, R. M. (1997). Developmental insanity or dementia praecox: was the wrong concept adopted? *Schizophrenia Research*, 23, 97–106.

Opjordsmoen, S. (1991). Long-term clinical outcome of schizophrenia with special reference to gender differences. *Acta Psychiatrica Scandinavica*, 83, 307–313.

Paavonen, T. (1994). Hormonal regulation of the immune response. *Annals of Medicine*, 26, 255–258.

Paikoff, R. L., and Brooks-Gunn, J. (1991). Do parent–child relationships change during puberty? *Psychological Bulletin*, 110, 47–66.

Perry, W., Geyer, M. A., and Braff, D. (1999). Sensorimotor gating and thought disturbance measured in close temporal proximity in schizophrenic patients. *Archives of General Psychiatry*, 56, 277–281.

Reagan, L. P., and McEwen, B. S. (1997). Controversies surrounding glucocorticoid-mediated cell death in the hippocampus. *Journal of Chemical Neuroanatomy*, 13, 149–167.

Sachser, N., Durchlag, M., and Hirzel, D. (1998). Social relationships and the management of stress. *Psychoneuroimmunology*, 23, 891–904.

Saugstad, L. F. (1989). Mental illness and cognition in relation to age at puberty: a hypothesis. *Clinical Genetics*, 36, 156–167.

Saugstad, L. F. (1994). The maturational theory of brain development and cerebral excitability in the multifactorially inherited manic-depressive psychosis and schizophrenia. *International Journal of Psychophysiology*, 18, 189–203.

Schlegel, A., and Barry, H. (1991). *Adolescence: an anthropological inquiry*. New York: Free Press.

Seeman, M. V., and Lang, M. (1990). The role of estrogens in schizophrenia gender differences. *Schizophrenia Bulletin*, 16, 185–194.

Shtasel, D. L., Gur, R. E., Gallacher, F., Heimber, C., and Gur, R. C. (1992). Gender differences in the clinical expression of schizophrenia. *Schizophrenia Research*, 7, 225–231.

Stansbury, K., and Gunnar, M. R. (1994). Adrenocortical activity and emotion regulation. *Monographs of the Society for Research in Child Development*, 59, 108–134.

Susser, E., Neugebauer, R., Hoek, H. W., Brown, A. S., Lin, S., Labovitz, D., and Gorman, J. M. (1996). Schizophrenia after prenatal famine. *Archives of General Psychiatry*, 53, 25–31.

Tremblay, R. E., Schaal, B., Boulerice, B., Arsenealt, L., Soussignan, R. G., Paquette, D., and Laurent, D. (1998). Testosterone, physical aggression, dominance, and physical development in early adolescence. *International Journal of Behavioral Development*, 22, 753–777.

Vaughn, C. E. (1989). Expressed emotion in family relationships. *Journal of Child Psychology and Psychiatry and Allied Disciplines*, 30, 13–22.

Walker, E. F., and Diforio, D. (1997). Schizophrenia: a neural diathesis-stress model. *Psychological Review*, 104, 667–685.

Walker, E. F., Neumann, C., Baum, K., and Davis, D. M. (1996). The developmental pathways to schizophrenia: potential moderating effects of stress. *Development and Psychopathology*, 8, 647–665.

Walker, E. F., Neumann, C., Baum, K. M., Davis, D., Diforio, D., and Bergman, A. (1996). Developmental pathways to schizophrenia. Moderating effects of stress. *Development and Psychopathology*, 8, 647–665.

Waltrip, R. W., Carrigan, D. R., and Carpenter, W. T. (1990). Immunopathology and viral reactivation. A general theory of schizophrenia. *Journal of Nervous and Mental Disease*, 178, 729–738.

Warner, R., and de Girolamo, G. (1995). *Schizophrenia*. Geneva: World Health Organization.

Weinberger, D. R. (1987). Implications of normal brain development for the pathogenesis of schizophrenia. *Archives of General Psychiatry*, **44**, 660–669.

Welham, J. L., Pemberton, M. R., and McGrath J. J. (1996). Incorporating lag effects in register-based age-of-onset distributions in schizophrenia. *Schizophrenia Research*, **20**, 125–132.

Young, E. A. (1995). The role of gonadal steroids in hypothalamic–pituitary–adrenal axis regulation. *Critical Reviews in Neurobiology*, **9**, 371–380.

Zuk, M. (1996). Disease, endocrine-immune interactions, and sexual selection. *Ecology*, **77**, 1037–1042.

*Part 5*

# Pubertal timing: antecedents

# 10 Childhood sexual abuse and pubertal timing: implications for long-term psychosocial adjustment

*Tanya A. Bergevin, William M. Bukowski, and Leigh Karavasilis*

Although puberty is a normative event that is experienced by virtually every adolescent, the experience of puberty varies widely across individuals. As other chapters in this volume clearly show, puberty varies according to several basic dimensions, including when it happens, how quickly it happens, and so on. In this chapter we consider variations in pubertal timing as a function of a prior form of experience, specifically that of sexual abuse. Our goals are as follows: first, to introduce the topic of sexual abuse and to explore how sexually abusive experiences predict early pubertal timing; second, using an integrated bio-psycho-social perspective, to discuss how early entry into puberty may, especially for girls, exacerbate the effects of sexual abuse and increase the risk of adverse outcomes in postpubescence; and finally, we present preliminary evidence linking childhood sexual victimization, pubertal timing, and adolescent maladjustment within intra- and interpersonal domains.

### What is sexual abuse?

The topic of sexual abuse has not been without its social and scientific controversies. Regarded as a relatively rare and innocuous event a half-century ago, the sexual abuse of children has reached the forefront of our collective awareness as a social problem of considerable proportion (Pilkington and Kremer, 1995). The first epidemiological studies of child sexual abuse (CSA) began in the 1920s; and research has long suggested that experiences of sexual victimization negatively impact a substantial number of children (Hamilton, 1929; Kinsey, *et al.*, 1953; Landis, *et al.*, 1940). Despite this, it was not until the mid 1970s, amidst a shifting sociopolitical landscape fueled largely by women's and victims' rights organizations, that the issue of CSA truly captured public attention (Myers, *et al.*, 1999). With nearly 7,000 papers published since 1977, the issue of CSA has become a central topic of research and discussion among social scientists, clinical practitioners, and educators alike (Oddone-Paolucci, Genius, and Violato, 2001).

As public interest intensified and the body of literature concerning childhood maltreatment rapidly expanded, so too did the more extreme perspectives regarding CSA. For example, conjectures suggesting that CSA was rampant, rarely erroneously or falsely alleged, and that it inevitably entailed devastating consequences for victims became commonplace. By the late 1980s extreme claims of this nature resulted in what some have called a "backlash" within the field (Ondersma, *et al.*, 2001). Shifting away from unearthing the "hidden problem" of CSA, public attention began to focus on issues surrounding false allegations, inflated incidence and prevalence rates, and the variability of outcomes following CSA, including the apparent absence of negative (i.e., problematic) symptoms among some survivors (Ondersma, *et al.*, 2001, p. 708).

These conflicts and controversies have been magnified by several challenges related to the scientific study of CSA. Researchers have been severely limited by important empirical inconsistencies, significant methodological shortcomings, and by research conclusions that are often stated more strongly than the actual data would indicate. At present, the major challenges associated with the study of childhood sexual maltreatment include: (1) reaching consensus on a clear operational definition of CSA; (2) determining accurate prevalence rates; and (3) disentangling CSA from other forms of childhood adversity. Until the latter goals are attained, disagreements concerning the study of CSA, and resulting implications for public policy, will undoubtedly continue to be hotly debated (for reviews, see Dallam, *et al.*, 2001; Demause, 1997; Rind, Tromovitch, and Bauserman, 1998, 2001).

One of the most important sources of variability across studies stems from the lack of a clear and consistent definition of CSA. The terms "child," "sex," and "abuse" represent social constructs that are shaped by often conflicting legal, cultural, and psychosocial considerations. Definitions of CSA are highly dependent on the context in which they are embedded. For example, it is often unclear whether 16- or 17-year-old teenagers should be conceptualized as children, and if perpetrators of abuse, by definition, need to be adults or even older than their victims. Similarly, it is unclear whether behaviors need to involve some form of coercion or direct contact in order to be considered sexually abusive. Generally speaking, sexual abuse has been defined as sexual interactions, manipulations, and/or coercions that may or may not involve direct contact between either (a) a nonadult who is incapable of giving informed consent, such as a child or an adolescent, and a dominant older individual, or (b) between two nonadults when coercion is employed (Abney and Priest,

1995; Rind and Tromovitch, 1997). According to the US Department of Health and Human Services National Center on Child Abuse and Neglect (1997), CSA also includes activities designed to entice a child for sexual purposes, the performance of sexual acts in the presence of a child, and the use of children in the creation or production of sexually explicit materials.

With definitions of CSA ranging from broad to narrow across studies, it has been nearly impossible to obtain precise prevalence rates. In addition to definitional problems, biased sampling techniques, such as relying on nonrepresentative clinical or college samples, have also contributed to widely discrepant prevalence rates (for a review, see Pilkington and Kremer, 1995). Even when broad-based community samples have been employed, problems associated with underreporting have also blurred the prevalence picture for some groups more than for others (e.g., males and certain ethnic groups), as well as for children who at the time of the abuse were too young to understand the nature and implications of their experiences (Kenny and McEachern, 2000; Romano and De Luca, 2001). Taken together, these factors explain why American population prevalence estimates of contact and/or noncontact sexual abuse experienced before the age of 18 range enormously from 11–62 percent for women, and 3–25 percent for men (for reviews, see Pilkington and Kremer, 1995; Salter, 1992).[1]

### An integrated psychophysiological perspective of childhood sexual abuse

Beyond simply defining CSA and estimating its prevalence, research has also focused on exploring the developmental repercussions of having been abused (Davis and Petretic-Jackson, 2000; Farley and Keaney, 1997; Fry, 1993; Neumann, et al., 1996; Jumper, 1995; Kendall-Tackett, Williams, and Finkelhor, 1993, 2001). Although the vast majority of CSA outcome studies have focused on the psychosocial repercussions of victimization, some authors have attempted to investigate the impact of CSA from an integrative psychophysiological perspective (Trickett and Putnam, 1993; Turner, Runtz, and Galambos, 1999). For example, Trickett and Putnam (1993) have advanced a set of proposals that, deeply rooted in established principles of child development, come together to build the argument that CSA not only interferes with psychological growth, but also interferes with physical growth and pubertal timing. Their psychophysiological perspective rests on two central premises: (1) CSA induces critical psychological stress prior to and during puberty; and (2) nonoptimal levels of psychological stress have attendant physiological repercussions for development, which result in early pubertal timing and accelerated sexual maturation. Before exploring these notions further, we must briefly review the role of stress in mediating pubertal timing.

### *The impact of stress on pubertal timing: a brief review*

Over the course of the last century, pubertal timing has evidenced an important decrease in most industrialized countries. Although some have attributed this phenomenon to overall improvements in general health care and nutrition (Tanner, 1990), others have pointed to increased stress associated with urbanization (Adams, 1981). The relation between stress and pubertal timing is complex and multidimensional, with cumulative research highlighting at least three general classes of stress (for reviews, see Ellis and Garber, 2000 and chapter 11 below). The first type of stress, referred to as ecological or physical stress, occurs under extreme conditions of physiological threat, such as those associated with severe malnutrition or disease. Evidence from human and animal models suggests that under such perilous conditions, finite energy reserves are allocated toward basic survival and maintenance needs, thereby inhibiting or delaying the costly process of reaching sexual maturation (Ellison, 1990; Olsson, *et al.*, 1999; Surbey, 1998).

In contrast to ecological stress, a second class of stress referred to as psychosocial stress is thought to expedite pubertal onset and accelerate sexual maturation. For instance, high levels of psychosocial stress evident in dysfunctional families characterized by poor cohesion, high parent–child conflict, and low parental investment may adaptively promote early sexual maturation in order to minimize the amount of time individuals spend in a "vulnerable juvenile state" (Surbey, 1998, p. 82). With a primary focus on girls, research has generally supported an inverse relationship between stressful family context and age of sexual maturation (Ellis and Garber, 2000; Ellis, *et al.*, 1999; Graber, Brooks-Gunn, and Warren, 1995; Moffitt, *et al.*, 1992; see also chapter 11). In a rare study contrasting the effects of different classes of stress, Hulanicka (1999) demonstrated that ecological stress (e.g., severe poverty) predicted later menarche, whereas psychosocial stress (e.g., father absence, parental alcohol abuse, and prolonged parent illness) predicted earlier menarche, despite the typically poorer ecological environments that accompany families characterized by psychosocial stress.

A third class of stress believed to affect pubertal timing is related to experiences of parental separation and/or a physical distancing from one's biological father. Compared to their counterparts from intact families, girls not living with biological fathers had earlier rates of sexual maturation (Kanazawa, 2001; Moffitt, *et al.*, 1992; Weirson, Long, and Forehand, 1993). Several hypotheses have been advanced to explain this phenomenon. One explanation is that father absence directly or indirectly leads to increased stress within the family unit, thus favoring early pubertal development. However, other explanations outside the stress paradigm are noteworthy. For example, it is also possible that, in the evolutionary service of preventing inbreeding, biological fathers exercise an inhibitory influence over female offspring's physical maturation (Hoogland, 1982; Lidicker, 1980).

In a somewhat related vein, recent evidence has suggested that it may be the positive aspects of paternal presence/investment that act to decelerate pubertal development in girls, rather than father absence per se, which acts to accelerate it (Ellis, *et al.*, 1999). Specifically, girls who experienced a warm and supportive relationship with their fathers were found to enter puberty later than others did. Finally, more biologically based accounts for the association between father-related factors and girls' pubertal timing stem from the conjecture that sexual maturation is hastened by pheromonal stimulation, which results from the likelihood of increased exposure to nonrelated adult males (i.e., stepfathers). Although further research is required to fully comprehend why this phenomenon occurs, existing empirical evidence for the association between psychosocial stress, father-related variables, and pubertal timing has important implications for the current discussion of CSA.

*Stressful family contexts: implications for childhood sexual abuse*

Although the current discussion is centrally premised on the notion that CSA functions as a stressor in its own right, it is also intricately connected to other types of adversities. Research reveals that childhood victimization occurs in highly stressed families characterized by parental unemployment, low income, poor education, and substance abuse (Newberger, *et al.*, 1986; Whipple and Webster-Stratton, 1991). According to the US Department of Health and Human Services National Center on Child Abuse and Neglect (1996), the highest incidence of CSA occurs in families with annual incomes of $15,000 or less. In fact, data suggest that the occurrence of CSA in these families is seventeen times more likely than in families with incomes averaging above $30,000 per year. With this said, it is important to note two cautionary points. First, conflicting and negative findings regarding the links between income and CSA have been recorded (Faller, 1989); second, it is quite possible that other factors related to lower social-economic status, such as having bleak expectations for the future, are more critically related to CSA than annual income per se.

It is clear, however, that incestual CSA occurs within dysfunctional family contexts (Alexander and Lupfer, 1987; for review, see Burke-Draucker, 1996, and Nash, *et al.*, 1993). Besides indices of intrafamilial dysfunction, victims also tend to grow up in families disadvantaged by poor access to resources and lower levels of extrafamilial social support. Even when CSA takes place outside the family unit, a similar picture emerges. For example, research indicates that boys raised by single mothers are at heightened risk of abuse than boys raised in dual-parent households (Watkins and Bentovim, 1992). Findings have been less consistent for girls, which stands to reason given that boys are typically abused outside the home by a nonrelative, whereas girls are more likely to be abused within the home by a father figure or family member (Kenny and McEachern, 2000; for review, see Romano and De Luca, 2001). Nevertheless, it seems reasonable to propose that a lower level of parental supervision and increased exposure to nonrelated adult males (e.g., mothers' romantic partners) may heighten the risk of CSA for both boys and girls.

To summarize thus far, different classes of stress, namely ecological, psychosocial, and divorce-related stress (i.e., characterized by biological-father absence/stepfather presence), have differential effects on pubertal timing. With research generally focusing on girls, psychosocial and divorce-related stressors have been linked to early pubertal timing. For some children, sexual abuse is experienced as a severe psychosocial stressor that negatively impacts their development over the short and long term (Bukowski, 1992; Finkelhor and Browne, 1985). Beyond this, CSA is likely to co-occur with other types of psychosocial adversities, which also moderate pubertal timing. Taken together, these propositions form the foundation for the contention that stress associated directly or indirectly with experiences of CSA will accelerate or hasten pubertal timing, especially in females. The sections that follow will discuss theory and evidence suggesting that, (1) CSA is a direct antecedent of early pubertal timing, and (2) that early puberty, in turn, may compound the long-term negative effects of CSA across development into postpubescence.

To this end, Belsky, Steinberg, and Draper's (1991) evolutionary theory of socialization will be outlined, as it provides a comprehensive framework for linking childhood psychosocial adversity to specific pre- and postpubertal developmental trajectories. Its integrated psychophysiological perspective, as well as its focus on developmental outcomes across adolescence and into adulthood, render it particularly propitious for discussing how CSA comes to accelerate pubertal timing, and also how early onset of puberty then acts to exacerbate the consequences of CSA in later life.

## Pre- and postpubertal outcomes of childhood adversity: an evolutionary perspective

Throughout their development, children learn about the availability and predictability of broadly defined environmental resources. They also learn about the reliability and trustworthiness of others, as well as the durability of close interpersonal relationships. Belsky and colleagues (1991) suggest that this information shapes developing beliefs and assumptions, adaptively preparing children for the environments that they will most likely encounter in adulthood. Differential availability of environmental resources shape two generally defined reproductive strategies. The first suggests that children reared in environments characterized by adequate resources and high parental warmth and sensitivity form secure attachments, reach sexual maturation and become sexually active later in their development, form longer-term pair bonds, and invest heavily in their offspring. Under conditions of contextual stress, however, parental care tends to be less sensitive, more inconsistent, and more affectively negative, which fosters more insecure attachments in children and more opportunistic styles of interaction with others. Increased internalizing and externalizing problems in prepubescence often ensue. Stressful rearing conditions and behavioral maladjustment are thought, in turn, to promote earlier pubertal maturation, earlier onset of sexual activity characterized by risky and opportunistic encounters, unstable pair bonds, and limited parental investment in the next generation.

Despite important criticisms on both theoretical and empirical grounds, and several alternative hypotheses that may, at least in part, account for such divergent developmental pathways (e.g., behavioral genetics, lifestyle factors), cumulative evidence has generally provided cautious support for the major tenets of Belsky and colleagues' (1991) model. Specifically, research indicates that psychosocial stress within the family, as measured by divorce/biological father absence, parent–child conflict, and parent–child emotional distance, accelerates sexual maturation in females and, to some extent, in males (Campbell and Udry, 1995; Ellis, 1991; Ellis, et al., 1999; Kim and Smith, 1998a, 1998b, 1999; Moffitt, et al., 1992; Surbey, 1990; Weirson, et al., 1993; see also chapter 11).

In contrast, fewer studies have considered the onset of puberty in relation to postpubertal reproductive behavior. Those that have, generally indicate that early maturers engage in dating earlier, have sex earlier, and generally give birth at an earlier age (Stattin and Magnusson, 1990; Udry and Cliquet, 1982). In direct relation to the propositions advanced by Belsky and colleagues (1991), Leek (1991) found that women who report early menarche relative to others, also report more negative and stressful childhood family experiences, an earlier age at first intercourse, and a greater number of sexual partners. These findings were further supported by Kim and Smith (1998a, 1998b, 1999), who suggested that early menarche is linked to increased family stress and parental conflict, early dating and sexual activity, and having a greater number of sexual partners.

Belsky and colleagues' (1991) model, however, remains controversial for a number of reasons; namely, for its provision of a single framework for understanding the psychophysiological trajectories of both boys and girls (Maccoby, 1991). Given the different types of reproductive challenges faced by males and females, it seems reasonable to assume that evolved environmental responses designed to increase reproductive fitness would differ across sex (Surbey, 1998). By providing a single unifying frame, the model fails to account for the evolution of sex-specific sensitivities within the highly sex-stratified domain of reproduction.

Understanding these often nebulous sex differences may help shed light on disparities in boys' and girls' psychophysiological reactions to psychosocial stress within the family context. Whereas some research has linked early spermarche to father absence, less emotional closeness to mother, more stress in quality of family life, as well as to earlier dating, younger age at first intercourse, and having more girlfriends (Kim and Smith, 1998b, 1999), others have reported incongruent findings. Malo and Tremblay (1997), for example, report that sons of alcoholic fathers experience a delay in pubertal timing relative to sons of nonalcoholics. Interestingly, though, sons of alcoholics had nevertheless experienced a greater number of sexual encounters, and reported a greater number of sexual partners than did other boys. In brief, besides elucidating how stress shapes and integrates psychological and physiological outcomes, Belsky and colleagues' (1991) model also provides the parameters to explore the impact of CSA within the specific context of pubertal development.

### Conceptualizing CSA as a direct predictor of pubertal timing

Despite the relatively voluminous literature investigating the short- and long-term effects of CSA, very little research has investigated the impact of CSA in direct relation to pubertal experiences. Among the only scholars to explore this relation, Trickett and Putnam (1993) have proposed several reasons why entry into puberty could be particularly distressing for victims of sexual abuse. First, puberty may recapitulate the trauma of abuse as adolescents struggle to come to terms with their sexual identity and with newly emerging sexual feelings and desires. A central task during adolescence is to achieve an integrated and unified sense of self, which through dynamics associated with abuse (e.g., traumatic sexualization, feelings of betrayal, powerlessness, and stigmatization) may be exceedingly difficult for survivors of CSA and, thereby, may compromise normal adolescent developmental processes (Finkelhor and Browne, 1985). Moreover, pubertal transitions may be particularly taxing for female survivors as a result of their more overt physiological manifestations of sexual maturation. Awareness of a public audience observing these potentially unwelcome physiological changes may heighten feelings of shame, while the inability to slow or stop these transformations may further promote feelings of powerlessness.

A second way that CSA may exacerbate potential difficulties for survivors at puberty is through damaging family relations and social support systems that may have otherwise buffered pubertal-related stress. At least for some adolescents, difficulties concomitant to puberty can be eased through support and acceptance from family and friends. Regardless of whether it occurred within or outside the parameters of the home, sexual abuse may compromise the developing individual's sense of basic trust, rendering him/her less likely to turn to others in times of distress, possibly promoting feelings of loneliness and rekindling earlier feelings of betrayal.

Finally, and of particular salience here, Trickett and Putnam (1993) also suggest that CSA may impact pubertal-related experiences by accelerating rates of sexual maturation and, hence, promoting early entry into puberty. They suggest that prepubertal sexual abuse can result in levels of psychosocial stress that alter the hormonal balance of a developing child, thereby triggering precocious physiological development. Interestingly, the authors also posit how these hormonal repercussions may, in part, help explain heightened levels of aggression and sexualization observed in some victims of CSA. Taken together, these processes may set the stage for a developmental trajectory that coincides with Belsky and colleagues' (1991) postpubertal predictions of early, risky sexuality, increased probability of early pregnancy, increased risk of unstable pair bonds, and ultimately, less skilled and invested parenting styles. With most observations being limited to clinical anecdotes, very few studies have empirically investigated, or even addressed, CSA as a possible predictor of accelerated pubertal timing. A study conducted by Herman-Giddens, Sandler, and Friedman (1988) was a rare exception to the rule. In examining a sample of 105 sexually abused girls, the authors have shown that female victims of CSA are approximately fifteen times more likely than others to experience the onset of puberty prior to age 8. Among abused girls, all precocious developers except for one had experienced more extreme forms of sexual abuse involving vaginal penetration. It has been suggested that more severe forms of abuse, such as those involving penetration, act as a powerful stressor that "in some way stimulates adrenal androgen secretion or early activation of the hypothalamic-pituitary axis," which results in hastened pubertal onset (p. 433).

In addition to this, it is also possible that prepubertal vaginal penetration may biochemically (e.g., via pheromones) act to sexualize the developing individual and activate physiological growth. Again, however, the correlational nature of the findings does not exclude the possibility of the inverse contingency, namely, that girls who show signs of early pubertal development are at an increased risk for sexual victimization. Given the sheer paucity of research exploring the connection between CSA and precocious puberty, it follows that, to date, directional relations remain largely speculative.

To our knowledge, the only other empirical investigation of the direct association between CSA and pubertal timing comes from Turner, Runtz, and Galambos (1999), who recruited twenty-two sexually abused girls from outpatient clinics and public high schools in western Canada, and matched them to controls based on age, current living situation, parental marital status, socioeconomic status, and family size. Official records including perpetrator information, available only for the twelve girls recruited from clinics, showed that eight of them, or 67 percent, had been victimized by fathers or father figures. Overall, for the entire sample the average age for onset of abuse was 8.6 years, with 42 percent of incidents involving forced intercourse and 36 percent of victims experiencing abuse from multiple perpetrators.

Using adapted versions of the Childhood Sexual Experiences Survey (Finkelhor, 1979), the Sexual Abuse Scale (DiTomasso and Routh, 1993), the Pubertal Development Scale (Petersen, *et al.*, 1988), and a measure of subjective age, Turner and colleagues (1999) revealed that sexually abused girls were more likely to experience early entry into puberty relative to their nonabused counterparts. Moreover, findings revealed that among the fourteen most precocious developers, eleven, or 79 percent, were identified as girls who had been sexually abused in prepubescence. Consistent with normative samples, the average age of menarche among nonabused girls was 12.5 years, while among abused girls it averaged 11.2 years of age – a difference of over one full year. Interestingly, the authors also demonstrated that a history of CSA positively predicted girls' subjective age, that is, their feelings of being significantly older than their nonabused age-mates. In fact, a history of CSA accounted for 13 percent of the variance in girls' assessments of their subjective age. Also noteworthy, main effects were not found for actual pubertal timing in predicting subjective age, nor were any interactions revealed among these variables.

Turner and colleagues' (1999) findings support the notion that, conceptualized as a stressor, CSA predicts pubertal acceleration and, thus, early sexual maturation. Findings that survivors also experience a higher subjective age may also shed light on how early puberty, especially among girls, can compound negative long-term consequences of CSA. Specifically, subjective age may represent an underlying mechanism that links a history of CSA to many of the postpubertal behavioral and psychological outcomes observed in victims. Before elaborating further, however, it is first important to address the above issues within the context of male CSA.

*Sexual abuse of boys*

There is clearly a relative deficiency in research focusing on the sexual abuse of males (Romano and De Luca, 2001; Violato and Genius, 1993; Watkins and Bentovim, 1992). Fueling this imbalance has been the social perspective that, at least in comparison to girls, the impact of sexual abuse on boys' development is relatively minimal, short-lived, and benign. Compounding these assumptions, and further deflecting empirical attention away from the study of male CSA, have been conjectures that the sexual abuse of boys is a relatively uncommon event. According to Romano and De Luca (2001), beliefs about the rarity of male CSA are the result of a serious underestimation in prevalence rates, which stem largely from males' general reluctance to report incidents and seek support following experiences of sexual victimization.

A number of factors may contribute to the problem of underreporting in male survivors. First, boys may feel increased pressure to remain silent because of the social ethics surrounding cultural ideals of male self-reliance. Males' social scripts may limit boys' opportunities to admit victimization and distress, hence, hampering their odds of reporting abuse and/or seeking support following their experiences. Second, because the vast majority of perpetrators are males, boys may have to deal with the additional social stigma associated with homosexuality, which may also act as a powerful deterrent. Third, because boys' sexual experiences typically involve more overt physiological reactions (e.g., erection, ejaculation), they may also be increasingly compelled to "own" the experience and, thus, be less likely to label it as victimization (Romano and De Luca, 2001). Finally, underreporting may also be attributable to perpetrator characteristics. Research suggests that relative to female victims, there tends to be a smaller age gap between male victims and their abusers (e.g., babysitters, neighbors), allowing incidents to be more easily minimized as inappropriate sex play (Finkelhor, *et al.*, 1990; Holmes, Offen, and Waller, 1997). Underreporting may also occur in situations involving female perpetrators. Contact between boys and women may not be considered as serious or traumatic due to generally positive societal views surrounding youthful male sexuality (Dhaliwal, *et al.*, 1996; Holmes, Offen, and Waller, 1997).

Despite these issues, empirical reviews have generally indicated that males' and females' responses to sexual abuse are, for the most part, rather equivalent (Finkelhor, 1990; Romano and De Luca, 2001). That is, although males display slightly higher rates of postabuse externalizing problems, while females tend to display higher rates of postabuse internalizing problems, the severity of resulting symptoms appears to be largely analogous. However, this being said, it is possible that sex differences in reactivity to CSA are confounded with the different features of abuse typically experienced by boys and girls. As previously stated, boys, for example, are likely to be abused outside the home while girls are likely to be abused within the family system (Kenny and McEachern, 2000). Because intrafamilial abuse is less likely to be discovered, it tends to occur over a longer period of time than extrafamilial abuse (Romano and De Luca, 2001). These features, combined with a heightened sense of betrayal that conceivably accompanies abuse by a family member, result in graver outcomes over the long term (Mendel, 1995; Crowder, 1995). Evidence also indicates that whereas girls are at heightened risk of being abused by multiple perpetrators, boys are more likely, overall, to experience direct contact abuse, to suffer concomitant physical abuse, and to experience a greater number of sexually abusive events (Finkelhor, *et al.*, 1990; Violato and Genius, 1993; Watkins and Bentovim, 1992). In brief, because longer-term abuse characterized by the use or threat of force, sexual penetration, and father-figure perpetration typically increases the severity of outcomes (Beitchman, *et al.*, 1992), drawing firm conclusions regarding sex differences in response to CSA without serious consideration of the latter dimensions remains premature.

A history of CSA in males is associated with a constellation of negative outcomes, including low self-esteem, depression, anxiety, substance abuse, problems in interpersonal relationships, and offending behavior (for review, see Romano and De Luca, 2001). However, virtually no research to date has investigated the impact of CSA on boys' psychophysiological development as it applies to pubertal timing and sexual maturation. Nevertheless, there are several reasons why CSA may be conjectured to be increasingly linked to early menarche in girls relative to early spermarche in boys. Early entry into puberty may be less adaptive and less biologically relevant for boys as a result of the context and characteristics of the abuse experienced. For example, the likely extrafamilial nature of boys' abusive experiences may be less associated with high levels of chronic familial dysfunction, which remains, according to evolutionary models of socialization, the active ingredient in predicting pubertal timing.

It could also be hypothesized that relative to girls, boys are less sensitive to certain environmental pressures that may otherwise act to shape reproductive strategies. Decreased sensitivity and reactivity to contextual pressures, at least as they pertain to reproductive development, may render boys less likely to demonstrate accelerated pubertal timing as a function of psychosocial stress (Surbey, 1990). Finally, biological frames, which cite abuse-related hormonal disruptions resulting from pheromonal stimulation as the primary culprit of accelerated puberty, can also be used to understand why boys' physiological responses to abuse may be less apparent given that their abusers are largely same-sex. In sum, several factors may elucidate why sex differences in psychophysiological responses may emerge as a function of CSA. This being said, the following section aims to shift attention away from discussing CSA as a predictor of early pubertal onset and toward focusing on how (1) early entry into puberty and (2) subjective feelings of being older than one's peers can promote the negative effects of CSA.

*Pubertal timing and subjective age: compounding the impact of CSA across development*

There exist two principal theories regarding the consequences of reaching puberty outside normative developmental time frames. The first, referred to as the deviance perspective, posits that when an adolescent's physical development is out of sync with that of the majority of their peers, they are placed in a socially deviant category that puts them at risk for adjustment difficulties (Alsaker, 1995; Petersen and Crockett, 1985). On the other hand, the early-stage perspective contends that it is early sexual maturation relative to peers that places one at risk of maladjustment. By interrupting a child's developing identity and thrusting them abruptly into adulthood, early entry into puberty limits a child's opportunities to consolidate emerging adaptive skills (Williams and Dunlop, 1999). Thus, the precocious termination of developmental stages is thought to render early maturers ill-prepared to cope with the stress associated with adolescent transitions.

Evidence has generally indicated that boys who are out of sync with their peers, particularly those who mature later, and girls who mature earlier than their age-mates are the most vulnerable to adjustment difficulties (Caspi and Moffitt, 1991; Ge, Conger, and Elder, 1996; Graber, *et al.*, 1997). For example, not only has early menarche been predicted from internalizing symptoms, but early puberty in turn predicts higher rates of depression, phobic disorders, and subclinical eating disorders during high school (Hayward, *et al.*, 1997). In addition, studies have also shown that both off-time boys and early-maturing girls are at increased risk for delinquency relative to on-time peers (Moffitt, 1993; Williams and Dunlop, 1999). Whereas later maturing boys may engage in increased levels of delinquent activity as a compensatory means of gaining status and prestige within the peer group, early-maturing boys and girls may do so in an effort to bridge what Moffitt has coined the "maturity gap." According to the author, the experience of puberty in western societies leads individuals to biological maturity much earlier than they are afforded social maturity and an adult social status. The resulting gap in identity is thought to promote delinquent activity as a means of increasing feelings of autonomy and independence (i.e., pseudo-freedom) from parental control.

Because the maturity gap is greater for early developers, so is their expected involvement in delinquent activity as a means of bridging this gap (Moffitt, 1993). Although several factors undoubtedly mediate this relation (e.g., behavioral predispositions, intelligence, peer group relationships, school contexts, personality, and self-esteem), research has shown that early entry into puberty predicts participation in a wide range of delinquent and/or risky activities, such as smoking, alcohol and drug abuse, precocious sexual activity, as well as oppositional and antisocial behavior (Dick, *et al.*, 2000; Tschann, *et al.*, 1994; Williams and Dunlop, 1999).

It is within this context that adolescents' assessment of their subjective age may also act to prematurely immerse them in activities considered "adult"; activities which by definition they may be ill-equipped to negotiate in an adaptive manner. Adolescents' actual and perceived pubertal timing (i.e., subjective age) are conceptualized as "overlapping but distinct timing measures that reflect different biological and social processes" (Dubas, Garber, and Pedersen, 1991, p. 580). With this distinction made, it is argued that perceived pubertal timing may be at least as important as actual timing in predicting adolescents' psychosocial adjustment (Alsaker, 1992). It is the current contention that, in addition to promoting early pubertal maturation, CSA may also forecast many of the postpubertal outcomes observed among survivors by increasing their sense of subjective age during adolescence.

Experiences of CSA may lead adolescents to look, act, and feel older. Taken together, these factors may steer already vulnerable adolescents toward deviant behaviors designed to promote feelings of autonomy, independence, and ultimately to achieve an integrated sense of self. In concordance with Belsky and colleagues' (1991) hypotheses, we contend that both early entry into puberty and increased subjective age compound the postpubertal effects of CSA via trajectories of precocious sexuality and delinquent activity, unstable pair bonding, heightened risks of revictimization, early pregnancy, and more negative self-views as parents later in life.

Girls who mature earlier – among them CSA survivors who report engaging in more frequent, more unprotected, and more rapidly initiated sexual activity with multiple partners – become sexually active earlier and become pregnant younger than do their peers (Udry and Cliquet, 1982). Perhaps as a direct result of CSA in some cases, evidence suggests that low self-worth and lowered expectations for the future strongly predict teenage pregnancy (Becker-Lausen and Rickel, 1995). Specifically, the authors have shown that psychoemotional impairments related to both depression and dissociative problems mediate the relationship between CSA and an increased risk of pregnancy in adolescence.

Moreover, the interrelation between low-quality romantic relationships, unstable pair bonds, and increased risks of sexual and physical revictimization are also well documented among survivors (Bergevin and Bukowski, 2002; for review see Messman and Long, 1996). For example, 65 percent of male and 72 percent of female survivors report experiences of abuse in later adolescence and young adulthood (Stevenson and Gajarsky, 1991). Moreover, 66 percent of all adult rape victims report a history of CSA (Koss and Dinero, 1989). Finally, investigations of community samples have shown that survivors, overall, are at least 2.4 times more likely than others to be revictimized as adults (Wyatt, Guthrie, and Notgrass, 1992). Referred to by Kluft (1990) as "Sitting Duck Syndrome," it is thought that dysfunctional individual dynamics, symptoms of maladjustment, and poor cognitive relational schemas combine to produce a greater vulnerability for revictimization in postpubescence.

Increased susceptibility to physical and sexual assault may also be amplified in survivors as a function of pubertal timing, as well as a function of feeling older than others. That is, early entry into puberty may directly or indirectly increase the odds of revictimization through involvement in delinquent activity (e.g., substance abuse), as well as through an association with delinquent peers. The combined factors of CSA and early entry into puberty may also aggregate risks for poor partner selection and participation in low-quality romantic relationships through coalescent feelings of powerlessness, negative self-perceptions, and low self-esteem. In turn, poor partner selection and low-quality relationships augment the risks of revictimization creating a "vicious circle" of events that may explain findings showing, alarmingly, that female survivors of intrafamilial abuse are roughly three times more likely than nonabused women to experience violence at the hands of their husbands (Russell, 1986).

Studies have also begun to examine the relation between experiences of CSA and survivors' later parenting practices with their own children. Generally speaking, survivors report feeling less adequate, less confident, and possessing less emotional control over their children relative to other parents (Cole, *et al.*, 1992). In demonstrating a tendency toward neglectful parenting in a sample of low-income adolescent mothers, Zuravin and DiBlasio (1992) showed that neglectful teen mothers were more likely, relative to their nonmaltreating counterparts, to be victims of CSA, to be less educated, to have given birth at a younger age, and to have had more than one child as a teen. Even after controlling for other related family-of-origin factors, studies have supported a direct link between CSA and possessing negative self-views as a parent, greater difficulties in coping with child discipline, and an increased reliance on physical means of punishment (Banyard, 1997). Although when taken together evidence suggests that a history of CSA may be conceptualized as a risk factor for more ineffective, less-skilled parenting, it is important to note that these dimensions of negative parenting are not necessarily evidenced across all, or perhaps even the majority of, survivors.

### Linking childhood physical and sexual abuse to pubertal timing and adolescent psychosocial adjustment in dating relationships

The ideas expressed in this chapter served as the conceptual basis of a study conducted by the first two authors. The central goals of the study were to construct and examine a model that integrates measures of childhood experiences of sexual and physical abuse, pubertal timing, adolescent experiences in dating relationships, and affective well-being. As shown in figure 10.1, our model is based on the hypotheses that (1) sexual and physical abuse predict early pubertal timing, (2) sexual abuse and early puberty would be associated with subsequent experiences in dating relationship as independent predictors as well as via an interaction between them, and (3) experiences in dating relationships would, at least in part, mediate the associations between sexual abuse and depressed affect, and between early puberty and depressed affect.

The participants in this study were 332 senior high school students (144 boys and 188 girls; mean age = 16.7 years) from four

English-speaking secondary schools in the province of Quebec. Participants completed four questionnaires, namely: (1) the Children's Experiences of Violence Questionnaire (CEVQ; Walsh, *et al.*, 2000), a recently developed measure of children's experiences of physical and sexual abuse; (2) the Pubertal Development Scale (Petersen, *et al.*, 1988), a self-report measure of pubertal status and pubertal timing; (3) the Revised Conflict Tactics Scale (CTS2; Straus, *et al.*, 1996); and (4) the Center for Epidemiological Studies – Depression Scale (CES-D, Radloff, 1977, 1991). The internal consistency of all measures ranged from reasonably reliable to highly reliable. For example, the measure of sexual abuse, as assessed by items such as "Did anyone ever touch you sexually or make you touch them sexually when you did not want them to?," and the measure of physical abuse, as assessed by items such as "How many times has an adult kicked, bit, or punched/hit you to hurt you?," yielded reliabilities of alpha = .69 and alpha = .72, respectively. Next, pubertal timing, which was measured by assessing whether participants experienced pubertal markers earlier, at the same time as, or later than their same-sex peers, was also found to be reasonably reliable with alpha = .71. Following this, a measure of compliance in dating/romantic relationships was computed from the CTS2. Items such as "I have put up with a boyfriend or girlfriend who has been physically abusive to me" and "I have put up with a boyfriend or girlfriend who has made me feel bad about myself" were used to assess the extent to which an individual has experienced physical or verbal maltreatment from a romantic partner. The dating compliance measure was found to be reliable with alpha = .86. Finally, a single reliable measure of depression, alpha = .88, was computed from the CES-D.

The results we report here are divided into three sections, each representing a different part of the schematic model shown in figure 10.1. Specifically, we first used measures of sexual and physical abuse to predict pubertal timing; second, measures of abuse were then used as univariate predictors of compliance in dating relationships, and finally, measures of abuse, pubertal timing, and dating compliance were used to predict depression. Multiple regression was used as the statistical technique for each of these analyses.

The most important finding revealed by our examination of the association between experiences of abuse and pubertal timing was a three-way interaction between sex, sexual abuse, and physical abuse. As shown in figure 10.2, sexual abuse predicted an early entry into puberty for girls, regardless of whether they had also been physically abused. For boys, however, sexual abuse was related to an early entry into puberty only in the presence of physical abuse. In the absence of physical abuse, sexual abuse was found to be associated with a late entry into puberty. That

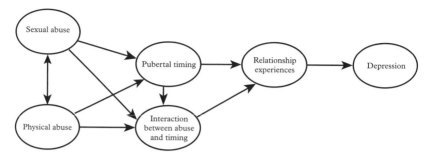

Figure 10.1 Schematic representation of the general model that guided the analyses of the associations between abuse history, pubertal timing, relationship experiences (i.e., compliance), and affective outcomes

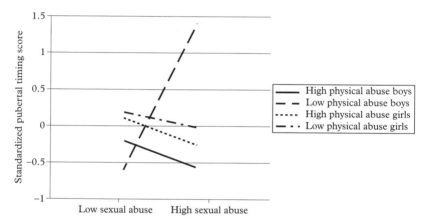

Figure 10.2 Association between sexual abuse and pubertal timing as a function of physical abuse for boys and girls (higher pubertal timing scores indicate a later entry into puberty)

is, boys who were sexually abused, but not physically abused, entered puberty later than did other boys. Thus, although these findings support the hypothesis that sexual abuse predicts precocious puberty in girls, the same association for boys occurs only under conditions of concomitant physical abuse. When sexual abuse is not accompanied by physical abuse among boys, entry into puberty is delayed. One explanation for the latter association is that late puberty itself renders boys more vulnerable to sexual abuse. It is conceivable that the more childlike cues and androgynous body characteristics of late maturing boys make them more appealing to sexual predators. Further analyses of the data that control for the timing of abuse are expected to help clarify this issue in the future.

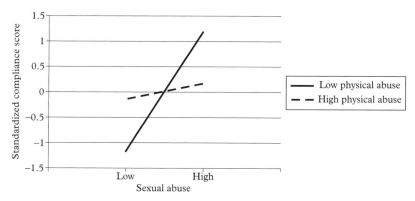

Figure 10.3 Association between sexual abuse, physical abuse, and compliance in dating relationships

Our next analysis examined how sexual abuse, physical abuse, and pubertal timing are associated with dating compliance (i.e., the likelihood that a person would allow oneself to be subjected to physical or verbal abuse in a dating relationship). This analysis revealed three important findings. First, a significant interaction emerged between sexual abuse and physical abuse in the prediction of compliance in dating relationships (see figure 10.3). Although we expected that the combination of these two forms of abuse would be a particularly potent predictor of compliance in dating, the pattern underlying the interaction indicated that the effect of sexual abuse was strongest in the absence, rather than in the presence, of physical abuse. In other words, adolescents who had been sexually abused were significantly more likely to be compliant (i.e., revictimized) when they *had not been* physically abused, relative to adolescents who had been both sexually and physically abused. Interestingly, this finding implies that the experience of physical abuse may reduce the risk of dating compliance usually associated with experiences of sexual abuse. Perhaps adolescents who have been sexually abused and physically abused know, more so than adolescents who have not been physically abused, to be extremely wary of physical and verbal maltreatment from others. Or, perhaps as a result of learning first-hand the powerful effects of physical force, sexually and physically abused individuals incorporate more coercive tactics into their own behavioural repertoire, rendering them less likely to manifest overtly compliant relational styles in dating relationships.

A second significant interaction between sexual abuse and pubertal timing also emerged in our investigation of dating compliance. For both boys and girls, a positive association between sexual abuse and dating compliance was stronger among adolescents who matured earlier rather

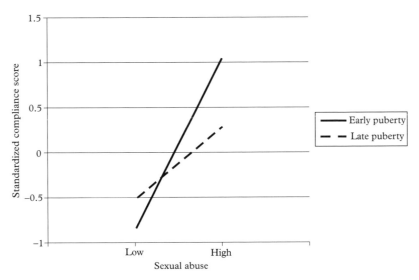

Figure 10.4 Association between sexual abuse and compliance as a function of pubertal timing

than later (see figure 10.4). This finding, seen both in males and females, shows that early puberty increases the likelihood that a sexually abused individual will be revictimized in a dating relationship during adolescence. Finally, a third interaction between physical abuse and pubertal timing in the prediction of dating compliance was also observed. Here, however, the findings were very different than those observed in the prediction of dating compliance from sexual abuse. As shown in figure 10.5, physical abuse was positively associated with dating compliance among boys and girls who matured early, but negatively associated with dating compliance among boys and girls who matured late. At this juncture, it is important to note the large difference between the pattern of findings associated with (1) the interaction between sexual abuse and pubertal timing and (2) the interaction between the physical abuse and pubertal timing. The slope for the association between sexual abuse and dating compliance was stronger for adolescents who matured earlier compared with those who matured later. The slope for the association between physical abuse and dating compliance, however, took on a completely different trajectory under conditions of early and late maturation. Specifically, physical abuse was positively related to dating compliance among adolescents who matured early, but it was negatively associated with dating compliance among adolescents who matured late. As figure 10.5 indicates, late puberty

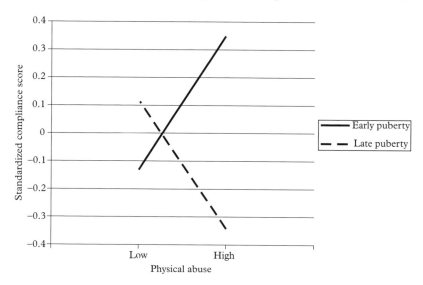

Figure 10.5 Association between physical abuse and compliance as a function of pubertal timing

is associated with a very low level of dating victimization among youth who have experienced physical abuse.

The final set of analyses aimed to explore the relation between experiences of sexual and physical abuse, pubertal timing, and dating compliance in predicting adolescent depression. In this analysis, the compliance score was entered on the first step. If compliance mediated the effects of abuse and puberty on depression, then these variables should be unrelated to depression after the effects of dating compliance were accounted for. Our findings showed that dating compliance was strongly associated with depression accounting for approximately 10 percent of its variance. However, even when dating compliance had been accounted for, the effects of abuse and pubertal timing still emerged as significant. Specifically, three findings were observed. First, depression was positively associated with physical abuse for both boys and girls (semipartial $r = .32$). Second, the effects of sexual abuse differed significantly for boys and girls, with the effects being positive for girls and negative for boys (see figure 10.6). Third, the effect of pubertal timing also differed for boys and girls, with early puberty being associated with high depression scores among girls, and late puberty being associated with higher depression scores among boys (see figure 10.7). The meaning of the sex difference in the association between sexual violence and depression is not immediately

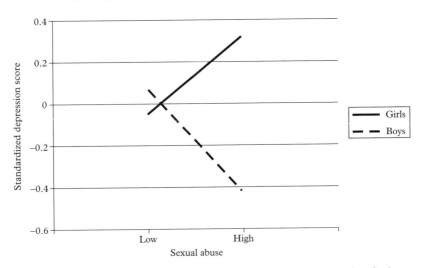

Figure 10.6 Association between sexual abuse and depression for boys and girls

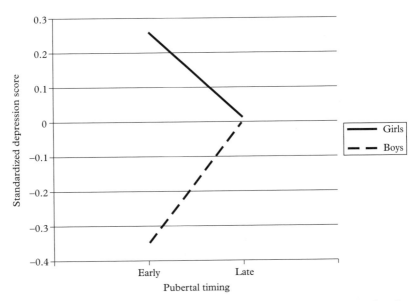

Figure 10.7 Association between pubertal timing and depression for boys and girls

clear. It is conceivable, however, that the experience of sexual abuse is more likely to be internalized by girls, resulting in depressed affect, whereas it may be externalized by boys, resulting in heightened anger and lower levels of reported depression, perhaps stemming from defensive processes. The pattern of findings regarding sex differences in the association between pubertal timing and depression confirms previous reports that early maturation is a risk factor for girls whereas late maturation is a risk factor for boys (Caspi and Moffitt, 1991; Ge, Conger, and Elder, 1996; for review, see Williams and Dunlop, 1999; see also chapter 12).

## Conclusion

The repeated observation that childhood sexual and physical abuse are related to subsequent negative outcomes have only rarely been studied in accordance with normal developmental events or experiences (Bukowski, 1992). In this chapter we have argued that sexual abuse may be related to the experience of puberty, a critical aspect of development during adolescence. From the perspective taken in this chapter, pubertal timing is viewed as both a consequence of prior experiences of childhood abuse and as a factor that moderates the association between abusive experiences and subsequent developmental outcomes. Also expressed in this chapter is the notion that one cannot reach simple conclusions about the impact of abusive experiences on development. The associations between experiences of childhood victimization and psychosocial adjustment over the short and long terms are necessarily complex, varying across individual and situational factors. As such, future approaches to the study of childhood sexual abuse require the use of an integrated biopsychosocial model in which the developmental significance of social experiences is not only viewed in terms of individual or biologically based events, but also in terms of the social context in which these events occur. Our findings show, for example, that abuse predicts pubertal timing in complex ways, and that the effects of abuse on outcomes of revictimization and depressed affect are moderated by pubertal timing. The present findings provide fresh evidence for the role of pubertal timing within particular developmental contexts. In doing so, they confirm prior speculation regarding the means by which childhood abuse affects psychological as well as physiological development (Bukowski, 1992; Finkelhor and Browne, 1985; Trickett and Putnam, 1993). The picture of how these phenomena operate is, however, remarkably incomplete. Only further integrative research will make this picture clearer.

NOTES

1. Moreover, prevalence studies have shed light on the demographic correlates of CSA as follows: mean age of onset is between 7 and 9 years of age; average duration of abuse is between two and six years; roughly half of all of survivors report experiencing attempted or completed vaginal, anal, or oral intercourse; the use of force is reported by 15 to 46 percent and 19 to 68 percent of abused males and females, respectively; 98 percent of perpetrators who abuse girls and 83 percent of those who abuse boys are male; finally, 42 percent of perpetrators of female victims are parental figures and another 22 percent are other relatives, indicating that the majority of abusers of female victims are family members (American Humane Association, 1993; Polusny and Follette, 1995).

## References

Abney, V. D., and Priest, R. (1995). African American and sexual child abuse. In L. Fontes (ed.), *Sexual abuse in nine North American cultures* (pp. 11–30). Thousand Oaks, CA: Sage.

Adams, J. F. (1981). Earlier menarche, greater height and weight: a stimulation-stress factor hypothesis. *Genetic Psychology Monographs*, **104**, 3–22.

Alsaker, F. D. (1992). Timing of puberty and reactions to pubertal changes. In M. Rutter (ed.), *Psychosocial disturbances in young people: challenges for prevention* (pp. 39–82). Cambridge: Cambridge University Press.

Alsaker, F. D. (1995). Pubertal timing, overweight and psychological adjustment. *Journal of Early Adolescence*, **12**, 396–419.

Alexander, P. C., and Lupfer, S. L. (1987). Family characteristics and long-term consequences associated with sexual abuse. *Archives of Sexual Behavior*, **16**, 235–245.

American Humane Association. (1993). *Child abuse and neglect data fact sheet. 1.* Englewood, CO: American Humane Association.

Banyard, V. L. (1997). The impact of childhood sexual abuse and family functioning on four dimensions of women's later parenting. *Child Abuse and Neglect*, **21(11)**, 1095–1107.

Becker-Lausen, E., and Rickel, A. U. (1995). Integration of teen pregnancy and child abuse research: identifying mediator variables for pregnancy outcome. *Journal of Primary Prevention*, **16(1)**, 39–53.

Beitchman, J. H., Zucker, K. J., Hood, J. E., daCosta, G. A., Akman, D., and Cassavia, E. (1992). A review of the long-term effects of child sexual abuse. *Child Abuse and Neglect*, **16(1)**, 101–118.

Belsky, J., Steinberg, L., and Draper P. (1991). Childhood experience, inter-personal development, and reproductive strategy: an evolutionary theory of socialization. *Child Development*, **62**, 647–670.

Bergevin, T., and Bukowski, W. M. (2002). Rejection sensitivity: a systems approach to understanding adolescent romantic development. Unpublished manuscript, Concordia University, Montreal, CA.

Bukowski, W. M. (1992). Sexual abuse and maladjustment considered from the perspective of normal developmental processes. In W. O'Donohue and

J. H. Geer (ed.), *The sexual abuse of children: theory and research* (vol. I, pp. 261–282). Hillsdale, NJ: Lawrence Erlbaum.

Burke-Draucker, C. (1996). Family-of-origin variables and adult female survivors of childhood sexual abuse: a review of the research. *Journal of Child Sexual Abuse*, 5(4), 35–63.

Campbell, B. C., and Udry, J. R. (1995). Stress and the age of menarche of mothers and daughters. *Journal of Biosocial Science*, 27, 127–134.

Caspi, A., and Moffitt, T. E. (1991). Individual differences are accentuated during periods of social change: the sample case of girls at puberty. *Journal of Personality and Social Psychology*, 61(1), 157–168.

Cole, P. M., Woolger, C., Power, T. G., and Smith, K. D. (1992). Parenting difficulties among adult survivors of father–daughter incest. *Child Abuse and Neglect*, 16(2), 239–249.

Crowder, A. (1995). *Opening the door: a treatment model for therapy with male survivors of sexual abuse*. New York: Brunner-Mazel.

Dallam, S. J., Gleaves, D. H., Cepeda-Benito, A., Silberg, J. L., Kraemer, H. C., and Spiegel, D. (2001). The effects of child sexual abuse: comment on Rind, Tromovitch, and Bauserman (1998). *Psychological Bulletin*, 127(6), 715–733.

Davis, J. L., and Petretic-Jackson, P. A. (2000). The impact of childhood sexual abuse on adult interpersonal functioning: a review and synthesis of the empirical literature. *Aggression and Violent Behavior*, 5(3), 291–328.

Demause, L. (1997). The history of child abuse. *Journal of Psychohistory*, 25(3), 216–236.

Dhaliwal, G. K., Gauzas, L., Antonowicz, D. H., and Ross, R. R. (1996). Adult male survivors of childhood sexual abuse: prevalence, sexual abuse characteristics, and long-term effects. *Clinical Psychology Review*, 16, 619–639.

Dick, D. M., Rose, R. J., Viken, R J., and Kaprio, J. (2000). Pubertal timing and substance use: association between and within families across late adolescence. *Developmental Psychology*, 36(2), 180–189.

DiTomasso, M., and Routh, D. (1993). Recall of abuse in childhood and three measures of dissociation. *Child Abuse and Neglect*, 17(4), 477–485.

Dubas, J. S., Garber, J. A., and Pedersen, A. C. (1991). A longitudinal investigation of adolescents' changing perceptions of pubertal timing. *Developmental Psychology*, 27, 580–586.

Ellis, C. T. (1991). An extension of the Steinberg accelerating hypothesis. *Journal of Early Adolescence*, 11, 221–235.

Ellis, B. J., and Garber, J. (2000). Psychological antecedents of variation in girls' pubertal timing: maternal depression, stepfather presence, and marital and family stress. *Child Development*, 71(2), 485–501.

Ellis, B. J., Mcfadyen-Ketchum, S., Dodge, K. A., Pettit, G. S., and Bates, J. E. (1999). Quality of early family relationships and individual differences in the timing of pubertal maturation in girls: a longitudinal test of an evolutionary model. *Journal of Personality and Social Psychology*, 77(2), 387–401.

Ellison, P. T. (1990). Human ovarian functioning and reproductive ecology: new hypotheses. *American Anthropologist*, 92, 933–952.

Faller, K. C. (1989). Characteristics of a clinical sample of sexually abused children: how boy and girl victims differ. *Child Abuse and Neglect*, 13(2), 281–291.

Farley, M., and Keaney, J. C. (1997). Physical symptoms, somatization, and dissociation in women survivors of childhood sexual assault. *Women and Health*, **25**(30), 33–45.

Finkelhor, D. (1979). *Sexually victimized children*. New York: Free Press.

Finkelhor, D. (1990). Early and long term-effects of child sexual abuse: an update. *Professional Psychology: Research and Practice*, **21**, 325–330.

Finkelhor, D., and Browne, A. (1985). The traumatic impact of child sexual abuse: a conceptualization. *American Journal of Orthopsychiatry*, **55**, 530–541.

Finkelhor, D., Hotaling, G., Lewis, I. A., and Smith, C. (1990). Sexual abuse in a national survey of adult men and women: prevalence, characteristics, and risk factors. *Child Abuse and Neglect*, **14**(1), 19–28.

Fry, R. (1993). Adult physical illness and childhood sexual abuse. *Journal of Psychosomatic Research*, **37**, 89–103.

Ge, X., Conger, R. D., and Elder, G. H. (1996). Coming of age too early: pubertal influences on girls' vulnerability to psychological distress. *Child Development*, **67**, 3386–3400.

Graber, J. A., Brooks-Gunn, J., and Warren, M. P. (1995). The antecedents of menarcheal age: heredity, family environment, and stressful life events. *Child Development*, **66**, 346–359.

Graber, J. A., Lewinsohn, P. M., Seeley, J. R., and Brooks-Gunn, J. (1997). Is psychopathology associated with the timing of pubertal development? *Journal of the American Academy of Child and Adolescent Psychiatry*, **36**(12), 1768–1776.

Hamilton, G. V. (1929). *A research in marriage*. New York: Albert and Charles Boni.

Hayward, C., Killen, J. D., Wilson, D. M., Hammer, L. D., Litt, I. F., Kraemer, H. C., Haydel, F., Varady, A., and Barr Taylor, C. (1997). Psychiatric risk associated with early puberty in adolescent girls. *Journal of the American Academy of Child and Adolescent Psychiatry*, **36**(2), 255–262.

Herman-Giddens, M. E., Sandler, A. D., and Friedman, N. E. (1988). Sexual precocity in girls: an association with sexual abuse? *American Journal of Diseases of Children*, **142**, 431–433.

Holmes, G. R., Offen, L., and Waller, G. (1997). See no evil, hear no evil, speak no evil: why do relatively few male victims of childhood sexual abuse receive help for abuse-related issues in adulthood? *Clinical Psychology Review*, **17**, 69–88.

Hoogland, J. L. (1982). Prairie dogs avoid extreme inbreeding. *Science*, **215**, 1639–1641.

Hulanicka, B. (1999). Acceleration of menarcheal age of girls from dysfunctional families. *Journal of Reproductive and Infant Psychology*, **17**, 119–132.

Jumper, S. A. (1995). A meta-analysis of the relationship of child sexual abuse to adult psychological adjustment. *Child Abuse and Neglect*, **19**(6), 715–728.

Kanazawa, S. (2001). Why father absence might precipitate early menarche: the role of polygyny. *Evolution and Human Behavior*, **22**, 329–334.

Kendall-Tackett, K. A., Williams, L. M., and Finkelhor, D. (1993). The impact of sexual abuse on children: a review and synthesis of recent empirical studies. *Psychological Bulletin*, **113** (1), 164–180.

Kendall-Tackett, K. A., Williams, L. M., and Finkelhor, D. (2001). The impact of sexual abuse on children: a review and synthesis of recent empirical studies. In R. Bull (ed.), *Children and the law: the essential readings. Essential readings in developmental psychology* (pp. 31–76). Oxford: Blackwell Scientific.

Kenny, M. C., and McEachern, A. G. (2000). Racial, ethnic, and cultural factors of childhood sexual abuse: a selected review of the literature. *Clinical Psychology Review*, **20**(7), 905–922.

Kim, K., and Smith, P. K. (1998a). Childhood stress, behavioral symptoms and mother–daughter pubertal development. *Journal of Adolescence*, **21**, 231–240.

Kim, K., and Smith, P. K. (1998b). Retrospective survey of parental marital relations and child reproductive development. *International Journal of Behavioral Development*, **22**(4), 729–751.

Kim, K., and Smith, P. K. (1999). Family relations in early childhood and reproductive development. *Journal of Reproductive and Infant Psychology*, **17**(2), 133–148.

Kinsey, A. C., Pomeroy, W. F., Martin, C. E., and Gebhard, P. H. (1953). *Sexual behavior in the human female*. Philadelphia, PN: W. B. Saunders.

Kluft, R. P. (1990). Incest and subsequent revictimization: the case of therapist–patient sexual exploitation, with a description of the sitting duck syndrome. In R. P. Kluft (ed.), *Incest-related syndromes of adult psychopathology* (pp. 263–287). Washington, DC: American Psychiatric Press.

Koss, M. P., and Dinero, T. E. (1989). Discriminant analysis of risk factors for sexual victimization among a sample of college women. *Journal of Consulting and Clinical Psychology*, **57**, 242–250.

Landis, C., Landis, A. T., Bolles, M. M., Metzger, H. F., Pitts, M. W., D'Esopo, D. A., Moloy, H. C., Kleegman, S. J., and Dickenson, R. L. (1940). *Sex in development*. New York: Paul B. Hoebert.

Leek, M. M. (1991). Genetic narcissism in the family unit: Genetic similarity theory as an extension of Hamilton's rule into the human domain. Unpublished Ph.D. thesis, University of Sheffield, UK.

Lidicker, W. Z. (1980). The social biology of the California vole. *Biologist*, **62**, 46–55.

Maccoby, E. E. (1991). Different reproductive strategies in males and females. *Child Development*, **62**, 676–681.

Malo, J., and Tremblay, R. E. (1997). The impact of paternal alcoholism and maternal social position on boys' school adjustment, pubertal maturation and sexual behavior: a test of two competing hypotheses. *Journal of Child Psychology and Psychiatry*, **38**(2), 187–197.

Mendel, M. P. (1995). *The male survivor: the impact of sexual abuse*. Thousand Oaks, CA: Sage.

Messman, T. L., and Long, P. J. (1996). Child sexual abuse and its relationship to revictimization in adult women: a review. *Clinical Psychology Review*, **16**(5), 397–420.

Moffitt, T. E. (1993). Adolescence-limited and life-persistent antisocial behavior: a developmental taxonomy. *Psychological Review*, **100**, 674–701.

Moffitt, T. E., Caspi, A., Belsky, J., and Silva, P. A. (1992). Childhood experience and the onset of menarche: a test of a sociobiological model. *Child Development*, **63**, 47–58.

Myers, J. E. B., Diedrich, S., Lee, D., Fincher, K. M., and Stern, R. (1999). Professional writing on child sexual abuse from 1900 to 1975: dominant themes and impact on prosecution. *Child Maltreatment*, **4**, 201–216.

Nash, M. R., Hulsey, T. L., Sexton, M. C., Harralson, T. L., and Lambert, W. (1993). Long-term sequelae of childhood sexual abuse: perceived family environment, psychopathology, and dissociation. *Journal of Consulting and Clinical Psychology*, **61**, 276–283.

Neumann, D. A., Houskamp, B. M., Pollock, V. E., and Briere, J. (1996). The long-term sequelae of childhood sexual abuse in women: a meta-analytic review. *Child Maltreatment*, **1**, 6–16.

Newberger, E. H., Hampton, R. L., Marx, T. J., and White, K. M. (1986). Child abuse and pediatric social illness: an epidemiological analysis and ecological reformulation. *American Journal of Orthopsychiatry*, **56(4)**, 589–601.

Oddone-Paolucci, E., Genius, M. L., and Violato, C. (2001). A meta-analysis of the published research on the effects of child sexual abuse. *Journal of Psychology*, **135(1)**, 17–36.

Olsson, I. A. S., de Jonge, F. H., Schuurman, T., and Helmond, F. A. (1999). Poor rearing conditions and social stress in pigs. *Behavioural Processes*, **46**, 201–215.

Ondersma, S. J., Chaffin, M., Berliner, L., Cordon, I., Goodman, G. S., and Barnett, D. (2001). Sex with children is abuse: comment on Rind, Tromovitch, and Bauserman (1998). *Psychological Bulletin*, **127(6)**, 707–714.

Petersen, A. C., and Crockett, L. J. (1985). Pubertal timing and grade effects on adjustment. *Journal of Youth and Adolescence*, **14**, 191–206.

Petersen, A. C., Crockett, L. J., Richards, M., and Boxer, A. (1988). A self-report measure of pubertal status: reliability, validity, and initial norms. *Journal of Youth and Adolescence*, **17**, 247–271.

Pilkington, B., and Kremer, J. (1995). A review of the epidemiological research on child sexual abuse. *Child Abuse Review*, **4**, 84–98.

Polusny, M. A., and Follette, V. M. (1995). Long-term correlates of child sexual abuse: theory and review of the empirical literature. *Applied and Preventive Psychology*, **4**, 143–166.

Radloff, L. S. (1977). The CES-D Scale: a self-report depression scale for research in the general population. *Applied Psychological Measurement*, **1**, 385–401.

Radloff, L. S. (1991). The use of the Center for Epidemiological Studies depression scale in adolescents and young adults. *Journal of Youth and Adolescence*, **20**, 149–166.

Rind, B., and Tromovitch, P. (1997). A meta-analytic review of findings from national samples on psychological correlates of child sexual abuse. *Journal of Sex Research*, **34(3)**, 237–255.

Rind, B., Tromovitch, P., and Bauserman, R. (1998). A meta-analytic examination of assumed properties of child sexual abuse using college samples. *Psychological Bulletin*, **124(1)**, 22–53.

Rind, B., Tromovitch, P., and Bauserman, R. (2001). The validity and appropriateness of methods: analyses and conclusions in Rind *et al.* (1998). A rebuttal of victimological critique from Ondersma *et al.* (2001) and Dallam *et al.* (2001). *Psychological Bulletin*, **127(6)**, 734–758.

Romano, E., and De Luca, R. V. (2001). Male sexual abuse: a review of effects, abuse characteristics, and links with later psychological functioning. *Aggression and Violent Behavior*, **6**, 55–78.

Russell, D. E. (1986). *The secret trauma: incest in the lives of girls and women.* New York: Basic Books.

Salter, A. C. (1992). Epidemiology of child sexual abuse. In W. O'Donohue and J. H. Geer (ed.), *The sexual abuse of children: theory and research* (vol. I, pp. 108–138). Hillsdale, NJ: Lawrence Erlbaum.

Stattin, H., and Magnusson, D. (1990). *Pubertal maturation in female development.* Hillsdale, NJ: Lawrence Erlbaum.

Stevenson, M. R., and Gajarsky, W. M. (1991). Unwanted childhood sexual experiences relate to later revictimization and male perpetration. *Journal of Psychology and Human Sexuality*, **4(4)**, 57–70.

Straus, M. A., Hamby, S. L., Boney-McCoy, S., and Sugarman, D. B. (1996). The revised Conflict Tactics Scales (CTS2): development and preliminary psychometric data. *Journal of Family Issues*, **17(3)**, 283–316.

Surbey, M. K. (1990). Family composition, stress, and the timing of human menarche. In T. E. Ziegler and F. B. Bercovitch (ed.), *Monographes in primatology, socioendocrinology of primate reproduction* (vol. XIII, pp. 11–32). New York: John Wiley–Liss.

Surbey, M. K. (1998). Parent and offspring strategies in the transition at adolescence. *Human Nature*, **9**, 67–94.

Tanner, M. J. (1990). *Foetus into man: physical growth from conception to maturity.* Cambridge, MA: Harvard University Press.

Trickett, P. K., and Putnam, F. W. (1993). Impact of child sexual abuse on females: toward a developmental, psychobiological integration. *Psychological Science*, **4(2)**, 81–87.

Tschann, J. M., Adler, N. E., Irwin, C. E., Millstein, S. G., Turner, R. A., and Kegeles, S. M. (1994). Initiation of substance use in early adolescence: the roles of pubertal timing and emotional distress. *Health Psychology*, **13(4)**, 326–333.

Turner, P. K., Runtz, M. G., and Galambos, N. L. (1999). Sexual abuse, pubertal timing, and subjective age in adolescent girls: a research note. *Journal of Reproductive and Infant Psychology*, **17(2)**, 111–118.

Udry, J. R., and Cliquet, R. L. (1982). A cross-cultural examination of the relationship between ages at menarche, marriage, and first birth. *Demography*, **19**, 53–63.

US Department of Health and Human Services National Center on Child Abuse and Neglect (1996). *The national incidence study of child abuse and neglect (NIS-3).* Washington, DC: US Government Printing Office.

US Department of Health and Human Services National Center on Child Abuse and Neglect (1997). *Child maltreatment 1995: reports from the states to the National Center on Child Abuse and Neglect.* Washington, DC: US Government Printing Office.

Violato, C., and Genius, M. (1993). Problems of research in male child sexual abuse: a review. *Journal of Child Sexual Abuse*, **2(3)**, 33–54.

Walsh, C. A., MacMillan, H. L., Trocme, N., Boyle, M., Jamieson, E., and Daciuk, J. (2000). The childhood experiences of violence questionnaire. Unpublished manuscript, McMaster University, Toronto, CA.

Watkins, B., and Bentovim, A. (1992). The sexual abuse of male children and adolescents: a review of current research. *Journal of Child Psychology and Psychiatry*, **33(1)**, 197–248.

Weirson, M., Long, P. J., and Forehand, R. L. (1993). Toward a new understanding of early menarche: the role of environmental stress in pubertal timing. *Adolescence*, **28(112)**, 913–924.

Whipple, E. E., and Webster-Stratton, C. (1991). The role of parental stress in physically abusive families. *Child Abuse and Neglect*, **15**, 279–291.

Williams, J. M., and Dunlop, L. C. (1999). Pubertal timing and self-reported delinquency among male adolescents. *Journal of Adolescence*, **22**, 157–171.

Wyatt, G. E., Guthrie, D., and Notgrass, C. M. (1992). Differential effects of women's child sexual abuse and subsequent sexual revictimization. *Journal of Consulting and Clinical Psychology*, **60**, 167–173.

Zuravin, S. J., and DiBlasio, F. A. (1992). Child-neglecting adolescent mothers: how do they differ from their non-maltreating counterparts? *Journal of Interpersonal Violence*, **7(4)**, 471–489.

# 11 Psychosocial factors predicting pubertal onset

*Laurie L. Meschke, Pamela Jo Johnson,*
*Bonnie L. Barber, and Jacquelynne S. Eccles*

Throughout the past century biopsychosocial models of adolescent development have increased in both their promotion and prevalence (reviewed by Susman, 1997). The biological process of puberty is the typical initiator of the adolescent period of human development (Petersen, 1985). Thus, it is not surprising that the majority of adolescent biopsychosocial research has considered pubertal timing or status (Graber, Petersen, and Brooks-Gunn, 1996) as predictors of social (e.g., Meschke and Silbereisen, 1997; Meschke, *et al.*, 2001) and psychological outcomes (Susman, *et al.*, 1985).

The timing of pubertal onset has potentially negative implications for subsequent psychological and physical health (see chapter 12). Research indicates that early onset of puberty is associated with an increased likelihood of adolescent problem behavior (Caspi and Moffitt, 1991; Steinberg, 1989), depression, anxiety (Brooks-Gunn, 1988; Susman, *et al.*, 1985), and breast cancer in women (Kampert, Whittemore, and Paffenbarger, 1988). The potential health consequences of early reproductive maturation have motivated researchers to investigate the possible predictors of pubertal timing.

Recently, environmental factors have been related to pubertal development (reviewed by Kim, Smith, and Palermiti, 1997). Stress is the environmental factor of interest and has typically been divided into two categories of predictors: physical stressors and psychosocial stressors. Increased physical stressors (e.g., decreased nutritional intake or increased exercise; Brooks-Gunn and Warren, 1985; Frisch, 1983) are more often associated with delayed pubertal timing. Psychosocial stressors (e.g., family conflict or depressed mood; Brooks-Gunn and Warren, 1985; Frisch, 1983; Graber, Brooks-Gunn, and Warren, 1995) are often associated with accelerated pubertal timing.

The goal of this chapter is to briefly review the literature describing the relation between psychosocial factors and pubertal timing, including an overview of specific models. Data from the Michigan Study of Adolescent

217

Life Transitions (MSALT) are then used to reexamine several established psychosocial predictors of puberty and also to introduce the potential relation between previously untested stressors and pubertal timing.

## Puberty prediction models

### *Neurobiological perspective*

Psychosocial predictors, particularly stress, have been associated with hormonal changes that could delay pubertal timing (Susman, *et al.*, 1989b). Stress (e.g., sexual abuse; Trickett and Putman, 1993, or living with an alcoholic parent; Malo and Tremblay, 1997) is believed to activate the hypothalamic-pituitary-adrenal (HPA) axis that results in an increase in adrenocorticotropin hormone (ACTH) and cortisol levels. This increase is accompanied by the suppression of gonadal steroids (Susman, Dorn, and Chrousos, 1991; Susman, *et al.*, 1989a; Susman, *et al.*, 1989b). Thus prepubescent stress mediated by gonadal functioning appears to delay pubertal timing (Susman, *et al.*, 1989b). For example, intensive exercise has been associated with high cortisol levels (Luger, *et al.*, 1987) and highly trained female ballet dancers compared to nonballet dancers have experienced a delay in pubertal timing (Warren, *et al.*, 1986).

### *Sociobiological perspective*

Expanding on the previous work of Draper and Harpending (1982), Belsky, Steinberg, and Draper (1991) developed a theoretical explanation for the potential hastening effect of stress on pubertal timing. In summary, they argued that high levels of stress, such as child abuse, economic deprivation, marital discord, and psychological distress, especially during ages 5 to 7 years, would accelerate pubertal development for boys and girls (see chapter 10). High levels of stress would encourage youth to perceive their environment as risky or harmful. Earlier pubertal timing would increase their chances of leaving the stressful environment earlier. In other words, early pubertal development ultimately allows adolescents to transition to adulthood earlier, including leaving the parental home and establishing their own families (Chisholm, 1993; Simpson, 1999).

Belsky and his colleagues (1991) assume that gender differences exist in the relation between stress and pubertal timing. Depression is thought to mediate the association between stress and accelerated pubertal timing for females, as depression is hypothesized to predict a higher proportion of body fat, which in turn increases the likelihood of earlier pubertal maturation. For males, high levels of stress may increase their androgen level, resulting in greater aggressive and noncompliant behavior and possibly earlier pubertal timing. Together, aggressiveness and early pubertal timing are likely to increase boys' risk of early fatherhood, providing the opportunity to leave a stressful family situation.

## Psychosocial factors associated with puberty

Both the neurobiological and sociobiological models of the relation between psychosocial issues and pubertal timing emphasize the effects of stress. Research to date on the psychosocial influences of pubertal timing have primarily focused on stress and stress responses associated with the family of origin, as suggested by Belsky and colleagues (1991). Studies have investigated both stressful family environments and stressful family relationships during the formative years.

*Family composition*

Family size has been examined in relation to pubertal timing for girls. Some have argued that increased family size reflects increased psychosocial stress due to a decrease in access to "parental resources" (Surbey, 1998), specifically limited availability of parental investment for each additional child. This psychosocial stress would in turn lead to earlier maturation. However, research suggests that increased family size, specifically a larger number of siblings, is associated with delayed menarche. Two studies have found that for each additional sibling, menarche is delayed by at least two months (Malina, *et al.*, 1997; Stukovsky, Valsik, and Bulaistirbu, 1967). Other studies have reported conflicting findings. Jones and colleagues (1972) found no association between total number of children in the family and menarcheal timing. However, they did find a significant association between number of younger brothers and delayed menarche. Surbey (1990) reported no association at all between number of siblings and menarche.

Father absence has been associated with accelerated menarcheal timing in several studies. Early research indicated that women whose fathers were absent before the age of 6, reached menarche earlier than those whose fathers were not absent (Jones, *et al.*, 1972). More recent studies of family composition and menarche revealed similar but more detailed results. Surbey (1990) found that girls who experienced father absence reached menarche earlier than those with both parents present or those who experienced mother absence. Similarly, girls who experienced the absence of both parents reached menarche earlier than those with both parents present or mother absence only. Further analyses were conducted to examine the effects of stepfather presence on girls with absent biological fathers. The presence of an unrelated male accelerated menarche among girls with absent fathers, but not significantly. The mean age of menarche was compared for girls who experienced father absence prior to the age of 10 and those who experienced father absence after the age of 10. The results were significant for earlier father absence and early menarche (Surbey, 1990).

Other studies have produced supporting results. Among those who experienced father absence, menarcheal age was significantly inversely associated with the number of years of father absence (Moffitt, *et al.*, 1992). Girls from divorced families also reported significantly earlier menarche than girls from intact families (Wierson, Long, and Forehand, 1993), however this sample only included families with married parents or those who had experienced divorce in the preceding twelve months. Girls who experienced father absence or divorce more than twelve months prior to the study were excluded.

Contrary to the aforementioned findings, one study found that while early menarche was significantly associated with father absence during late adolescence, it was not associated with father absence in early or late childhood (Campbell and Udry, 1995). These findings seem to contradict the sociobiological argument, in that father absence in the causally relevant time period does not appear to be associated with early menarche. However, marital conflict and/or a stressful family environment during early childhood may have preceded father absence in late adolescence.

Most recently, two studies have sought to clarify the role of father absence in predicting pubertal timing. Ellis and colleagues (1999) examined the timing of menarche in girls from single-mother households as compared with two-parent households. Significant associations were detected between living in a single-mother home at age 5 and earlier menarche, as compared with always married two-parent households and compared with all two-parent households.

Ellis and Garber (2000) also found a significant association between father absence and early menarche.[1] However, they further examined this association in light of stepfather presence. These analyses revealed no association of pubertal timing with the age of the girl at the time of father absence. However, there was a significant relation between pubertal timing and age at which an unrelated father figure became present. The younger the daughter when the unrelated father figure arrived, the more likely she was to report earlier onset of puberty.

Although antecedents to reproductive development in boys are studied much less frequently, the effects of father absence on spermarche were examined in one study. In this case, father absence for at least one year during childhood was associated with earlier spermarche (Kim and Smith, 1998b).

*Family environments*

Stressful relationships in childhood revolve primarily around parent–child relationships. Several studies have examined the association of specific parent–child relationships with pubertal timing. To date, the findings have been somewhat inconsistent and also indicate distinct gender-specific effects of conflictual parent–child relationships on the timing of puberty. For girls, mother–daughter conflict has been associated consistently with earlier menarche (Kim and Smith, 1998a; Kim, Smith, and Palermiti, 1997; Steinberg, 1988), as has parent–child conflict in general (Graber, Brooks-Gunn, and Warren, 1995; Moffitt, *et al.*, 1992). Father–daughter conflict, however, has not shown the same significant association with early menarche (Kim, Smith, and Palermiti, 1997; Steinberg, 1988).

For boys, parent–child conflict has not been consistently associated with age at spermarche. One study found no association between parent–child conflict and maturational development in boys (Steinberg, 1988). Another found that greater emotional distance from mother throughout childhood was associated with earlier spermarche (Kim and Smith, 1999). Malo and Tremblay (1997) found that boys with alcoholic fathers reported being punished more often than boys with nonalcoholic fathers (possibly indicating parent–child conflict) and were more likely to have delayed pubertal onset.

Stressful environments during childhood are predominantly located in the family and the home. Stress-filled environments may be the result of marital conflict or parental stress and their subsequent coping behaviors. Several studies have examined the influence of stressful family environments on pubertal timing.

In one study, greater family conflict at age 7 was significantly associated with early menarche, regardless of the girl's body weight at age 9 (Moffitt, *et al.*, 1992). In another study, more parental marital conflict (as reported by the mother) was associated with earlier menarche (Wierson, Long, and Forehand, 1993). However, no association between the adolescent's reported perception of marital conflict and earlier menarche was detected. Early menarche has been associated with a stressful family life (Kim and Smith, 1998a), as well as with parental marital conflict in early childhood and parental marital unhappiness throughout childhood (Kim

222    *Laurie Meschke, Pamela Jo Johnson, Bonnie Barber, and Jacquelynne Eccles*

and Smith, 1998b; Kim and Smith, 1999). Parental marital conflict and parental marital unhappiness in early childhood were also associated with early spermarche (Kim and Smith, 1998b; Kim, Smith, and Palermiti, 1997).

*Internalizing/externalizing behavior*

Researchers have investigated the possible association between internalizing (depression, anxiety) and externalizing (aggression) behaviors and early onset of puberty. Early studies produced somewhat conflicting results. This may not be surprising, however, if body weight is the hypothesized intermediary between depression and menarcheal timing. While overeating behaviors may characterize a stress response for some, others may engage in anorexic eating behaviors. Thus, depressive affect could be associated with either extreme of the body weight spectrum.

Moffit and colleagues (1992) found no significant association between internalizing or externalizing behavior at age 7 and subsequent early menarche. However, they did note a trend for behavior problems and later menarche. Graber, Brooks-Gunn, and Warren (1995) also found no significant association between internalizing or externalizing behaviors and early menarche. However, they reported a significant association between depressive affect and earlier maturation. More recently, Kim and Smith (1998a) reported that more anxiety and internalizing symptoms were associated with earlier menarche.

Malo and Tremblay (1997) found that boys with alcoholic fathers were more likely to be rated by their teachers as anxious or disruptive and were more likely to have delayed maturation. However, the association between these two variables was not directly evaluated. Conversely, two other studies reported that boys with more externalizing (aggressive/unruly) symptoms (Kim, Smith, and Palermiti, 1997), and less anxiety/depression in later childhood (Kim and Smith, 1999) were more likely to experience earlier spermarche.

**Expanding the types of stressors to examine: results of a study**

To date, most of the stressors examined in relation to pubertal timing have been related primarily to family stressors (e.g., family–teen conflict, father absence). Youth are also likely to experience stress from a variety of sources that previously have not been considered as predictors of pubertal timing (Susman, *et al.*, 1989a; D'Aurora and Fimian, 1988). For the purpose of this chapter, three stressors, unexamined previously in relation to pubertal timing, were included: (1) math anxiety, (2) school anxiety, and (3) economic anxiety.

## Method

### Sample

The data we used came from waves 1, 2, 5, and 6 of the Michigan Study of Adolescent Life Transitions (MSALT) (see Eccles, *et al*., 1989 for full sample details). MSALT began in 1983, when the respondents were in sixth grade in ten school districts in southeastern Michigan. Wave 1 data were collected in 1983, when the participants were ages 9.7 to 12.9 years (over 87% of the youth were 10.5 to 11 years of age). Wave 2 data were collected six months later. Wave 5 data were collected in 1988, when the respondents were in tenth grade. Wave 6 data were collected two years later. The students were in their senior year of high school.

Data from these waves were used to examine the proximal correlates of pubertal timing. In this sample, 22.7 percent of the sample reported reaching puberty prior to wave 1 data collection and approximately 84.2 percent of the respondents reported having reached puberty by wave 5 of data collection. Retrospective reports of pubertal timing from wave 5 data were used to measure pubertal timing and status. Requiring that respondents participated in waves 1 and 2, and either wave 5 or 6, yielded a subsample of 412 males and 484 females. The sample is primarily middle or working class, from small urban or suburban communities, and White (over 90%).

### Measures

The dependent variable was pubertal timing. Because Cox regression analysis was conducted, both a censoring and a timing variable were necessary for the dependent measure. The censoring and timing variables were based on wave 5 data. Males and females responded to the question: "Kids your age grow at different rates, but usually everyone has a time when they grew faster than at other ages. Has this happened to you yet? Yes (*1*; postpubertal) or no (*0*; prepubertal)." The timing variable for the postpubertal respondents was based on the question: "If yes, what grade were you in when this happened (grade and season)?" The timing variable for the prepubescent respondents was their grade at the time they answered the survey.

The reliability of the participants' subjective account of growth spurt was examined using two methods. Growth spurt measure was measured for boys (not girls) at wave 6. The correlation coefficient between these two measures was .47 ($p<.001$). When the difference between the two waves of data was calculated, 66 percent of the boys had a difference of one year or less. Over 28 percent of the boys reported the same grade of growth spurt for waves 5 (tenth grade) and 6 (twelfth grade) of data collection. For girls, grade of breast development and growth spurt were both measured at wave 5. These measures were also significantly correlated ($r=.21$; $p<.01$). The reliability of the dependent measure must be taken into account in relation to the findings. An objective, prospective measure of growth spurt would have been more ideal.

Self-reports of pubertal timing appear to be quite reliable. A strong positive relation exists between subjective pubertal timing and biological development, particularly in regards to height and weight (Silbereisen and Kracke, 1997). Self-reported fast developers recounted higher height and weight levels than their slower developing peers (Silbereisen and Kracke, 1993). Height spurt also provided a salient experience on which to base subjective pubertal timing. In addition to height and weight, research has shown a significant positive correlation between subjective pubertal timing and menarche for girls (Silbereisen, *et al.*, 1989). Subjective pubertal timing has also displayed moderate stability over time (Dubas, Graber, and Petersen, 1991).

These measures were structured for proportional hazards regression. If the person had experienced puberty, then the timing value was based on the grade and season that the event was reported. If the person reported being prepubescent, then timing was the grade of the person at wave 5 (n = 150). Based on timing of growth spurt, postpubertal females reported earlier pubertal timing than postpubertal males (females ($M = 7.31$, $SD = 1.26$); males ($M = 8.06$, $SD = 1.43$), $t(744) = -7.61$, $p<.001$).

The predictors, drawn primarily from wave 1 data, represent a variety of psychosocial stressors. Measures of family structure included (a) time spent in a divorced family and (b) total number of siblings. Parent–adolescent conflict was included as the family stress measure. Adolescent stressors included self-esteem and risk-taking behavior. Finally, several new stressors were considered: math anxiety, school anxiety, and economic anxiety.

*Time with divorced parents* ($M = .87$; $SD = 2.32$), from waves 5 and 6, was based on the question: "What is your parents' current marital status?" (1 = *married*; 2 = *divorced*; 3 = *widowed*; 4 = *separated*; 5 = *other*). If the students reported their parents as either divorced or separated, the time spent with divorced parents was calculated with the question: "How long has this been their marital status?" The categorical responses were converted to reflect the mean time of each interval. Thus, .5 = *less than 6 months*; .75 = *6 months to a year*; 1.5 = *1.1 to 2 years*; 2.5 = *2.1 to 3 years*; 4 = *3.1–5 years*; 7.5 = *5.1 to 10 years*; 12.5 = *10.1 to 15 years*; and 15 = *over 15 years*. If the question was not answered in wave 5, wave 6 responses to the same question were used. In both cases the value was adjusted to reflect the number of years spent with divorced parents at the time of wave 1 data collection.

*Total number of siblings* ($M = 1.78$; $SD = 1.27$) was also from waves 5 or 6 data. Only biological and adopted siblings were included in this tally. If data from wave 5 were not available, wave 6 data were used.

*Parent–teen conflict* ($M = 1.79$; $SD = .87$) is measured as: "I have a lot of fights with my parents about their rules and decisions for me" (1 = *never true*; 4 = *always true*).

*Self-esteem* ($\alpha = .66$; $M = 2.87$; $SD = .71$) is based on the mean of four items. Two items were reverse coded so that a high score reflects a high level of self-esteem. An example is "Some kids wish they were different." Responses fell on a 4-point scale with 1 = "*really true for me*" and 4 = "*really not true for me*," as based on the work of Harder (1979). Threats to one's self-esteem have been noted as sources of childhood stress (D'Aurora and Fimian, 1988).

*Risk-taking, wave 2* ($\alpha = .78$; $M = 10.46$; $SD = 13.13$) included eight items. Each of the items was prefaced by "In the last three weeks at school, about how many times did you . . ." Examples of risk-taking activities were "punch or push around another student," "wise off and disrupt class," and "bring alcohol or drugs to school." Responses could range from 0 to 12 or more. The composite risk-taking measure is the sum of events reported by the respondents.

Three anxiety or stress measures were included as predictors. Reported alpha levels refer to the subsample of MSALT participants included in this study. The scale score for each respondent was the unit-weight mean value of all the items included in the scale.

*Math anxiety, wave 1* ($\alpha = .89$; $M = 3.26$; $SD = 1.43$) included ten items such as "Before you take a test in math, how nervous do you get?" (1 = *I'm not nervous at all*; 7 = *I'm very nervous*) and "Math makes me feel like I'm lost in a jungle of numbers and I can't find my way out" (1 = *I never feel this way*; 7 = *I often feel this way*).

*School anxiety, wave 1* ($\alpha = .69$; $M = 2.53$; $SD = .82$) was measured with three items: "How worried do you get about getting your school work in on time" (1 = *not at all worried*; 4 = *very worried*); "How nervous do you get when the teacher hands back grades on a class assignment"; and "How nervous do you get when you only have a short time to do a hard assignment?" (1 = *not at all nervous*; 4 = *very nervous*).

*Economic anxiety* ($\alpha = .76$; $M = 2.90$; $SD = .96$) included three items: "Do you worry that your parents might not have a job in the future?"; "Do you worry that you will not be able to get a good job when you are an adult?"; "Do you ever worry that your family might not have enough money to pay for things?" ($1 = never$; $7 = always$).

## Results

### Descriptive analyses

All analyses were conducted using the SAS statistical package. Prior to conducting the primary analyses, correlation matrixes of the predictors and dependent variable (whether or not the person had experienced puberty) by gender were analyzed. In examining the correlation matrixes, particular attention was given to the correlation values between the various predictors. A high correlation value between the predictors increases the likelihood of multicollinearity. The correlation coefficients ranged from $-.33$ to $.37$, thus issues of multicollinearity were not considered to be a substantial threat (Affifi and Clark, 1990).

### Predicting pubertal timing

Event history analysis was utilized to examine pubertal timing and its association with psychosocial predictors. In event history analysis a hazard rate, or the instantaneous risk that the event (puberty) will occur at a given moment if the event has not occurred before this time (Yamaguchi, 1991), is calculated. The results of proportional hazards regression are interpreted using risk ratios based on parameter estimates. If the risk ratio is less than 1.0 then an increase in the predictor value would be related to later timing of the event, or a decrease in the hazard rate. A risk ratio exceeding 1.0 means that as the unit value of the predictor increases, the hazard rate also increases, that is, earlier timing of the event (SAS Institute, 1990). For example, if math anxiety has a risk ratio of 1.75 regarding pubertal timing, for each unit of increase in math anxiety, persons who have not yet experienced puberty would increase their hazard rate, or likelihood of entering puberty, by 75 percent.

Two hierarchical models predicting pubertal timing were analyzed by gender. An ecological approach guides both models (Bronfenbrenner, 1988). Specifically, family composition members are entered first, followed by individual stress issues. Stressors related to family and school issues are entered into the model last. With each new step added to the models, it was of interest whether additional predictors increased the

Table 11.1. *Proportional hazards regression to pubertal timing: hierarchical family composition, adolescent stress, and family stress models of pubertal timing for females and males*

| Predictor | Risk ratios | | | | | |
|---|---|---|---|---|---|---|
| | Female | Female | Female | Male | Male | Male |
| *Family composition* | | | | | | |
| Time with divorced parents, wave 1 | 1.02 | 1.02 | 1.02 | 1.00 | 1.00 | 1.00 |
| Total number of siblings, waves 5, 6 | 0.92* | 0.92* | 0.92+ | 1.01 | 1.01 | 1.01 |
| *Adolescent stress* | | | | | | |
| Self-esteem, wave 1 | | 1.02 | 1.08 | | 1.01 | 1.02 |
| Risk-taking behavior, wave 2 | | 0.99 | 0.99 | | 1.00 | 1.00 |
| *Family stress* | | | | | | |
| Parent–teen conflict | | | 1.28*** | | | 1.03 |
| Total subjects | 484 | 484 | 484 | 412 | 412 | 412 |
| Number who are postpubertal | 381 | 381 | 381 | 365 | 365 | 365 |
| Number censored | 103 | 103 | 103 | 47 | 47 | 47 |
| Percent censored | 21.28 | 21.28 | 21.28 | 11.41 | 11.41 | 11.41 |
| Chi-squared | 5.39 | 6.68 | 20.28** | 0.07 | 1.76 | 1.99 |
| Change in chi-squared | | 1.29 | 13.60*** | | 1.69 | 0.23 |

$+ \, p<.10$    $^*p<.05$    $^{**}p<.01$    $^{***}p<.001$

strength of the model. This was determined by calculating whether there was a significant increase in the chi-squared value of the expanded model, as compared to the previous model.

The first model incorporates stressors associated with the sociobiological model (Belsky, Steinberg, and Draper, 1991; Chisholm, 1993) as predictors of pubertal timing. The first step included time with divorced parents and total number of siblings (see table 11.1). This model was not significant for males or females. Adolescent self-esteem and risk-taking were added in step two of the model. Again, this model was not significant for males or females. Parent–teen conflict was added in the final step of the model. This model was significant for females and resulted in a significant increase in the model's chi-squared value [$\chi^2$ (1, $N = 484$) = 13.60, $p<.001$]. Higher levels of parent–teen conflict were associated with earlier pubertal timing for females. In addition, total number of siblings approached significance for females. Females with more siblings reported somewhat later pubertal timing.

Table 11.2. *Proportional hazards regression to pubertal timing: hierarchical family composition, family stress, and adolescent stress models of pubertal timing for females and males*

| Predictor | Risk ratios | | | | | | | |
|---|---|---|---|---|---|---|---|---|
| | Female | Female | Female | Female | Male | Male | Male | Male |
| *Family composition* | | | | | | | | |
| Time with divorced parents, wave 1 | 1.02 | 1.02 | 1.02 | 1.02 | 1.00 | 1.00 | 1.00 | 1.00 |
| Total number of siblings, waves 5, 6 | 0.92* | 0.92+ | 0.93+ | 0.93 | 1.01 | 1.01 | 1.01 | 1.01 |
| *Family and adolescent stress* | | | | | | | | |
| Self-esteem, wave 1 | | 1.08 | 1.06 | 1.07 | | 1.02 | 0.96 | 0.97 |
| Risk-taking behavior, wave 2 | | 0.99 | 0.99+ | 0.99 | | 1.00 | 0.99+ | 1.00 |
| Parent–teen conflict, wave 1 | | 1.28*** | 1.30*** | 1.29*** | | 1.03 | 1.05 | 1.03 |
| *School stress* | | | | | | | | |
| Math anxiety, wave 1 | | | 0.97 | 0.97 | | | 1.01 | 0.98 |
| School anxiety, wave 1 | | | 1.00 | 1.00 | | | 0.78*** | 0.76*** |
| *Future worries* | | | | | | | | |
| Economic anxiety, wave 1 | | | | 1.04 | | | | 1.14* |
| Total subjects | 484 | 484 | 484 | 484 | 412 | 412 | 412 | 412 |
| Number who are postpubertal | 381 | 381 | 381 | 381 | 365 | 365 | 365 | 365 |
| Number censored | 103 | 103 | 103 | 103 | 47 | 47 | 47 | 47 |
| Percent censored | 21.28 | 21.28 | 21.28 | 21.28 | 11.41 | 11.41 | 11.41 | 11.41 |
| Chi-squared | 5.36 | 20.28** | 20.85** | 21.37** | 0.07 | 1.99 | 14.40* | 19.26* |
| Change in chi-squared | | 14.92** | 0.57 | 0.52 | | 1.92 | 12.41** | 4.86* |

+ p<.10    * p<.05    ** p<.01    *** p<.001

The first step of the second model (see table 11.2) included family composition measures. Again this step was not significant for males or females. In the second step, family and adolescent stressors (conflict, self-esteem, and risk-taking behavior) were added. This model was significant only for females [$\chi^2$ (3, $N = 484$) $= 14.92, p<.01$]. Higher levels of parent–teen conflict were associated with earlier pubertal timing. Also, as in the previous model, total number of siblings was approaching significance. School-related stressors were added in the second step of the model. These additional predictors resulted in a significant increase in the model's chi-squared value for males [$\chi^2$ (2, $N = 412$) $= 12.41, p<.01$]. This model was significant for males and females. Higher levels of conflict were associated with earlier pubertal timing for females. Higher levels of school anxiety were related to delayed pubertal timing for males.

In the final step of the second model, the measure of economic anxiety was added. This addition resulted in a significant increase in the chi-squared value for males [($\chi^2$ (1, $N = 412$) $= 4.86, p<.05$]. The model was significant for males and females. Parent–teen conflict was still a significant predictor for females. For males, school anxiety remained a significant predictor, and, in addition, higher levels of economic anxiety were associated with earlier pubertal development ($p<.05$).

### Discussion

A number of precarious outcomes have been associated with earlier pubertal timing, including earlier initiation of intercourse (Meschke, et al., 2001; Meschke and Silbereisen, 1997) and higher levels of risk-taking behavior (Caspi and Moffit, 1991; see also chapter 12). Researchers have recently put forth efforts to understand factors influencing pubertal timing (e.g., Surbey, 1990; Belsky, Steinberg, and Draper, 1991). In particular, the relation between stress and pubertal timing demands further attention. Based on the review of the literature and subsequent analyses, several recommendations for future research can be made.

Gender differences in the patterns of predictors of pubertal timing are quite pervasive. Previous research has focused primarily on females. In turn, readers might be quick to conclude that female pubertal timing is particularly sensitive to stressors. However, based on the analyses conducted here, male pubertal timing can also be related to stress. Inconsistency in the significance of predictors by gender occurs frequently, as exemplified by this chapter's analyses. Perhaps most interesting is the significant relation between social stressors and pubertal timing for females (e.g., parent–teen conflict) compared with the significance of economic anxiety as a predictor of male pubertal timing.

These results may reflect the effects of gender socialization (Lytton and Romney, 1991). In a metaanalysis including 172 studies, Lytton and Romney (1991) concluded that parents emphasize achievement, restrictiveness, and disciplinary strictness to boys, whereas warmth and encouragement of dependence are emphasized slightly more to girls. The effects of differential parental encouragement of same gender-typed activities could have broader implications. Differential encouragement to various tasks in early childhood may account for the differences in responsibility.

Similar findings by gender have been reported by a number of researchers. Elder and his colleagues (1985) reported a differential effect of economic hardship by gender for parents of adolescents. Specifically, the parenting skills of fathers were negatively impacted by economic hardship, whereas maternal parenting behavior did not vary significantly with income loss. In examining the reasons underlying suicide in Japan, Lester and Saito (1999) found that job stress was prominent for males, whereas psychiatric problems were most common for female suicide victims. Hraba and his colleagues (1996) examined the association of social network events and economic events with depression. Although males and females reported similar exposure levels to social network events and economic events, male depression was more closely linked to economic events and female depression was significantly associated with social network events.

Future research should also examine more closely the relation between the timing of the stressor and pubertal timing. Different findings and assumptions support the possibility of various critical periods regarding stress and pubertal timing. Nottelmann and Susman (1989, as in Susman, Dorn, and Chrousos, 1991) suggested that during puberty the gonadal axis might be more sensitive to changes in the adrenal axis related to stress. Stimulation of adrenaline secretion due to stress would then be more likely to stimulate the secretion of growth hormones. Belsky and his colleagues (1991) emphasized the importance of stressors prior to age 7. Despite the various assumptions, very few studies have successfully tracked youth from middle childhood through puberty (Moffit, *et al.*, 1992, Ellis *et al.*, 2000).

The initial wave of MSALT data, presented in this chapter, was collected when the students were approximately 11 years old. Yet, several significant relations emerged between the psychosocial stressors and pubertal timing. These findings seem to indicate that stressors during early adolescence also play a role in pubertal timing. More studies should be initiated with respondents younger than 7 that continue to track participants through puberty. Longitudinal studies that are initiated prior to age 7 and which continue throughout adolescence would help identify critical periods regarding the relation between psychosocial predictors and pubertal timing. In this case, the MSALT data are limited, as over 20 percent of the respondents had experienced puberty prior to the initial wave of data collection. Yet, despite the potential benefits to be gained from earlier initiation of longitudinal data collection, the potential enduring nature of the included predictors implies that information about the early developing youth is known.

The analyses conducted in this chapter introduced some psychosocial stressors that were not previously examined in relation to pubertal timing. Two of these new stressors – school anxiety and economic anxiety – were significantly related to male pubertal timing. These findings encourage the incorporation of a greater variety of stressors in studies of pubertal timing.

Interestingly, higher levels of school anxiety were associated with delayed pubertal timing, whereas greater economic anxiety was related to earlier pubertal timing. It can be noted that school anxiety is an internal reaction, that is, all children experience school and regardless of ability or performance, all children can potentially experience school anxiety. This is an experience internal to each child. However, economic anxiety could potentially be relieved if the youth acquired a job. Thus, economic anxiety could serve as an environmental press for maturity, whereas little relief from school anxiety related to physical maturation is likely to occur.

Nottelmann and Welsh (1986) indicated a potential conundrum when examining the relation between stressors and pubertal timing. "tAdjustment and social stressors, adrenal activation, and reproductive maturation may constitute a 'vicious' cycle of interrelated factors during adolescence. Adjustment problems could cause activation of the adrenal glands that would cause gonadal suppression and later maturation. The latter could constitute an added stressor reentering the cycle and potentiating the 'abnormality'" (as in Susman, et al., 1989, p. 349). Greater efforts need to be made to tease out this possible feedback reaction. In addition to various stress measures, more biological predictors need to be measured, including hormone levels. In time, less invasive techniques by which to collect hormonal level data may be developed, increasing the likelihood of standard inclusion of such measures in various studies.

Indeed, the relation between parent–teen conflict and pubertal timing may exemplify such a relation. Specifically, growth spurt is a pubertal event that can be considered midpuberty. Prior to this event hormonal changes have occurred. Although only 20 percent of the sample reported having experienced growth spurt at the time the wave 1 data were

Table 11.3. *Cross-tabulation of parent–adolescent
conflict and grade of growth spurt (Percent within grade)*

| Grade of growth spurt | Low conflict (value of 1 or 2) | High conflict (value of 3 or 4) |
|---|---|---|
| 5 | 78.8 | 21.2 |
| 6 | 84.3 | 15.7 |
| 7 | 85.2 | 14.8 |
| 8 | 87.4 | 12.6 |
| 9 | 84.3 | 15.7 |
| 10 | 86.4 | 13.6 |

c2 (5, N = 637) = 2.75; p = .74

collected, it is most likely that a substantial portion of the youth had already experienced hormonal changes associated with puberty. Hormonal
changes could be influencing greater levels of conflict and not vice versa,
as tested in these analyses. However, it is important to note that many
researchers have found the *quality* of parent–adolescent conflict may increase but that the *quantity* of conflict remains relatively stable during adolescence (Dekovic, 1999; Galambos and Almeida, 1992; Laursen, Coy,
and Collins, 1998). Indeed, a follow-up chi-squared analysis of grade of
growth spurt and a dichotomized conflict measure was not significant
(see table 11.3).

Existing research, including the analyses presented in this chapter, has
taken a variable-centered approach to data interpretation. This approach
utilizes methods such as correlational, regression, and structural equa-
tion analyses. Such approaches assume that values on a continuous scale
for any given variable can be interpreted in a meaningful way for all individuals, without regard to the context in which they exist, including
the presence of other behaviors (Magnusson, 1998). For example, high
levels of stress may be considered problematic for any adolescent, regardless of the levels of other factors, such as social support or psychological
well-being. That is, with this type of approach high levels of stress could
be viewed as being as problematic for the straight-A student with high
self-esteem as it is for the adolescent who is taking drugs and reporting
high levels of depressed mood. Under the variable-centered approach, individuals are considered to differ quantitatively, rather than qualitatively
on the dimension under consideration (Magnusson, 1998).

The person-centered approach could supplement our understanding
of stress and pubertal timing by taking patterns of behaviors or characteristics within the individual into consideration (Magnusson, 1988). These

patterns of variables within the individual are applied in the formation of groups or typologies. In comparison to the traditional variable-centered approach, the person-centered approach directly accounts for interactions between variables. It is believed that a single variable cannot be fully understood when taken out of context (Magnusson, 1998). The person-centered approach might provide better understanding of why some stressors appear to accelerate pubertal timing (e.g., single mother homes; Ellis and Graber, 2000), whereas other stressors tend to delay puberty (e.g., alcoholic fathers; Malo and Tremblay, 1997).

Potential mediators and moderators of stress levels such as social support and coping mechanisms should be included in future analyses. For example, girls tend to adopt rumination as a coping strategy much more often than boys (Broderick, 1998). Rumination has been associated with greater risk of depression (Fleming and Offord, 1990), which in turn has been associated with a delay in pubertal development (Nottelmann, et al., 1990; Nottelmann and Susman, 1989, as in Susman, Dorn, and Chrousos, 1991). Interaction models, multistep regressions (Baron and Kenny, 1986), and path analyses (Jöreskog and Sörbom, 1996) are likely to more accurately capture mediating and moderating effects. This approach will be pursued in the future.

Over the centuries an acceleration of pubertal timing has been observed (Eveleth and Tanner, 1976). Nutrition has often been cited as the primary influence of this trend (e.g., Brooks-Gunn and Reiter, 1990). Yet in this chapter's analyses, family–teen conflict emerged as a significant factor in the acceleration of female pubertal timing and economic anxiety was associated with accelerated male pubertal timing. On the other hand, school anxiety was related to delayed pubertal timing for males. How do psychosocial measures factor into the observed pubertal timing trends?

The sophistication of research addressing the relation between psychosocial factors and pubertal timing has developed considerably over the past decade. The MSALT analyses included in this chapter further explore gender differences and the variety of psychosocial factors that are associated with puberty. Despite these contributions, it is obvious that greater efforts need to be applied to develop a more solid understanding of the experiences of youth in today's society.

NOTES

1. Ellis and Garber, 2000 found time with a stepfather to be a significant accelerator of female pubertal timing. A measure was created for time spent with a stepparent. This measure was substituted time with divorced parents in the first regression model. Time with a stepparent was not significant for males or females and no changes in the other significant predictors emerged.

## References

Afifi, A. A., and Clark, V. (1990). *Computer-aided multivariate analysis*, 2nd edn. New York: Van Nostrand Reinhold.

Baron, R. M., and Kenny, D. A. (1986). The moderator-mediator variable distinction in social psychological research: conceptual, strategic, and statistical considerations. *Journal of Personality and Social Psychology*, **51**, 1173–1182.

Belsky, J., Steinberg, L., and Draper, P. (1991). Childhood experience, interpersonal development and reproductive strategy: an evolutionary theory of socialization. *Child Development*, **62**, 647–670.

Broderick, P. C. (1998). Early adolescent gender differences in the use of ruminative and distracting coping strategies. *Journal of Early Adolescence*, **18**, 173–191.

Bronfenbrenner, U. (1988). Interacting systems in human development. Research paradigms: present and future. In N. Bolger, A. Caspi, G. Downey, and M. Moorehouse (ed.), *Persons in context: developmental processes* (pp. 25–49). Cambridge: Cambridge University Press.

Brooks-Gunn, J. (1988). Antecedents and consequences of variations in girls' maturational timing. *Journal of Adolescent Health Care*, **9**, 365–373.

Brooks-Gunn, J., and Reiter, E. O. (1990). The role of pubertal processes. In S. S. Feldman and G. R. Elliott (ed.), *At the threshold: the developing adolescent* (pp. 15–54). Cambridge, MA: Harvard University Press.

Brooks-Gunn, J., and Warren, M. P. (1985). Effects of delayed menarche in different contexts: dance and nondance students. *Journal of Youth and Adolescence*, **14**, 285–300.

Brooks-Gunn, J. and Warren, M. P. (1988). Mother–daughter differences in menarcheal age in adolescent dancers and nondancers. *Annals of Human Biology*, **15**, 35–43.

Brooks-Gunn, J., Petersen, A. C., and Eichorn, D. (1985). The study of maturational timing effects in adolescence. *Journal of Youth and Adolescence*, **14**, 149–161.

Campbell, B. C., and Udry, J. R. (1995). Stress and age at menarche of mothers and daughters. *Journal of Biosocial Science*, **27(2)**, 127–134.

Caspi, A., and Moffitt, T. E. (1991). Individual differences are accentuated during periods of social change: the sample case of girls at puberty. *Journal of Personality and Social Psychology*, **61**, 157–168.

Chisholm, J. S. (1993). Death, hope and sex: life-history theory and the development of reproductive strategies. *Current Anthropology*, **34**, 1–24.

D'Aurora, D. L., and Fimian, M. J. (1988). Dimensions of life and school stress experienced by young people. *Psychology in the Schools*, **25**, 44–53.

Dekovic, M. (1999). Parent–adolescent conflict: possible determinants and consequences. *International Journal of Behavioral Development*, **23 (4)**, 977–1000.

Draper, P., and Harpending, H. (1982). Father absence and reproductive strategy: an evolutionary perspective. *Journal of Anthropological Research*, **38**, 255–273.

Dubas, J. S., Graber, J. A., and Petersen, A. C. (1991). A longitudinal investigation of adolescents' changing perceptions of pubertal timing. *Developmental Psychology*, **27**, 580–586.

Eccles, J. S., Wigfield, A., Flanagan, C. A., Miller, C., Reuman, D. A., and Yee, D. (1989). Self-concepts, domain values, and self-esteem: relations and changes at early adolescence. *Journal of Personality*, **57**, 283–310.

Elder, G. H., Nguyen, T. V., and Caspi, A. (1985). Linking family hardship to children's lives. *Child Development*, **56**, 361–375.

Ellis, B. J., and Garber, J. (2000). Psychosocial antecedents of variation in girls' pubertal timing: maternal depression, stepfather presence, and marital and family stress. *Child Development*, **71(2)**, 485–501.

Ellis, B. J., McFadyen-Ketchum, S., Dodge, K. A., Pettit, G. S., and Bates, J. E. (1999). Quality of early family relationships and individual differences in the timing of pubertal maturation in girls: a longitudinal test of an evolutionary model. *Journal of Personality and Social Psychology*, **77(2)**, 387–401.

Ellis, N. B. (1991). An extension of the Steinberg Accelerating Hypothesis. *Journal of Early Adolescence*, **11**, 221–235.

Eveleth, P., and Tanner, J. (1976). *Worldwide variation in human growth*. Cambridge: Cambridge University Press.

Fleming, J. E., and Offord, D. R. (1990). Epidemiology of childhood depressive disorders: a critical review. *Journal of the American Academy of Child and Adolescent Psychiatry*, **29(4)**, 571–580.

Frisch, R. E. (1983). Fatness, puberty, and fertility: the effects of nutrition and physical training on menarche and ovulation. In J. Brooks-Gunn and A. C. Petersen (ed.), *Girls at puberty: biological and psychosocial perspectives* (pp. 29–55). New York: Plenum.

Galambos, N. L., and Almeida, D. M. (1992). Does parent–adolescent conflict increase in early adolescence? *Journal of Marriage and the Family*, **54(4)**, 737–747.

Graber, J. A., Brooks-Gunn, J., and Warren, M. P. (1995). The antecedents of menarcheal age: heredity, family environment, and stressful life events. *Child Development*, **66(2)**, 346–359.

Graber, J. A., Petersen, A. C., and Brooks-Gunn, J. (1996). Pubertal processes: methods, measures, and models. In J. A. Graber, J. Brooks-Gunn, and A. C. Petersen (ed.), *Transitions through adolescence: interpersonal domains and context* (pp. 23–53). Hillsdale, NJ: Lawrence Erlbaum.

Harter, S. (1979). *Manual: perceived competence scale for children*. Denver, Co: University of Denver Press.

Himes, J. H., and Dietz, W. H. (1994). Guidelines for overweight in adolescent preventive services: recommendations from an expert committee. *American Journal of Clinical Nutrition*, **59**, 307–316.

Hraba, J., Lorenz, F. O., Lee, G., and Pechacova, Z. (1996). Gender and well-being in the Czech Republic. *Sex Roles*, **34**, 517–533.

Jones, B., Leeton, J., McLeod, I., and Wood, C. (1972). Factors influencing the age of menarche in a lower socioeconomic group in Melbourne. *Medical Journal of Australia*, **21**, 533–535.

Jöreskog, K. G., and Sörbom, D. (1996). Lisrel 8: user's reference guide. Chicago, IL: Scientific Software International.

Kampert, J. B., Whittemore, A. S., and Paffenbarger, R. S. (1988). Combined effects of childbearing, menstrual events, and body size on age-specific breast cancer risk. *American Journal of Epidemiology*, **128**, 962–979.

Kim, K., and Smith, P. K. (1998a). Childhood stress, behavioral symptoms and mother–daughter pubertal development. *Journal of Adolescence*, 21, 231–240.

Kim, K., and Smith, P. K. (1998b). Retrospective survey of parental marital relations and child reproductive development. *International Journal of Behavioral Development*, 22(4), 729–751.

Kim, K., and Smith, P. K. (1999). Family relations in early childhood and reproductive development. *Journal of Reproductive Infant Psychology*, 17, 133.

Kim, K., Smith, P. K., and Palermiti, A. (1997). Conflict in childhood and reproductive development. *Evolution and Human Behavior*, 18, 109–142.

Laursen, B., Coy, K. C., and Collins, W. A. (1998). Reconsidering changes in parent–child conflict across adolescence: a metaanalysis. *Child Development*, 69(3), 817–832.

Lester, D., and Saito, Y. (1999). The reasons for suicide in Japan. *Omega: Journal of Death and Dying*, 38, 65–68.

Luger, A., Deuster, P. A., Kyle, S. B., Gallucci, B. S., Montgomery, L. C., Gold, P. W., Loriaux, D. L., and Chrousos, G. P. (1987). Acute hypothalamic-pituitary-adrenal responses to the stress of treadmill exercise: physiologic adaptations to physical training. *New England Journal of Medicine*, 316, 1309–1315.

Lytton, H., and Romney, D. (1991). Parents' differential socialization of boys and girls: a meta-analysis. *Psychological Bulletin*, 109, 267–296.

Magnusson, D. (1988). *Individual development from an interactional perspective*, vol. I of D. Magnusson (ed.), *Paths through life: a longitudinal research program*. Hillsdale, NJ: Lawrence Erlbaum.

Magnusson, D. (1998). The logic and implications of a person-oriented approach. In R. B. Cairns, M. Radke-Yarrow, L. R., and J. Kagan Bergman (ed.), *Methods and models for studying the individual* (pp. 33–64). Thousand Oaks, CA: Sage.

Malina, R. M., Katzmarzyk, P. T., Bonci, C. M., Ryan, R. C., and Wellens, R. E. (1997). Family size and age at menarche in athletes. *Medicine and Science in Sports and Exercise*, 29(1), 99–106.

Malo, J., and Tremblay, R. E. (1997). The impact of paternal alcoholism and maternal social position on boys' school adjustment, pubertal maturation and sexual behavior: a test of two competing hypotheses. *Journal of Child Psychology and Psychiatry*, 38, 187–197.

Meschke, L. L., and Silbereisen, R. K. (1997). The influence of puberty, family processes, and leisure activities on the timing of first sexual experience. *Journal of Adolescence*, 20, 403–418.

Meschke, L. L., Zweig, J. M., Barber, B. L., and Eccles, J. S. (2001). Demographic, biological, psychological, and social predictors of the timing of first intercourse. *Journal of Research on Adolescence*, 10, 317–341.

Moffitt, T. E., Caspi, A., Belsky, J., and Silva, P. A. (1992). Childhood experience and the onset of menarche: a test of a sociobiological model. *Child Development*, 63, 47–58.

Nottelmann, E. D., and Welsh, C. J. (1986). The long and short of physical stature in early adolescence. *Journal of Early Adolescence*, 6, 15–27.

Nottelmann, E. D., Inoff-Germain, G., Susman, E. J., and Chrousos, G. P. (1990). Hormones and behavior at puberty. In J. Bancroft and J. M.

Reinisch (ed.), *Adolescence and puberty* (pp. 88–123). Oxford: Oxford University Press.

Petersen, A. C. (1985). Pubertal development as a cause of disturbance: myths, realities, and unanswered questions. *Genetic, Social, and General Psychology Monographs*, 111, 205–232.

SAS Institute (1990). SAS technical report P-217 SAS/STAT software: the PHRGG procedure, version 6. Cary, NC: SAS Institute Inc.

Silbereisen, R. K., and Kracke, B. (1993). Variation in maturational timing and adjustment in adolescence. In S. Jackson and H. Rodriguez-Tomé (ed.), *Adolescence and its social worlds* (pp. 67–94). Hillsdale, NJ: Lawrence Erlbaum.

Silbereisen, R. K., and Kracke, B. (1997). Self-reported maturational timing and adaptation in adolescence. In J. Schulenberg, J. Maggs, and K. Hurrelmann (ed.), *Health risks and developmental transitions during adolescence* (pp. 85–109). Cambridge: Cambridge University Press.

Silbereisen, R. K., Petersen, A. C., Albrecht, H. T., and Kracke, B. (1989). Maturational timing and development of problem behavior: longitudinal studies in adolescence. *Journal of Early Adolescence*, 9, 247–268.

Simpson, J. (1999). Attachment theory in modern evolutionary perspective. In J. Cassidy and P. R. Shaver (ed.). *Handbook of attachment: theory, research, and clinical applications*. New York: Guilford Press.

Steinberg, L. (1988). Reciprocal relation between parent–child distance and pubertal maturation. *Developmental Psychology*, 24, 122–128.

Steinberg, L. (1989). Pubertal maturation and parent–adolescent distance: an evolutionary perspective. In G. R. Adams, R. Montemayor, and T. P. Gullotta (ed.), *Advances in adolescent development: an annual book series*. Volume I, *Biology of adolescent behavior and development* (pp. 71–97). Thousand Oaks, CA: Sage.

Stukovsky, R., Valsik, J. A., and Bulaistirbu, M. (1967). Family size and menarcheal age in Costanza, Romania. *Human Biology*, 39, 277–283.

Surbey, M. K. (1990). Family composition, stress, and the timing of human menarche. In T. E. Ziegler and F. B. Bercovitch (ed.), *Socioendocrinology of primate reproduction. Monographs in primatology* (vol. XIII, pp. 11–32). New York: John Wiley–Liss.

Surbey, M. K. (1998). Parent and offspring strategies in the transition at adolescence. *Human Nature*, 9(1), 67–94.

Susman, E. J. (1997). Modeling developmental complexity in adolescence: hormones and behavior in context. *Journal of Research on Adolescence*, 7, 283–306.

Susman, E. J., Dorn, L. D., and Chrousos, G. P. (1991). Negative affect and hormone levels in young adolescents: concurrent and predictive perspectives. *Journal of Youth and Adolescence*, 20, 167–190.

Susman, E. J., Nottelmann, E. D., Dorn, L. D., Gold, P. W., and Chrousos, G. P. (1989a). The physiology of stress and behavioral development. In D. S. Palermo (ed.), *Coping with uncertainty: behavioral and development perspectives* (pp. 17–37). Hillsdale, NJ: Lawrence Erlbaum.

Susman, E. J., Nottelmann, E. D., Inoff-Germain, G., and Chrousos, G. P. (1989b). Physiological and behavioral aspects of stress in adolescence. In

G. P. Chrousos, D. L. Loriaux, and P. W. Gold (ed.), *Physical and emotional stress: biochemical mechanisms and clinical implications*. New York: Plenum.

Susman, E. J., Nottleman, E. D., Inoff-Germain, G. E., Loriaux, D. L., and Chrousos, G. P. (1985). The relation of relative hormonal levels and physical development and social-emotional behavior in young adolescents. *Journal of Youth and Adolescence*, **14**, 245–264.

Trickett, P. K., and Putnam, F. W. (1993). Impact of child sexual abuse on females: towards a developmental, psychobiological integration. *Psychological Science*, **4**, 81–87.

Warren, M. P. (1980). The effects of exercise on pubertal progression and reproductive function in girls. *Journal of Clinical Endocrinology and Metabolism*, **51**, 1150–1157.

Warren, M. P., Brooks-Gunn, J., Hamilton, L. H., Hamilton, W. G., and Warren, L. F. (1986). Scoliosis and fractures in young ballet dancers: relationship to delayed menarcheal age and secondary amenorrhea. *New England Journal of Medicine*, **314**, 1348–1353.

Wierson, M., Long, P. J., and Forehand, R. L. (1993). Toward a new understanding of early menarche: the role of environmental stress in pubertal timing. *Adolescence*, **28(112)**, 913–924.

Yamagnchi, K. (1991). *Event history analysis*. Wewbury Park, CA: Sage.

*Part 6*

# Pubertal timing: consequences

# 12 Short-term and long-term consequences of early versus late physical maturation in adolescents

*Karina Weichold, Rainer K. Silbereisen, and Eva Schmitt-Rodermund*

We are all confronted almost daily with a major source of interindividual variation – people of the same chronological age vary tremendously in physical attributes and behaviors. Some look younger (and consequently may feel younger) than their age would predict, whereas others look older (and may disregard this entirely). A particularly impressive case of variation occurs during puberty: whereas some early adolescents appear physically almost fully grown, others still remind one of a child, and yet both may attend the same classroom and share the same chronological age. In the many domains of everyday interactions we adapt our behavior to the perceived age of others, our expectations and behavioral overtures toward young people may be inadequate; either we treat them like grown-ups (thus overtaxing capabilities) or like children (thereby underestimating potential). At any rate, it is likely that such behaviors, if persistent, could lead to age-inappropriate changes in the behavior of the young. Social reactions to physical maturation also vary widely across cultures. The onset of puberty in girls is universally followed by more restrictions than is observed for boys. Girls are subjected to menstrual taboos, dress codes, and limitations of their activities, whereas boys usually do not have to deal with increased supervision and limitations of their freedom (Petersen, Silbereisen, and Sörensen, 1996).

This chapter deals with interindividual variation in the timing of puberty and its association with differences in psychosocial functioning; as will be seen, this relationship is complex and goes well beyond the role of the social processes just mentioned. More specifically, we describe these associations in detail, as well as reveal the mediating processes. As an advanced organizer for the variables involved, we rely on a model introduced by Brooks-Gunn, Graber, and Paikoff (1994), but before turning to concepts and substantive results, we need to provide some groundwork on pubertal changes, the causes of differences in timing, and how pubertal timing can be assessed.

## Puberty: variation in timing

The period between childhood and adulthood is characterized by the most rapid and extensive biological changes since the endocrinological organization during the fetal period (Tanner, 1975; Brooks-Gunn and Reiter, 1990; see also chapter 2). Puberty is considered a major developmental milestone both for the physical and social transitions into adolescence and adulthood; it is a key developmental challenge for the developing individual. In addition to the effects hormonal changes have on mood, body, cognition, and personality, young people face others' reactions to their more mature appearance. They need to learn to cope with feelings of sexual arousal and issues of sexual relationships, as well as adjust their self-image to their new appearance and feelings.

The timing of the various changes during puberty shows a tremendous variation across individuals. For a long time genetic differences were seen as the only determinant of variation in pubertal timing (Tanner, 1962). Indeed, mothers' and daughters' timing of menarche correlate about .26 to .45 (Brooks-Gunn and Warren, 1985; Zacharias and Wurtman, 1969), and differences in pubertal timing of girls of different ethnic groups also suggest that heredity has at least some influence (Herman-Giddens, *et al.*, 1997). Nevertheless, the most powerful determinant of variation in maturational timing is socioeconomic status, mediated by differences in nutrition and health status. Puberty typically is delayed in poor or rural settings, with the age of menarche in girls and growth in boys being about a year or two later in such populations (Eveleth and Tanner, 1976; Ezeome, *et al.*, 1997).

In addition, specific activities such as professional sports or dancing have been shown to delay menarche. Adolescent ballet dancers' age at menarche was considerably delayed, with 15 years of age being the average, and their body weight was 10 to 15 percent below the norm (Warren, 1983). Similar mechanisms have also been shown for boys (Frisch, 1983). The average age at menarche in girls who were blind or who did not participate in sports was earlier as compared to the general population (Zacharias and Wurtman, 1969; Malina, *et al.*, 1973). Thus, limited activity seems to accelerate the accumulation of body fat at an earlier age, whereas strict training seems to delay weight gain. A critical amount of body fat, in turn, is assumed to be relevant for the onset of reproductivity (Warren, 1983; Frisch, 1983; see also chapter 2).

The status and timing of puberty have been measured with a range of different methods (see Graber, Petersen, and Brooks-Gunn, 1996, and chapter 1 of this volume, for an overview). Pubertal status is usually assessed using pictures of boys and girls in the five stages of pubertal development, according to Tanner (1974). The raters are physicians or parents, but self-descriptions were shown to be as reliable (Duke, Litt, and Gross, 1980). The use of the Tanner scales in nonmedical contexts, however, has been considered problematic by school authorities and parents. Thus, for such purposes, a scale of pubertal maturation was developed that required self-ratings and did not involve any picture material. Petersen and colleagues' (1988) Pubertal Development Scale uses a four-point rating format to assess the status of development of several secondary sex characteristics, such as breast development. No age norms are given, but results proved to be very close to other measures of pubertal status at a given age. Other methods, such as endocrinological ratings of pubertal status, are expensive, and, consequently are not used often in the context of studies with larger samples (Susman, 1997).

Pubertal timing represents an index of pubertal status relative to a given age (see chapter 1). In many studies, adolescents were grouped using population norms (Duke-Duncan, *et al.*, 1985) or classified according to the sample distribution into early, on-time, and late developers. Others used sample values in order to indicate the deviation from the mean: more than one standard deviation above or below the group mean is seen as the threshold for early or late pubertal maturation (Alsaker, 1992). Alternatively, subjective ratings of pubertal timing have been used; adolescents were asked to assess their pubertal timing as earlier, same, or later than their peers (Dubas, Graber, and Petersen, 1991a). The results show rather high correlations to other more objective measures and moderate stability when assessed over time (Silbereisen and Kracke, 1993).

### Consequences of early versus late pubertal development in boys and girls for various domains of psychosocial functioning

We will now concentrate on differences in pubertal timing and try to extract from a diverse range of literature the gist of what is known about its consequences for psychosocial functioning. Therefore, we are not interested in the association between pubertal status and behavior, but rather in the role of the interindividual differences in the timing of pubertal and physical changes. From the outset it should be clear that virtually all of the studies reported are correlational (sometimes longitudinal) in nature, with no experimental control of the crucial timing variable. Although this is necessary for ethical reasons, it should be clear that the "consequences" discussed qualify as such, not by virtue of systematic variation, but due to the conceptual framework.

*Theoretical approaches*

Concerning the role of variation in pubertal timing on immediate behavioral consequences and long-term adjustment, a number of conceptual approaches have been developed, which basically fall into two categories. The first specifies a relation between timing and behavior, but is rather silent as to the nature of the biopsychosocial processes mediating the relationship. The second, and more recent, approach concerns such processes and distinguishes various models with regard to the complexity of the mechanisms postulated.

As far as the first type of conceptualizations is concerned, there are two propositions that differ in the role given to early timing (Brooks-Gunn, Petersen, and Eichorn, 1985) versus off-timing. According to the "deviance hypothesis," every deviation from the norm perceived by the individual and others implies difficulties for psychosocial development. Consequently, one would expect early and late timing to be equally problematic for adjustment (although not necessarily of the same nature). Thus, if a girl who developed earlier than others feels negative concerning her body due to untimely (relative to others) body fat and resulting feminine appearance, a girl who developed later may also suffer concerning her body image, but, rather, due to her childlike body.

In contrast, the "stage termination hypothesis" predicts difficulties concerning adjustment, particularly for adolescents revealing early pubertal timing. The basic notion behind this model is that these youngsters lack the time to adapt gradually (intellectually as well as emotionally) to pubertal changes and their social consequences (e.g., the reactions of others to their more mature body). Thus, using the same example as above, only early-maturing girls would develop negative feelings toward their bodies, probably because they lack the foresight that this is a transitional period and have not yet developed skills to deal with the resulting expectation of others (e.g., boys).

Particularly concerning the deviance hypothesis, a number of qualifications were suggested in the literature. Depending on ethnic background (or other group membership) the threshold for acceptable deviations from the norm (not only related to puberty) may vary (Lerner, 1985), and girls may be affected more than boys due to the generally stronger normative expectations for females concerning psychosexual issues (Zakin, Blyth, and Simmons, 1984).

Moreover, it looks as if the two models do not fit equally to all behavioral domains affected by timing differences (see chapter 13). In our own research on subjective developmental timing relative to peers (Silbereisen and Kracke, 1997), we found a clear difference between adjustment difficulties in the internalizing (e.g., depressive mood) and the external-izing (e.g., underage drinking) domains. The stage termination model seems to fit better to externalizing behaviors. Adolescents with early pu-bertal timing cannot resist contact with older peers, for whom behaviors such as alcohol use are already normative, and they may even actively seek such contact. Among boys, older peers were important in helping to gain access to relevant leisure settings, whilst among girls, older peers of-fer better empathy concerning the unsettling feelings of early-developing girls. In contrast, internalizing adjustment problems seem to match the deviance hypothesis better. Early and late developing girls were irritated and upset by boys' comments about their bodies, and particularly late developing boys felt inferior in social comparisons with other boys and girls. It should be noted that girls on average mature about one to two years earlier than boys, which means that a late developing boy is very obvious in a coeducational setting.

Although experiences in social interactions obviously play a role in these models, the relationship with the pubertal processes is not really made explicit. The second type of model mentioned earlier details such pathways between the pubertal changes and the developmental outcomes in adjustment. According to Graber, Petersen, and Brooks-Gunn (1996; see also chapter 14), any model specifying the relationship between pu-bertal and social events in adjustment needs to be mediative rather than direct, bidirectional rather than unidirectional, and interactive rather than additive. Concerning mediation, past research that tried to show direct hormone-behavior effects did not meet expectations (see chapters 3 and 8). It is known, for instance, that levels of testosterone are related to sexual activity in boys (Udry, et al., 1985), although initiation of sexuality may be more related to behavioral standards in peer groups. Likewise, sexual intercourse itself may increase androgen levels, thus demonstrating a bidirectional influence. Finally, effects of pubertal tim-ing are probably best described according to the active and evocative genotype–environment covariation postulated by Scarr and McCartney (1983). It states that depending on the timing, adolescents will actively look for environments that match their potential or avoid those that do not, which will also evoke certain behaviors. Note that such a framework nicely suits the result of Silbereisen and Kracke (1997) reported earlier: timing and environmental opportunities interact, rather than just having independent additive effects.

Brooks-Gunn, Graber, and Paikoff (1994) introduced the most com-prehensive and still up-to-date conceptualization of a model satisfying the criteria mentioned above. Its target variable is affective states, either favoring internalizing or externalizing behaviors. The model, as depicted

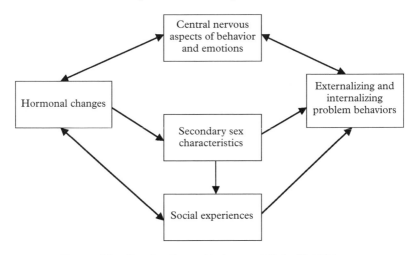

Source: After Brooks-Gunn, Graber, and Paikoff, 1994
Figure 12.1 Model for development of problem behaviors during puberty

in figure 12.1, postulates three mediational processes between hormonal changes during puberty and the short-term outcomes. The first concerns the well-documented effect that the timing of the development of secondary sexual characteristics (e.g., breast development, menarche, etc.) links hormonal changes and affective states. The second mediational pathway concerns the external perspective, that is, the behavior of others toward the adolescent, including the experiences of the adolescent that result from this attention, and its effect on affective states. This contextual effect is in part provoked directly by the hormonal changes; it is a response to the changed bodily characteristics, particular those directly visible. These two mediational processes were obviously addressed in the stage termination and the deviance hypothesis.

The third mediational link shown in figure 12.1 is new and refers to central nervous processes instigated by the hormonal changes that consequently have an effect on behavioral outcomes. Although recent research has revealed functional and structural brain changes during adolescence that are related to externalizing problem behaviors (Spear, 2000), the hormonal influences still need to be clarified. The same caution applies to the view that the secular acceleration of puberty (about three to four months per decade during the last century; Tanner, 1975) has resulted in a previously unknown discrepancy between advanced behavioral options (e.g., concerning sexuality) and cognitive development. In our research (Miltner, *et al.*, 2001, see below) we tried to shed more light on differences in information processing as a function of pubertal timing.

Some of the pathways depicted are bidirectional, indicating that adolescents' experiences with others and their own behavior may feed back into the central nervous and hormonal systems, and may even have a delaying or promoting effect on puberty itself (see Belsky, Steinberg, and Draper, 1991 for an overview).

The main objective of the remainder of this chapter is to provide information on associations between pubertal timing and adjustment variables seen in short- and long-term perspective, and to discuss what is known about the mediating mechanisms. The model by Brooks-Gunn and colleagues (1994) represents a point of reference that allows the processes of the larger framework to be emitted from recent research. As noted, the original model does not specify how a change in affective states should result in a change in adolescents' short- or long-term adjustment and development. Upon closer inspection this is not a weakness but is actually a strength; a specific linkage with maladjustment is not claimed, rather, it is a tendency for heightened depressive or aggressive affect that puts adolescents on a somewhat deviant trajectory. This can lead to long-term maladjustment, provided other risk factors provoked by the heightened affect come into play.

## Short-term consequences of pubertal timing in boys and girls

### Behavioral differences in different contexts

During puberty, increasing conflict at home cause adolescents to see their parents in a different light and to develop a sense of individuation (Hofer, et al., 1993). Individuation is characterized by an increase of autonomy accompanied by the maintenance of emotional connectedness between adolescents and parents (Youniss and Smollar, 1985). In this process, parents lose their influence as primary socialization agents. This begins typically during puberty and is especially true for families of early-maturing adolescents, where older peers become socialization forces in their own right (Stattin and Magnusson, 1990).

*Peer context*  Early-maturing girls tend to associate with older male peers (Magnusson, Stattin, and Allen, 1985; Stattin and Magnusson, 1990; Weichold and Silbereisen, 2001). For early-maturing girls, older males are more attractive than boys of their own age, who are perceived as less socially mature (Kracke, 1993). With regard to same-sex peer relations, Hannover (1997) reported that early-maturing girls prefer early and on-time (but not late maturing) girls as friends among their peers. Socializing with other adolescents of the same maturational age leads to more frequent visits of leisure places, such as clubs, that present them with a variety of age-inappropriate opportunities (Weichold and Silbereisen, 2001; Silbereisen and Kracke, 1997). Furthermore, early-maturing girls entertain more intensive contacts with norm-violating peers and share a higher proportion of friends that approve of drinking alcohol and truancy (Silbereisen and Kracke, 1997).

Moreover, early-maturing girls enjoy romantic relationships earlier (Silbereisen and Kracke, 1997), think about sex more often, have unsupervised outings with boys, and feel more sexually experienced in comparison to their peers (Prokopáková, 1998). Among early-maturing German girls, ages 13 through 16, 80 percent reported having a steady boyfriend, compared with 50 percent among late maturers (Silbereisen, Kracke, and Nowak, 1992). Attempts have been made to explain these timing differences with the role of hormones and social experiences. Studies including hormonal measures found that serum concentrations of adrenal androgens had a strong effect on girls' sexual behaviors, but not on their experience of intercourse (Udry, *et al.*, 1985). Furthermore, testosterone levels were related to the timing of subsequent transition to first coitus (Tucker-Halpern, Udry, and Suchindran, 1997). Concerning social experiences, attendance at religious services played a moderating role in white females, probably due to the social control involved. American female virgins (11–17 years old) whose best friends were sexually experienced were almost certain to experience intercourse within two years of the study (Billy and Udry, 1985). Moreover, having an older boyfriend increased the risk for early sexual experiences in early-maturing girls (Stattin and Magnusson, 1990).

The findings for boys are less consistent. There is a tendency in early-maturing boys to report more frequent contacts with norm-violating peers as compared to on-time and late maturing age-mates during early adolescence, but these effects were not found later in adolescence (Silbereisen and Kracke, 1997). Furthermore, early maturation in boys was related to early sexual experiences. For instance, in a German sample (Silbereisen, Kracke, and Nowak, 1992) at ages 13 to 16, the proportion of early-maturing boys having a steady girlfriend was 50 percent, as compared to 15 percent among late maturing boys. Studies measuring pubertal timing by using hormonal indices found high-for-age adrenal androgen levels in boys to be related to a higher likelihood of engagement into dating (Susman, *et al.*, 1987), and for serum concentration of testosterone to predict sexual motivations and behaviors in adolescent boys (Udry, *et al.*, 1985). Further investigations revealed that there was no direct hormone–behavior association, but rather change in pubertal development was related to sexual activity due to its social stimulus value (Tucker-Halpern, *et al.*, 1993). This, again, may interact with experiences in the peer group. Smith, Udry, and Morris (1985) concluded that advancements in pubertal development and friends' sexual behaviors clearly predict an adolescent's own sexual behaviors.

*Family context*    Adolescents often envision status passages at an earlier age than their parents (Dekovic, Noom, and Meeus, 1997), whereas parents are more likely to orient themselves on the social norms conveyed by adolescents' chronological age. In families with early-maturing adolescents, the discrepancy between parental and adolescent expectations toward developmental timetables seems to be even larger than in most other families. Furthermore, this discrepancy might be particularly pronounced in most families of early-maturing girls, because parents are willing to revise their timetables for daughters to a lesser extent than for sons (Paikoff and Brooks-Gunn, 1992). The following studies mainly concern girls.

According to Laursen and Collins (1994), close systems such as families are prone to increasing conflicts when the interaction partners have to revise expectations toward each other. A case in point is families with children of nonnormative pubertal development. Parents are confused about how to react adequately toward seemingly age-inappropriate striving for autonomy and individuation (Alsaker, 1995). According to questionnaire data, conflicts in families of early-maturing adolescents, regardless of the topic, seem to be more frequent and intense than in other families (Savin-Williams and Small, 1986; Steinberg, 1988; Sagrestano, McCormick, and Holmbeck, 1999). For early-maturing girls, research showed that interactions at home were more conflictual and restrictive (Hill and Holmbeck, 1987), and that they had more interpersonal problems with parents, especially when the girls were both objectively and subjectively early maturing (Ruiselová, 1998). Moreover, late maturation in boys and girls seems to be linked with more authoritarian parental reactions, which is associated with higher rates of family conflict (Steinberg, 1988). This result, however, was not replicated in boys only (Peskin and Livson, 1972), which might be due to the fact that late maturation in girls is more socially accepted than in boys.

Two studies utilized observation methodologies in order to look more closely at the concrete interactions between early maturers and their parents during conflict discussions. First, during mother–daughter conflict discussions, on-time maturing girls showed more mutually accepting

behaviors than did other girls. Furthermore, girls with off-time maturation were highest in explaining and arguing to make their points clear
(Hauser, *et al.*, 1985). Second, a recent German investigation of dyadic
interactions between early adolescent girls and their mothers revealed
that both early- and late maturing girls were higher in their striving for
individuation toward their mothers. This was evident in these girls caring
more for the flow of interchange and soliciting input from their mothers
than on-time maturers. Only mothers of the early maturers, however, re-
ciprocated the behaviors in a symmetric way; they were lowest in control
and power, indicating higher individuation. In contrast, late maturers also
strove for autonomy, but their behavior was not accepted by their mothers
(Weichold, *et al.*, in press). In this sense, late maturers' behaviors might
be a strategy to compensate for their less advanced physical development,
whereas in the dyads with early-maturing girls the relationship appears
to be more on an equal footing.

In sum, early-maturing girls and boys, especially during early and mid
adolescence, tend to socialize with older peers, engage in norm-breaking
activities, and entertain earlier romantic and sexual experiences. There is
little evidence for a direct relationship between sex hormones and sexual
experiences during adolescence. Rather, behavioral differences among
adolescents can be explained by their advanced pubertal development
and the influence of sexually experienced peers. In their family contexts,
early maturers (especially girls) experience more conflicts associated with
higher levels of individuation and autonomy within parent–adolescent interactions in midadolescence. Thus, relationships in the peer and family
context of early maturers appear to be more advanced and mature as
compared to their age-mates. With regard to the model by Brooks-Gunn,
Graber, and Paikoff (1994), the evidence is most prominent for the pathway from own experiences with others' reactions to the outcome.

### Internalizing problems and affective experiences

*Eating behaviors*

During puberty, adolescents (especially girls) are at increased risk for developing eating problems, which range from body dissatisfaction, through
nonpathological dieting, to serious eating disorders. Although less than
10 percent of adolescent girls suffer from eating disorders, the majority
engages in special diets or in excessive exercise, even though they are
not clinically overweight (Davies and Furnham, 1986). Various findings
indicate that negative body image is a risk factor for eating problems
(e.g., Wichstrøm, 1995; Koff and Rierdan, 1993). Furthermore,

excessive weight concerns in female adolescents are predicted by the importance their peers put on weight, being teased about their weight, or trying to copy females in the media (Taylor, *et al.*, 1998). Thus, it seems plausible that early pubertal timing, associated with early increase in body fat, has an effect on girls' eating behaviors. No studies on the relationship between pubertal timing and problematic eating during adolescence exist for boys.

Results indicate that early-maturing girls are more negative about their bodies and have higher rates of dieting, even after their later maturing peers have caught up and reached puberty (Brooks-Gunn, 1987; see also chapter 4). Various studies from different countries support a link between early maturation in puberty and problematic eating habits, a drive for thinness, and bulimia in girls (e.g., Keel, Fulkerson, and Leon, 1997; Wichstrøm, 1995). This might be explained by the high weight, low body satisfaction, and high feelings of worthlessness in early-maturing girls (Killen, *et al.*, 1994). Graber and colleagues (1994) reported results from an eight-year longitudinal study where early menarche and a higher percentage of body fat predicted eating problems in midadolescence, as well as subsequent chronological eating problems.

The particular experiences in family and peer contexts seem to modify the risk for eating disorders. For instance, self-perceived early maturation in 15- to 17-year-old girls with distant family relationships was linked with eating problems (Swarr and Richards, 1996). Furthermore, early-maturing girls who were already dating at ages 13 and 14 appeared to be at highest risk for problem eating behaviors among their age cohort (Smolak, Levine, and Gralen, 1993).

In sum, girls with early pubertal timing appear to be at particular risk for problematic eating habits throughout adolescence (see chapter 4). Beyond lower body image as a mediating factor, the timing effects can be exacerbated by precocious dating and strained family relationships, which may or may not be seen as consequences of early maturation.

*Moods and emotions*

Pubertal timing has been linked repeatedly with internalizing problems, such as depressive mood, including major depression; during adolescence the rate of depression increases. Among prepubescent children, no gender differences in the prevalence of depressive symptoms have been obtained, however by midadolescence girls show higher rates of depressive disorders, symptoms, and depressive affect than boys (Nolen-Hoeksema, 1994; Ge, Conger, and Elder, 2001; Wichstrøm, 1999; see also chapter 8). Self-worth and self-evaluations, which are reportedly lower in early-maturing girls and late maturing boys, are predictors of depression during adolescence (Harter and Whitesell, 1996). Furthermore, body image and eating-related risk factors contribute to elevated levels of depression in girls (Stice, *et al.*, 2000). Thus, there is a common assumption that early-maturing girls and late maturing boys might be at risk for negative moods and emotions.

A large body of research supports the prediction that early-maturing girls are particularly at risk for depressed mood or emotional distress during midadolescence. Also, early timing in girls has been linked with more severe expression of internalized symptoms, such as depressive symptoms, panic attacks (Hayward, *et al.*, 1997), and suicide attempts (Wichstrøm, 1998).

Using objective measures for pubertal timing, some studies have associated early maturation with higher depressed mood in adolescence, even in late adolescence (e.g., Petersen and Crockett, 1985; Petersen, Sarigiani, and Kennedy, 1991; Ge, *et al.*, 1996). In other studies, however, objective pubertal timing (based on breast development) was not linked with depressive symptoms (Angold, Costello, and Worthman, 1998) or emotional distress during early adolescence (Tschann, *et al.*, 1994). With respect to self-perceived pubertal timing, in a nationally representative Norwegian sample, depressive mood was predicted by perceived advanced pubertal development in 12- to 20-year-old females (Wichstrøm, 1999). Further, perceived early maturation was linked with depression and negative mood in midadolescence (Alsaker, 1992; Schmitt-Rodermund and Ittel, 1999; Richards and Larson, 1993), but not with objective pubertal timing (Alsaker, 1992).

Silbereisen and Kracke (1997) investigated the relation between self-perceived and objective maturational timing and emotional problems (i.e., feelings of aggression and anxiety) in a sample of 13/14- and 15/16-year-old girls. No systematic difference in depression by perceived pubertal timing was found, but early objective timing based on age at menarche was linked with more anxiety and depressed feelings in younger girls. In older girls, no significant difference between pubertal timing groups emerged. These results are in line with Stattin and Magnusson (1990), who reported no association between perceived timing and depressive moods, but who did find a distinct relationship between objective measures of pubertal timing and depression in girls. The results of both studies support a link between physical changes, their hormonal background, and emotional difficulties rather than a pathway mediated through perceived timing differences and thus social reactions (see chapter 13). Furthermore, as the study by Silbereisen and Kracke suggests, the effects of pubertal timing seem to be rather circumscribed and short-lived (restricted to the beginning of puberty). Several studies investigated the actual interplay of hormones and emotions during puberty. Results indicate that depressive symptoms and withdrawal are highest in girls during the period of fastest increase in estradiol concentrations, which occurs at the beginning of puberty. Conversely, secondary sex characteristics (e.g., Tanner stages), pubertal timing, and age of first menarche show no effect on depressive mood (Brooks-Gunn and Warren, 1989). High levels of testosterone and high levels of cortisol in girls have been related to sad affect (Susman, Dorn, and Chrousos, 1991), and high-for-age follicle-stimulating hormones were positively associated with depressed affect (Buchanan, Eccles, and Becker, 1992). These results suggest a link between high levels of puberty-related hormones and depressive mood in girls of the same chronological age (see chapter 8). In their study, Paikoff, Brooks-Gunn, and Warren (1991) found hormones and pubertal stages to be linked with depressed affect in 10- to 14-year-old girls, but not with objective pubertal timing. In this way, girls' moods and emotions seem to be influenced by hormonal and physiological changes, primarily during early adolescence.

In addition to hormones predicting negative moods and emotions in early maturers, psychological mechanisms, particularly related to body dissatisfaction, are likely to play a role in the increase of depressive mood in early-maturing girls (see chapter 4). Throughout adolescence, girls become more dissatisfied with their bodies, regardless of objective ratings of attractiveness and actual body fat proportion (Rosenblum and Lewis, 1999). Body image, in turn, has been found to be a key determinant of self-esteem (and depressive mood) in adolescents (Cairns, et al., 1990). Early maturation in girls has been linked with negative body image and low body satisfaction (e.g., Blyth, Simmons, and Zakin, 1985; Richards and Larson, 1993; O'Dea and Abraham, 1999). Early maturers were more dissatisfied with their own weight (Stattin and Magnusson, 1990), with 69 percent of the girls wishing to be thinner (Duke-Duncan, et al., 1985). These associations were explained by an early confrontation with the thin body ideal preferred in western cultures (Cash and Henry, 1995), social experiences in the peer context (i.e., teasing; Silbereisen and Kracke, 1997), or the lower satisfaction with specific parts of the body, such as the buttocks (Dorn, Crockett, and Petersen, 1988). Dissatisfaction with the body, in turn, seems to mediate the association between early maturation and low self-esteem in girls at the beginning of puberty (Williams and Currie, 2000). Moreover, weight dissatisfaction (Wichstrøm, 1999) and body dissatisfaction (Rierdan, Koff, and Stubbs, 1989; Stice, et al., 2000; see also chapter 4) were identified as predictors of depressive symptoms in girls during puberty.

Research including both indicators of biological changes (e.g., body fat proportion) and psychological measures of body image for the prediction of depressive symptoms in early-maturing girls during puberty is rare. Studies attempting to identify the relative importance of biological changes and perceptions of the body showed BMI (Body Mass Index) not to be a prospective predictor of depression in girls, whereas body dissatisfaction predicted depression successfully (Lewinsohn, *et al.*, 1994; Stice, *et al.*, 2000). Thus, actual weight does not play such an important role for depression compared to perceptions of body change and social reactions.

The traditional view holds that early maturation in boys has more positive consequences for psychosocial adaptation than late maturation. Research showed that boys' early pubertal maturation, in particular, appears to be experienced positively (Blyth, *et al.*, 1982; Petersen and Taylor, 1980). Early-maturing boys share positive attitudes toward puberty, mostly centered on advantages for sports and social relationships (Silbereisen and Kracke, 1997). Whereas early-maturing boys are more satisfied with their bodies (Simmons and Blyth, 1987), late maturing boys hope for growth in order to catch up with the majority of their age-mates and suffer from teasing by peers (Kracke, 1993). Late maturing boys tend to be less satisfied with themselves, and show higher levels of self-derogation, particularly during midadolescence (Kracke, 1993; O'Dea and Abraham, 1999). Given the hypotheses of low body satisfaction mediating the effect between pubertal timing and depressive affect, these findings would suggest higher depression in late maturing boys. Indeed, Nottelmann and colleagues (1987) found a higher rate of sad affect in late maturing boys in mid and late adolescence as compared to their age-mates. Other authors, however, have reported no link between pubertal timing and depressive mood in early adolescent boys (e.g., Simmons and Blyth, 1987; Angold, Costello, and Worthman, 1998).

Contrary to the aforementioned traditional view, several investigations of larger samples supported a link between perceived, as well as objective, early maturation in boys and emotional problems (Petersen and Crockett, 1985), depressive feelings, and anxiety, especially in mid to late adolescence (Silbereisen and Kracke, 1997; Alsaker, 1992). In a recent longitudinal sample Ge, Conger, and Elder (2001) also found that objective early maturation in boys was associated with higher emotional distress in grades eight and twelve as compared to their age-mates (see chapter 7). Pubertal timing at grade seven was a more powerful predictor of psychological distress in boys than was earlier distress or concurrent life events. Moreover, pubertal timing interacting with stressful life events predicted later symptoms of distress.

In sum, girls of early maturational timing are at risk for depressive mood, especially during the early adolescent years. In the main, two mechanisms might be the reasons for this: first, biological changes (i.e., rapid hormonal changes) are likely to trigger an increase of negative mood in early-maturing girls; second, dissatisfaction with own weight and body interacting with social experiences and cultural attitudes may explain negative moods and emotions. In the latter, actual weight and proportion of fat were less important than negative attitudes toward their own bodies. Moreover, early maturation in boys also seems to be accompanied by emotional risks during adolescence. In addition, early and rapid biological transitions may increase the vulnerability to other stressors, such as negative social experiences, changing social demands, or life events.

### Externalizing problem behavior

The increasing levels of externalizing behavior problems during puberty and adolescence may be linked with maturational events (Moffitt, 1993; see also chapter 6). Most adolescents face a mismatch between biological maturation, especially if experienced earlier in life, and social autonomy ("maturity gap"). Whereas for the majority in midadolescence, at least some forms of externalizing behaviors become functional in demonstrating adult social status, for early maturers, norm-violating behaviors, such as early substance use, precocious sexual activities, and other status offenses, may be more prominent means to demonstrate adult status.

*Substance use*

A large body of research indicates that early-maturing girls display earlier onset and higher levels of substance use behaviors, such as cigarette smoking or alcohol drinking, compared to their on-time and late maturing age-mates (e.g., Aro and Taipale, 1987; Magnusson, Stattin, and Allen, 1985; Dick, et al., 2000; Petersen, Graber, and Sullivan, 1990). They also show a higher current and lifetime prevalence for substance use (Graber, et al., 1997) associated with higher frequency of alcohol intoxication, number of units per drinking occasion, and higher frequency of drinking between ages 13 and 18 (Wichstrøm, 1999). Moreover, 15-year-old early-maturing girls smoke marihuana and try other drugs more frequently than other girls of the same age (Prokopáková, 1998). Longitudinal data suggest that the association between early timing and substance use in girls holds only for those whose advanced developmental level, relative to same-age peers, remained stable between the ages of 12 and 14 (Dick, *et al.*, 2001).

Several studies focused on the likely mechanisms involved in these results. Tschann and colleagues (1994) reported that early timing in girls was related to higher levels of substance use and emotional distress. However, emotional distress did not mediate the relationship between pubertal timing and substance use, but instead contributed independently to subsequent substance use. Particular social experiences of early-maturing girls seem to be linked with their earlier substance use. Magnusson, Stattin, and Allen (1985) found that early-maturing girls socialize with older peers, and as a result may have more opportunities, and perhaps pressure, to engage in age-inappropriate behaviors, such as precocious substance use. Moreover, in a Norwegian study the association between timing and more frequent alcohol intoxication was mediated through friends' problem behaviors (Wichstrøm, 1999). Results on 14-year-old German girls provide further support; the association between early maturation and higher frequency of drinking and cigarette smoking was mediated by male-oriented peer and leisure contexts (Weichold and Silbereisen, 2001). Male peers who are older but of a similar maturational status and for whom consumption is a part of everyday life, become socialization agents and behavioral role models for early-maturing girls (Alsaker, 1995). Following them can be a means to overcome the contrast between their actual social status and others' reactions to their more mature physical appearance (Silbereisen, Noack, and von Eye, 1992). Thus, greater and earlier substance use among early maturers does not necessarily indicate deviant behavior per se, but may actually represent girls' attempts to match their older peers' behavior and appearance, regardless of their chronological age (Silbereisen and Kastner, 1987).

Empirical studies on the relationship between pubertal timing and substance use in boys have revealed somewhat inconsistent results. Some researchers suggest that the link between early maturation and substance use is the same in boys as it is in girls (e.g., Tschann, *et al.*, 1994; Udry, 1991; Dick, *et al.*, 2001; Wichstrøm, 1999). In addition, both early- and late maturing boys drank more frequently than their on-time age-mates (Andersson and Magnusson, 1990). These results were supported by a German sample, which showed early and late timing to be related to higher frequency of drinking and drunkenness (Silbereisen and Kracke, 1993).

Research is limited regarding the mechanisms behind the link between off-timing and high substance use in boys. It is known that in contrast to girls, higher substance use in early-maturing boys is not accompanied by negative emotions; rather, social processes play a role similar to those of advanced peer activities (Tschann, *et al.*, 1994). According to interview data, late maturing boys cited the need to feel more relaxed or the desire to appear strong in social situations as reasons for getting drunk (Kracke, 1993). Thus, the more frequent drunkenness in boys of late pubertal timing can be seen as attempts to gain prestige among age-mates.

In sum, early maturation in both genders was linked to higher substance use during midadolescence, which could be explained by advanced peer activities and socialization with older or deviant peers. Contrary to this, for boys of late pubertal timing the consumption of alcohol and other substances may reflect a compensation for their suspected low status among peers. Seen against the backdrop of Brooks-Gunn, Petersen, and Eichorn's 1994 model, the pathway to substance use seems to be primarily related to particular experiences with others that are triggered by the deviant appearance of the adolescents.

*Aggression and deviant behaviors*

The majority of studies identified early maturation in girls as a risk factor for aggressive or delinquent behavior (see chapter 6). Early-maturing girls engage in risky behaviors, such as delinquency, earlier in adolescence and more frequently than their age-mates (Caspi and Moffitt, 1991; Magnusson, Stattin, and Allen, 1985; Petersen, Graber, and Sullivan, 1990; Flannery, Rowe, and Gulley, 1993). This effect can be observed primarily in midadolescence, but not in late adolescence (Duke-Duncan, *et al.*, 1985). Other research on 10- to 14-year-old girls, including endocrinological measures, found hormone profiles (e.g., estradiol, testosterone, follicle-stimulating hormones), but not maturational timing, to be related with delinquent behaviors and aggressive affect (Paikoff, Brooks-Gunn, and Warren, 1991).

Meaningful interactions with social and biological influences have also been identified. For girls with early timing, more adverse outcomes were reported if there was a history of adaptation problems prior to puberty (Caspi and Moffitt, 1991), and higher delinquency was found in early-maturing girls involved with older peer groups (Magnusson, 1988). Finally, contact with older male peers resulted in deviant activities in early-maturing girls only if they were exposed to boys in school, which is the case in coeducation classrooms (Caspi, *et al.*, 1993).

The results reported on the relation between aggression or delinquency and pubertal timing are less consistent for boys. Findings suggest that early maturation in boys is linked with behavioral problems (e.g., Dubas, Graber, and Petersen, 1991b; Buchanan, Eccles, and Becker, 1992), deviant behaviors (Duke-Duncan, *et al.*, 1985), and delinquent activities during adolescence (Flannery, Rome, and Gulley, 1993). In addition, Williams and Dunlop (1999) showed that both early- and late maturing 14-year-old boys showed a wider range and a greater incidence of delinquent behaviors (including higher levels of crime and school opposition) compared to on-time boys.

Studies involving hormones revealed a relation of aggression and levels of adrenal androgens (Susman, *et al.*, 1987). Moreover, in a sample of 6- to 13-year-old boys, testosterone concentrations and BMI predicted social dominance (Tremblay, *et al.*, 1998). Thus, male adolescents with high-for-age levels of testosterone (referring to early maturation) were more likely to be aggressive and socially dominant, especially if they had a high BMI.

Taken together, levels of aggressive or delinquent behaviors are higher in early-maturing girls and boys during midadolescence as compared to their age-mates; limited empirical evidence is available on the mechanisms of this. Effects of pubertal timing on aggression and delinquency may be mediated through contextual factors, such as more advanced peer activities and deviant peer contacts, similar to the effects on substance use. Note, however, that there are also differences, particularly concerning the role of late maturation in boys.

### School adaptation and achievement

Taking into account pubertal timing effects on internalizing and externalizing problems, it seems plausible to assume that timing also has an impact on school adaptation and academic achievement, probably triggered by the interference of such behaviors with school activities.

Using data from the US National Health Examination Survey, Duke and colleagues (1982) did not find differences in academic aspirations and attainment in 13- to 17-year-old girls of different pubertal timing (based on Tanner stages). Conversely, a more recent investigation found that in 12- to 14-year-old girls, late maturation was linked with the highest school accomplishment, independent of the girls' achievement orientation (Dubas, Graber, and Petersen, 1991b). This result may reflect a strategy to compensate for a lack of popularity by expending more energy on their schoolwork (Simmons and Blyth, 1987). In contrast, early-maturing girls received lower grades and reported getting in trouble at school more frequently than on-time and late maturers. Results from a Swedish sample also indicated that early-maturing girls experienced school more negatively, had higher absenteeism, and were increasingly less satisfied with school during adolescence (Stattin and Magnusson, 1990).

Late maturing males between the ages of 13 and 17 ranked lower than on-time and early maturers on IQ tests, standardized achievement tests, and educational attainment in adolescence. Early-maturing boys, in turn, ranked higher in educational measures and parental reports of achievement (Duke, *et al.*, 1982). Moreover, even after controlling for the effect of IQ on outcomes, late maturers were still viewed as less capable academically. Recent results support findings that late maturing boys have the lowest grades in various subjects, and the lowest academic achievement (Dubas, Graber, and Petersen, 1991b). Other studies did not find an effect of pubertal timing on boys' average school achievement (Simmons and Blyth, 1987).

Attempts have been made to explain differences in academic achievement possibly associated with pubertal timing by focusing on adolescents' differences in cognitive abilities and information processing. However, only a small advantage in general cognitive abilities has been reported for early maturers (Newcombe and Dubas, 1987). Nevertheless, studies on more specific cognition abilities (Hassler, 1991) found differences between pubertal timing groups in spatial abilities, but not in verbal fluency, which may be more closely linked to school achievement. More specifically, when adolescents were tested at age 11.5, late maturing girls and boys attained the highest scores in spatial abilities. Thus, perhaps the conclusion is that the school-related differences originate in differences in distracting behaviors (such as precocious romantic relationships).

### Summary short-term consequences

In girls, early maturation was linked with more mature interpersonal relationships within family and peer contexts as compared to age-mates of on-time and late maturation, probably due to their more grown-up appearance and socializing with peers of similar maturational age. Moreover, within their particular peer context, early-maturing girls tend to engage in externalizing behaviors, such as substance use or delinquency, which may reflect attempts to demonstrate their desire for a more adult-like social status. Moreover, the increased involvement with older peers and romantic relationships may also explain their lower academic achievement. Early-maturing girls tend to show more internalizing problems, such as poor body image, low self-esteem, associated problematic eating habits, and depressive symptoms. This may originate in their own and others' reactions to the physical changes that are seen to be incongruous with typical culturally accepted body ideals that emphasize the desirability of thinness. Regarding the effects of early pubertal timing on girls' moods and emotions, hormonal changes also seem to play a crucial role.

In boys another picture emerges. Late rather than early-maturing boys were more at risk for poor body image, although the mediating processes may be similar to those experienced by early-maturing girls. Likewise, late maturation in boys was linked with lower academic achievement. In spite of early-maturing boys' more positive body image, they were more likely to show depressive tendencies, which seemed to be linked to hormonal changes and heightened vulnerability toward life stress. Furthermore, they were more involved with older peer groups, an aspect which is associated with their elevated externalizing problem behaviors, such as substance use and delinquency.

Referring to the model by Brooks-Gunn, Graber, and Paikoff (1994), it becomes obvious that in explaining adolescents' problem behaviors most research has focused on the interplay between secondary sex characteristics and social experiences, whereas hormonal changes and, particularly, processes related to the central nervous system were rarely addressed. Because pubertal brain processes seem to be related to the heightened risk-taking behaviors and sensitivity to alcohol during adolescence (Spear, 2000), future research should focus on a possible link to hormonal changes that may trigger changes in the brain (see chapter 3). At this time, there is still too little empirical evidence on the complex causal mechanisms and moderating factors involved in the relationship between pubertal timing and psychosocial adaptation.

In line with the postulated pathway through central nervous processes as delineated in the model by Brooks-Gunn, Graber, and Paikoff (1994), behaviors typical of early or late maturers may be enhanced by a particular sensitivity to relevant social models. Miltner and colleagues (2001) addressed this topic in an unprecedented study that tested whether early-maturing girls differ in their sensitivity toward puberty and sexuality related information (e.g., words like *petting* or *kissing*). Sensitivity was evidenced by specific patterns of neural activities and longer reaction times in a task that required them to decide whether the briefly exposed words were typed in small or capital letters. The results based on EEG data (i.e., the expression of P300-measurement and brain activation) suggested that pubertal timing was related to significant differences of drive-related attention sets functional during information processing or dispositions to respond to environmental stimuli (organized in approach versus defensive responses). More specifically, the hypothesis was supported that early maturers are more sensitive toward puberty and sexuality related information and this sensitivity was shown to be associated with neural activities related to approach activities of information processing. At the same time, the higher interest of the early-maturing girls in the content of such words resulted in delayed task solution, as indicated by longer reaction times. In late maturing girls the same words also attracted attention, but the allocation of attention toward these stimuli seem to be associated with neural activities that are indicative of withdrawal or embarrassment. Although the results were based on a small sample, they give unprecedented insights into the actual link between social experiences, brain functioning, and information processing in early-maturing girls.

The effects of pubertal timing on short-term adaptation seem to be pronounced during early adolescence and tend to diminish during late adolescence (see chapter 1). This might be due to the fact that interindividual variation in biological maturation is especially pronounced in early adolescence. Thus, the need for longitudinal studies covering the entire pubertal period in large samples becomes evident. Furthermore, inconsistency remains in the findings concerning short-term consequences of pubertal timing. First, this might be due to the different measurement methods of pubertal timing (objective timing based on various specific indicators versus subjective overall rating of timing), and also concerning outcome variables (e.g., questionnaire data on psychopathological symptoms versus multiple measurements of moods and emotions *in vivo*). Second, where the consistency of pubertal timing across a period of time was assessed, such as in the research on substance use by Dick and colleagues (2000), results suggest that effects of pubertal timing were only observed when interindividual differences in timing remained stable over adolescence. Thus, it might be possible that the short-term consequences of pubertal timing (particularly beyond early adolescence) may be valid only among those adolescents who remain consistently early or late, compared to their age-mates, over a longer period of time. In order to investigate this open question, more prospective longitudinal data are clearly necessary.

### Long-term consequences of off-time pubertal development

Overall, there is a scarcity of research addressing the issue of long-term effects of interindividual differences in the timing of biological maturation. The existing studies concern personality features and psychological health, and adult domains of functioning in work, occupation, and family life.

### Normative personality development

Using longitudinal data from the Oakland Growth Study, Jones and Mussen (e.g., Jones, 1957; Mussen and Jones, 1957, 1958) reported results on personality differences in late adolescence and adulthood (for the latter, males aged 30 only) by the subjects' objective pubertal timing. The study design was replicated by Livson and Peskin (e.g., Livson and Peskin, 1980; Peskin, 1973) utilizing data from the Berkeley Guidance Study. In both studies, personality features were assessed by interviews with the target adolescent, parents, and teachers (the latter two reporting on the target adolescents). Moreover, Q-sort techniques were used for the individuals' personality assessments. In the following summary of results, the personality features reported are organized according to basic personality traits (i.e., the "big five" – extroversion, agreeableness, conscientiousness, emotional stability, and openness to experiences; Pervin, 1993). Note that this is simply meant for the ease of communication.

In the Jones and Mussen study, early-maturing girls (age at menarche approximately 11 years) in late adolescence revealed high levels of social inhibition, irritability, shyness, and the tendency to react with temper tantrums and whining, pointing to low agreeableness and low emotional stability. On the contrary, late-maturing girls in late adolescence were less shy and introverted, and showed lower social inhibition and a lower tendency to react with temper tantrums, indicating high agreeableness and high emotional stability. Data from the replication study by Peskin (1973) showed that early-maturing females at age 30, however, were more self-possessed and self-directed than their late maturing peers, for example, they were highly responsible and productive persons with a wide range of interests, suggesting high conscientiousness, high emotional stability, and high agreeableness. Thus, the early-maturing female had developed from a quite unpromising adolescent to a psychologically integrated woman. Contrary to that, late maturing females showed lower overall psychological integration at age 30, that is, they were more likely to give up or to withdraw in the face of frustrating events, had more fluctuating moods, and felt more often victimized by life as compared to their early-maturing age-mates. This indicates low emotional stability, low extroversion, and low agreeableness.

The apparent discrepancy between late adolescence and adulthood was interpreted as a kind of inoculation process: early-maturing girls were confronted with the stress and tension of puberty, at a time when they were barely prepared for it or the accompanying physical changes. But this experience might nevertheless have prepared them to deal successfully with future stressful events. In this way, stress and social interactions in the early-maturing girls' adolescence may have fostered learning processes that modified further coping strategies and personality development to their advantage (Livson and Peskin, 1980). In late maturing girls, however, pubertal development and behavioral consequences were more in compliance with social expectations, with the repercussion that life was less challenging without the need to struggle with external or internal problems. This may have resulted in an overprotective climate, lacking the sense of real mastery experiences and challenges. This, in turn, may lead to adult problems in coping capabilities (Livson and Peskin, 1980; Peskin, 1973).

Mussen and Jones (1957) described early-maturing boys during late adolescence (17–18 years) as having higher self-esteem and self-confidence, a more positive self-image, and as being more socially mature, which may have led to more favorable perceptions of early maturation in males by the adult world. Contrary to this, late maturing boys were described as energetic, bouncy, and bossy, indicating higher extraversion, low agreeableness, and low conscientiousness, which was interpreted as reflecting attempts to compensate for physical inferiority. Most interestingly, the effects of greater prestige experienced by early maturing males was still evident at age 33, when they were found to be more responsible, cooperative, sociable, and self-controlled compared to late maturers. However, they were also found to be more rigid, moralistic, humorless, and conformist (i.e., indicating high conscientiousness, high agreeableness, but low openness to experiences). Adult males of late pubertal timing, on the other hand, were more impulsive, assertive, insightful, and receptive. In addition, they were more able to cope effectively with ambiguity in new situations (Livson and Peskin, 1980), which refers to high extraversion, high emotional stability, and high openness to experiences.

Using a German sample, Ewert (1984) found that early-maturing boys in late adolescence (age 18) were no longer superior to late maturers in physical appearance and interests, as was the case during early adolescence. They were, however, rated as being more dominant in social interactions (i.e., taking over responsibility), which indicates higher conscientiousness than found in their age-mates at age 18. Conversely, late maturing boys displayed higher sensibility to the feelings and opinions of others. Unfortunately, this study did not report results on adult personality development, but given the secular trends in pubertal timing, it is conceivable that the difference between the older US and the newer German study actually reveal the same tendencies concerning personality development.

In sum, the link between pubertal timing and adult personality development seems to be different in adult males and females. In females, the more negative adaptation of early maturers in adolescence changes to high integration and effective problem-solving capacities in adulthood. Contrary to this, the situation of late maturing girls worsened over time, and revealed lower psychological integration and ineffective coping strategies. The explanation seems to rest on the varying degree of exposure to stress and conflicts during adolescence. In males, however, the more favorable situation of early-maturing adolescents was maintained through to adulthood. This may be due to the generally positive perception of early maturation in males, and to their less stressful experiences in adolescence. Given the pronounced historical change in gender equality, it is particularly problematic that no data of more recent cohorts are available. This is particularly so because the long-term advantage of early-maturing girls may no longer exist, as girls today are generally confronted with challenges that promote strength in the long term.

### Problem behaviors

Stattin and Magnusson (1990) investigated the relationship between females' pubertal timing and adult social adjustment. They found no relationship between pubertal timing and substance use at age 25 (i.e., alcohol abuse, drug use, cigarette use). Thus, adolescent norm-breaking activities in early maturers, such as precocious and severe consumption of substances, were not a risk factor for the development of chronically problematic consumption patterns. Rather, early maturation seems to have an impact on deviant involvement (Stattin and Magnusson, 1990). More specifically, early-maturing girls were overrepresented in official criminal records covering the age range 18–33. Probably earlier heterosexual contacts in adolescence mediated the relationship between early age at menarche and criminal offenses.

A study that included data on consumption at ages 14, 16, and 24 investigated the effects of pubertal maturation on adult alcohol consumption in males (Andersson and Magnusson, 1990). The results showed that objectively early- and late maturing boys showed more advanced drinking habits (e.g., were more frequently drunk) at age 14 as compared with on-time maturers. At age 16, however, these differences diminished. Interestingly enough, in young adulthood only 14 percent of the former early-maturing males, but more than one-third of the late maturers, were registered for alcohol abuse. The latter figure entailed entries such as public drunkenness, driving under the influence of alcohol, or psychiatric care. The results concerning the late maturers were interpreted as the delayed consequence of intensive striving for participation in "high-status" activities, serving as compensation for their relative low social status among same-aged friends in adolescence.

Taken together, early maturation in girls and late maturation in boys seem to be linked to maladjustment not only in adolescence but also in adulthood. Early heterosexual contacts among early-maturing females may especially increase the risk of deviant behavior in adulthood. In our view, the continuity in problematic behaviors is at least in part due to environmental effects – once a driving license is obtained, the likelihood that excessive drinking results in convictions is increased, which, in turn, may provoke other norm violations. In other words, the behavior as such is not simply maintained but earlier problematic behaviors provoke reaction from the environment that result in new adaptational problems.

**Work and career aspirations**

The study by Stattin and Magnusson (1990) provides empirical evidence for a link between pubertal timing and work and career conditions in adulthood. Although the actual work history at age 25 (e.g., length of time employed or unemployed) and the type of occupation did not differ by age at menarche, early-maturing females held lower employment positions than late maturing age-mates. Among the early maturers, 36 percent had jobs that only required obligatory compulsory schooling, compared to 14 percent for the rest of the sample.

As to the mechanisms behind these results, either the particular domestic situation of the early-maturing females (i.e., higher involvement in child care, household duties) prevents them from taking jobs that match their actual and probably higher educational level, or early maturers have lower educational achievement, which is then reflected in their lower occupational attainment. Further analyses supported the second interpretation; early maturers indeed revealed the lowest educational attainment. More specifically, among those maturing really early (age at menarche before or at 11 years), only a minority reported education beyond the obligatory nine-year compulsory schooling (Magnusson, Stattin, and Allen, 1985), and only 2 percent of these girls entered university or academic careers, compared to about 15 percent among the rest. Additional analyses showed that the effect of maturational timing was not confounded with differences in the parental education or intelligence of the girls. Instead, contacts with older working peers and early heterosexual relationships in adolescence seem to function as mediating mechanisms.

For boys, again, research is scarce. The only study on the association between pubertal development and work and career status in adulthood is reminiscent of the positive effects of early pubertal maturation on males' psychosocial functioning. In the Oakland Growth Study, early-maturing boys were found to hold higher occupational positions in adulthood as compared to their age-mates (Ames, 1957).

In sum, early timing of pubertal events seems to be linked to adult work and career development. Whereas in females early timing (especially very early pubertal timing) was associated with earlier family formation and lower occupational attainment, in males early maturation was linked with occupational success in adulthood. The outcomes in early-maturing females were explained as a consequence of their early engagement in romantic relationships, particularly with older working peers. The results on early-maturing males seem to be a function of a better match of their psychosocial functioning with their job demands.

### Family life

Using data from two cohorts of a British large-scale investigation, Sandler, Wilcox, and Horney (1984) showed that early maturation in girls (indicated by age at menarche) was linked with earlier marriage and timing of first conception. Stattin and Magnusson (1990) reported no systematic relationship between age at menarche and living under stable family circumstances (i.e., marriage or stable relationship with a partner). Interestingly enough, early-maturing girls, especially those who had experienced menarche before or at age 11, more frequently reported having abortions during adolescence and were more likely to be mothers at age 25. Thus, early engagement in motherhood and marriage may be a long-term consequence, particularly for girls of extreme early maturation.

Searching for the mechanisms, it can be concluded that more developed maturational status in girls is connected with earlier and greater involvement in heterosexual contacts during adolescence. As a result, early-maturing girls are more likely to live in adulthood under stable family conditions and to have children.

Unfortunately, no analogous studies have been undertaken to investigate the effect of pubertal timing on adult family circumstances in males. If at all, however, associations may point in a direction different from that reported for girls. This is so because their higher levels of drinking are likely to delay family formations.

Taken together, females of very early pubertal timing begin heterosexual relationships and marry at an earlier age during adolescence than age-mates; they also seem to foreclose partnership choices earlier and subsequently become mothers earlier than their age-mates.

### Summary long-term consequences

Interindividual differences in pubertal timing obviously play a gender-specific role in adult psychosocial functioning. Among females, early age at menarche, and in particular very early age at menarche, is linked with problems concerning norm-obeying in adulthood. Moreover, these females were less successful in their occupational attainment, and entered family formation, such as marriage and motherhood, earlier than their age-mates. The stepping-stone for these long-lasting effects seems to be their precocious involvement in heterosexual contacts during adolescence, especially with older, working, or deviant males. Associating with these males is subsequently more likely to interfere with their school achievement and educational attainment, the latter representing an obstacle against aspiring for higher occupational development. Either dependent on this (and perhaps as compensation for lacking job commitment), or already fostered by earlier sexual commitments, motherhood and marriage follow earlier for these early-maturing females than is common for their age-mates.

In males, however, adverse effects of differences in pubertal timing on long-term adult adaptation appear to be limited to excessive alcohol consumption and related concerns in late maturing men. These behaviors were interpreted as reminiscent of activities meant to compensate for their low status among peers during adolescence.

Why are there so few long-term consequences of pubertal timing in males as compared to females? First, females' life paths and future careers in general might be particularly influenced by early motherhood and associated family responsibilities, which seem to be a consequence of precocious heterosexual contacts and truncated school careers. Conversely, for males, stable family conditions and fatherhood do not, at least under traditional circumstances, change their work and career life. Note also that only very early maturation in females seems to be linked with profound psychosocial consequences in adulthood. Second, measurement problems may also play a role. The age at menarche, the most often used index of maturational timing in these studies, can be assessed with high precision, even retrospectively in adulthood (Bean, et al., 1979). Timing in males, based on indicators such as growth spurt, voice break, or nocturnal emission (Peskin, 1973), however, is much less accurately recalled.

Taken together, explanations for long-term consequences of early versus late pubertal timing refer primarily to social relationships and preoccupying experiences in adolescence (e.g., early heterosexual relationships) that shape adult development. Most of the published studies on long-term consequences of pubertal timing did not address the complexity of processes entailed in the model by Brooks-Gunn, Graber, and Paikoff (1994). This certainly limits insights into the mechanisms behind the results. Moreover, a great deal of information on long-term consequences of variations in pubertal maturation was drawn from data sets collected several decades ago. Finally, we lack studies on the consequences of pubertal timing beyond the third decade of life, and it would certainly be interesting to investigate whether early and late maturers still differ in their psychosocial adaptation in later adulthood. In sum, there is clearly a need for longitudinal studies that investigate the long-term effects of (more or less consistent) variations in pubertal timing in adulthood.

## References

Alsaker, F. D. (1992). Pubertal timing, overweight, and psychological adjustment. *Journal of Early Adolescence*, **12(4)**, 396–419.
Alsaker, F. D. (1995). Timing of puberty and reactions to pubertal changes. In M. Rutter (ed.), *Psychosocial disturbances in young people: challenges for prevention* (pp. 37–67). Cambridge: Cambridge University Press.
Ames, R. (1957). Physical maturing among boys as related to adult social behavior: a longitudinal study. *California Journal of Educational Research*, **8**, 69–75.
Andersson, T., and Magnusson, D. (1990). Biological maturation in adolescence and the development of drinking habits and alcohol abuse among young males: a prospective longitudinal study. *Journal of Youth and Adolescence*, **19(1)**, 33–41.
Angold, A., Costello, E. J. and Worthman, C. M. (1998). Puberty and depression: the roles of age, pubertal status and pubertal timing. *Psychological Medicine*, **28(1)**, 51–61.
Aro, H. and Taipale, V. (1987). The impact of timing of puberty on psychosomatic symptoms among fourteen- to sixteen-year-old Finnish girls. *Child Development*, **58(1)**, 261–268.
Bean, J. A., Leeper, J. D., Wallace, R. B., Sherman, B. M., and Jagger, H. J. (1979). Variations in the reporting of menstrual histories. *American Journal of Epidemiology*, **109**, 181–185.
Belsky, J., Steinberg, L., and Draper, P. (1991). Further reflections on an evolutionary theory of socialization. *Child Development*, **62**, 682–685.
Billy, J. O. G., and Udry, J. R. (1985). The influence of male and female best friends on adolescent sexual behavior. *Adolescence*, **20(77)**, 21–32.
Blyth, D. A., Simmons, R. G., and Zakin, D. F. (1985). Satisfaction with body image for early adolescent females: the impact of pubertal timing within different school environments. *Journal of Youth and Adolescence*, **14(3)**, 205–225.
Blyth, D. A., Simmons, R. G., Bulcroft, R., Felt, D., Van Claeve, E. F., and Bush, D. M. (1982). The effects of physical development on self-image and satisfaction with body image for early adolescents. *Research in Community and Mental Health*, **2**, 43–73.
Brooks-Gunn, J. (1987). Pubertal processes and girls' psychological adaptation. In R. M. Lerner and T. T. Foch (ed.), *Biological-psychosocial interactions in early adolescence* (pp. 123–154). Hillsdale, NJ: Lawrence Erlbaum.
Brooks-Gunn, J., and Reiter, E. O. (1990). The role of pubertal processes. In S. S. Feldman and E. O. Elliott (ed.), *At the threshold: the developing adolescent*, (pp. 16–53). Cambridge, MA: Harvard University Press.

Brooks-Gunn, J., and Warren, M. P. (1985). The effects of delayed menarche in different contexts: dance and non-dance students. Special issue: time of maturation and psychosocial functioning in adolescence II. *Journal of Youth and Adolescence*, **14**, 285–300.

Brooks-Gunn, J., and Warren, M. P. (1989). Biological and social contributions to negative affect in young adolescent girls. *Child Development*, **60**, 40–55.

Brooks-Gunn, J., Graber, J. A., and Paikoff, R. L. (1994). Studying links between hormones and negative affect: models and measures. *Journal of Research on Adolescence*, **4**, 469–486.

Brooks-Gunn, J., Petersen, A. C., and Eichorn, D. (1985). The study of maturational timing effects in adolescence. *Journal of Youth and Adolescence*, **14**, 149–161.

Buchanan, C. M., Eccles, J. S., and Becker, J. B. (1992). Are adolescents the victims of their raging hormones? Evidence for activational effects of hormones on moods and behavior at adolescence. *Psychological Bulletin*, **111(1)**, 62–107.

Cairns, E., McWhirter, L., Duffy, U., and Barry, R. (1990). The stability of self-concept in late adolescence: gender and situational effects. *Personality and Individual Differences*, **11(9)**, 937–944.

Cash, T. F., and Henry, P. E. (1995). Women's body images: the results of a national survey in the USA. *Sex Roles*, **33**, 19–28.

Caspi, A., and Moffitt, T. E. (1991). Individual differences are accentuated during periods of social change: the sample case of girls at puberty. *Journal of Personality and Social Psychology*, **61(1)**, 157–168.

Caspi, A., Lynam, D., Moffitt, T. E., and Silva, P. A. (1993). Unraveling girls' delinquency: biological dispositions and contextual contributions to adolescent misbehavior. *Developmental Psychology*, **29**, 19–30.

Davies, E., and Furnham, A. (1986). Body satisfaction in adolescent girls. *British Journal of Medical Psychology*, **59**, 279–287.

Dekovi, M., Noom, M. J., and Meeus, W. (1997). Expectations regarding development during adolescence: parental and adolescent perceptions. *Journal of Youth and Adolescence*, **26(3)**, 253–272.

Dick, D. M., Rose, R. J., Pulkkinen, L., and Kapiro, J. (2001). Measuring puberty and understanding its impact: a longitudinal study of adolescent twins. *Journal of Youth and Adolescence*, **30(4)**, 385–399.

Dick, D. M., Rose, R. J., Viken, R. J., and Kaprio, J. (2000). Pubertal timing and substance use: associations between and within families across late adolescence. *Developmental Psychology*, **36(2)**, 180–189.

Dorn, L. D., Crockett, L. J., and Petersen, A. C. (1988). The relations of pubertal status to intrapersonal changes in young adolescents. *Journal of Early Adolescence*, **8(4)**, 405–419.

Dubas, J. S., Graber, J. A., and Petersen, A. C. (1991a). A longitudinal investigation of adolescents' changing perceptions of pubertal timing. *Developmental Psychology*, **27**, 580–586.

Dubas, J. S., Graber, J. A., and Petersen, A. C. (1991b). The effects of pubertal development on achievement during adolescence. *American Journal of Education*, **99(4)**, 444–460.

Duke, P. M., Carlsmith, J. M., Jennings, D., Martin, J. A., Dornbusch, S. M., Gross, R. T., and Siegel-Gorelick, B. (1982). Educational correlates of early and late sexual maturation in adolescence. *Journal of Pediatrics*, **100**, 633–637.

Duke, P. M., Litt, I. F., and Gross, R. T. (1980). Adolescents self-assessment of sexual maturation. *Pediatrics*, **66**, 918–920.

Duke-Duncan, P. M., Ritter, P., Dornbusch, S. M., Gross, R. T., and Carlsmith, J. M. (1985). The effects of pubertal timing on body image, school behavior and deviance. *Journal of Early Adolescence*, **14**, 227–235.

Eveleth, P. B., and Tanner, J. M. (1976). *Worldwide variation in human growth*. Cambridge: Cambridge University Press.

Ewert, O. M. (1984). Psychische Begleiterscheinungen des puberalen Wachstummschubs bei männlichen Jugendlichen. Eine retrospektive Untersuchung [Psychological effects of pubertal growth spurts in male adolescents. A retrospective study]. *Zeitschrift für Entwicklungspsychologie und Pädagogische Psychologie*, **16(1)**, 1–11.

Ezeome, E. R., Ekenze, S. O., Obanye, R. O., Onyeagocha, A. C., Adibe, L. N., Chigbo, J., and Onuigbo, W. I. (1997). Normal pattern of pubertal changes in Nigerian boys. *West-African Journal of Medicine*, **16**, 6–11.

Flannery, D. J., Rowe, D. C., and Gulley, B. L. (1993). Impact of pubertal status, timing, and age on adolescent sexual experience and delinquency. *Journal of Adolescent Research*, **8(1)**, 21–40.

Frisch, R. E. (1983). Fatness, puberty, and fertility: the effects of nutrition and physical training on menarche and ovulation. In J. Brooks-Gunn and A. C. Petersen (ed.), *Girls at puberty: biological and psychosocial perspectives*. New York: Plenum.

Ge, X., Best, K. M., Conger, R. D., and Simons, R. L. (1996). Parenting behaviors and the occurrence and co-occurrence of adolescent depressive symptoms and conduct problems. *Developmental Psychology*, **32(4)**, 717–731.

Ge, X., Conger, R. D., and G. H. Elder, Jr. (2001). Pubertal transition, stressful life events, and the emergence of gender differences in adolescent depressive symptoms. *Developmental Psychology*, **37(3)**, 404–417.

Graber, J. A., Brooks-Gunn, J., Paikoff, R. L., and Warren, M. P. (1994). Prediction of eating problems: An eight-year study of adolescent girls. *Child Development*, **30(6)**, 823–834.

Graber, J. A., Lewinsohn, P. M., Seeley, J. R., and Brooks-Gunn, J. (1997). Is psychopathology associated with the timing of pubertal development? *Journal of the American Academy of Child and Adolescent Psychiatry*, **36(12)**, 1768–1776.

Graber, J. A., Petersen, A. C., and Brooks-Gunn, J. (1996). Pubertal processes: methods, measures, and models. In J. A. Graber, J. Brooks-Gunn, and A. C. Petersen (ed.), *Transitions through adolescence: interpersonal domains and context* (pp. 23–53). Hillsdale, NJ: Lawrence Erlbaum.

Hannover, B. (1997). Die Bedeutung des pubertaeren Reifestatus fuer die Herausbildung informeller Interaktionsgruppen in koedukativen Klassen und Maedchenschulklassen [Effects of pubertal maturation upon the formation of informal interaction groups in coeducational school classes and in girls' school classes]. *Zeitschrift für Pädagogische Psychologie*, **11(1)**, 3–13.

Harter, S., and Whitesell, N. R. (1996). Multiple pathways to self-reported depression and psychological adjustment among adolescents. *Development and Psychopathology*, **8**, 761–777.

Hassler, M. (1991). Maturation rate and spatial, verbal, and musical abilities: a seven-year longitudinal study. *International Journal of Neuroscience*, **58**, 183–198.

Hauser, S. T., Liebmann, W., Houlihan, J., Powers, S. I., Jacobson, A. M., Noam, G. G., Weiss, B., and Follansbee, D. (1985). Family contexts of pubertal timing. *Journal of Youth and Adolescence*, **14(4)**, 317–337.

Hayward, C., Killen, J. D., Darrell, M. W., Hammer, L. D., Litt, I. F., Kraemer, H. C., Haydel, F., Varady, A., and Taylor, C. B. (1997). Psychiatric risk associated with early puberty in adolescent girls. *Journal of the American Academy of Child and Adolescent Psychiatry*, **36**, 255–262.

Herman-Giddens, M. E., Slora, E. J., *et al.* (1997). Secondary sexual characteristics and menses in young girls seen in the office practice: a study from the Pediatric Research in Office Settings network. *Pediatrics*, **99(4)**, 502–512.

Hill, J. P., and Holmbeck, G. N. (1987). Familial adaptation to biological change during adolescence. In R. M. Lerner *et al.* (ed.), *Biological-psychosocial interactions in early adolescence.* Child Psychology (pp. 207–223). Hillsdale, NJ: Lawrence Erlbaum.

Hofer, M., Pikowsky, B., Fleischmann, T., and Spranz-Fogasy, T. (1993). Argumentationssequenzen in Konfliktgespraechen [Argument sequences in conflict discourses]. *Zeitschrift für Sozialpsychologie*, **24(1)**, 15–24.

Jones, M. C. (1957). The later careers of boys who were early or late-maturing. *Child Development*, **28**, 113–128.

Keel, P. K., Fulkerson, J. A., and Leon, G. R. (1997). Disordered eating precursors in pre- and early adolescent girls and boys. *Journal of Youth and Adolescence*, **26(2)**, 203–216.

Killen, J. D., Hayward, C., Wilson, D. M., Taylor, C. B., Hammer, L. D., Litt, I., Simmons, B., and Haydel, F. (1994). Factors associated with eating disorder symptoms in a community sample of 6th and 7th grade girls. *International Journal of Eating Disorders*, **15(4)**, 357–367.

Koff, E., and Rierdan, J. (1993). Advanced pubertal development and eating disturbance in early adolescent girls. *Journal of Adolescent Health*, **14**, 433–439.

Kracke, B. (1993). *Pubertaet und Problemverhalten bei Jungen* [Puberty and behavior problems of male adolescents]. Weinheim: Beltz, PVU.

Laursen, B., and Collins, W. A. (1994). Interpersonal conflict during adolescence. *Psychological Bulletin*, **115**, 197–209.

Lerner, R. M. (1985). Adolescent maturational changes and psychosocial development: a dynamic interactional perspective. *Journal of Youth and Adolescence*, **14**, 355–372.

Lewinsohn, P. M., Roberts, R. E., Seeley, J. R., Rohde, P., Gotlib, I. H., and Hops, H. (1994). Adolescent psychopathology II: psychosocial risk factors for depression. *Journal of Abnormal Psychology*, **103**, 302–315.

Livson, N., and Peskin, H. (1980). Perspectives on adolescence from longitudinal research. In J. Adelson (ed.), *Handbook of Adolescent Psychology* (pp. 47–68). New York: John Wiley.

272     *Karina Weichold, Rainer Silbereisen, and Eva Schmitt-Rodermund*

Magnusson, D. (1988). Individual development from an interactional perspective: a longitudinal study. In D. Magnusson (ed.), *Paths through life*, vol. I. Hillsdale, NJ: Lawrence Erlbaum.

Magnusson, D., Stattin, H., and Allen, V. L. (1985). Biological maturation and social development: a longitudinal study of some adjustment processes from midadolescence to adulthood. *Journal of Youth and Adolescence*, 14(4), 267–283.

Malina, R. M., Harper, A. B., Avent, H. H., and Campbell, D. E. (1973). Age at menarche in athletes and non-athletes. *Medicine and Science in Sports*, 5, 11–13.

Miltner, W., Vorwerk, L., Weichold, K., and Silbereisen, R. K. (2001). How does the brain of girls at different states of puberty process puberty-related semantic stimuli? Paper presented at the seventh European Congress of Psychology, July 1–6, 2001, London.

Moffitt, T. E. (1993). Adolescence-limited and life-course-persistent antisocial behavior. A developmental taxonomy. *Psychological Review*, 100, 674–701.

Mussen, P. H., and Jones, M. C. (1957). Self-conceptions, motivations, and interpersonal attitudes of late- and early maturing boys. *Child Development*, 28, 243–256.

Mussen, P. H., and Jones, M. C. (1958). The behavior inferred motivations of late- and early maturing boys. *Child Development*, 29, 61–67.

Newcombe, N., and Dubas, J. S. (1987). Individual differences in cognitive ability: are they related to timing of puberty? In R. M. Lerner and T. T. Foch (ed.), *Biological-psychosocial interactions in early adolescence* (pp. 249–302). Hillsdale, NJ: Lawrence Erlbaum.

Nolen-Hoeksema, S. (1994). An interactive model for the emergence of gender differences in depression in adolescence. *Journal of Research on Adolescence*, 4(4), 519–534.

Nottelmann, E. D., Susman, E. J., Inoff-Germain, G., Cutler, Jr., G. B., Loriaux, D. L., and Chrousos, G. P. (1987). Developmental processes in early adolescence: relationships between adolescent adjustment problems and chronological age, pubertal stage, and puberty related serum hormone levels. *Journal of Pediatrics*, 110(3), 473–480.

O'Dea, J., and Abraham, S. (1999). Association between self-concept and body weight, gender, and pubertal development among male and female adolescents. *Adolescence*, 34 (133), 69–79.

Paikoff, R. L., and Brooks-Gunn, J. (1992). Do parent–child relationships change during puberty? *Psychological Bulletin*, 110, 47–66.

Paikoff, R. L., Brooks-Gunn, J., and Warren, M. P. (1991). Effects of girls' hormonal status on depressive and aggressive symptoms over the course of one year. *Journal of Youth and Adolescence*, 20(2), 191–215.

Pervin, L. A. (1993). *Personality: theory and research*. Munich: Ernst Reinhardt.

Peskin, H., and Livson, N. (1972). Pre- and post-pubertal personality and adult psychological functioning. *Seminars in Psychiatry*, 4(4), 343–353.

Peskin, H. (1973). Influence of the developmental schedule of puberty on learning and ego functioning. *Journal of Youth and Adolescence*, 2(4), 273–290.

Petersen, A. C., and Crockett, L. J. (1985). Pubertal timing and grade effects on adjustment. *Journal of Youth and Adolescence*, 14, 191–206.

Petersen, A. C., and Taylor, B. (1980). Puberty: biological change and psychological adaptation. In J. Adelson (ed.), *Handbook of adolescent psychology* (pp. 117–158). New York: John Wiley.

Petersen, A. C., Crockett, L. J., Richards, M., and Boxer, A. M. (1988). A self-report measure of pubertal status: reliability, validity, and initial norms. *Journal of Youth and Adolescence*, 17, 117–133.

Petersen, A. C., Graber, J. A., and Sullivan, P. (1990). Pubertal timing and problem behavior: variations in effects. In D. Magnusson (Chair), Timing of maturation and adolescent problem behavior, symposium conducted at the meeting of the Society for Research on Adolescence, Atlanta, GA.

Petersen, A. C., Sarigiani, P. A., and Kennedy, R. E. (1991). Adolescent depression: why more girls?. *Journal of Youth and Adolescence*, 20, 247–271.

Petersen, A. C., Silbereisen, R. K., and Sörensen, S. (1996). Adolescent development: a global perspective. In K. Hurrelmann, S. F. Hamilton, *et al.* (ed.), *Social problems and social contexts in adolescence: perspectives across boundaries* (pp. 3–37). Hawthorne, NY: De Gruyter.

Prokopáková, A. (1998). Drug experimenting and pubertal maturation in girls. *Studia Psychologica*, 40, 287–290.

Richards, M. H., and Larson, R. (1993). Pubertal development and the daily subjective states of young adolescents. *Journal for Research on Adolescence*, 3(2), 146–169.

Rierdan, J., Koff, E., and Stubbs, M. L. (1989). A longitudinal analysis of body image as a predictor of the onset and persistence of adolescent girls' depression. *Journal of Early Adolescence*, 9, 454–466.

Rosenblum, G. D., and Lewis, M. (1999). The relations among body image, physical attractiveness, and body mass index. *Child Development*, 70(1), 50–64.

Ruiselová, Z. (1998). Relationships with parents and teachers in connection with pubertal maturation timing in girls. *Studia Psychologica*, 40(4), 277–281.

Sagrestano, L. M., McCormick, S. H., and Holmbeck, G. H. (1999). Pubertal development and parent–child conflict in low-income, urban, African American adolescents. *Journal of Research on Adolescence*, 9(1), 85–107.

Sandler, D. P., Wilcox, A. J., and Horney, L. F. (1984). Age at menarche and subsequent reproductive events. *American Journal of Epideminology*, 119, 765–774.

Savin-Williams, R. C., and Small, S. A. (1986). The timing of puberty and its relationship to adolescent and parent perceptions of family interactions. *Developmental Psychology*, 22, 342–347.

Scarr, S., and McCartney, K. (1983). How people make their own environments: a theory of genotype environment effects. *Child Development*, 54, 424–435.

Schmitt-Rodermund, E., and Ittel, A. (1999). Noch Kind oder schon Frau – was macht den Zeitpunkt aus? Voraussetzungen für Unterschiede im Entwicklungstempo bei Mädchen [Girl or woman – what makes the difference? Antecedents of differences in girls' pubertal timing]. In R. K. Silbereisen and J. Zinnecker (ed.), *Entwicklung im sozialen Wandel: Kindheit, Jugend und junges Erwachsenenalter im wiedervereinigten Deutschland 1991 bis 1996* (pp. 203–220). Weinheim: Beltz, PVU.

Silbereisen, R. K., and Kastner, P. (1987). Jugend und Problemverhalten: Entwicklungspsychologische Perspektiven [Youth and problem behavior:

Developmental psychological perspectives]. In R. Oerter and L. Montada (Hrsg.), *Entwicklungspsychologie. Ein Lehrbuch* (pp. 882–919). Weinheim: Beltz, PVU.

Silbereisen, R. K., and Kracke, B. (1993). Variation in maturational timing and adjustment in adolescence. In S. Jackson and H. Rodriguez-Tomèé (ed.), *The social worlds of adolescence* (pp. 67–94). Hillsdale, NJ: Lawrence Erlbaum.

Silbereisen, R. K., and Kracke, B. (1997). Self-reported maturational timing and adaptation in adolescence. In J. Schulenberg, J. L. Maggs, and K. Hurrelman (ed.), *Health risks and developmental transitions during adolescence* (pp. 85–109). Cambridge: Cambridge University Press.

Silbereisen, R. K., Kracke, B., and Nowak, M. (1992). Koerperliches Entwicklungstempo und jugendtypische Uebergaenge [Maturational timing and adolescent transitions]. In J. Zinnecker (ed.), *Jugend '92: Lebenslagen, Orientierungen und Entwicklungsperspektiven im vereinigten Deutschland.* Vol. II, *Im Spiegel der Wissenschaften* (pp. 171–196). Opladen: Leske and Budrich.

Silbereisen, R. K., Noack, P., and von Eye, A. (1992). Adolescents' development of romantic friendship and change in favorite leisure contexts. *Journal of Adolescent Research*, 7, 80–93.

Simmons, R. G., and Blyth, D. A. (ed.) (1987). *Moving into adolescence. The impact of pubertal change and school context.* Hawthorne, NY: De Gruyter.

Sinkkonen, J., Anttila, R., and Siimes, M. A. (1998). Pubertal maturation and changes in self-image in early adolescent Finnish boys. *Journal of Youth and Adolescence*, **27**(2), 209–218.

Smith, E. A., Udry, J. R., and Morris, N. M. (1985). Pubertal development and friends: a biosocial explanation of adolescent sexual behavior. *Journal of Health and Social Behavior*, **26**, 183–192.

Smolak, L., Levine, M. P., and Gralen, S. (1993). The impact of puberty and dating on eating problems among middle school girls. *Journal of Youth and Adolescence*, **22**(4), 355–368.

Spear, L. P. (2000). The adolescent brain and age-related behavioral manifestations. *Neuroscience and Behavioral Reviews*, **24**, 417–463.

Stattin, H., and Magnusson, D. (1990). *Pubertal maturation in female development.* Hillsdale, NJ: Lawrence Erlbaum.

Steinberg, L. (1988). Reciprocal relation between parent–child distance and pubertal maturation. *Developmental Psychology*, **24**(1), 122–128.

Stice, E., Hayward, C., Cameron, R. P., Killen, J. D., and Taylor, C. B. (2000). Body image and eating disturbances predict onset of depression among female adolescents: a longitudinal study. *Journal of Abnormal Psychology*, **109**(3), 438–444.

Susman, E. (1997). Modeling developmental complexity in adolescence: hormones and behavior in context. *Journal of Research on Adolescence*, 7, 283–306.

Susman, E. J., Dorn, L. D., and Chrousos, G. P. (1991). Negative affect and hormone levels in young adolescents: concurrent and predictive perspectives. *Journal of Youth and Adolescence*, **20**, 167–190.

Susman, E. J., Inoff-Germain, G., Nottelmann, E. D., Loriaux, D. L., Cutler, Jr., G. B., and Chrousos, G. P. (1987). Hormones, emotional dispositions, and aggressive attributes in young adolescents. *Child Development*, **58(4)**, 1114–1134.

Swarr, A. E., and Richards, M. H. (1996). Longitudinal effects of adolescent girls' pubertal development, perceptions of pubertal timing, and parental relations on eating problems. *Developmental Psychology*, **32(4)**, 636–646.

Tanner, J. M. (1962). *Growth at adolescence*, 2nd edn. Oxford: Blackwell Scientific.

Tanner, J. M. (1974). Sequence and tempo in the somatic changes of puberty. In M. M. Grumbach, G. D. Grave, and F. E. Mayer (ed.), *Control of the onset of puberty* (pp. 448–472). New York: John Wiley.

Tanner, J. M. (1975). Growth and endocrinology of the adolescent. In L. I. Gardner (ed.), *Endocrine and genetic diseases of childhood and adolescence* (pp. 14–64). Philadelphia, PN: W. B. Saunders.

Taylor, C. B., Sharpe, T., Shisslak, C., Bryson, S., Estes, L. S., Gray, N., McKnight, K. M., Crago, M., Kraemer, H., and Killen, J. D. (1998). Factors associated with weight concerns in adolescent girls. *International Journal of Eating Disorders*, **24(1)**, 31–42.

Tremblay, R. E., Schaal, B., Boulerice, B., Arseneault, L., Soussignan, R. G., Paquette, D., and Laurent, D. (1998). Testosterone, physical aggression, dominance, and physical development in early adolescence. *International Journal of Behavioral Development*, **22(4)**, 753–777.

Tschann, J. M., Adler, N. E., Irwin, C. E., Millstein, S. G., Turner, R. A., and Kegeles, S. M. (1994). Initiation of substance use in early adolescence: the roles of pubertal timing and emotional distress. *Health Psychology*, **13(4)**, 326–333.

Tucker-Halpern, C., Udry, J. R., Cambell, B., Campbell, B., and Suchindran, C. (1993). Testosterone and pubertal development as predictors of sexual activity: a panel analysis of adolescent males. *Psychosomatic Medicine*, **55**, 436–447.

Tucker-Halpern, C., Udry, J. R., and Suchindran, C. (1997). Testosterone predicts initiation of coitus in adolescent females. *Psychosomatic Medicine*, **59**, 161–171.

Udry, J. R. (1991). Predicting alcohol use by adolescent males. *Journal of Biosocial Science*, **23(4)**, 381–386.

Udry, J. R., Billy, J. O. G., Morris, N. M., Groff, T. R., and Raj, M. H. (1985). Serum androgenic hormones motivate sexual behavior in adolescent boys. *Fertility and Sterility*, **43**, 90–94.

Warren, M. P. (1983). Physical and biological aspects of puberty. In J. Brooks-Gunn and A. C. Petersen (ed.), *Girls at puberty* (pp. 3–28). New York: Plenum.

Weichold, K., and Silbereisen, R. K. (2001). Pubertal timing and substance use: the role of peers and leisure context. Paper presented at the seventh European Congress of Psychology, July 1–6, 2001, London.

Weichold, K., Silbereisen, R. K., Schmitt-Rodermund, E., Vorwerk, L., and Miltner, W. H. R. (in press). Links between timing of puberty and behavioral indicators of individuation. *Journal of Youth and Adolescence*.

Wichstrøm, L. (1995). Social, psychological and physical correlates of eating problems. A study of the general adolescent population in Norway. *Psychological Medicine*, **25**, 567–579.

Wichstrøm, L. (1998). Self-concept development during adolescence. In E. E. A. Skoe and A. L. von der Lippe (ed.), *Personality development in adolescence* (pp. 99–122). New York: Routledge.

Wichstrøm, L. (1999). The emergence of gender difference in depressed mood during adolescence: the role of intensified gender socialization. *Developmental Psychology*, **35(1)**, 232–245.

Williams, J. M., and Currie, C. (2000). Self-esteem and physical development in early adolescence: pubertal timing and body image. *Journal of Early Adolescence*, **20(2)**, 2000.

Williams, J. M., and Dunlop, L. C. (1999). Pubertal timing and self-reported delinquency among male adolescents. *Journal of Adolescence*, **22**, 157–171.

Youniss, J., and Smollar, J. (1985). *Adolescent relations with mothers, fathers, and friends*. Chicago: Chicago University Press.

Zacharias, L., and Wurtman, R. J. (1969). Age at menarche: genetic and environmental influences. *New England Journal of Medicine*, **280**, 868–875.

Zakin, D. F., Blyth, D. A., and Simmons, R. G. (1984). Physical attractiveness as a mediator of the impact of early pubertal changes for girls. *Journal of Youth and Adolescence*, **13(5)**, 439–450.

# 13 When coming of age means coming undone: links between puberty and psychosocial adjustment among European American and African American girls

*Alice Michael and Jacquelynne S. Eccles*

### What does "coming undone" look like among European American and African American girls?

Societal concerns for boys and girls during their teenage years tend to be compartmentalized into a stereotyped dichotomy, where our concerns for boys typically center around problems such as delinquency, gang involvement, school disengagement, and substance abuse, and our concerns for girls are typically more inclined toward the internalizing spectrum, such as depression, eating disorders, or low self-esteem. To use recent examples in the psychological literature, adolescent boys may become lost in rage and disconnection and end up imprisoned, literally (Garbarino, 1999), while girls are at risk of being figuratively imprisoned by the social surrounds that leave them with low self-esteem, diminished sense of agency, depressed, and despondent (Pipher, 1994).

Similarly, the pitfalls most frequently encountered by adolescent girls have been described and investigated within a dichotomy of race/ethnicity and class. In the world of European American middle- and upper-class girls, concerns continue to center around the development of internalizing spectrum mental health difficulties: eating disorders, depression, low self-esteem, and disturbed body image. In contrast, African American (or ethnic minority or impoverished) adolescent girls are viewed to be most at risk for the development of more externalizing manifestations of adolescent problems, such as delinquency, school disengagement, early or risky sexual behavior, or teen pregnancy.

As is the case for most stereotypes, there is some foundation for this dichotomy when current estimates of mental disorder and social behavior are considered. For example, the prevalence of the eating disorders anorexia and bulimia nervosa in the US population are substantially greater in European American than in African American women (American Psychiatric Association, 1994), and the rates of teen

277

pregnancy are higher among African Americans than among European Americans (Zabin and Hayward, 1993), although reports also indicate that rates are decreasing more rapidly among African Americans (Alan Guttmacher Institute, 1994). Although ethnic group membership is often used as the comparative index, the majority of studies have either not included individuals from varying ethnic/racial groups in the same study, or have confounded race with socioeconomic conditions (i.e., African Americans are overrepresented in the lower socioeconomic groups) (Hamburg and Takanishi, 1996; Jenkins, 1983). We have had limited opportunity to view development in comparable socioeconomic conditions across racial or ethnic groups. As such, "problems" have often been narrowly defined and studied in isolation (Jessor and Jessor, 1977), thereby decreasing our understanding of more generalized patterns or recognition of distinct and contextually specific expression of possibly similar underlying disturbance (i.e., overeating and undereating might both be a response to feeling not in control of other aspects of one's life). This dichotomy has begun to be challenged by researchers (see Leadbeater and Way, 1996) dedicated to unpacking the stereotypes and to examining the processes underlying adolescent girls' adaptation and development within different social contexts.

### Pubertal timing reviewed: developmentally ready or not

As in the other chapters of this volume, we turn to pubertal development as one important aspect of early adolescent development that may play a role in the subsequent trajectories of youth's lives. We, like many others, focus on the issue of the timing of pubertal changes as particularly relevant to girls' adaptation. Two contrasting hypotheses, the stage-termination (also called developmental-readiness) hypothesis and the social deviance hypothesis have been offered to explain vulnerabilities that can arise as a function of maturing significantly earlier or "off-time" relative to one's peers. According to the stage-termination hypothesis, early maturation does not allow for consolidation of the developmental tasks of the preadolescent latency period, thus precipitating problems for these adolescents as they grapple with the pubertal or social changes of early adolescence with fewer cognitive and emotional skills than their later developing peers. That is, they are not "developmentally ready" for the changes, and therefore, the stage-termination hypothesis predicts difficulties only for early maturers (Rierdan and Koff, 1993).

In contrast, according to the social deviance hypothesis, distress is associated with passage through salient developmental transitions either significantly earlier or later than peers, due to the perceived lack of shared experience with others and the feeling of difference from peers (Neugarten, 1969, 1979). Although popularized by the book *Are You There God, It's Me, Margaret* (Blume, 1971), about a girl who longs for her period and bigger breasts, the distress of late development has been less born out by empirical investigations of pubertal maturation among middle-class European American girls.

## The assessment of puberty and pubertal timing

Previous investigations of maturational timing during early adolescence have used a number of different indicators to assess adolescents' development as on or off-time. Frequently, studies have used a salient biological marker, such as age at menarche for girls and age of peak-height velocity for boys. Researchers have typically regarded the earliest 20 percent within the distribution for that sample as the "early" developers, and designated the latest 20 percent as the "late" developers (see Graber, Petersen, and Brooks-Gunn 1996 for review). Alternately, the Pubertal Development Scale (PDS, Petersen, *et al.*, 1988), which aggregates several measures of pubertal status (e.g., growth spurt, acne, and acquisition of secondary sex characteristics) for boys and girls separately, has been widely used over the past decade.

One of the questions included in the PDS has also received particular attention because it affords the opportunity to index a more psychologically textured aspect of pubertal timing. Adolescents are asked to assess their own pubertal timing relative to peers of the same sex and age (Graber, *et al.*, 1997; Silbereisen, *et al.*, 1989; Simmons and Blyth, 1987; Wilen and Petersen, 1980). This question has been of particular interest, given early adolescents' heightened self-consciousness and the significant psychological challenge of adapting to and making sense of the physical changes of puberty. Therefore, developmental researchers anticipate that perceiving oneself to be experiencing these changes in temporal isolation from one's peer group would be particularly associated with difficulties in psychological adjustment. Indeed, a number of studies using this question as a means to assess pubertal timing have demonstrated greater psychological and social difficulties among those who perceive themselves to be either early or "off-time" in their development (Graber, *et al.*, 1997; Silbereisen, *et al.*, 1989; Wilen and Petersen, 1980).

Because reporting on one's perception of developmental timing leaves open more room for interpretation on the part of the respondent than does direct inquiry regarding the onset of menstruation, there is also greater potential for individual concerns to influence a girl's assessment of her own timing. For example, studies have demonstrated that girls' affective response to menarche is related to how prepared the girl felt for the event (Ruble and Brooks-Gunn, 1982). Thus, a girl might perceive herself to be an early maturer not only because it reflects her status relative to her peers, but because it, in part, reflects her lack of developmental readiness for maturation. Although little empirical research to date sheds light on girls' feelings about developing later than their peers (see Martin, 1996 for exception), it could be that feeling oneself to be a "late" maturer could reflect a desire to grow up more quickly, to be taken seriously, or to be treated as an adult or a woman, or a curiosity about bodily changes and peer attention afforded to some peers. Thus, perceived late maturers could also be indicating greater dissatisfaction with the pace of their maturation for reasons other than actual maturational timing. These ideas regarding possible intrapsychic influences on girls' perceptions of their pubertal timing are relatively unexamined by academic psychology to date. However, they are offered here as potential "antecedents" of girls' perceptions of timing in order to illuminate one of the central goals of this study. That is, to better understand the ways in which the biological events of puberty are made meaningful to and interpreted by the adolescent, and, in turn, become associated with mental health or social problems.

## Context as one lens through which meaning is made and seeds of distress may be sown

As noted in the preface to this volume, as well as in the previous section of this chapter, puberty may be linked with adjustment problems through several different pathways or interactions among physiologic, psychological, and social changes. In this chapter we focus on links between puberty and adjustment with an emphasis on ethnic context. This interest stems from two related goals: to better understand developmental experiences of African American girls, and to test the generalizability of work on the timing of pubertal development that has been conducted primarily within European American samples of girls. Several authors have noted the importance of particular demands or expectations within different contexts (e.g., family, school, and peers) in shaping girls' experience of "coming of age." Environmental expectations for, and responses to, development serve as important sources of information for adolescents experiencing these changes (Brooks-Gunn and Warren, 1985; Caspi, Lynam, Moffitt, and Silva, 1993; Simmons and Blyth, 1987). Hence, social contexts will vary in the extent to which they either contribute to girls' vulnerability to "coming undone" (i.e., developing psychological or social difficulties) or resilience as they physically mature.

Several previous studies have demonstrated the importance of context on the links between the timing of development and the emergence of psychopathology. For example, Brooks-Gunn and colleagues' studies of ballet dancers suggested that seeing oneself as "early" is a subjective experience dependent on one's surroundings and goals. In these studies, serious ballet students who were "on-time" by population-based standards felt "early" compared to their fellow-ballerinas; were more likely to respond to their own pubertal development with attempts to slow or reverse its effects. Consequently, they were more likely to restrict their diet or engage in excessive exercise, precisely because the physical changes associated with female pubertal development are in direct opposition to the physical ideals prevalent in their primary "culture" – that of competitive ballet schools (Brooks-Gunn, *et al.*, 1989; Brooks-Gunn and Warren, 1985).

Alternately, as suggested by the "developmental readiness" hypothesis, difficulties with the timing of pubertal development can also result from psychological immaturity. For example, Rierdan and Koff (1993) found that European American girls who were both less mature in terms of their ego development and more physically mature than their peers reported higher levels of depressive symptoms than girls for whom cognitive and physical development were more evenly paced. These examples illustrate that a girl's developmental readiness is influenced by both her own rate of maturation across different areas of development and the expectations of or responses to her physical development by the people in her social and cultural environment.

### Ethnic context of development

Conducting research with African American adolescents is important for several reasons. First, African American adolescents have been grossly neglected in mainstream developmental research. Second, African Americans differ from European Americans in ways that are theoretically important.

For example, on average African American girls have been shown to reach menarche seven months earlier than European Americans (mean age = 12.16 years in African Americans, and 12.88 in European Americans) (Herman-Giddens, *et al.*, 1997; Striegel-Moore, *et al.*, 2001; see Obeidallah, *et al.*, 2000 for data that do not support this conclusion). If early maturation is in and of itself a problematic event, as suggested by stage-termination theory, early-maturing African American girls should be the most likely to manifest evidence of this "crisis" (Neugarten, 1979), because they tend to be the "earliest" as compared to other girls across racial/ethnic groups, and perhaps therefore also the least developmentally ready for the events of maturation, having spent the least time consolidating childhood skills and capacities. Consequently, comparing the association of early maturation with psychosocial development in these two ethnic groups provides an important test of the stage-termination hypothesis.

Similarly, it is likely that African American and European American girls differ in both their preparation for puberty and the responses of important others to their pubertal development. For example, Scott and colleagues (1989a, 1989b) examined African American girls' expectations and responses to menarche, and compared their reports to studies conducted on European American samples (e.g., Ruble and Brooks-Gunn, 1982). Findings across ethnic groups indicate that girls report "surprise" as the most common response to menarche, and similar ratios of positive and negative emotional responses (Scott, *et al.*, 1989a, 1989b). In addition, these studies also suggest important differences between racial/ethnic groups. First, African American girls reported more positive responses from their mothers than did European American girls. Second, results suggest an ethnic group difference in the kinds of responses likely to accompany the changes of puberty. African American girls were more likely to offer reassurance than were European American girls in response to a projective task, in which the girls were asked what they would tell a younger sister about menarche. In addition, because sexuality is implicit in pubertal development, the changes of puberty are more likely to be met with indirect or conflictual communications if the social environment has conflicted values and ideas about sex. European American families may be more likely than African American families to hold and transmit conflicted values about sexuality. This is consistent with findings from studies of European American girls who report teasing instead of congratulations and feelings of shame and embarrassment as well as pride and excitement about their experience of pubertal changes (Brooks-Gunn, *et al.*, 1994; Grief and Ulman, 1982; Ruble and Brooks-Gunn, 1982).

Finally, the differentiated body preferences within African American and European American cultures may serve to affect girls' responses to their developing bodies. For European American girls, puberty constitutes both changes toward societally valued body shape (e.g., breasts), but also away from the "slim-ideal" that defines contemporary white feminine standards of beauty. In contrast, African American men and women have more flexible ideas about beauty, and they prefer larger female body size and more marked secondary sex characteristics than do European

American men and women (Parker, *et al.*, 1995; Rucker and Cash, 1992; Thompson, Sargent, and Kemper, 1996). These findings suggest that African American girls would be less distressed and more welcoming of the physical changes and weight gain associated with puberty than are European American girls. Some initial support for this idea has been provided by Hayward and colleagues (1999), who found that pubertal status was related to girls' depressive symptoms among Caucasian, but not African American or Hispanic girls (Hayward, *et al.*, 1999). In contrast, a recent study by Striegel-Moore and colleagues (2001) reports that both African American and European American early-maturing girls expressed more dissatisfaction with their bodies and more dieting behaviors than did later maturers, suggesting that African American girls are not wholly immune from distress generated by the weight gain of puberty.

### Maryland study of adolescent development in context

In the next part of this chapter we summarize findings from an ongoing study of adolescent development being conducted by Jacque Eccles and her colleagues. By so doing, we hope to expand our understanding of the social contexts in which girls' pubertal development corresponds with their experience of mental health or social problems.

In keeping with the ideas outlined above, we expected to find that ethnic group membership would be associated with different experiences of maturation, and thus would be linked with different patterns of association between the timing of maturation and girls' adjustment. As reviewed above, the existing literature on African American girls as compared to European American girls suggests two competing hypotheses. First, if lack of "developmental readiness" due to less time spent in latency-stage development is the primary reason for early maturers' distress, then early-maturing African American girls should evidence more distress than European American girls because they experience puberty earlier. In contrast, to the degree that environmental/ethnic response and preparation of girls is important to girls' adjustment, African American girls should be less likely than European American girls to experience distress as early developers. Indeed, late developing African American girls may be expected to feel greater distress if development is connected with more positive attention and is viewed as more desirable by girls and those around them. In particular, given the difference between these two ethnic groups regarding body size, we expect to find that African American girls would be less likely to develop eating disturbance or body image concerns as a function of their pubertal timing.

In addition, we are interested in understanding how both reports of pubertal timing (e.g., menarche) and more psychologically mediated impressions of pubertal development (e.g., perception of pubertal timing relative to one's peers) relate to girls' psychosocial adjustment in both ethnic groups. Girls' reports of pubertal development should differ for these two measures depending on their ethnic group membership. African American girls should report menarche at a younger average age than European American girls. In contrast, since perception of pubertal timing is more subjective and based (at least in part) on girls' sense of their own maturation relative to their peers, there may be no ethnic differences in this report. This would be true if each ethnic group is primarily using peers of their own ethnicity as their basis of comparison.

### Background of the study

In order to investigate these questions, we used data collected as part of the third wave of the Maryland Adolescent Development in Context (MADIC) study, an ongoing longitudinal investigation of adolescent development across multiple contexts (Eccles and Sameroff, PIs). The MADIC study includes questionnaire and interview data gathered from adolescents, as well as their primary and secondary care-givers. For this report, we examined data gathered from adolescent girls and their primary care-givers in the summer following the girls' eighth grade year in school (age 13–14 years).

One of the particularly compelling aspects of this set of data is its inclusion of large samples of both African American and European American families of fairly comparable socioeconomic status. In 1993, for example, mean annual income was $43,700 for African American families and $50,200 for European American families. Although the majority of girls in both ethnic groups lived with both biological parents, more African American girls lived in single-parent families than did European American girls. The sample includes roughly two-thirds African American (n=270) and one-third European American (n=177) girls and their primary care-givers, who were typically (90%) mothers.

### Measures

Girls were asked about their pubertal development and timing using the Pubertal Development Scale (PDS: Petersen, *et al.*, 1988). In order to contrast a rather more pure "biological" marker with a more subjective index of puberty, we separated two different indicators of pubertal development rather than using the composite scale. The timing of girls' first

Table 13.1. *Menarcheal timing distribution*

| Timing group | African American N (266) | Percentage | European American N (172) | Percentage |
|---|---|---|---|---|
| Early (20%) | 56 | 22.3 | 32 | 19.2 |
| On time (60%) | 135 | 53.8 | 96 | 57.5 |
| Late (20%) | 60 | 23.9 | 39 | 22.7 |

period was assessed by asking the girls the grade and season in which it had occurred. Self-reported menarcheal age is a valid indicator of the timing of pubertal maturation (Brooks-Gunn, *et al.*, 1987; Morris and Udry, 1980). A small number of girls (8 African Americans and 18 European Americans) had not yet experienced their first period at the time of the eighth grade assessment. As predicted, African American girls reported experiencing menarche about six months earlier than did European Americans. On average, African American girls experienced menarche in the spring of the sixth grade; European American girls reached menarche in the late fall of the seventh grade. The percentage of girls reaching menarche in each grade is presented in figure 13.1.

Given this ethnic difference in timing, girls were divided into timing categories within ethnic groups: we created "early," "on-time," and "late" maturing groups using a 20–60–20 split. That is, the earliest 20 percent of girls within each race were specified as belonging to the "early" group, the latest 20 percent of girls within each race formed the "late" group, and the middle 60 percent were specified as "on-time." Using this classification, African American girls were "early" if menarche occurred before the spring of their fifth grade, and "late" if they reached menarche after the spring of their seventh grade. For European Americans, "early" maturers experienced menarche prior to the beginning of their sixth grade, and were considered "late" if they reached menarche after the winter of their eighth grade. The resultant groupings are detailed in table 13.1.

Perception of timing was assessed using one five-point question asking each girl if she felt that she was developing earlier, about the same, or later than most girls her age. Girls who selected a "one" on this scale indicated that their physical development was occurring "a lot before most girls," while those who selected a "five" on this item assessed their physical development as occurring "a lot later than most girls" their age. Girls' perceptions of their pubertal timing demonstrated mild to moderate relations with their ratings of other aspects of pubertal maturation, such as skin changes and menarche, with the highest relation between perception of timing and breast development ($r = .45$). Overall, 28 percent

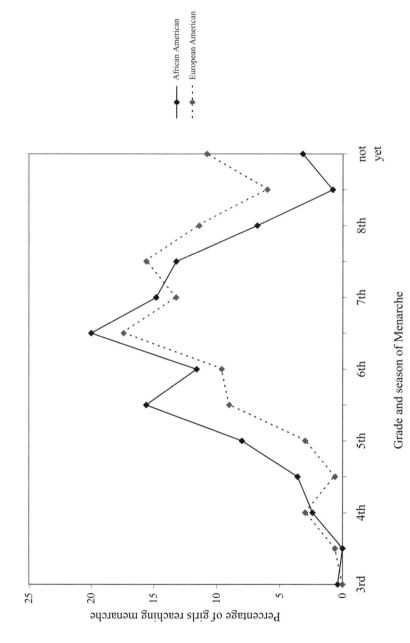

Figure 13.1 Timing of menarche for African American and European American girls

of girls reported either "much earlier" or "earlier" development, 44 percent reported development "about the same" as others, and 28 percent reporting "later" or "much later" development for both European American and African American girls. A greater percentage of African American girls endorsed the "very early" category, which mirrors the pattern for their reports of their timing of menarche (that is, more African American girls were indeed "very early" in their experience of menarche). There was not, however, an overall difference in girls' perceived timing between European American and African American girls.

**Adolescent adjustment**

In order to assess girls' adjustment, we focused our assessment on two broad and related areas of functioning: mental health and sense of self. The appendix below includes greater detail about the scales in each of these areas.

To assess mental health, adolescent girls reported on four different kinds of symptoms: (1) depressive symptoms (CDI; Kovacs, 1992); (2) eating disturbance (EDI-2; Garner, Olmstead, and Polivy, 1983); (3) experience of strong feelings of anger (Achenbach and Edelbrock, 1983); and (4) involvement in problem behaviors (Jessor and Jessor, 1977). In addition, their mothers reported on girls' mental health, including both internalizing and externalizing symptoms (CBCL; Achenbach and Edelbrock, 1983). These areas were selected in order to gain information about the kinds of symptoms or difficulties typically assessed for both European American and African American adolescent girls.

To assess girls' sense of self we used measures tapping the following areas: (1) global self-esteem, (2) popularity, (3) attractiveness, and (4) satisfaction with body weight. Each of these areas was selected due to its relevance to the period of early adolescence generally, but also because concerns about adequacy in these areas is thought to underlie some of the more serious mental health or social difficulties experienced during adolescence. That is, girls who feel inadequate with regard to these issues of "self" may be at heightened risk for the development of more serious psychological problems or for making poor or risky social choices (Fredrickson and Roberts, 1997).

Finally, we included assessments made by both girls and mothers regarding their estimations of the likelihood of future negative sexual events for the girl. Girls and mothers were asked to assess the chances that the adolescent would experience a range of outcomes, including becoming pregnant, being sexually assaulted or raped, getting AIDS or other sexually transmitted diseases, or having sex "too young." Separate scales were computed for girls and their mothers. We included these questions in order to include sexually linked occurrences in our investigation, given concerns about adolescent girls' sexuality and to examine whether girls and mothers in these ethnic groups believe that girls are at increased risk of sexual victimization of one kind or another due to early pubertal development.

### Findings and discussion

We examined the data in three steps. First, we compared African American and European American girls on their overall adjustment in eighth grade. Next, we considered whether their adjustment was related to their pubertal timing (timing of menarche), and whether there were differences in these relations for African American girls as compared to European American girls. We then asked this question using girls' perception of their pubertal timing in order to compare results with those obtained using timing of menarche as the critical index.

How psychologically "undone" do these adolescent girls appear to be? As one would anticipate from a community sample, girls did not evidence particularly high rates of psychological distress. Very few of the girls indicated levels of distress consistent with a clinical diagnosis of depression or eating disorder. However, the subclinical variation in their levels of distress is still noteworthy. When we looked at African American and European American girls separately, we found that European American girls reported higher levels of eating disturbance and less anger than African American girls. Girls' depression and involvement in problem behaviors did not differ between ethnic groups, nor did their mothers' reports of internalizing or externalizing symptoms. When we looked at girls' sense of self, we found that African American girls reported significantly higher levels of self-esteem across each of the areas assessed. That is, African American girls reported themselves to have higher self-esteem, to be more popular, better-looking, and more satisfied with their weight than did European American girls. Finally, girls and mothers reported only mild concern about future sexually related events, and there were no differences in these estimations between the two ethnic groups.

In sum, we found mixed evidence for differences in the expression of disturbance among girls from these two groups. African American girls' consistently higher endorsement of positive sense of self suggests that African American girls do not tend to be as vulnerable to the concerns so often typified in the literature on European American girls. The source of

African American girls' ability to maintain a more positive sense of self on our measures of self is particularly interesting, given that these girls are presumably managing experiences linked to discrimination or minority status in addition to the transitions of adolescence that could erode self-esteem (Simmons, Black, and Zhou, 1991). As suggested by the work of Dubois and colleagues (1996), African American girls' positive esteem in the areas of appearance and body image may be crucial to their overall maintenance of global esteem during early adolescence. In addition, African American girls (and boys) likely rely on more internally based sources of esteem and affirmation, and develop a "thicker skin" against discriminatory remarks from an early age, which may then translate into greater "protection" from the often cruel remarks, looks, or behaviors of peers during adolescence (Wong, Eccles, and Sameroff, 2000).

Given that African American girls report more anger than European American girls, it may be the case that African American girls have more tacit permission or ability to express a broader range of emotions, which may in turn serve to protect them against the development of more serious internalizing symptoms or disorders (e.g., depression and eating disorders). This idea is particularly compelling when noting that, on average, African American girls reported experiencing anger somewhere between "once in a while" and "sometimes," which is unlikely to constitute a clinically concerning level of anger.

In summary, the girls and mothers in this study are not reporting high levels of distress. In addition, African American girls showed some potentially "protective" features in their more positive sense of self, as well as a greater willingness to report feelings of anger as well as sadness.

### Timing of menarche

We next assessed whether girls' adjustment was related to the timing of menarche. Table 13.2 shows the results of analyses comparing the levels of each adjustment indicator as a function of when the girls experienced menarche for African Americans and European Americans separately. As can be seen in table 13.2, there are more significant effects among European American girls, particularly in the area of mental health. Indeed, European American girls who experienced menarche in the earliest 20 percent of their peers reported greater levels of depressive affect, eating disturbance, and anger, as well as more negative expectations about their "sexual futures" than did girls in the later maturing groups. In addition, European American mothers concurred with these assessments, as they reported greater internalizing and externalizing symptoms in the early

Table 13.2. *Relations between timing of menarche and adjustment*

|  | Group differences | |
| --- | --- | --- |
| Adjustment | European Americans | African Americans |
| *Mental health: girls' report* | | |
| Depressive symptoms | Early > on time, late | None |
| Eating disturbance | Early > on time, late | None |
| Anger | Early > on time, late | None |
| Problem behaviors | None | None |
| *Mental health: mothers' report* | | |
| Internalizing symptoms | Early > on time, late | None |
| Externalizing symptoms | Early > on time, late | None |
| *Sense of self* | | |
| Self-esteem | None | On time < late |
| Popularity | On time > late | On time > late |
| Attractiveness | None | None |
| Satisfaction with weight | Early < on time, late | Early < on time, late |
| *Chances of negative events* | | |
| Girls' reports | Early > late | None |
| Mothers' reports | None | None |

maturing group. Among African American girls, in contrast, there were no significant effects of menarcheal timing on either their own, or their mothers' assessments of mental health or expectations for future sexual concerns. To illustrate the pattern of these differences, we have graphed some of the effects in figures 13.2 and 13.3.

When girls' sense of self is considered, the findings are more consistent across the two ethnic groups: girls who were "on-time" reported themselves to be more popular than girls who were "late" across ethnic groups, and girls who were "early" reported a desire to lose more weight than their later maturing peers. Unexpectedly, later maturing African American girls reported significantly greater self-esteem than their on-time African American peers.

The overall pattern of results from this set of analyses offers support for the stage-termination hypothesis among European American girls only, casting doubt on the idea that "early" puberty is troublesome because it disrupts the necessary consolidation of childhood skills and capacities. In keeping with previous studies (i.e., Hayward, *et al.*, 1997; Simmons and Blyth, 1987; Stattin and Magnussen, 1990), we find support for the idea that earlier maturation is a risk for mental health distress among European American or European girls. However, the different pattern of findings among African American girls leads us to speculate about

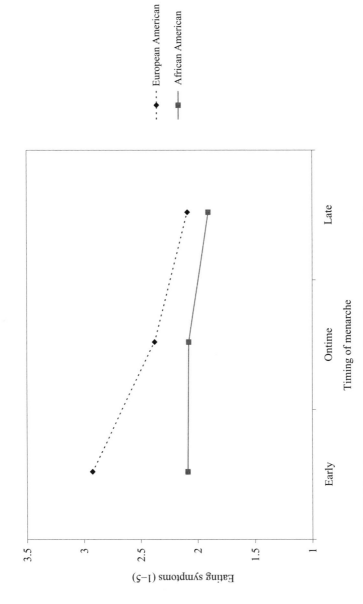

Figure 13.2 Girls' eating symptoms: interaction of menarche and ethnic group

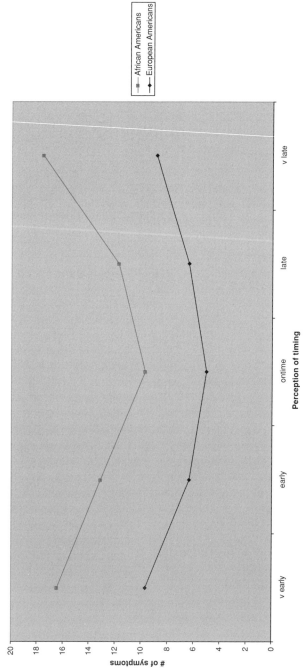

Figure 13.3 Girls' self-esteem: interaction of menarche and ethnic group

the reasons for the differences. An examination of both communications from her social world and girls' own developmental functioning would provide a more comprehensive model for predicting which girls will experience adjustment difficulties as a function of maturational timing, and can help account for the distress of European American early menarcheal girls as well as the lack of distress among early menarcheal African American girls (Holmbeck, 1996; Graber and Brooks-Gunn, 1996). That is, "developmental readiness" may in fact aptly describe the difference between these two groups of girls. It may not be the case that early-maturing African American girls are more "done" with the tasks of childhood, necessarily, but rather that they perceive there to be more to look forward to, and less to beware of, regarding pubertal development regardless of its timing. They feel more "ready" for these changes than do European American girls, on the whole, and therefore do not experience or anticipate the dysregulation of emotions or behaviors that are more common among European American girls. Interestingly, like other researchers using quantitative data, we did not find evidence that later development is particularly hazardous to girls' mental health, at least as assessed in the eighth grade on the measures we used. Across ethnic group, girls did report feeling less popular if they were less developed, paralleling findings from qualitative data (Martin, 1996), quantitative data (Simmons and Blyth, 1987), and popular literature (Blume, 1971).

### Perception of timing

When we asked the same questions using girls' perception of maturational timing as the basis on which to make distinctions between "early," "on-time," and "late" maturation, we found a very different pattern of results. These results are summarized in table 13.3. Generally, girls reported feeling most psychologically healthy (that is, less depressed or inclined toward disturbed eating patterns or angry) when they felt themselves to be "on-time" in their physical development. Girls who perceived themselves to be either earlier or later than their peers were reporting more mental health distress. Similarly, girls' mothers reported more symptoms when their daughter's reported feeling either "earlier" or "later" in their development. Moreover, these patterns of results were basically the same for African American and European American girls. In general, the pattern of results here is more consistent with the "social deviance" hypothesis, in that girls who reported feeling more off-time (regardless of whether they felt early or late) reported more psychological distress.

Interestingly, those European American girls who reported their maturation to be "much earlier than other girls" were typically the most

Table 13.3. *Relations between perception of timing and adjustment*

| Adjustment | Group differences | |
| --- | --- | --- |
| | European Americans | African Americans |
| *Mental health: girls' report* | | |
| Depressive symptoms | Early, late > on time | Early, late > on time |
| Eating disturbance | Early > on time, late | Early, late > on time |
| Anger | Early > on time > late | Early, late > on time |
| Problem behaviors | None | None |
| *Mental health: mothers' report* | | |
| Internalizing symptoms | Early, late > on time | Early, late > on time |
| Externalizing symptoms | Early, late > on time | Early, late > on time |
| *Sense of self* | | |
| Self-esteem | Early, late < on time | None |
| Popularity | Early > on time > late | Early > on time > late |
| Attractiveness | Early > on time > late | Early > on time > late |
| Satisfaction with weight | Early < on time < late | Early < on time < late |
| *Chances of negative events* | | |
| Girls' reports | Early > on time > late | None |
| Mothers' reports | None | None |

distressed, indicating that early development may indeed be uniquely distressing among this ethnic group. In contrast, African American girls who felt that their development was "much later than others" were more often the most symptomatic. These findings provide some support for the differential meaning of early versus late maturation as a function of ethnic group membership. For some African American girls, feeling "late" does correspond to somewhat greater mental health distress, perhaps due to the desire to join the ranks of the physically more mature, in much the same way that later developing boys have been noted to want to catch up to their earlier peers because of the perceived typical benefits of development (Crockett and Petersen, 1987).

When girls' sense of self was considered, a different pattern of results was apparent; girls who perceived themselves to be early developers felt more popular and attractive than did "on-time" girls, who reported feeling more popular and attractive than did "late" girls. That is, we find a gradual decrement in girls' reports of popularity and attractiveness, whereby feeling "early" coincides with a heightened sense of being popular and attractive, while feeling "late" co-occurs with feeling less popular and attractive. The opposite pattern was true for girls' satisfaction with their weight; girls who felt "earliest" also thought that they needed to lose the most weight, while girls who felt "latest" were more satisfied with their weight, and those who saw themselves as "on-time" were in the middle. This pattern closely mirrors the girls' actual weight; the girls who developed early also tended to have a higher body mass, as would be expected. In addition, this pattern held for European American girls' expectations regarding the future – "early" girls reported greater likelihood that they would be involved in a negative sexually related event in their future than did girls who perceived their development as "on-time" or "late." Finally, among European American girls, feeling "on-time" was associated with higher self-esteem than was reported by girls who felt either "early" or "late." Interestingly, girls' reports of their involvement in problem behavior did not differ as a function of their perceived timing.

Perceiving oneself to be an earlier maturing girl appears to be associated with an interesting pattern of both benefits (i.e., popularity) and liabilities (i.e., body dissatisfaction) to one's psychological and social development. Perceived late development is associated with liabilities in terms of mental health distress, as well as viewing oneself as less attractive or popular. In contrast, perceived lateness is linked to greater body satisfaction. In comparison to both perceived earliness and lateness, feeling "on-time" is uniformly beneficial. Girls who perceive themselves to be "on-time" report fewer symptoms of mental health distress, and a sense of "average" popularity and attractiveness. For both European American and African American girls who perceive themselves as "early," it appears that popularity and attractiveness are "benefits" of their maturation. As Stattin and Magnussen (1990) found, this pattern could lead these girls to focus on relationships with older boys, leading them to forgo investments in developing other aspects of themselves, such as other talents, for example, sports or academics (Eccles, et al., in press; Pipher, 1994). According to these results, African American girls are potentially also at risk for the development of this "shell-self" where beauty or peer status is privileged over what is "inside" with respect to their perceived timing of development. Clearly, we would need to know more about how important or salient these elements are to girls, as well as other contributions to their overall sense of self, in order to know whether this indeed translates into a risk for early-developing girls.

As expected, girls' perception of pubertal timing appears to be quite subjective. Although African American girls experienced menarche substantially earlier than did European American girls, they were not substantially more likely than European American girls to see themselves as early maturers. European American and African American girls were equally likely to report themselves to be "off-time" in their development, and were basing this estimation on their actual developmental timing (i.e., menarche, breast development) to a roughly comparable degree. In addition, this rating was only moderately related to the more objective indicators of pubertal timing. These results suggest that there are other significant influences on girls' perceptions of their pubertal timing that were not accounted for in this study, which lead girls to see themselves as either "in sync" or "socially deviant" with regard to pubertal development. In turn, this sense of being "socially deviant" is linked to mental health distress in both of these ethnic groups. Thus, results using perceived timing suggest some internal sense of "developmental readiness" over and above the effects of actual development that is somewhat independent of ethnic context. Although ethnicity moderated the association of pubertal development and psychological/social adjustment when menarcheal timing is examined, this is much less the case when girls' perception of timing is used as the marker of maturation. Continuing to develop an understanding of the influences on perceived timing is a worthy goal, as both African American and European American girls who are inclined to view themselves as "off-time" report similar adjustment difficulties.

## Final thoughts

Clearly, although we assume that processes of socialization at work on the family, peer, and neighborhood levels are important elements of "ethnic group context," it is quite difficult to measure the attitudes, ideas, or behaviors of those people who truly make up the "context" of these girls' development on a moment-to-moment basis. Although we have not yet included family processes in our study of these issues, the findings reported here suggest many hypotheses regarding the ethnic differences associated with the impact of menarcheal timing. Because the girls in this study live in the same communities and attend the same schools, we can assume they were exposed to similar sex education in the classroom, and therefore we can interpret the findings as a more likely product of familial and peer influences rather than they are of differences in formal educational attention to preparation for the events of puberty. For example, African American families may better prepare girls for menarche, be more unconditionally welcoming of the event, celebrate it as an important milestone, and imbue it with less shame and stigma (Martin, 1996) than is typical in European American families. Perhaps African American girls are afforded more positive and sustained close relations during pubertal development, which serves to assist them in successful adaptation to these bodily changes and their corresponding social definition (Michael, 1997). Thus, in line with previous studies demonstrating the importance of context (e.g., Brooks-Gunn, *et al.*, 1989; see also chapter 14) on the interpretation of, and behavioral adaptation to, pubertal development, it appears that we need to enhance our understanding of developmental processes by paying close attention to the locales in which they take place.

In pulling together a "wish list" of things to include as these studies progress, we believe that future research would do well to include assessments of more positive aspects of maturation and social behavior, particularly regarding dating and sexual activities (see Paikoff, 1995 and also chapter 5). For example, only negative events related to sexual behavior (e.g., having sex "too early," experiencing rape) were assessed here. Although these are important aspects of social development or experiences, they bias findings toward identifying problematic rather than positive aspects of development. Particularly given societal views of adolescence as a problem-filled phase of life, it would be useful to investigate and describe adaptive functioning as well as maladaptive functioning.

If our goal is to minimize the distress and tendency to "come undone" sometimes experienced during early adolescence, our results suggest that helping youth of both sexes and all ethnic groups to feel "developmentally ready" for the changes of puberty would be useful. The mental health and social pitfalls of adolescence are not inevitable, and are informed, at least in part, by social expectations and pressures that make the kinds of mental health problems experienced by adolescents limited to those that have relevance in their salient communities. Preventive intervention should address cultural expectations regarding what kids will do with their developing bodies. There is also a cultural need for "developmental readiness" – society needs to be ready for children to develop, and to assist in their adaptation, particularly as the average age of pubertal development stretches downward. Although pubertal development, like the shift to middle school, can feel like a very discontinuous set of experiences, these also happen within the context of an individual's overall life and circumstances.

Coming of age does not need to imply "coming undone." The inclusion of youth from a range of circumstances, ethnicities, and settings in studies of adolescent development is critical to allow us to further circumscribe and refine our understanding of the links between "early" or "off-time" development and the various risks to successful adaptation during the adolescent years.

**Appendix**

MENARCHE

Have you had your first period yet? (1) = yes   (2) = no
(if yes) Please circle the grade in which your period first occurred

| 3rd grade (1) | 4th grade (2) | 5th grade (3) | 6th grade (4) | 7th grade (5) | 8th grade (6) |
|---|---|---|---|---|---|

Now please circle the time of year it first occurred.

| fall (1) | winter (2) | spring (3) | summer after that grade (4) |
|---|---|---|---|

PERCEPTION OF TIMING

Compared to OTHER GIRLS YOUR AGE, would you say you are physically developing:

| A lot before most girls (1) | A little before most girls (2) | About the same time as most girls (3) | A little later than most girls (4) | A lot later than most girls (5) |
|---|---|---|---|---|

Adolescent Adjustment Measures

| Scale | Number of items | Examples of items | Internal consistency (alpha) |
|---|---|---|---|
| *Mental health: girls' report* | | | |
| Depressive symptoms (CDI)   1–44 | 27 | Mood, vegatative symptoms, anhedonia, hopeless- ness | .88 |
| Eating disturbance (EDI)   1–6 | 9 | Dieting, binging, worries about weight gain | .89 |

| | | | | |
|---|---|---|---|---|
| Anger | 1–5 | 3 | Wanting to hurt people or property because angry | .87 |
| Problem behaviors | 0–1 | 9 | Lying to parents, substance use, criminal behavior | .82 |
| *Mental health: mothers' report (CBCL)* | | | | |
| Internalizing symptoms | 0–40 | 3 scales | Withdrawn, anxious, depressed | NA |
| Externalizing symptoms | 0–49 | 2 scales | Aggressive, oppositional, cruel | NA |
| *Sense of self* | | | | |
| Self-esteem | 1–5 | 3 | "How often are you . . . pretty sure about yourself?" | .73 |
| Popularity | 1–7 | 1 | "Compared to others . . . how popular are you?" | NA |
| Attractiveness | 1–7 | 2 | "How good looking are you?" | .85 |
| Satisfaction with weight | 1–5 | 1 | "How do you feel about your weight" (lose weight vs gain) | NA |
| *Chances of negative events* | | | | |
| Girls' reports | 1–6 | 4 | What are the chances that you will start having sex too young? | .59 |

| Mothers' reports | 1–6 | 4 | Same as above ("your child") | .77 |

*Notes*

CBCL = Child Behavior Checklist
CDI = Childrens' Depression Inventory
EDI = Eating Disorders Inventory ("drive for thinness" and "bulimia" subscales used)

## References

Achenbach, T. M., and Edelbrock, C. S. (1983). *Manual for the child behavior checklist and revised child behavior profile.* Burlington, VT: University of Vermont Press.

Alan Guttmacher Institute (1994). *Sex and America's teenagers.* New York: Alan Guttmacher Institute.

American Psychiatric Association (1994). *Diagnostic and statistical manual of mental disorders,* 4th edn. Washington, DC: American Psychiatric Association.

Attie, I., and Brooks-Gunn, J. (1989). Development of eating problems in adolescent girls: a longitudinal study. *Developmental Psychology,* 25(1), 70–79.

Blume, J. (1971). *Are you there God, it's me, Margaret.* New York: Dell.

Brooks-Gunn, J., and Warren, M. (1985). The effects of delayed menarche in different contexts: dance and non-dance students. *Journal of Youth and Adolescence,* 14, 285–300.

Brooks-Gunn, J., Attie, I., Burrow, C., Rosso, J., and Warren, M. (1989). The impact of puberty on body and eating concerns in athletic and non-athletic contexts. *Journal of Early Adolescence. Special issue: Early adolescent transitions: longitudinal studies of biological, psychological and social interactions,* 9(3), 269–290.

Brooks-Gunn, J., Newman, D. L., Holderness, C. C., and Warren, M. P. (1994). The experience of breast development and girls' stories about the purchase of a bra. *Journal of Youth and Adolescence,* 23(5), 539–565.

Brooks-Gunn, J., Warren, M., Rosso, J., and Gargiulo, J. (1987). Validity of self-report measures of girls' pubertal status. *Child Development,* 58, 829–841.

Caspi, A., Lynam, D., Moffitt, T. E., and Silva, P. A. (1993). Unraveling girls' delinquency: biological, dispositional and contextual contributions to adolescent misbehavior. *Developmental Psychology,* 29, 19–30.

Crockett, L., and Petersen, A. C. (1987). Pubertal status and psychosocial development: findings from the Early Adolescence Study. In R. M. Lerner and T. T. Foch (ed.), *Biological-psychosocial interactions in early adolescence: a life-Span perspective.* Hillsdale, NJ: Lawrence Erlbaum.

DuBois, D. L., Felner, R. D., Brand, S., Phillips, R. S., and Lease, A. M. (1996). Early adolescent self-esteem: a developmental-ecological framework and assessment strategy. *Journal of Research on Adolescence,* 6(4), 543–579.

Eccles, J. S., Barber, B., Jozefowicz, D., Malanchuk, O., and Vida, M. (in press). Self-evaluations of competence, task values and self-esteem. In J. Warrell (ed.), *Girls and adolescence.* Washington, DC: American Psychiatric Association.

Eccles, J. S., Wigfield, A., Flanagan, C., Miller, C., Reuman, D., and Yee, D. (1989). Self-concepts, domain values, and self-esteem: relations and changes at early adolescence. *Journal of Personality*, 57, 283–310.

Fredrickson, B., and Roberts, T.-A. (1997). Objectification theory: towards an understanding of women's lived experiences and mental health risks. *Psychology of Women Quarterly*, 21, 173–206.

Garbarino, J. (1999). *Lost boys*. New York: Free Press.

Garner, D. M., Olmstead, M. P., and Polivy, J. (1983). Development and validation of a multi-dimensional eating disorders inventory for anorexia nervosa and bulimia. *International Journal of Eating Disorders*, 2(2), 15–34.

Graber, J. A., and Brooks-Gunn, J. (1996). Transitions and turning points: navigating the passage from childhood through adolescence. *Developmental Psychology*, 32(4), 768–776.

Graber, J. A., Lewinsohn, P. M., Seeley, J. R., and Brooks-Gunn, J. (1997). Is psychopathology associated with the timing of pubertal development? *Journal of the American Academy of Child and Adolescent Psychiatry*, 36(12), 1768–1776.

Graber, J. A., Petersen, A. C., and Brooks-Gunn, J. (1996). Pubertal processes: methods, measures, and models. In J. A. Graber. (ed.), *Transitions through adolescence: interpersonal domains and contexts*. Hillsdale, NJ: Lawrence Erlbaum.

Grief, E. B., and Ulman, K. J. (1982). The psychological impact of menarche on early adolescent females: a review of the literature. *Child Development*, 53, 1413–1430.

Hamburg, D. A., and Takanishi, R. (1996). Great transitions: preparing American youth for the 21st century – the role of research. *Journal of Research on Adolescence*, 6(4), 379–396.

Hayward, C., Gotlib, I., Schraedley, P., and Litt, I. (1999). Ethnic differences in the association between pubertal status and symptoms of depression in adolescent girls. *Journal of Adolescent Health*, 25(2), 143–149.

Hayward, C., Killen, J. D., Wilson, D. M., and Hammer, L. (1997). Psychiatric risk associated with early puberty in adolescent girls. *Journal of the American Academy of Child and Adolescent Psychiatry*, 36, 255–262.

Herman-Giddings, M. E., Slora, E. J., et al. (1997). Secondary sexual characteristics and menses in young girls seen in office practice: a study from the Pediatric Research in Office Settings network. *Pediatrics*, 99(4), 505–512.

Holmbeck, G. (1996). A model of family relational transformations during the transition to adolescence: parent–adolescent conflict and adaptation. In J. A. Graber, J. Brooks-Gunn, and A. C. Petersen (ed.), *Transitions through adolescence: interpersonal domains and contexts*. Hillsdale, NJ: Lawrence Erlbaum.

Jenkins, R. R. (1983). Future directions in research. In J. Brooks-Gunn and A. C. Petersen (ed.), *Girls at puberty: biological and psychosocial perspectives* (pp. 325–338). New York: Plenum.

Jessor, R., and Jessor, S. L. (1977). *Problem behavior and psychosocial development: a longitudinal study of youth*. New York: Academic Press.

Kovacs, M. (1992). *Children's Depression Inventory manual*. North Tonawanda, NY: Multi-Health Systems.

Leadbeater, B., and Way, N. (ed.) (1996). *Urban girls: resisting stereotypes, creating identities*. New York: New York University Press.

Martin, K. A. (1996). *Puberty, sexuality and the self: girls and boys at adolescence.* New York: Routledge.

Michael, A. (1997). Family relations during puberty: parent and adolescent perspectives. Poster presented at the biennial meeting of the Society for Research in Child Development, Washington, DC.

Morris, N. M., and Udry, J. R. (1980). Validation of self-administered instrument to assess stage of adolescent development. *Journal of Youth and Adolescence,* **9,** 271–280.

Neugarten, B. L. (1969). Continuities and discontinuities of psychological issues into adult life. *Human Development,* **12,** 121–130.

Neugarten, B. L. (1979). Time, age, and the life cycle. *American Journal of Psychiatry,* **136,** 887–894.

Obeidallah, D. A., Brennan, R. T., Brooks-Gunn, J., Kindlon, D., and Earls, F. (2000). Socioeconomic status, race and girls' pubertal maturation: results from the project on human development in Chicago neighborhoods. *Journal of Research on Adolescence,* **10**(4), 443–464.

Paikoff, R. L. (1995). Early heterosexual debut: situations of sexual possibility during the transition to adolescence. *American Journal of Orthopsychiatry,* **65**(3), 389–401.

Parker, S., Nichter, M., Vuckovic, N., Sims, C., and Ritenbaugh, C. (1995). Body-image and weight concerns about African American and white adolescent females – differences that make a difference. *Human Organization,* **54,** 103–114.

Petersen, A. C., Crockett, L., Richards, M., and Boxer, A. (1988). A self-report measure of pubertal status: reliability, validity and initial norms. *Journal of Youth and Adolescence,* **17**(2), 117–133.

Pipher, M. (1994). *Reviving Ophelia.* New York: Ballantine.

Rierdan, J., and Koff, E. (1993). Developmental variables in relation to depressive symptoms in adolescent girls. *Development and Psychopathology,* **5,** 485–496.

Ruble, D. N., and Brooks-Gunn, J. (1982). The experience of menarche. *Child Development,* **53,** 1557–1566.

Rucker, C. E., and Cash, T. F. (1992). Body images, body-size perceptions, and eating behaviors among African American and white college women. *International Journal of Eating Disorders,* **12**(3), 291–299.

Scott, C. S., Arthur, D., Panizo, M. I., and Owen, R. (1989a). Menarche: the black American experience. *Journal of Adolescent Health Care,* **10,** 363–368.

Scott, C. S., Arthur, D., Owen, R., and Panizo, M. I. (1989b). Black adolescents' emotional response to menarche. *Journal of the National Medical Association,* **81**(3), 285–290.

Silbereisen, R. K., Petersen, A. C., Albrecht, H. T., and Kracke, B. (1989). Maturational timing and the development of problem behavior: longitudinal studies in adolescence. *Journal of Early Adolescence,* **9**(3), 247–268.

Simmons, R. G., and Blyth, D. A. (1987). *Moving into adolescence: the impact of pubertal change and school context.* Hawthorne, NY: De Gruyter.

Simmons, R. G., Black, A., and Zhou, Y. (1991). African American versus white children and the transition into junior high school. *American Journal of Education. Special issue: development and education across education,* **99**(4), 481–520.

Stattin, H., and Magnussen, D. (1990). *Pubertal maturation in female development*. Hillsdale, NJ: Lawrence Erlbaum.

Streigel-Moore, R. H., McMahon, R. P., Biro, F. M., Schreiber, G., Crawford, P. B., and Voorhees, C. (2001). Exploring the relationship between timing of menarche and eating disorder symptoms in black and white adolescent girls. *International Journal of Eating Disorders*, **30(4)**, 421–433.

Thompson, S. H., Sargent, R. G., and Kemper, K. A. (1996). Black and white adolescent males' perceptions of ideal body size. *Sex Roles*, **34(5–6)**, 391–406.

Udry, J. R. (1988). Biological predispositions and social control in adolescent sexual behavior. *American Sociological Review*, **53**, 709–722.

Wilen, J. B., and Petersen, A. C. (1980). Young adolescents' responses to the timing of pubertal chances. Paper presented at the annual meeting of the American Psychological Association, Montreal, CA.

Wong, C. A., Eccles, J. S., and Sameroff, A. J. (n.d.). Ethnic discrimination and ethnic identification: the influence of African Americans' and whites' school and social-emotional adjustment. Manuscript under review.

Zabin, L., and Hayward, S. (1993). *Adolescent sexual behavior and childbearing*. Thousand Oaks, CA: Sage.

# Part 7

# Puberty and context

# 14 Puberty in context

*Julia A. Graber*

Examinations of links between pubertal development and various outcomes (e.g., psychopathology, reproductive behaviors) have focused on
both the effects of puberty on behavior as well as on how context and behavior influence the course of puberty. The interest in puberty as a defining transition in the course of development is in many ways based on
circumstantial evidence. That is, rates of psychopathology change dramatically in the late pubertal to postpubertal period for several common
disorders, such as depression and conduct disorder (e.g., Lewinsohn,
*et al.*, 1993; Loeber and Keenan, 1994). In addition, gender differences
in rates of depression also emerge at this time (see chapter 8). The challenge to researchers interested in developmental process and the health
outcomes of adolescents has been to demonstrate that some link or links
actually exist between pubertal development and these behavioral and adjustment changes. Furthermore, if such links exist to what extent are they
explanatory in rates of psychopathology in adolescence and to what extent
do they identify strategies for prevention and intervention for adolescent
mental health.

Historically, it has long been assumed that puberty was an important
causal element in adolescent adjustment and behavior. This "assumption" is no small factor in our understanding of adolescent development
and prevention and intervention for mental health. Although Buchanan
and her colleagues (Buchanan, Eccles, and Becker, 1992) attempted to
lay to rest the notion of "raging hormones" in their now classic review of
the hormone and behavior literature prior to 1992, the reality is that most
parents, teachers, and even adolescents themselves believe that raging
hormones exist and that they explain behavior. It should be noted that the
theory is fairly simple and has two main interpretations. First, hormonal
changes at puberty lead to sexual arousal and interest and these desires
make adolescents crazy. The second interpretation is that hormones lead
to some type of arousal or perturbation in affect, which causes the mood-
iness, irritability, and irrational behavior that makes parents crazy. The

informed reader will undoubtedly note that these overviews of popular belief are also based on conjecture and anecdote.

Despite widespread beliefs, empirical findings have not demonstrated such resounding effects of puberty on behavior. In part, few studies examined puberty at all up until about twenty to twenty-five years ago. A notable exception was the work of Mary Cover Jones and her colleagues (Jones, 1965; Jones and Mussen, 1958). Using the Oakland Growth Studies, Jones and her colleagues investigated the effect of how puberty was experienced within a social context or time frame (e.g., timing). Thus, from the beginning, empirical examinations of puberty have expected that puberty works in an individual differences framework rather than as something that influences all children in the same manner. Also, from the beginning, it was not puberty per se but the context in which it occurred that was salient to understanding subsequent adjustment in boys and girls.

The notion that puberty would be an important predictor of adolescent adjustment is particularly appealing, given that puberty exerts such a profound influence on the body and its functioning. That is, the hormonal changes and external physical changes that occur result in an individual who looks more like an adult than a child and, moreover, now has the reproductive capacity of an adult. The pervasive nature of the changes cannot be overemphasized. Along with the commonly observed development of secondary sexual characteristics and growth spurts in height and weight, puberty influences internal maturation of the reproductive organs, the circulatory and respiratory systems, as well as the central nervous system and endocrine systems (Marshall and Tanner, 1986; see also chapter 2). As such, it would seem naïve to presume that these changes had no psychological effect on the developing individual. At the individual level, certainly the changes of puberty have personal meaning (e.g., Brooks-Gunn, 1984). However, puberty does not happen just at the personal level; rather, how the changes of puberty are experienced is dependent upon what those changes mean in a larger social context. An individual's interpretation of physical change is dependent upon how others respond to those changes. For example, increases in conflict between parents and children during the midpubertal period may be due to the effect that external signs of adulthood have on an individual's desire to be more autonomous (Paikoff and Brooks-Gunn, 1991). Beyond the family environment, individuals also redefine themselves at puberty in the context of peers, communities, and larger cultural systems.

The most important fact in the study of puberty and its effect on adolescence is that most individuals do not have significant mental health problems during or after puberty (e.g., Offer, 1987). Thus, the simple models of direct effects of hormones or status cannot predict mental health outcomes; it is an impossibility, as all boys and girls will experience hormonal and secondary sexual characteristic changes. Even if specific hormonal changes unique to girls were associated with onset or increased rates of a particular disorder, models would still have to explain why all girls do not develop the disorder. That is, individual differences either in the adolescent's context or internal functioning must interact with hormonal changes or pubertal status (see chapter 3). Inasmuch as Buchanan and her colleagues (1992) attempted to drive a stake through the heart of "raging hormones" as the explanation for all adolescent behavior, it is essential to perform a similar act on the notion of direct effect models. Interactive models that account for either internal characteristics of the individual or variations in the individual's environment are the only approaches to explaining puberty–psychopathology links that have any basis in logic or support from the literature. Much like Buchanan's assertion that most researchers interested in development at puberty did not truly believe that raging hormones were in and of themselves explanatory, most studies of puberty do not believe in direct effect models (Brooks-Gunn, Graber, and Paikoff, 1994). Regardless, in both cases many studies, including my own, still report on such models and discuss them as though they were explanatory.

Whereas everyone notes that puberty is a process that spans four to five years for the individual and includes multiple physiological and physical changes, most studies that include "puberty" as a construct have simply examined one dimension, one event, or one point in time (see Graber, Petersen, and Brooks-Gunn, 1996 for a review of the methods of measuring puberty; see also chapter 1). Because of the focus on single points in time, even fewer studies have considered how puberty may connect prepubertal development and postpubertal outcomes and how pathways from childhood to adolescence may differ depending on the broader context of an individual's development.

In general, there have been three main dimensions of puberty that are thought to influence aspects of psychopathology during adolescence. Specifically, effects on psychopathology, or more generally adjustment, have been examined in connection with hormonal changes at puberty, level of development of secondary sexual characteristics (i.e., pubertal status), and timing of pubertal development in comparison to the norms for age or peer group (Graber, Brooks-Gunn, and Warren, in press). Other chapters in this volume have examined one or more of these areas (see chapters 3, 8, 9, 12, and 13); as such, it is not the purpose of this discussion to review the literature in each area, but rather to discuss how contextual factors may be involved in when, for whom, and how effects of puberty on psychopathology are demonstrated.

As indicated, one of the drawbacks in the literature to date is that researchers have generally not followed individuals through the entirety of puberty. As Petersen (1987) pointed out, if most adolescents take four to five years to progress through the development of secondary sexual characteristics and given the range of variability among individuals in terms of when they begin and how quickly they progress through puberty, it would take at least ten years to follow one cohort of children through puberty. Subsequent studies have used innovative designs to truncate the time needed to examine pubertal variation among age cohorts (e.g., Angold, Costello, and Worthman, 1998). In addition to the time necessary to follow a cohort through puberty, when effects of puberty on psychopathology are found among adolescents, the question of whether or not and to what extent effects persist over longer periods of time requires an even more extensive time frame for studying these issues (see Stattin and Magnusson, 1990 as one of the few studies to extend into adulthood).

Moreover, an almost completely separate literature exists on the factors that influence the onset of puberty (see chapters 10 and 11). Even though factors have been identified that influence hormonal changes, status, and timing, the more comprehensive examinations that consider how or whether processes that influence onset of puberty also play a role in how or whether puberty influences subsequent psychopathology have rarely been conducted. That is, the precursors of puberty and outcomes of puberty literature are often not viewed jointly. As such, a brief review of different factors that influence the onset of puberty is in order before moving on to connections to outcomes. In this discussion, attention is paid to the extent to which each hypothesis focuses on contextual factors that would account for individual differences in the experience of puberty.

### Factors that influence the onset of puberty

The actual mechanisms and systems that begin the initial changes of puberty are documented in several comprehensive reviews (e.g., Grumbach and Styne, 1998; Reiter and Grumbach, 1982; see also chapter 2), and will not be reviewed here. A few points are noteworthy, however. The biological and physiological systems that will ultimately develop to mature functioning at puberty are established prenatally. At birth the hypothalamic regulatory system that controls pituitary hormones is active, although not fully mature, and the gonadotropins, LH and FSH, may exhibit "adult-like" patterns in their levels and excretion (Grumbach and Styne,

1998). This hormonal activity often persists until late infancy or early childhood. Once greater maturation in the regulatory areas of the hypothalamus is attained, pituitary release of LH and FSH is suppressed, from late infancy or early childhood until mid or late childhood; as such, these hormones do not exert influence on the adrenal or gonadal systems during this time, and maturation of the reproductive system remains in stasis for much of childhood (see chapter 2).

The question of what exactly initiates the hypothalamus-pituitary system to start releasing gonadotropins again in mid to late childhood is not fully answered (Grumbach and Styne, 1998; Reiter and Grumbach, 1982). Rather, the hypotheses regarding factors that influence the timing of onset of puberty have some support in research, but often have not provided substantial evidence for the mechanisms involved. Also, and of particular relevance to the present volume on gender differences, most hypotheses are either specific to the onset of puberty in girls or have only been tested in girls. Even less is known about the processes that influence the onset of puberty in boys.

As might be expected, one factor that influences the timing of the onset of puberty in girls is genetics. For studies that have examined correspondence of age at menarche between mothers and daughters moderate correlations (often between 0.30 and 0.40) are reported (e.g., Brooks-Gunn and Warren, 1988; Zacharias and Wurtman, 1969). Notably, these correlations may tap in to genetic factors but may also tap in to behaviors that mothers and daughters share that influence pubertal development (Belsky, Steinberg, and Draper, 1991; Graber, Brooks-Gunn, and Warren, 1995). These may include behavioral patterns such as dieting and exercise, in which mothers may engage and model for their daughters (see Graber, Archibald, and Brooks-Gunn, 1999 for a review); for example, intense exercise and lean body mass are linked to later onset of puberty (e.g., Warren, 1980). As such, basic correlational studies of correspondence of mothers and daughters for a pubertal event such as menarche include a genetic contribution along with environmental factors (which may, of course, also have a genetic contribution).

In addition, paternal contribution to the onset of puberty for girls is typically not included in studies of heritability. In general, studies of puberty in adult women have relied on the ability of the women to accurately recall their age at menarche (Bean, *et al.*, 1979), whereas studies of puberty have not assessed which indicators of puberty are recalled most accurately for adult men. The absence of this information in the literature may in part explain why studies of potential heritability of puberty from father to son have rarely been conducted. Rather, it is assumed that genetics play some role in the onset of the timing of puberty, but research in this area is sparse and findings for girls are inconclusive as to the extent of genetic versus contextual influence.

Another factor associated with stimulating the onset of puberty that has recently gained attention is exposure to environmental toxins. Again, this research has focused on effects on girls and suggests that some chemicals, such as DDE (produced when the pesticide DDT breaks down) mimic estrogens in the body (e.g., Gladen, Ragan, and Rogan, 2000). As such, these "estrogens" may act directly on organs to promote development and may trigger hypothalamus activity that begins activation of the pubertal system. Certainly, the influence of toxins on the developing system is a contextual or environmental factor that might predict why girls in a particular environmental context, that is, neighborhood or community, might mature earlier than girls in different neighborhoods. To date, studies of neighborhoods and puberty have been limited and have not assessed environmental hazards or pollutants in order to see if subgroups of girls in these environments might account for a subset of earlier maturers among girls. Interestingly, environmental toxins that act as estrogens may also influence puberty prenatally when the hypothalamus-pituitary-gonadal system first develops or is organized (Gladen, Ragan, and Rogan, 2000). In this case, contextual factors would have to be studied in connection with mothers' environments during pregnancy, which may or may not match the environment of the girls in the prepubertal years of childhood. Whereas this model discusses mechanisms that would apply to variations in girls' pubertal development, it does not address normative developmental contexts and processes, but only those contexts that include sufficient toxin exposure to alter development. The term "sufficient" is perhaps misleading as these processes have mainly been studied in extreme conditions, when exposure that is dramatically atypical is observed. Whether or not more subtle effects are demonstrated on a gradient is not known.

As indicated, nutritional and diet-related behaviors have been associated with onset of puberty. Whereas lowered nutritional intake, at extreme levels, delays the onset of puberty, it has long been suggested that body fat was associated with the onset of puberty, again, at least for girls (Frisch, 1983). Frisch has suggested that menarche is reached once body fat attains particular levels; certainly menarche frequently follows the peak in weight gain at puberty for girls (Marshall and Tanner, 1986). However, menarche is one of the last pubertal events and it is not clear to what extent prepubertal weight is associated with onset of puberty. Recent studies have focused on the role of the hormone leptin in onset of puberty and regulation of body fat (e.g., Clayton and Trueman, 2000; see also chapter 2). Leptin appears to increase dramatically during periods of rapid weight gain in humans (Horlick, *et al.*, 2000). In addition, leptin seems to influence gonadotropin activity. Despite much speculation, to date, studies have only found correlations of levels of pubertal development, weight, and leptin levels, but no indications that leptin in fact causes pubertal changes or onset (Clayton and Trueman, 2000). Weight may still be a factor in the onset of puberty, but the mechanism seems unlikely to be via leptin. Weight-related behaviors clearly have a basis in context and environment. In the United States, obesity rates among adults and children have been increasing as activity levels have dropped and dietary patterns have changed (Himes and Dietz, 1994; Lewis, *et al.*, 2000).

As for the hypotheses reviewed thus far, some are more based in contextual influences on puberty than others. More importantly, some have stronger potential connections to the adjustment outcomes of individual differences in pubertal development. For example, how exposure to increased environmental toxins would be associated with subsequent psychopathology outcomes of puberty is not entirely clear. In contrast, behaviors that influence pubertal development, such as weight gain or aspects of shared environments, may have more direct links to subsequent adjustment and pathology.

Along these lines, the final hypothesis outlining influences on the onset of puberty is more closely tied to potential dysfunction postpubertally. Over the past ten years several studies have documented that psychosocial stress influences the timing and perhaps the rate of pubertal development in girls (e.g., Graber, Brooks-Gunn, and Warren, 1995; Moffitt, *et al.*, 1992; Steinberg, 1988; Surbey, 1990). In particular, stressful familial contexts have been the focus of much research. Father absence in the childhood years was associated with earlier maturation in a retrospective study of college-age women (Surbey, 1990). Subsequent prospective studies found that the quality of family relations, specifically low warmth in family relations, was associated with earlier maturation even in families that did not have father absence (Graber, Brooks-Gunn, and Warren, 1995; Moffitt, *et al.*, 1992). In fact, Ellis and his colleagues (1999) reported that quality of parent–child interaction in early childhood was associated with earlier maturation in girls. A second study by Ellis and Garber (2000) reported that maternal mood disorders were associated with earlier maturation in girls, but the association was mediated by poor quality of family relationships and father absence; both factors seemed to be independent pathways to earlier maturation in girls. The investigations of Trickett and Putnam (1993) of childhood sexual abuse would also be an example of this type of psychosocial stress model, which may be particularly useful in explaining subsequent psychopathology (see chapter 10).

Such findings are particularly intriguing for understanding how factors that are precursors to puberty may also relate to subsequent psychopathology outcomes of pubertal development. The mechanisms that link family relationships to pubertal development have yet to be identified, but are presumably through the hormonal pathways controlling puberty. As adrenal hormones (e.g., cortisol) have been associated with stressful conditions, and as poorer family relations may produce physiological stress responses, the hypothalamus-pituitary-adrenal (HPA) axis is hypothetically the path linking family stress and pubertal maturation. However, research on hormonal activity has found that elevated secretion of cortisol from the adrenals suppresses androgen secretion in the hypothalamus-pituitary-gonadal (HPG) system; development should be slowed rather than accelerated. Unfortunately, hormonal regulation and interaction between the HPA and HPG axes are not well understood at this time. Even if gonadal secretion of sex steroids (i.e., androgens) is suppressed, the adrenal glands may increase both androgen and other adrenal hormone secretion with stress. Notably, in studies of adult women and in animal models psychosocial or environmental stress influences the estrogen system and a range of health outcomes (e.g., McEwen, 1994). Again, in the studies on sexual abuse the experience of sexual abuse may influence pubertal development either via estrogen/stress pathways or via other systems.

To reiterate, the family stress and father absence models were developed almost exclusively based on malleability of the estrogen system in girls' pubertal development. Much of the attention to variations in the onset of puberty for girls stemmed from reports that menarche was possibly occurring at earlier ages over the past few decades, despite expectations that it would not change as dramatically as it had over the past century, and that menarche was occurring earlier for certain subgroups of girls (e.g., African American/black girls versus white girls; see chapter 2). In addition, earlier maturation was also being identified as a risk for psychopathology for girls during adolescence, at least for white girls. As has been the case with much of the focus on pubertal effects on behavior or behavioral effects on puberty, the documentation of group differences in timing of pubertal onset has not been well connected to whether or not there are also group differences in pubertal effects on psychopathology.

### *Racial/ethnic and SES differences in onset of puberty*

Recent studies have found that African American girls are starting puberty at earlier ages and reaching menarche about six months earlier than their white counterparts (Herman-Giddens, *et al.*, 1997; Kaplowitz, *et al.*,

1999; see also chapters 1 and 2). It is not known when these differences first began to emerge; that is, it is not clear whether or not these differences were simply not detected in prior studies due to the absence of nonwhite participants, or whether these differences have only recently appeared in the population. For boys, two recent studies have examined this question. Biro and his colleagues (1995) did not find differences between African American and white boys in patterns of pubertal stages (although there was a race effect for testosterone). In contrast, Herman-Giddens, Wang, and Koch (2001) found that African American males started puberty earlier than white or Hispanic males. Methodological debates regarding these studies and the assessment of puberty in boys indicate that more data are needed before conclusions can be drawn about variations in puberty by race in boys (Reiter and Lee, 2001).

When examining girls' puberty, some of the group differences in the onset of puberty may be explained by some of the aforementioned hypotheses. For example, differences in diet and weight may in part play a role in explaining differences between white and African American/black girls. Even environmental hazards, or estrogens, may in part explain racial differences. Many communities are still heavily segregated and predominantly African American/ black areas, at least in urban areas, often have higher reports of other known environmental health risks resulting in higher rates of mortality for same age African American and white adults (Geronimus, Bound, and Waidman, 1999). Unfortunately, many potentially hazardous substances are simply not tracked, making this explanation for racial differences an extrapolation from the data.

In addition, psychosocial or contextual stress likely varies by race. Certainly, African American/black girls experience stress in connection with discrimination that is not experienced by white girls in the United States. These girls are also more likely to live in father-absent households than their white counterparts (Hernandez, 1993). It has been suggested that the disproportionate number of African American children living in poverty in comparison to the proportion of white children may also account for maturational differences, especially as persistent poverty may be experienced as stress or may serve as a stress factor on parental behaviors and quality of family relationships (Conger, et al., 1994; McLoyd, et al., 1994).

Again, this conjecture pieces together literatures on the effects of familial and environmental stress on puberty and the effects of poverty on families. As yet, only a few studies have attempted to test whether racial differences in puberty are the result of economic or SES differences. In one study, controlling for SES reduced differences between groups in age of menarche between white and Hispanic girls in a neighborhood study that sampled neighborhoods based on race and SES (Obeidallah, *et al.*, 2000). In contrast, controlling for SES indicators did not influence race differences in onset of puberty between African American and white girls in a large representative study of 9- and 10-year-old girls (National Heart, Lung, and Blood Institute Growth and Health Study Research Group, 1992); in this study, SES indicators were not assessed in depth. The methodological differences between these two studies, and the few others that have investigated this issue, make it difficult to draw conclusions about the extent to which race differences may or may not be explained by SES.

As to whether or not racial or ethnic group differences exist in the effects of puberty on adjustment, work presented in the present volume (see chapter 13) provides one of the few investigations of whether or to what extent pubertal timing influences adjustment among African American adolescents. Notably, in one of the few prior studies connecting puberty to psychopathology with the specific examination to ethnic differences, Hayward and his colleagues (1999) found effects in white girls but not African American or Hispanic girls. Thus, whereas in this and other studies more advanced development at a particular age (that is, being earlier in maturation than one's peers) was associated with greater psychopathology, in this case, depressive symptoms, the effect was only found for white girls, even though more African American girls would be in a situation in which they are more advanced in their development in comparison to the group. Of course, an important caveat of this point is that within an immediate peer group these girls may not be particularly out of sync or off-time, as their immediate peer group may be other African American girls. Hence, the effects on psychopathology of being earlier than other girls is likely to be associated with some contextual factor that confers risk to earlier development or individual difference factors that may moderate effects of puberty on psychopathology.

## Models that explain outcomes of variations in pubertal onset

As indicated, historically the models that have explained why some individuals experience difficulties at puberty and others do not have been connected to differences in context. In terms of variations in the onset of puberty, the psychological experience of the timing of puberty has long been thought to be based on the experience of being off-time from peers or norms. For example, the "deviancy" hypothesis suggests that being off-time has negative effects, as individuals are out of sync with the normative experiences of their peers (Brooks-Gunn, Petersen, and Elchorn, 1985;

Neugarten, 1979; Petersen and Taylor, 1980). However, not all hypotheses linking timing to outcomes focus on context; the stage-termination hypothesis suggests that early maturation is difficult as individuals have less time to develop in other areas, such as cognitive and coping skills, prior to the challenges of puberty (Brooks-Gunn, Petersen, and Eichorn, 1985; Petersen and Taylor, 1980). Thus, earlier maturers have fewer skills entering the transition than their peers. In this case, it is a characteristic of the individual rather than the context that determines whether or not puberty is linked to subsequent psychopathology. Research to date has not universally supported one hypothesis over the other, but rather has been a mix of the two (see chapter 13). A series of studies have focused on identifying whether or not variations in pubertal timing are linked to psychopathology, and if so, for whom. A second set of studies have focused on mechanisms for effects and understanding individual differences within different timing groups; that is, why do some early-maturing girls have difficulties and others do not (see chapter 12)? The literature in these two areas has amassed in parallel rather than sequentially.

*Establishing for whom effects occur*

As noted by other chapters in this volume (e.g., chapters 12–13) and previous reviews (Archibald, Graber, and Brooks-Gunn, 2003; Graber and Brooks-Gunn, 2003), there is increasing convergence that variations in pubertal timing are linked to subclinical and serious psychopathology for girls and to a lesser extent for boys. A surge of recent studies have reported links between earlier pubertal maturation in girls and depressive disorders and symptoms (e.g., Ge, Conger, and Elder, 2001a; Graber, *et al.*, 1997; Hayward, *et al.*, 1997; Stice, Presnell, and Bearman, 2001), alcohol, tobacco, and/or substance use (e.g., Dick, *et al.*, 2000; Graber, *et al.*, 1997; Stice, *et al.*, 2001; Wichstrom, 2001), conduct disorders (e.g., Graber, *et al.*, 1997), and eating disorders and symptoms (e.g., Graber, *et al.*, 1994; Graber, *et al.*, 1997). While methods and nature of effects vary across studies, a pattern seems to have established that earlier maturation for girls is associated with psychopathology during adolescence. Using data from the Oregon Adolescent Depression Study, my colleagues and I also found elevated depressive symptoms and higher rates of major depressive disorder in comparisons of late maturing girls with on-time maturers (Graber, *et al.*, 1997). In general, though, late maturation among girls appears to have more positive than negative associations.

Examinations of links between psychopathology and variations in pubertal timing among boys have also begun to reveal some consistent findings, although the pattern is not as consistent as the one for girls. In part, the absence of a clearer picture for boys may be because several of the studies referenced above only included girls (e.g., Dick, *et al.*, 2000; Hayward, *et al.*, 1997; Stice, *et al.*, 2001). Also, when effects are found for boys, it is more often for elevated symptoms rather than disorders (e.g., Graber, *et al.*, 1997). Specifically, early maturation in boys has been associated with increased depressive symptoms or internalizing types of psychological distress (e.g., Ge, Conger, and Elder, 2001b; see also chapter 7; Graber, *et al.*, 1997), alcohol use and or abuse (Wichstrom, 2001; Williams and Dunlop, 1999), as well as delinquent or externalizing behaviors (Ge, Conger, and Elder, 2001b; Williams and Dunlop, 1999). Late maturation for boys also seems to confer some risk for psychopathology with elevated psychological distress during mid-adolescence (Graber, *et al.*, 1997) and increased alcohol use and/or abuse in young adulthood (Andersson and Magnusson, 1990).

Notably, off-time maturation in boys has not, in general, been considered to be a particular concern in terms of adjustment. Prior studies had either found few effects or positive effects of early maturation for boys (see Graber, Petersen, and Brooks-Gunn, 1996 for a review); it had frequently been suggested that maturing earlier was good for boys, as some of the physical changes of puberty – muscle gain, increased strength, and endurance – are likely to be beneficial in stereotypic male behaviors (i.e., sports). However, the emergence of negative consequences of early and late maturation in boys suggests that new contextual factors may be shaping how early maturation is experienced for boys (see chapter 7). Increased alcohol and tobacco use among early-maturing boys may indicate that they are experimenting with these behaviors at younger ages; earlier age of initiation for these substances has long been linked to subsequent development of more serious problems (Jessor, 1992). In addition, psychological distress among early maturers may be due to changing pressures on youth, in general, that are experienced by earlier maturing boys at younger ages.

*Explanatory models for effects*

Processes or mechanisms through which variations in pubertal timing influence psychopathology has begun to amass for girls. Many of these specifically relate to how puberty is experienced within a context and/or individual differences among individuals that may have existed prior to puberty. Also, the models of interest here are those that would explain individual differences within timing groups; as such, models are most salient in explaining why some girls experience psychopathology and others do not. For example, Stattin and Magnusson (1990) have found that early maturation was problematic for the subset of early maturers who also associated with older peers. Presumably, older peers were engaging in more "problem behaviors" and the early girls were becoming involved in these behaviors before they had developed the skills needed to manage the situations.

Others have suggested that it may not be early maturation per se that confers risk for psychopathology for girls, but rather, that early maturers may experience unique patterns of cumulative or simultaneous stress (Petersen, Sarigiani, and Kennedy, 1991; Simmons and Blyth, 1987). For example, going through puberty just before making a school change was predictive of having a depressive episode or depressive problems in late adolescence (Petersen, Sarigiani, and Kennedy, 1991; Simmons and Blyth, 1987). The school transition is most likely to overlap with the peak of pubertal development for early-maturing girls. Thus, girls who fared the worst in the study by Petersen, Sarigiani, and Kennedy (1991) were those who matured early and had a simultaneous school transition; the simultaneity of the transitions was the determinant of subsequent problems, rather than one or the other transition.

In addition to the immediate context or environment in which puberty occurs, Caspi and Moffitt (1991) have proposed that it is the accentuation of prior problems by early maturation that leads to greater psychopathology for some girls. In their study, not all early-maturing girls had an increase in behavioral problems in the postpubertal years. Only early-maturing girls who had prior behavioral problems in the pre- or beginning pubertal years demonstrated sharp increases in problems postpubertally.

Interestingly, two of the explanations for why early maturation may confer risk for psychopathology in girls focus on factors in the immediate context or environment of girls; that is, patterns of involvement with peers and patterns of school transitions. As such, these may represent unique stressors or stressful contexts that emerge in adolescence. These models may also be equally likely to apply to off-time development in boys. Regardless of gender, involvement with deviant or older peers may lead to some of the problem behaviors for which timing effects have been demonstrated. In contrast, the accentuation hypothesis focuses on prior development as a factor in the development of psychopathology. One question that immediately arises from the findings of Caspi and Moffitt (1991) is what factors were associated with problem behaviors at the prepubertal period? Were these the result of familial stressors that were, in part, one reason why these girls matured earlier than their peers?

In recent work that I and my colleagues have done Graber, Brooks-Gunn, and Warren (in press), we have tried to examine individual characteristics of young adolescent girls that may differentiate what places some girls at risk. We have examined the effects of three aspects of pubertal development (patterns of estradiol activity, DHEAS levels, and pubertal timing) on depressive symptoms. Three potential mediators were also examined: emotional arousal, attention difficulties, and negative life events. Tests of mediated models indicated that early pubertal timing predicted higher emotional arousal, which subsequently predicted increased depressive affect. Follow-up analyses focusing on emotional arousal indicated, as would be expected, that not all early-maturing girls experienced high emotional arousal and depression. Those girls with high levels of adrenal activity (as tapped by DHEAS) and early maturation were those who had the highest emotional arousal and depressive affect scores. It should be noted that DHEAS levels did not differ substantially by timing group and higher DHEAS levels alone did not predict emotional arousal or depressive affect. This interaction has multiple possible interpretations. That is, DHEAS may be an indicator of a preexisting physiological disposition that is exacerbated or activated by the contextual demands placed on early-maturing girls. This predisposition itself may be associated with the propensity to mature early for some girls. Or, some early-maturing girls who are experiencing difficulties coping with their maturation may have elevated adrenal activity as a product of this stress.

## Conclusions

As studies of puberty and psychopathology progress, the goal will certainly be to move beyond demonstrating effects, to a better understanding of why effects occur, for whom, and for how long. In my experience, each investigation of a potential pathway seems to identify other constructs that merit future and fuller examination. In the present discussion I have highlighted precursors and outcomes of pubertal development, but the connections among these constructs have yet to be made in any comprehensive manner. I have also argued that contextual factors are important as potential predictors of variations in pubertal development (e.g., family context) and as factors that determine who has difficulties at puberty (e.g., peer associations). In addition, contextual factors clearly interact with individual differences in determining who is at risk and for what. For example, my colleagues and I have now demonstrated in two studies (the one discussed and a second study) that certain patterns of adrenal response interact with pubertal timing to predict depressive symptoms (see chapter 8). However, when looking at the initiation of sexual behaviors in one of these studies a different pattern emerges; that is, early-maturing girls who do not have elevated adrenal activity are the most advanced in heterosocial behaviors in comparison to other girls. Of course, early engagement in heterosocial behaviors may also put girls at risk for depression or other psychopathology, as well as other health risks. Thus, two different pathways to depression in adolescence would exist for early-maturing girls. As such, different types of prevention would potentially stem from different pathways to the same outcome. It may be that the task of including multiple hormonal pathways, multiple contextual factors, multiple outcomes, and both genders will not be achieved in any single definitive study, but via several investigations that examine pieces of the puzzle. However, within any given study some effort must be made to capture the causes and outcomes of individual variation in development.

## References

Andersson, T., and Magnusson, D. (1990). Biological maturation in adolescence and the development of drinking habits and alcohol abuse among young males: a prospective longitudinal study. *Journal of Youth and Adolescence*, **19**, 33–41.

Angold, A., Costello, E. J., and Worthman, C. M. (1998). Puberty and depression: the roles of age, pubertal status and pubertal timing. *Psychological Medicine*, **28**, 51–61.

Archibald, A. B., Graber, J. A., and Brooks-Gunn, J. (2003). Physical development and the adolescent. In G. R. Adams and M. Berzonsky (ed.), *Handbook on adolescence*. Oxford: Blackwell.

Bean, J. A., Leeper, J. D., Wallace, R. B., Sherman, B. M., and Jagger, H. J. (1979). Variations in the reporting of menstrual histories. *American Journal of Epidemiology*, **109**, 181–185.

Belsky, J., Steinberg, L., and Draper, P. (1991). Childhood experience, interpersonal development, and reproductive strategy: an evolutionary theory of socialization. *Child Development*, **62**, 647–670.

Biro, F. M., Lucky, A. W., Huster, G. A., and Morrison, J. A. (1995). Pubertal staging in boys. *Journal of Pediatrics*, **127**, 100–102.

Brooks-Gunn, J. (1984). The psychological significance of different pubertal events to young girls. *Journal of Early Adolescence*, **4(4)**, 315–327.

Brooks-Gunn, J., and Warren, M. P. (1988). Mother–daughter differences in menarcheal age in adolescent girls attending national dance company schools and non-dancers. *Annals of Human Biology*, **15(1)**, 35–43.

Brooks-Gunn, J., Graber, J. A., and Paikoff, R. L. (1994). Studying links between hormones and negative affect: models and measures. *Journal of Research on Adolescence*, **4(4)**, 469–486.

Brooks-Gunn, J., Petersen, A. C., and Elchorn, D. (1985). The study of maturational timing effects in adolescence. *Journal of Youth and Adolescence*, **14(3)**, 149–161.

Buchanan, C. M., Eccles, J. S., and Becker, J. B. (1992). Are adolescents the victims of raging hormones: evidence for activational effects of hormones on moods and behavior at adolescence. *Psychological Bulletin*, **111**, 62–107.

Caspi, A., and Moffitt, T. E. (1991). Individual differences are accentuated during periods of social change: the sample case of girls at puberty. *Journal of Personality and Social Psychology*, **61**, 157–168.

Clayton, P. E., and Trueman, J. A. (2000). Leptin and puberty. *Archives of Disease in Childhood*, **83**, 1–4.

Conger, R. D., Ge, X., Elder, G. H., Jr., Lorenz, F. O., and Simons, R. L. (1994). Economic stress, coercive family process, and developmental problems of adolescents. *Child Development*, **65**, 541–561.

Dick, D. M., Rose, R. J., Kaprio, J., and Viken, R. J. (2000). Pubertal timing and substance use: associations between and within families across late adolescence. *Developmental Psychology*, **36**, 180–189.

Ellis, B. J., and Garber, J. (2000). Psychosocial antecedents of variation in girls' pubertal timing: maternal depression, stepfather presence, and marital and family stress. *Child Development*, **71**, 485–501.

Ellis, B. J., McFadyen-Ketchum, S., Dodge, K. A., Pettit, G. S., and Bates, J. E. (1999). Quality of early family relationships and individual differences in the timing of pubertal maturation in girls: a longitudinal test of an evolutionary model. *Journal of Personality and Social Psychology*, **77**, 387–401.

Frisch, R. E. (1983). Fatness, puberty, and fertility: the effects of nutrition and physical training on menarche and ovulation. In J. Brooks-Gunn and A. C. Petersen, *Girls at puberty: biological and psychosocial perspectives* (pp. 29–50). New York: Plenum.

Ge, X., Conger, R. D., and Elder, G. H., Jr. (2001a). Pubertal transition, stressful life events, and the emergence of gender differences in adolescent depressive symptoms. *Developmental Psychology*, **37**, 404–417.

Ge, X., Conger, R. D., and Elder, G. H., Jr. (2001b). The relationship between puberty and psychological distress in adolescent boys. *Journal of Research on Adolescence*, **11**, 49–70.

Geronimus, A. T., Bound, J., and Waidmann, T. A. (1999). Poverty, time, and place: variation in excess mortality across selected US populations, 1980–1990. *Journal of Epidemiology and Community Health*, **53**, 325–334.

Gladen, B. C., Ragan, N. B., and Rogan, W. J. (2000). Pubertal growth and development and prenatal and lactational exposure to polychlorinated biphenyls and dichlorodiphenyl dichloroethene. *Journal of Pediatrics*, **136**, 490–496.

Graber, J. A., and Brooks-Gunn, J. (2002). Adolescent females' sexual development. In G. M. Wingood and R. J. DiClemente (ed.), *Women's sexual and reproductive health: social, psychological and public health perspectives* (pp. 21–42). New York: Plenum.

Graber, J. A., Archibald, A. B., and Brooks-Gunn, J. (1999). The role of parents in the emergence, maintenance, and prevention of eating problems and disorders. In N. Piran, M. P. Levine, and C. Steiner-Adair (ed.), *Preventing eating disorders: a handbook of interventions and special challenges* (pp. 44–62). Philadelphia, PN: Brunner/Mazel.

Graber, J. A., Brooks-Gunn, J., Paikoff, R. L., and Warren, M. P. (1994). Prediction of eating problems: an eight-year study of adolescent girls. *Developmental Psychology*, **30**, 823–834.

Graber, J. A., Brooks-Gunn, J., and Warren, M. P. (1995). The antecedents of menarcheal age: heredity, family environment, and stressful life events. *Child Development*, **66**, 346–359.

Graber, J. A., Brooks-Gunn, J., and Warren, M. P. (in press). Pubertal effects on adjustment in girls: moving from demonstrating effects to identifying pathways. *Journal of Youth and Adolescence*.

Graber, J. A., Lewinsohn, P. M., Seeley, J. R., and Brooks-Gunn, J. (1997). Is psychopathology associated with the timing of pubertal development? *Journal of the American Academy of Child and Adolescent Psychiatry*, **36**, 1768–1776.

Graber, J. A., Petersen, A. C., and Brooks-Gunn, J. (1996). Pubertal processes: methods, measures, and models. In J. A. Graber, J. Brooks-Gunn, and A. C. Petersen (ed.), *Transitions through adolescence: interpersonal domains and context* (pp. 23–53). Hillsdale, NJ: Lawrence Erlbaum.

Grumbach, M. M., and Styne, D. M. (1998). Puberty: ontogeny, neuroendocrinology, physiology, and disorders. In J. D. Wilson, D. W. Fostor, and H. M. Kronenberg (ed.), *Williams textbook of endocrinology* (pp. 1509–1625). Philadelphia, PN: W. B. Saunders.

Hayward, C., Gotlib, I. H., Schraedley, P. K., and Litt, I. F. (1999). Ethnic differences in the association between pubertal status and symptoms of depression in adolescent girls. *Journal of Adolescent Health*, **25**, 143–149.

Hayward, C., Killen, J. D., Wilson, D. M., Hammer, L. D., Litt, I. F., Kraemer, H. C., Haydel, F., Varady, A., and Taylor, C. B. (1997). Psychiatric risk associated with early puberty in adolescent girls. *Journal of the American Academy of Child and Adolescent Psychiatry*, **36**, 255–262.

Herman-Giddens, M. E., Slora, *et al*., (1997). Secondary sexual characteristics and menses in young girls seen in office practice: a study from the Pediatric Research in Office Settings network. *Pediatrics*, **99(4)**, 505–512.

Herman-Giddens, M. E., Wang, L., and Koch, G. (2001). Secondary sexual characteristics in boys. *Archives of Pediatric and Adolescent Medicine*, **155(9)**, 1022–1028.

Hernandez, D. J. (1993). *America's children: resources from family, government, and the economy*. New York: Russell Sage Foundation.

Himes, J. H., and Dietz, W. H. (1994). Guidelines of overweight in adolescent preventive services: recommendations from an expert committee. *American Journal of Clinical Nutrition*, **59**, 307–316.

Horlick, M. B., Rosenbaum, M., Nicolson, M., Levine, L. S., Fedun, B., Wang, J., Pierson, R. N., Jr., and Leibel, R. L. (2000). Effect of puberty on the relationship between circulating leptin and body composition. *Journal of Clinical Endocrinology and Metabolism*, **85**, 2509–2518.

Jessor, R. (1992). Risk behavior in adolescence: a psychosocial framework for understanding and action. In D. E. Rogers and E. Ginzberg (ed.), *Adolescents at risk: medical and social perspectives* (pp. 19–34). Boulder, CO: Westview.

Jones, M. C. (1965). Psychological correlates of somatic development. *Child Development*, **56**, 899–911.

Jones, M. C., and Mussen, P. H. (1958). Self-conceptions, motivations, and interpersonal attitudes of early and late-maturing girls. *Child Development*, 29, 491–501.

Kaplowitz, P. B., Oberfield, S. E., and Drug and Therapeutics and Executive Committees of the Lawson Wilkins Pediatric Endocrine Society (1999). Reexamination of the age limit for defining when puberty is precocious in girls in the United States: implications for evaluation and treatment. *Pediatrics*, 104, 936–941.

Lewinsohn, P. M., Hops, H., Roberts, R. E., Seeley, J. R., and Andrews, J. A. (1993). Adolescent psychopathology. I: Prevalence and incidence of depression and other DSM III-R disorders in high school students. *Journal of Abnormal Psychology*, 102, 133–144.

Lewis, C. E., Jacobs, D. R., Jr., McCreath, H., Kiefe, C. I., Schreiner, P. J., Smith, D. E., and Williams, O. D. (2000). Weight gain continues in the 1990s: ten-year trends in weight and overweight from the CARDIA study. *American Journal of Epidemiology*, 151, 1172–1181.

Loeber, R., and Keenan, K. (1994). Interaction between conduct disorder and its comorbid conditions: effects of age and gender. *Clinical Psychology Review*, 14, 497–523.

Marshall, W. A., and Tanner, J. M. (1986). Puberty. In F. Falkner and J. M. Tanner (ed.), *Human growth*, vol. II, *Postnatal growth neurobiology* (pp. 171–209). New York: Plenum.

McEwen, B. S. (1994). How do sex and stress hormones affect nerve cells? *Annals New York Academy of Sciences*, 743, 1–18.

McLoyd, V. C., Jayaratne, T. E., Ceballo, R., and Borquez, J. (1994). Unemployment and work interruption among African American single mothers: effects on parenting and adolescent socioemotional functioning. *Child Development*, 65, 562–589.

Moffitt, T. E., Caspi, A., Belsky, J., and Silva, P. A. (1992). Childhood experience and the onset of menarche: a test of a sociobiological model. *Child Development*, 63, 47–58.

National Heart, Lung, and Blood Institute Growth and Health Study Research Group (1992). Obesity and cardiovascular disease risk factors in black and white girls: the NHLBI growth and health study. *American Journal of Public Health*, 82, 1613–1620.

Neugarten, B. L. (1979). Time, age and life cycle. *American Journal of Psychiatry*, 136, 887–894.

Obeidallah, D. A., Brennan, R., Brooks-Gunn, J., Kindlon, D., and Earls, F. E. (2000). Socioeconomic status, race, and girls' pubertal maturation: results from the Project on Human Development in Chicago Neighborhoods. *Journal of Research on Adolescence*, 10, 443–464.

Offer, D. (1987). In defense of adolescents. *Journal of the American Medical Association*, 257, 3407–3408.

Paikoff, R., and Brooks-Gunn, J. (1991). Do parent–child relationships change during puberty? *Psychological Bulletin*, 110(1), 47–66.

Petersen, A. C. (1987). The nature of biological-psychosocial interactions: the sample case of early adolescence. In R. M. Lerner and T. T. Foch (ed.),

*Biological-psychosocial interactions in early adolescence: a life-span perspective* (pp. 35–61). Hillsdale, NJ: Lawrence Erlbaum.

Petersen, A. C., Sarigiani, P. A., and Kennedy, R. E. (1991). Adolescent depression: why more girls? *Journal of Youth and Adolescence*, **20**, 247–271.

Petersen, A. C., and Taylor, B. (1980). The biological approach to adolescence: biological change and psychological adaptation. In J. Adelson (ed.), *Handbook of adolescent psychology* (pp. 117–155). New York: John Wiley.

Reiter, E. O., and Grumbach, M. M. (1982). Neuroendocrine control mechanisms and the onset of puberty. *Annual Review of Physiology*, **44**, 595–613.

Reiter, E. O., and Lee, P. A. (2001). Have the onset and tempo of puberty changed? *Archives of Pediatric and Adolescent Medicine*, **155**, 988–989.

Simmons, R. G., and Blyth, D. A. (1987). *Moving into adolescence: the impact of pubertal change and school context*. Hawthorne, NY: De Gruyter.

Stattin, H., and Magnusson, D. (1990). *Paths through life*, vol. II, *Pubertal maturation in female development*. Hillsdale, NJ: Lawrence Erlbaum.

Steinberg, L. (1988). Reciprocal relation between parent–child distance and pubertal maturation. *Developmental Psychology*, **24**, 122–128.

Stice, E., Presnell, K., and Bearman, S. K. (2001). Relation of early menarche to depression, eating disorders, substance abuse, and comorbid psychopathology among adolescent girls. *Developmental Psychology*, **37**, 608–619.

Surbey, M. K. (1990). Family composition, stress, and the timing of human menarche. In T. E. Ziegler and F. B. Bercovitch (ed.), *Socioendocrinology of primate reproduction* (pp. 11–32). New York: John Wiley.

Trickett, P. K., and Putnam, F. W. (1993). Impact of child sexual abuse on females: toward a developmental, psychobiological integration. *Psychological Science*, **4**, 81–87.

Warren, M. P. (1980). The effects of exercise on pubertal progression and reproductive function in girls. *Journal of Clinical Endocrinology and Metabolism*, **51**, 1150–1157.

Wichstrom, L. (2001). The impact of pubertal timing on adolescents' alcohol use. *Journal of Research on Adolescence*, **11**, 131–150.

Williams, J. M., and Dunlop, L. C. (1999). Pubertal timing and self-reported delinquency among male adolescents. *Journal of Adolescence*, **22**, 157–171.

Zacharias, L., and Wurtman, R. J. (1969). Age at menarche: genetic and environmental influences. *New England Journal of Medicine*, **280**, 868–875.

# Index